THE HISTORY OF THE IRISH FAMINE

THE HISTORY OF THE IRISH FAMINE

Edited by
Christine Kinealy, Gerard Moran
and Jason King

Volume II

The Irish Famine Migration Narratives:
Eye-Witness Testimonies

Edited by Jason King

LONDON AND NEW YORK

First published 2019
by Routledge
2 Park Square, Milton Park, Abingdon, Oxon OX14 4RN

and by Routledge
711 Third Avenue, New York, NY 10017

Routledge is an imprint of the Taylor & Francis Group, an informa business

© 2019 selection and editorial matter, Christine Kinealy, Gerard Moran and Jason King; individual owners retain copyright in their own material.

The right of Christine Kinealy, Gerard Moran and Jason King to be identified as the authors of the editorial material, and of the authors for their individual chapters, has been asserted in accordance with sections 77 and 78 of the Copyright, Designs and Patents Act 1988.

All rights reserved. No part of this book may be reprinted or reproduced or utilised in any form or by any electronic, mechanical, or other means, now known or hereafter invented, including photocopying and recording, or in any information storage or retrieval system, without permission in writing from the publishers.

Trademark notice: Product or corporate names may be trademarks or registered trademarks, and are used only for identification and explanation without intent to infringe.

British Library Cataloguing-in-Publication Data
A catalogue record for this book is available from the British Library

Library of Congress Cataloging-in-Publication Data
A catalog record for this book has been requested

ISBN: 978-1-138-20077-7 (set)
ISBN: 978-1-138-20089-0 (volume II)
eISBN: 978-1-315-51389-8 (set)
eISBN: 978-1-315-51369-0 (volume II)

Typeset in Times New Roman
by Apex CoVantage, LLC

CONTENTS

Introduction   1

PART I
Irish Famine migration narratives   **43**

1   Stephen De Vere to T. F. Elliot, 30 November, 1847, *Minutes of evidence before Select Committee on Colonisation from Ireland, British Parliamentary Papers, Emigration*, v 5, pp. 45–48   45

2   Stephen De Vere, unpublished 'America journals' 1847–1848 (Trinity College Dublin Manuscripts Department, MSS 5061–5062)   52

3   John Burke, 'Reminiscences', or 'Migration of seven brothers' (MS John Burke, 'Reminiscences', New York Historical Society Library, New York, 1891)   69

4   John Young, 'Diary of John Young' (Nancy Mallett Archive and Museum of St. James' Cathedral, Toronto)   72

5   Robert Whyte, *The ocean plague: a voyage to Quebec in an Irish emigrant vessel, embracing a quarantine at Grosse Isle in 1847. With notes illustrative of the ship-pestilence of that fatal year. By a cabin passenger* (Boston: Coolidge and Wiley, 1848)   88

6   Herman Melville, *Redburn: his first voyage* (New York: Harper and Brothers, 1849)   138

v

CONTENTS

7 William Smith, *An emigrant's narrative, or, a voice from the steerage: being a brief account of the sufferings of the emigrants in the ship 'India,' on her voyage from Liverpool to New-York, in the winter of 1847–8, together with a statement of the cruelties practiced upon the emigrants in the Staten Island Hospital* (New York: published by the author, 1850)   152

8 Henry Johnson to Jane Johnson, 18 September 1848, in L. Wyatt (ed.), 'The Johnson letters', *Ontario History* (1948), pp. 7–52, on pp. 34–38   177

9 Jane White to Eleanor, 29 June, 1849. Public Record Office of Northern Ireland. D.1195/3/5, 8B, 9–15   181

10 Sir Robert Gore-Booth letters (1846–1849), *Appendix x, minutes of evidence before Select Committee on Colonisation from Ireland, submitted by Sir Robert Gore-Booth, British Parliamentary Papers, Emigration*, v 5, pp. 122–132   184

11 Henry David Thoreau, *The shipwreck, Putnam's Monthly* 5.30 (1855), pp. 632–637   190

PART II
Eyewitness testimonies: Famine Irish caregivers   **195**

12 Grey Nuns, or Sisters of Charity, Famine annal, *Ancien Journal*, vol. I. Translated by Jean-François Bernard   197

13 Grey Nuns, or Sisters of Charity, Famine annal, *Ancien Journal*, vol. II. *The typhus of 1847*. Translated by Philip O'Gorman   209

14 Grey Nuns, or Sisters of Charity, Famine annals, *Foundation of St. Patrick's Orphan Asylum* (1849). Translated by Philip O'Gorman   215

15 Anon. *The emigrant ship. Written for the Protestant Orphan Bazaar*, in the *Literary Garland, and the British North American Museum* (Montreal: Lowell and Gibson, 1850)   217

CONTENTS

16 Fr. Bernard O'Reilly to *Quebec Mercury* (letter written on Grosse Isle quarantine station, 11 July, 1847; published in the *Quebec Mercury* on 27 July, 1847)   224

17 Fr. Bernard O'Reilly, testimony for *Report of the Special Committee appointed to inquire into the management of the quarantine station at Grosse Isle, . . . on behalf of the Board of Health of the City of Montreal* (23 July 1847). Canada. Legislature. Legislative Assembly. Special Committee appointed to inquire into the management of the quarantine station at Grosse Isle   227

18 Fr. Bernard O'Reilly, 'Settlement of the eastern townships', *Quebec Mercury* (30 March. 1848)   231

19 Fr. Bernard O'Reilly, 'The Irish emigration of 1847', *True Witness and Catholic Chronicle* (17 December 1852)   233

20 Fr. Bernard O'Reilly, *The mirror of true womanhood; a book of instruction for women in the world* (New York: P. J. Kennedy, Excelsior Publishing House, 1877), pp. 96–99   242

21 John Francis Maguire, *The Irish in America* (New York: D & J Sadlier and Co, 1868), pp. 134–153   245

22 Robert Walsh to unnamed Irish bishop (1857). (Archives du Séminaire de Nicolet, F091/B1/5/2 & F091/B1/5/3). Translated by Jason King   257

23 Thomas Quinn, 'Une voix d'Irlande', in *Premier Congrès de La Langue Français au Canada. Québec 24–30 Juin 1912* (Québec, 1913), pp. 227–232. Translated by Jason King   260

Bibliography   264
Keywords   268

vii

INTRODUCTION

I

On 21 September 1847, the *Times* published an editorial that was both strident and strikingly atypical in its denunciation of the horrific conditions of the Irish Famine migration:

> Did Ireland possess a writer endued with the laborious truth of Thucydides, the graceful felicity of Virgil, or the happy invention of De Foe, the events of this miserable year might be quoted by the scholar for ages to come, together with the sufferings of the pent-up multitudes of Athens, the distempered plains of northern Italy, or the hideous ravages of our great plague . . . The fact of more than a hundred thousand souls flying from the very midst of the great calamity, across a great ocean, to a new world, crowding into insufficient vessels, scrambling for a footing on a deck and a berth in a hold, committing themselves to these worse than prisons, while their frames were wasted with ill fare and blood infested with disease, fighting for months of unutterable wretchedness against the elements without and pestilence within, giving almost hourly victims to the deep, landing at lengths on shores already terrified and diseased, consigned to encampments of the dying and of the dead, spreading death wherever they roam, and having no other prospect before them than a long continuance of these horrors in a still farther flight across forests and lakes under a Canadian sun and a Canadian frost – all these are the circumstances beyond the Greek historian or Latin poet, and such as an Irish pestilence alone could produce . . .
>
> The worst horrors of the slave trade . . . have been reenacted in the flight of British subjects from their native shores . . . The Blackhole of Calcutta was a mercy compared to the holds of those vessles.
>
> Of these awful occurrences some account must be given. Historians and politicians will some day sift and weigh the conflicting narratives and documents of this lamentable year, and pronounce with or without affectation, how much is due to the inclemency of heaven, and how

INTRODUCTION

much to the cruelty, heartlessness or improvidence of man. The boasted
institutions and spirit of the empire are on trial.[1]

This volume of *Irish Famine Migration Narratives: Eye-witness Testimonies*
brings together primary sources and first-hand accounts of the Irish Famine
migration of 1847 that attest to 'these awful occurences'. During the summer of
1847, approximately 117,000 Irish emigrants sailed to the United States with a
mortality rate of 10 per cent; 100,000 of the most destitute took the cheaper passage to British North America, and up to a third of them perished at sea or in the
fever sheds at the quarantine stations at Grosse Isle, Montreal, further upriver on
the St Lawrence to Kingston and Toronto, and to a lesser extent in New York, Boston and Philadelphia.[2] The ramshackle vessels on which they crossed the Atlantic
became known as 'sailing coffins' or 'coffin ships'.[3]

This book comprises the diaries, journals and letters written on board these 'coffin ships' by the Famine migrants themselves as well as the eyewitness accounts of
those who first encountered and cared for them in British North America and the
United States. It consists almost entirely of first person testimonies that describe
the harrowing experiences of Irish emigrants at sea and in the fever sheds in which
they were quarantined, augmented by a couple of fictional texts, survivor recollections and orphan stories from those who endured the calamity. The book features newly discovered, unpublished primary source material such as the journals
and letters of Stephen De Vere and the Grey Nuns annals that have never before
appeared in print. The first section contains the eyewitness accounts of the Famine
Irish themselves, and the second section that of their caregivers. Classic literary
works such as Herman Melville's *Redburn* (1849) and Henry David Thoreau's
The Shipwreck (1855) are set alongside little known emigrant diaries. They attest
not only to the suffering of Famine emigrants but also to the compassion of their
caregivers.

Irish Famine Migration Narratives: Eye-witness Testimonies breaks new
ground in bringing together these published and unpublished primary sources into
a single volume. Recent studies have focused on the political impact and policy
implications of the Irish Famine migration and assisted colonization under the
auspices of the Irish landlords, the British government and Poor Law;[4] Famine
Irish interethnic encounters and conflicts with other racialized groups such as
African-Americans and French-Canadians in the United States and Quebec;[5] their
reception and experiences of community and institution building in British and
North American cities such as Liverpool, Philadelphia, Montreal and Toronto;[6]
the influence of the Famine Irish in stimulating American nativism and the development of restrictive immigrant legislation;[7] and their patterns of remembrance,
memorialization and fictional recollections of the Famine migration in Ireland,
Great Britain and North America.[8] Yet the eyewitness accounts of the Famine
migrants themselves and their caregivers have been largely neglected in professional scholarship. One reason for this is that the very genre of the Famine
journal has remained under a veneer of suspicion since the publication of Gerald

2

INTRODUCTION

Keegan's fraudulent best-seller *Famine Diary: Journey to a New World* in 1991 and the controversy surrounding its exposure as a fabricated text.[9] The reluctance of professional scholars to examine these primary sources has left a significant historiographical gap – one that this volume aims to fill. Indeed, the untold story of Stephen De Vere's influence on Passenger Act reform and inadvertent curtailment of Canadian Irish immigration can be traced to his unpublished journals and letters in this volume.[10]

These eyewitness narratives attest to the Irish Famine migration as a mid-Victorian refugee crisis. The 1847 Famine exodus featured a sudden influx of desperate Irish emigrants travelling along well established passenger routes in rapidly deteriorating conditions on board ship and in the cities and fever sheds of British North America and the United States: a 'sudden, unanticipated and disorderly movement involving considerable degrees of force . . . which profoundly upsets the prior migration order'.[11] It was a crisis more keenly felt in Canada than the United States. The most destitute and assisted emigrants availed of cheaper fares to British North America; immigration restrictions and 'head money' largely excluded them from the U.S.[12] 'The arrival of the Famine Irish, however', notes Hirota

> compelled Massachusetts and New York, the two major [U.S.] destination states for them, to centralize the authority over immigration at the state rather than municipal level for the stricter supervision of foreign passengers. By the 1840s, both Massachusetts and New York had pioneered measures for pauper deportation and exclusion. Irish famine immigration stimulated the formation of state-level immigration control, and it was during the famine period that Massachusetts and New York solidified their leading positions in immigration control in antebellum America.[13]

These immigration restrictions ultimately became national in scope, and anti-Irish nativism 'critically influenced' later measures such as federal Chinese exclusion.[14] By contrast, British North America gained control over its immigration policy only as a result of the public outcry following the arrival of Famine emigrants in 1847, which brought Irish mass migration to the colonies to an end.[15] Thus, although 1847 marked the 'Famine foundations'[16] of increasing U.S. Irish immigration, the vast majority who perished did so at Grosse Isle (6,000), Montreal (6,000) and Quebec City (1,100) in Canada East (Quebec), further up the St Lawrence River at Kingston (1,400) and Toronto (1,200) in Canada West (Ontario), in Saint John and Partridge Island quarantine station (1,200), New Brunswick, while up to a thousand emigrants were buried in mass graves on Staten Island, New York, and Deer Island in Boston.

This geography of migrant mortality is reflected in the testimonies in this book.[17] The migration narratives in the first half of this volume are arranged chronologically in relation to when their voyages took place between April 1847

3

INTRODUCTION

and 1850. They include Stephen De Vere's unpublished journal and letter entries from his voyage to Canada in 1847–1848 that appear here for the first time in print, as well as his famous letter of 30 November 1847 to Thomas Frederick Elliot that exposed the harrowing conditions on the coffin ships;[18] John Burke's unpublished memoirs ('Reminiscences') and recollections of the Famine migration to New York City;[19] John Young's unpublished diary of his journey from Glasgow to Ancaster, Ontario, in the company of Famine migrants (1847);[20] Robert Whyte's *The Ocean Plague, or A Voyage to Quebec in an Irish Emigrant Vessel by 'A Cabin Passenger'* (1848);[21] Herman Melville's *Redburn* (1849), a fictional account of an emigrant voyage from Liverpool to New York in 1847 'with elements of autobiography';[22] a collection of emigrant letters from the former tenants of the Gore-Booth estate at Lissadell in County Sligo in 1847;[23] Henry Johnson's 1848 letter from British North America describing his voyage to New York and Canada West;[24] Jane White's 29 June 1849 letter from 'Grosse Island';[25] and William Smith's *An Emigrant's Narrative, Or, A Voice from the Steerage: Being a Brief Account of the Sufferings of the Emigrants in the Ship 'India,' on Her Voyage from Liverpool to New-York, in the Winter of 1847–8, Together with a Statement of the Cruelties Practiced Upon the Emigrants in the Staten Island Hospital* (1850).[26]

These testimonies tend to be written from the perspective of more affluent, often Protestant passengers who bear witness to suffering in the steerage. Kerby Miller notes in *Emigrants and Exiles* 'that Famine emigrants *were* generally poorer and less skilled than those who embarked before the potato blights'.[27] He distinguishes between an earlier, pre-Famine model of 'purposeful' and systematic migration by 'able' and 'calculating' emigrants who would become upwardly mobile in the New World, and the eruption of a more spontaneous and impulsive flight of desperate, impoverished 'traditionalist peasants' and 'refugees', more often Roman Catholics and Gaelic speaking than their predecessors, and 'economically as well as temperamentally less prepared . . . for material achievement and assimilation abroad'.[28] They were also predisposed to regard themselves as involuntary exiles, Miller claims, attributing their misfortune to English misgovernment and the Irish landlords. 'As the year [1847] progressed', adds Christine Kinealy, 'it was obvious that emigration was no longer the preserve of able-bodied labourers and professionals who, in an orderly and rational manner, had sought an increase in their fortune elsewhere', but rather, it 'had increasingly become the last refuge of a desperate population who believed that their only hope of survival lay outside Ireland'.[29] 'A progressive and natural system of emigration gave place within the last few years', observes Robert Whyte in *The Ocean Plague*, 'to a violent rush of famished, reckless, human beings, flying from their native land, to seek food in a distant and unknown country'.[30] Cecil Woodham-Smith describes the Famine migrants most succinctly as 'the reverse of pioneers'.[31]

Nevertheless, the voices of the steerage class do surface in the vernacular in some unlikely primary sources, such as testimonial letters from former tenants of the Gore-Booth estate at Lissadell in County Sligo who emigrated to Saint John,

New Brunswick, in 1847. These letters often enjoin friends and relatives remaining in Ireland to cross the Atlantic, but they also tend to report upon the harrowing conditions of the transatlantic voyage, describing in clipped and neutral tones the deaths of shipmates and even loved ones on board. 'I am very glad you did not come out here', writes Ference M'Gowan to her parents on 13 October 1847, after arriving in Saint John, as 'they are comeing here and dieing in Dozens[,] their is not a vassal comes here but the feaver is on Board'.[32] 'Dear Father Pen could not write of the distress of the Irish Passengers which arrived here thro Sickness death and distress of every Kind', writes Catherine Hennigan on 15 February 1848:

> The Irish I know have suffered much and is still suffering but the Situation of them here even the Survivors at that awful time was lamentable in the extreme there are thousands of them buried on [Partridge] Island and those who could not go to the States are in the Poorhouse or beggin thro the streets of St John.[33]

In a similar vein, Mary McBride notifies her friend William Gifcut about the deaths she witnessed when 'the most of the people that came out in your vessels have died in st johns'.[34]

The vast majority of eyewitness accounts of the Famine exodus are not written, though, by members of the steerage class. Rather, the social and occupational profiles of most emigrant narrators reveal them to be a subset of artisans, entrepreneurs and lower gentry who almost invariably travelled cabin class. De Vere was quite exceptional as a landowner who subjected himself to the steerage in order to report on the hardships of the transatlantic voyage. Robert Whyte led Anglican religious services for his fellow passengers at sea; John Young was equally devout and removed from the steerage class, though impressed by 'the cook [who] is a black man and rather an original; he talks Gaelic to the Highlanders'.[35] Jane White's letters reveal 'the unabashed and simple prejudices that marked much of the Protestant Irish bourgeoisie'.[36] Smith was a highly skilled power-loom weaver and Burke a successful shoe merchant. Only Johnson emigrated as a common labourer, but with considerable resources in hand. *Redburn* is written from the perspective of a young boy in the crew, but from an affluent middle-class family. Each of these authors thus travelled on the crest of the wave of the Irish Famine migration.

These more affluent passengers did not regard themselves as exiles but often saw evidence of emigrant disaffection and hostility towards the Irish landlords. They also tended to distinguish themselves along religious and social lines from the steerage class. 'There was fur-five hundred on board[,] all Roman Catholics with the exception of about forty protestants', writes Henry Johnson in a letter to his wife in 1848, 'and a more Cowardly Set of hounds than the same papists I never seen'.[37] Robert Whyte also disapproved of his fellow Catholic, Gaelic-speaking passengers, who did not 'seem to have any regard for the sanctity of the Sabbath; . . . in the evening they had prayers in the hold; and were divided into two parties – those who spoke Irish, and those who did not; each section having a leader, who gabbled in his respective language a number of "Paters and Aves", as quickly as the devotees could count their beads'.[38] 'Poor little things', he adds:

> I learned that many of these emigrants had never seen the sea nor a ship, until they were on board. They were chiefly from the county Meath, and sent out at the expense of their landlord, without any knowledge of the country to which they were going, or means of livelihood, except the labour of the father of each family. All they knew concerning Canada was, that they were to land in Quebec, and to go up the country; moreover, they had a settled conviction that the voyage was to last exactly three weeks.[39]

'They were the most simple people I had ever seen', asserts Melville's Redburn in like fashion: 'they seemed to have no adequate idea of distances; and to them, America must have seemed a place just over a river'.[40] '*Those* poor creatures', '*they* were of the very poorest class',[41] '*these* emigrants', 'to *them*': these third person pronouns reveal the narrators' sense of religious and social differentiation from the steerage.

The hold of the emigrant vessel thus functioned as a forum for religious and social contact and conflict between various emigrant groups that could exacerbate their confessional and class divisions. This compression of social and spatial tension into the confined setting of the coffin ship both encapsulated and precipitated a wider sense of conflict that became one of its defining features as a literary motif and site of memory. Marguérite Corporaal and Christopher Cusack have tracked this memory to a corpus of nineteenth century novels in which, they argue, 'the coffin ships facilitate the development of microcosmic Irish "imagined communities", functioning as "heterotopias" where the cultural clashes experienced in the homeland and the pending assimilation in the New World have to be negotiated'.[42] On the other hand, the intermingling of migrants from vastly different backgrounds who were brought into close proximity on board ship often exhibited what Mikhail Bakhtin describes as 'carnivalesque' tendencies of licenced transgression, for the temporary suspension of social norms and the levelling of hierarchical class, gender and religious distinctions that had defined their identities prior to the voyage.[43] Moreover, like in the hold of the emigrant vessel, later incarceration in the fever sheds at Grosse Isle and Montreal also brought migrants across confessional and social lines into intimate and prolonged contact that could aggravate conflict between them.[44]

These 'carnivalesque' festivities could at different times either uphold or undermine the established social order, rigidly hierarchical class structure, gender norms and expression of religious pieties on board ship. Robert Whyte expresses dismay at the intermixture and intermingling of 'young men and young women' who, during St John festivities (24 June 1847), 'got up a dance in the evening regardless of the moans and cries of those who were tortured by the fiery fever' in a maritime dance-macabre. After the mate 'spoke to them of the impropriety of such conduct, they desisted and retired to the bow where they sat down and spent the remainder of the evening singing[,] the monotonous howling they kept up . . . quite in unison with the scene of desolation within and the dreary expanse of ocean without'.[45] 'The dancing continues every night', observes Young, 'though some people are complaining of it, both on account of the sin and of the noise'.[46] Despite such spontaneous festivities, the intimate and prolonged contact necessitated on board deck and in the steerage clearly also caused tensions between the emigrants and exacerbated their confessional and social divisions, especially when rival groups were forced to live together in close proximity, in times of sickness,[47] or, Redburn and Smith each note, in settings where the emigrants were particularly vulnerable and forced to compete with one another, as in the emigrants' kitchen.[48] 'Had social worship . . . at 7 o'clock [and] the 2nd Cabin was crowded to excess with all denominations . . . in attendance', records Samuel Harvey Craigy in his 'Journal of a Passage from Belfast to New York' (26 August 1849).[49] 'After our exercises', he adds, 'I was scarcely able to prevent the young man, Magill ['a staunch Orangeman but kind hearted'], . . . from taking summary vengeance on a couple of young men (R. Catholics) who trampled and made much noise above our heads during worship'. Later in the voyage (29 August), Craigy also notes that 'a laughable scene occurred at one of the fires on Friday last, from a few drops of gravy flying from the frying pan of a protestant into the saucepan of a R. Catholic female. The unfortunate offender in order to save his head had to beat an immediate and hasty retreat'.[50] 'Many similar scenes occurred every day', claims Melville's Redburn; 'nor did a single day pass, but scores of the poor people got no chance whatever to do their cooking . . . But it was still a more miserable thing to see these poor emigrants wrangling and fighting together for the want of the most ordinary accommodations'.[51] Not only that, tensions would also often surface on the passenger vessels between the emigrants and the crews whose function it was to transport them.

These religious and social frictions in the steerage were particularly aggravated during ocean storms. Under such circumstances, the emigrants evinced varying degrees of leadership,[52] instinct for self-preservation, sheer panic, awe-struck immobility and intimations of the sublime, many of them agreeing with Edmund Burke that in its power, vastness, infinite expanse, turbulence and sheer capacity to take life, 'the ocean is an object of no small terror'.[53] 'The lesson of a storm is humility', records William Smith in *A Voice from the Steerage*:

> Each cloud may be the engine of destruction, each sea may capsize or overwhelm your ark; you cannot lighten its stroke by a single drop. Surrounded by objects, all potent to destroy, there is nought on which your skill can work the least amelioration. The sky, the wind, the waves, are eloquent with the announcement, 'God is all in all;' you can do nought but meekly crave his compassion, or humbly await his will, and when the danger is passed, man has had no hand in averting it . . . You see

INTRODUCTION

his agency through no obstructive instrument, you have been dealing directly with your Maker.[54]

'Here the Almighty displays the strength of his omnipotent arm', writes Craigy in his 'Journal of a Passage from Belfast to New York' (1849), 'and performs a hymn to his praise on the strings of the storm, awakening the terror' of those who apprehend it. 'Oh it is a fearful but sublime scene, surpassing description', but 'I wish however that it was over'.[55]

Other emigrants perceived the storm at sea as evidence of the human frailty of their fellow passengers. Henry Johnson ridicules the supplications and terror of Irish Catholic emigrants during an ocean gale. 'In the time of danger they would do nothing', he complains,

> but sprinkle holy water, cry, pray, cross themselves and all sorts of Tom-foolery instead of giving a hand to pump the ship and then when danger was over they would Carry on all sorts of wickedness and they are just the same any place you meet them at home or abroad . . . One old fellow Kept me laughing nearly the whole time at the way he was getting on. The very Senses were frightened out of him. Cursing & praying in one breath. I got such a disgust at the party of papists at this Scene that I felt almost as if I could have submitted to go down if I had got them all with me.[56]

For Johnson, the ocean storm serves only to confirm his prejudices about 'papists' 'at home and abroad' in relation to his own religious beliefs. He finds proof of their pusillanimity and of the shortcomings of their faith.

Emigrants also often felt a sense of deliverance after such travails when they first encountered the pilot at the end of the transatlantic voyage. As ships approached New York City or navigated the dangerous shoals of the Gulf of St Lawrence they would take a pilot on board, who would often provide the emigrant's first moment of contact with a citizen of the New World. It is true that, on occasion, such first impressions of the pilot could be negative, especially when he was French-Canadian. 'The pilot was a heavy, stupid fellow – a Canadian, speaking a horrible patois, and broken English', writes Robert Whyte in *The Ocean Plague*.[57] First impressions of African-American cabin boys[58] and indigenous peoples could also be quite negative. 'Some Indians prowling about the quay tried to come on board to spy out the land', writes John Young after his arrival at Montreal's fever sheds, 'but they were prevented, partly for fear of infection and partly to prevent theft and there was almost a battle about it'.[59] More often, the approach of the pilot was greeted with considerable enthusiasm. According to Redburn: 'when, among sea-worn people, a strange man from shore suddenly stands among them, with the smell of the land in his beard, it conveys a realization of the vicinity of the green grass, that not even the distant sight of the shore itself can transcend'[60] – an impression that is confirmed by Burke and William Smith on their respective approaches to New

8

York harbour in 1847.[61] Even more effusive is Samuel Harvey Craigy's description of the first sight of land in his 'Journal of a Passage from Belfast to New York' (20 September 1849):

> First sight of land from the Masthead at N½ o'clock A.M.
> I must leave the reader to his imagination for a description of the thoughts & feelings which thronged in quick succession upon our hearts, as the glad announcement rung in our ears from the lips of the keen-sighted tar on his lofty perch . . . And now as if inspired with love of Country, your speed seems to outstrip the winds of heaven – while your tall masts bend as if in homage to the land from which you have been for a time an exile! Every available spot is now occupied – four hundred eyes strive to pierce that far off verge, where sky & water seems to meet . . . The musings of our hearts are at length interrupted by the appearance of the Pilot Boat, which is approaching us . . . The beautiful stranger approaches – our signal for him floats from our Mast-head; . . . Many an eye gaze with curiosity at their swarthy complexions, & huge whiskers . . . Hail, happy Columbia! No wonder thy soil was kissed when first pressed by the foot of a European, for how sweet to the seasick wanderer is thy smiling shore![62]

Ultimately, the approach of the pilot represents a form of first contact with a citizen of the New World – 'a strange man from shore'; 'the beautiful stranger' – as well as immanent disembarkation in British North America or the United States. Indeed, Henry David Thoreau further transforms this figure of the 'skilful pilot' into an emblem of American Transcendentalism and a spiritual guide, a harbinger of deliverance from the material world. 'The mariner who makes the safest port in Heaven, perchance, seems to his friends on earth to be shipwrecked, for they deem Boston Harbor the better place', he contends.[63]

The prospect of shipwreck and threat of epidemic disease were all too real, however, for most emigrant writers. They were often shocked when they first arrived at the quarantine station at Grosse Isle 30 miles downriver from Quebec City. Observers were struck in particular by the incongruity of the intense human misery they witnessed in a setting of spectacular natural beauty. Joseph Pugliese notes a similar phenomenon in a more current context in which tourist places of leisure have become migrant destinations and sites of mass mortality as a result of twenty-first century refugee crises. He describes the Italian island of Lampedusa and Christmas Island near Australia, which were nineteenth-century penal colonies and twenty-first century sites of immigrant detention, as past and present 'border zones of the dead'.[64] Grosse Isle's profusion of natural splendour and human horror similarly led observers to remark upon its recurring mortuary spectacles on 'the Isle of Death'.[65] As a liminal 'scene of natural beauty sadly deformed by the dismal display of human suffering that it presented',[66] the island was envisioned as death's border zone.

Thus emigrant authors would often enthuse about its natural beauty while recoiling from the human calamity in their midst. They wrote effusive, panoramic and rhapsodic descriptions of the 'beautiful islets'[67] surrounding Grosse Isle from the vantage point of their ships, their effusions no doubt augmented by long weeks of prior confinement spent gazing at monotonous Atlantic expanses and endless vistas of water. Those emigrants who passed through the quarantine station when its facilities operated efficiently, aside from the crisis years of 1832 and 1847, usually referred in passing to the routine screening for infectious diseases taking place upon the island, and their descriptions of its scenic environs often appear subsumed within a more sweeping and panoramic tableau of the environmental and social features of the Gulf of St Lawrence region as a whole.

A case in point is the genteel, Anglo-Irishwoman Jane White, who depicts Grosse Isle not only as a quarantine station for the 'reception of the sick', but also as a social microcosm of Quebec. 'My dearest Elinor', she writes to a friend in her native Newtownards, 'I am glad to inform you we are so far on, on our long tedious journey. We are anchored at Grose Isle 36 miles below Quebec' (29 June 1849). She adds: 'The quarantine station is here, and I assure you the passengers all feel very discontented at being kept here . . . We have had fever and small pox on board so that is the reason the sick persons were taken on shore in a boat to the hospital. There have been a great many sheds erected on the Island which have been very useful for sick passengers'.[68] As a cabin passenger, however, White is not subjected to quarantine procedures, and only visits Grosse Isle of her own accord on a recreational excursion on which she 'had a sort of picnic'.[69] Moreover, she observes the mundane day to day activities that take place within the vicinity of the island and its various leisurely pursuits:

> The scenery on the banks of the river is delightful, especially at this season of the year, hill and valley, the beautiful towns and villages sloping to the river's edge together with fertile Islands form the most beautiful landscape I ever saw . . . The inhabitants are mostly of French descent and speak the French Language. The Roman Catholic religion is established here.
>
> I saw a very pretty steam boat on Sunday afternoon last which was St John's Day. It came past here on a pleasure excursion from Quebec, full of people gaily dressed, they stopped here and came past our ship. They were accompanied by a [?] band and played the Troubadour Garry Owen and other tunes, it was a very handsome sight. The day was warm and the sun [?] bright but it showed a very bad respect for the Lord's day. They are only to be excused on account of being Papists.
>
> You would be surprised to see the number of Brigs crowded here all full of emigrants trying their fortunes in America.[70]

From the detached vantage point of her emigrant vessel, Jane White turns her gaze from the expansive natural environs and picturesque scenery surrounding Grosse

INTRODUCTION

Isle to focus upon the signs of human activity and the customs of the inhabitants of the region. The 'most beautiful landscape' and the 'delightful scenery on the banks of the river' appear to frame and compensate somewhat for the less congenial aspects of life in the New World, such as the predominance of 'Papists' and the levelling ethos of emigrants all opportunistically arriving 'to try their fortunes in America'.

Such evocations of natural beauty could not mask the intense human misery on Grosse Isle at the height of the Irish Famine migration in 1847. Consider, for example, an article in the Toronto *Globe* entitled 'Notes of a Trip to Canada East' (1 September 1847) about an excursion on the St Lawrence River as the vessel passes the quarantine station:

> When the words Grosse Isle, Grosse Isle sounding in our ears – all arose, intent upon getting a sight of this Isle of graves. Its shores were covered with shining tents without, all beautiful and fair – within the abode of sighs and moans, and death; around it lay, at anchor, eighteen ships whose passengers were now ashore, and afterwards we met four others crowded with immigrants, to add their quota to this scene of death.[71]

By September 1847, the words 'Grosse Isle, Grosse Isle' had already become iconic and synonymous with a 'scene of death' amidst 'beautiful and fair' surroundings.

The island's stark contrast of natural beauty and human calamity is further emphasized by Robert Whyte in *The Ocean Plague*. 'A few miles further sail brought us among a number of beautiful islets', he observes, 'so beautiful that they seemed like a fairy scene; their verdant turf was almost level with the blue water that wound amongst them, submerging not a few, so that the first [trees] that grew upon them appeared to rise from the river' – but 'Oh! what a contrast to this magic beauty was presented within our floating pest-house'.[72] Whyte employs the conventions of travel narrative and landscape painting – the broad, expansive vista, intricately etched with naturalistic detail – to accentuate the spectacle of human suffering in its incongruous 'fairy scene'. Consider, for example, his extended, panoramic description of Grosse Isle, its natural environs and the frenetic human activity in his purview:

> We lay at some distance from the island, the distant view of which was exceedingly beautiful: At the far end were rows of white tents and marquees, resembling the encampment of an army; somewhat nearer was the little fort, and residence of the superintendent physician, and nearer still the chapel, seaman's hospital, and little village, with its wharf and a few sail boats; the most adjacent extremity being rugged rocks, among which grew beautiful fir trees. At high water this portion was detached from the main island, and formed a most picturesque islet. But this scene of natural beauty was sadly deformed by the dismal display of human suffering

11

that it presented; – helpless creatures being carried by sailors over the rocks, on their way to the hospital, – boats arriving with patients, some of whom died in their transmission from their ships. Another, and still more awful sight, was a continuous line of boats, each carrying its freight of dead to the burial ground, and forming an endless funeral procession. Some had several corpses, so tied up in canvass that the stiff, sharp outline of death was easily traceable . . . In a few, a solitary mourner attended the remains; but the majority contained no living beings save the rowers. I would not remove my eyes until boat after boat was hid by the projecting point of the island, round which they steered their gloomy way . . . I ventured to count the number of boats that passed, but had to give up the sickening task.[73]

Whyte's panoramic view shifts from a wide angle view of Grosse Isle and its natural environs, the architecture and settlements on the island, to focus on the individual examples of 'human suffering' and emigrant fatalities that occupy his immediate foreground. His line of vision moves from nature to culture to the lone figure of the 'solitary mourner'. But this movement is disrupted and Whyte's vision 'deformed' by an 'endless funeral procession' and continuous line of boats, upon which his eyes remain transfixed yet unable to count or quantify, until the mortuary spectacle of death on Grosse Isle takes on the properties of a landscape painting. Indeed, Whyte employs the lexicon of a visual artist and presents Grosse Isle as a static landscape that is 'exceedingly beautiful' and affords a 'distant view', replete with 'rugged rocks' and 'beautiful fir trees' that form 'a most picturesque islet'. His line of vision is disrupted, however, by the 'endless funeral procession' and 'continuous line of boats' – so that the artist's canvas becomes substituted for the canvas of burial shrouds and the numerous 'stiff, sharp outlines of death' they contain.

Stephen De Vere also discovered a death zone at Grosse Isle within a verdant natural setting.[74] Shortly before his arrival at the quarantine station, he noted in his unpublished journal the 'picturesque scenery' of the St Lawrence River valley with 'rolling ground soft perfumed sod. . . [and] lawns with occasional thickets of dwarf spruce firs', all of which he describes as a 'beautiful pleasure ground of vast extent'.[75] De Vere's tone abruptly changes, however, when he reaches Grosse Isle on 16 June 1847:

Arrived at Grosse isle quarantine about 7 am. Detained waiting for dr till evening, when he inspected & gave us clean bill of health – abt. 40 ships detained there – villages of white tents on shore for the sick. Daily mortality about 150. One ship, Sisters of Liverpool, in with all passengers & crew in fever of this ship, all but the Cap'n and one girl died.

Laid alongside of 'Jessy' in which many ill. Water covered with beds, cooking utensils refuse of the dead. Ghastly appearance of boats full of sick going ashore never to return. Several died between ship and shore.

INTRODUCTION

Wives separated from husbands, children from parents. Ascertained by
subsequent enquiry that funds in agents hands altogether insufficient for
care. Medical attendance bad. Exemplary conduct of Catholic Clergy.[76]

Stephen De Vere's diary entries are evocative and emotionally gripping, but
were never intended for public consumption. As his vessel lay at anchor off
Grosse Isle, he bears witness to the grim traffic all around him of small vessels
ferrying the sick and the dead from the coffin ships to the fever sheds and mass
graves on the island. De Vere's journal records the spectacle of sundered families,
that moment of separation in which Irish children were orphaned and left bereft
of their parents.

De Vere also anticipates many of the themes in his famous letter of 30 Novem-
ber 1847 to T. F. Elliot that exposed the harrowing conditions on the coffin ships.
He had sailed steerage with former tenants from his estate at Curragh Chase in
County Limerick to bear witness to the hardships of the transatlantic voyage.
'Having myself submitted to the Privations of a Steerage Passage in an Emigrant
Ship for nearly Two Months, in order to make myself acquainted with the Condition of the Emigrant from the Beginning', De Vere recounts in his letter: 'I can
state from Experience that the present Regulation[s] for ensuring Health and com-
parative Comfort to Passengers are wholly insufficient'.[77] His eyewitness account
of the steerage passage would become the most widely cited description of the
Famine voyage. In De Vere's own words:

> Before the emigrant has been a week at sea he is an altered man. How
> can it be otherwise? Hundreds of poor people, men, women, and children
> of all ages, from the drivelling idiot of ninety to the babe just born, hud-
> dled together without light, without air, wallowing in filth, and breathing
> a fetid atmosphere, sick in body and despair at heart, the fevered patients
> lying between the sound in sleeping places so narrow as almost to deny
> them the power of indulging, by a change of position, the natural rest-
> lessness of the disease, by their agonized ravings disturbing those around
> them and predisposing them, through the effects of the imagination, to
> imbibe the contagion; living without food or medicine except as admin-
> istered by the hand of casual charity, dying without the voice of spiritual
> consolation and buried in the deep without the rites of the Church.[78]

De Vere then goes on to describe the condition of the fever sheds at the quarantine
station on Grosse Isle: 'They were very miserable', he writes,

> so slightly built as to exclude neither the heat nor the cold. No sufficient
> care was taken to remove the sick from the sound, or to disinfect and
> clean the bedding after the removal of the sick to hospitals. The very
> straw upon which they had lain was often allowed to become a bed for
> their successor; and I have known many poor families prefer to burrow

INTRODUCTION

under heaps of loose stones which happened to pile up near the shore rather than accept the shelter of the infected sheds.

Finally, he describes the deplorably over-crowded conditions prevailing aboard the steamers chartered to convey convalescing emigrants away from Grosse Isle further inland.[79] 'I have seen small, incommodious, and ill-ventilated steamers', he recalls,

> arriving at the quay in Toronto, after a forty-eight hours passage from Montreal, freighted with fetid cargoes of 1,100 and 1,200 Government emigrants of all ages and sexes. The healthy who had just arrived from Europe, mixed with the half-recovered convalescents of the hospitals, unable, during that time, to lie down, almost to sit. In almost every boat were clearly marked cases of actual fever – in some were deaths – the dead and the living huddled together.[80]

De Vere's harrowing testimony shocked a House of Lords Select Committee on Colonisation from Ireland, chaired by his uncle Lord Monteagle, into recommending comprehensive Passenger Act reform.[81] T. F. Elliot testified before the committee and entered De Vere's letter of 30 November 1847 into the Minutes of Evidence on 9 March 1848. Years later, De Vere's younger brother, the poet Aubrey, recalled that Stephen had risked his life when

> he took passage for Canada with a considerable number of those who had been employed . . . under his supervision, and conducted them to Quebec, sharing with them all the sufferings and perils which then belonged to a crowded steerage passage. Those who escaped fever on their sea-passage frequently caught it on landing, the dormant seeds of disease becoming rapidly developed by the stimulus of better air and food, and by infection. It was so on this occasion. They reached Quebec in June of 1847, and in a short time nearly all of those whom he had taken with him and lodged in a large, healthy house were stricken down in succession, during a period covering about eight months, and received from him personally all the ministrations which they could have had from a hospital nurse . . . His letter describing the sufferings of emigrants was read aloud in the House of Lords by Earl Grey, then Secretary for the Colonies, and the 'Passengers Act' was amended, due accommodations of all sorts being provided in the emigrant vessels. Most of those emigrants who on reaching Quebec went into the crowded and infected hospitals died there. It is impossible to guess how many thousands of emigrants may have been saved by this enterprise.[82]

Such was De Vere's influence, contends MacDonagh, that 'it is scarcely too much to regard it as the basis of most of their future legislation for ship life'.[83]

14

INTRODUCTION

Despite his influence, however, the fact that Stephen De Vere kept copious journals and wrote extensive letters during his voyage to Canada in 1847–1848 remains little known. The little red journal in which he jotted his impressions on a daily basis that is published in this volume is one of the most important documents of the Irish Famine migration and an invaluable cultural and historical resource. It is also a hidden gem of mid-Victorian travelogue.

After he left Grosse Isle on 16 June 1847, De Vere remained a keen observer of his surroundings as he travelled upriver. He arrived in Quebec City the next day on 17 June where he lodged a complaint against the ship's captain, donated the £10 fine 'for the use of destitute Emigrants' and noted that the 'Irish and [French-] Canadians dislike one another'.[84] At 6am on 24 June, De Vere reached Montreal, where he observed 'Frightful mortality in the Emigrant Sheds hospitals & generally Throughout the town'.[85] He remained in Montreal until 13 July and then embarked for Toronto, marvelling at the beauty of the Canadian countryside, especially around Thousand Islands, from the deck of his steamship. In his own words:

> From Brockville to Kingston. This an archipelago of islands. Perfect labyrinth. The larger ones with large trees. The smaller ones with brushwood & dwarf pines. Landed in one. Beautiful andromeda. Narrow channels where hardly room for steamers suddenly spreading out. Great inland seas, & then as suddenly contracted. Lavish profusion of vegetation. The most barren rock has its tree – tree arboretum. At Kingston change steamers. New fortifications Kingston in a great scale for the protection of harbour. Immense crowd of German and Irish Emigrants on board of the worst description. Great apparent disease. Pay difference for cabin Passage to Toronto $6. Pass Cobourg and Port Hope at night. Wednesday July 14th Arrive at Toronto at 11am.[86]

His first impression of Toronto was of St Michael's nearly completed 'Magnificent Catholic Cathedral . . . building. Brick with cut stone door'.[87]

De Vere remained in Ontario for a year between July 1847 and 1848, though his plan to purchase land and establish a settlement near London never came to fruition. He was a keen observer of Canadian colonial growth and the cultivation of the wilderness. Indeed, De Vere was especially interested in the varieties of Canadian foliage, as his estate at Curragh Chase is in an area of old growth, hardwood forest – now a publicly owned Coillte forest park – with its own arboretum. Through his eyes, the cultivation of the Canadian forests was seen in each stage of its development. More broadly, De Vere was highly sensitive to the Canadian landscapes he observed as he travelled extensively through Canada West in 1847–1848. His impressions of Niagara Falls on 25 May 1848 are beautifully rendered over several pages in his journals and letters,[88] as are his records of everyday Canadian life at that time, whether it is Christmas festivities,[89] his frequent hunting excursions, his encounters with First Nations peoples on 23 June 1848[90] or trying to purchase a farm in the early settlement of London, Ontario.[91] What recurs again and again in the unpublished De Vere journals are his perceptions and feelings of joy at the beauty of the Canadian landscape.

Ultimately, however, De Vere did not purchase land or remain in Canada West. In fact, he had an ulterior motive for his migration. As he wrote to his elder brother Vere Edward on 11 February 1848:

> In my letters home I have left one thing unsaid, which is for you alone. You know what had been for a considerable time (8 or 9 years) the tendency of my religious opinions. I could no longer, when thrown independently upon the world, reconcile it to my conscience to conceal them & I have, since I reached America, conformed to the ordinances of the Catholic Church. Whether this has got wind at home, or not I do not know. My principal reason for leaving my own country was to save my mother the pain which I feared the avowal of my convictions would have caused to her, nor will I ever reside in Ireland if that avowal gives her more pain than my presence would give pleasure . . . I leave the matter wholly in your hands to disclose or conceal as you <u>think best for my mother</u>. Should your reply be unfavourable, I am determined, at any cost, to remain an exile for conscience sake. If favourable, being 'functus officis' here, & having probably laid the foundation of much benefit to my native land, I am ready to return and share the fortunes of my family & home; but I will never live again at home concealing my faith, a faith from which I have derived strength to bear every hardship & consolation under every misfortune & privation.[92]

There is no record of a reply to De Vere's letter, but it must have been favourable, because he did return to Ireland in 1848 as an openly practicing Catholic, facilitating Aubrey De Vere's conversion a few years later.

As a convert to Catholicism, a proponent of assisted emigration and philanthropic colonist who personally led his former tenants to resettle in British North America, Stephen De Vere hardly fits the stereotype of the absentee proprietor or rapacious landlord. Yet he was highly atypical in relation to his former tenants, as he himself came to realize. De Vere's papers indicate that he decided not to purchase land because of their increasing sense of disaffection, 'disrespectful'[93] attitude and defections to the United States. In his own words, written in a letter on 12 April 1848: 'every man of them becomes an American sympathizer', 'a bitter enemy to England, + to the Anglo-Canadian connection[,] . . . + every man, through the relation which he carefully keeps up with his old country, contributes to increase Irish disaffection'.[94] He was also inadvertently denounced from the pulpit as an Irish property owner on his first occasion of Catholic worship in Montreal's newly consecrated St Patrick's Church on 11 July 1847, when Kingston Bishop Patrick Phelan 'attributed [the] Misfortunes of Ireland to the atrocious avarice of the landlords'.[95] Bishop Phelan's sermon made such an impression on

De Vere that he cited it six months later in a letter dated 23 December 1847 to his younger brother Aubrey as evidence of Canadian sentiment:

> The outcry against the Irish landlords here is furious. They are said to have produced all the miseries of Ireland, &, by their 'heartless shoveling out of pauper emigrants' to be now working the ruin of Canada. I have done all I can to stem the tide, but it is too strong. I have heard the evils of this year's emigration attributed in the pulpit to the 'atrocious avarice of the Irish landlords'.[96]

De Vere perceived these sentiments to be widespread among the Famine Irish in Canada and the United States and feared they could be mobilized by a host of potential enemies. He was also particularly disturbed while abroad by the upheaval of the Young Ireland movement culminating in the uprising which was led by his brother-in-law William Smith O'Brien in 1848. When he learned of O'Brien's role in fomenting unrest on 10 April, De Vere described his 'motives' as 'always pure, honorable + patriotic', though he was 'dazzled by the wonderful progress of Revolutionary principle over all Europe' that 'allowed him to be hurried to the pitch of revolutionary folly'.[97] The agitation also caused a conflict of loyalties for De Vere himself, who wrote to Aubrey on 14 May 1848:

> People may say I remain absent and this is cowardice, [but] you fully appreciate the extreme pain of the position in which I should be placed if home at present. I could not + would not be disloyal even if I thought the rising had a chance of success; but I never could bring myself to aid in spilling the blood of the noble deluded people who are entwined with my heart strings.[98]

De Vere felt a sense of divided allegiance between loyalty to crown and country, and his love of the 'noble, deluded people' who did not reciprocate his affection. In his view, their delusions were inspired by Republican ideals that exacerbated social divisions and aggravated political tensions which he had hoped but failed to resolve through emigration to Canada.

Nevertheless, De Vere did come to increasingly admire the Canadian caregivers of the Famine Irish.[99] He paid tribute to Toronto emigration agent Edward McElderry and Bishop Michael Power who perished in the autumn of 1847. De Vere also bore witness to the intense suffering of the Famine Irish in Ontario. On 20 November 1847, he wrote:

> A family from Mayo came out this year apparently in the most abject poverty. They consisted of a father mother uncle a little boy about 12 years old. They were transmitted to Toronto at the govt. expense. The mother was there taken into hospital suffering from a rapid cancer in the breast. She soon died. The father, uncle, little boy took a poor lodging close to

INTRODUCTION

me. I frequently met them and the father complaining to me of dysentery. I recommended him to send for a doctor, but he said he was too poor. He at last went into hospital, and died, from want of care in the early stage of the disease, leaving his little son in possession of 300 sovereigns tied up in an old rag, which had, during the voyage, had been tied under the mother's breast and had produced the cancer of which she died.[100]

Moreover, on 9 January 1848, De Vere was in Port Stanley when he learned of

a beggar in a lonely part of the bush heading towards an old burial ground [with] three coffins, [for each of his daughters] who had all died together of fever. So great was the fear of infection that none of the neighbors would attend the funeral. The old father . . . with the assistance of his wife, herself in fever, dug his daughters graves & buried their remains. In a few days the wife died, & the old man still survives, the last of his race.[101]

These diary entries were never intended for public consumption, but reinforce the impression of Irish emigrants in the Canadas as objects of fear and loathing.

Their suffering also inspired De Vere to seek to remedy their plight. His famous letter that Lord Grey read aloud in the House of Lords exposing the harrowing conditions on coffin ships can be traced to De Vere's unpublished diary entries and letters he wrote in Toronto. De Vere's journal entry on 19 July 1847 is: 'wrote a paper describing the treatment of passengers on board emigrant ships with sundry suggestions for ensuring better arrangements'.[102] On 30 November, he records 'preparing dispatch' and then 'dispatch my letter' the following day.[103] Two months later, on 12 February 1848, De Vere notes with satisfaction

a report of a public meeting in Toronto, adopting almost verbatim my views as to the necessity of improvement in the emigration system. Thus I have the satisfaction of finding my opinions supported by the Canadian public, & at the same time likely to be adopted by the English ministry.[104]

Indeed, the very moment his impressions of the coffin ships began to shape government policy was recorded in a letter on 31 January 1848 from Eliot Warbourton to Aubrey De Vere. 'I was at the Colonial Office on Saturday, where I found its secretary [Lord Grey] . . . in raptures', Warbourton writes, 'about a letter he had received from Stephen. He said [it] was just what he wanted in stating his experience in his brave enterprise of emigrating as a pauper – he had 'made the dumb to speak'.[105] In 'emigrating as a pauper' and ostensibly giving 'the dumb' a voice 'to speak', De Vere defined the lasting image of the coffin ship and helped shape 'future legislation' for emigrant protection. He registered the predicament of migrants in transit that led to a change in policy. Ultimately, though, he was dismayed that the legislation he inspired increased fares and thereby undermined the Canadian passenger trade he had sought to safeguard.[106]

Irish Famine emigrants had much less influence than De Vere on the development of passenger legislation in the United States. Even so, Melville and Smith sought to motivate readers to feel empathy for the Irish migrants in their midst. Smith describes himself as an ardent Republican who spent 'many happy hours . . . reading a history of the United States, and contemplating the circumstances which had given a Washington to the world[,] the noble devotion of Americans to the cause of liberty, their struggle with their tyrants in 1776, and the declaration of Independence'.[107] He expresses indignation about the betrayal of these values by the apathetic and brutalizing medical staff he finds in New York's Staten Island hospital:

> In a country blessed with a free government, with a people possessing the highest order of intelligence, and in the highest state of civilization, the existence of such a system of heartless cruelty, perpetrated upon the poor unoffending immigrants, and that too in the hour of sickness, and on the confines of eternity, may well indeed be doubted. But experience has taught me that neither the character nor the manners of a nation are to be judged by what may be found to exist in some of its institutions, particularly in a hospital.

'Reader, if you are an American', Smith implores, 'let your sympathy be extended to the honest immigrants, whom tyranny, overpopulation, and taxation has forced upon your shores, and may the star-spangled banner protect your noble institutions, and triumph over liberty's foes till time shall be no more'.[108]

Melville's Redburn is equally forthright in calling for an open immigration policy, although he concedes that 'no legislation, even nominally, reaches the hard lot of the emigrant'.[109] Nevertheless, he entreats his readership to 'waive that agitated national topic, as to whether such multitudes of foreign poor should be landed on our American shores; . . . with one only thought, that if they can get here, they have God's right to come; though they bring all Ireland and her miseries with them'.[110] Redburn also expresses outrage about the suffering of Irish emigrants at sea. He seeks to recuperate their voices that are constantly under threat of erasure in official records like parliamentary papers, captains' logs[111] and shipping news columns in the popular press. 'The only account you obtain' of maritime distress, he claims,

> is generally contained in a newspaper paragraph, under the shipping-head. *There* is the obituary of the destitute dead, who die on the sea. They die, like billows that break on the shore, and never more are heard or seen. But in the events, thus merely initialized in the catalogue of passing occurrences, and but glanced at by the readers of news, who are more taken up with paragraphs of fuller flavour; what a world of life and

death, what a world of humanity and its woes, lies shrunk into a three-worded sentence!

You see no plague-ship driving through a stormy sea; you hear no groans of despair; you see no corpses thrown over the bulwarks; you mark not the wringing hands and torn hair of widows and orphans: – all is a blank. And one of these blanks I have but filled up, in recounting the details of the *Highlander's* calamity.[112]

Plague-ships and storms at sea; multitudes of emaciated emigrants racked with hunger, sickness, delirium and despair; the anonymity of an ocean burial; and the frenzied anguish of those who remain behind: this is the harrowing 'catalogue of passing occurrences' documented in the Irish Famine migration narratives in this volume. They give voice to Irish emigrants and preserve from 'oblivion the last woes of the poor'.[113]

The most jarring account of 'the destitute dead' who 'die, like billows that break on the shore' can be found in Henry David Thoreau's essay *The Shipwreck* (1855) about the wreck of the brig *St John* from Galway in Cohasset, Massachusetts, in 1849. Like Melville, Thoreau envisioned the Irish Famine migration through the prism of American romanticism. His description of people 'bound for the beach', 'flocking' and 'streaming' to the site of the Cohasset shipwreck which is strewn with emigrant corpses – such as 'one livid, swollen, and mangled body of a drowned girl' – seems a harbinger of more recent 'border zones of the dead'.[114] Thoreau is often accused of insensitivity and having a lack of empathy for the 'poor human bodies' he comes across amidst scenes of natural splendour. In his own words:

On the whole, it was not so impressive a scene as I might have expected. If I had found one body cast upon the beach in some lonely place, it would have affected me more. I sympathized rather with the winds and waves, as if to toss and mangle these poor human bodies was the order of the day. If this was the law of Nature, why waste any time in awe or pity? . . . I saw that corpses might be multiplied, as on the field of battle, till they no longer affected us in any degree, as exceptions to the common lot of humanity . . . It is the individual and private that demands our sympathy.[115]

Thoreau's sympathy for 'the winds and waves' is a typical romantic conceit of embracing nature as an imaginative vehicle to transport him beyond his immediate physical surroundings. His seemingly callous observation that the shoreline's 'beauty was enhanced by wrecks like this' and refined into a 'rarer and sublimer beauty' can be attributed to belief in nature's restorative power. Likewise, his final insight that 'the strongest wind cannot stagger a Spirit; it is a Spirit's breath' is the revelation of a romantic aesthetic. Yet there is something strikingly modern in Thoreau's recognition that 'one body cast upon the beach' commands empathy

INTRODUCTION

and elicits an emotional reaction, whereas the multitude of shipwreck victims becomes only an abstraction. It is the very public exposure of the Famine dead in such places of leisure as Cohasset that links its multiplied corpses with more recent mortuary spectacles in death's border zones.

II

The influx of Famine emigrants was also documented by their caregivers whose eyewitness testimonies are comprised by the second part of this volume. The most detailed and evocative accounts of the Famine Irish can be found in the annals of the Grey Nuns and female religious orders who cared for them in the fever sheds of Montreal during the summer of 1847, which are published for the first time in this book. These annals contain more than 500 pages of first-hand testimonies about the suffering of typhus stricken fever patients, up to 6,000 of whom would perish and lie buried in North America's largest Famine mass grave. They provide the most complete and continuous narrative of the Irish Famine migration on either side of the Atlantic. The full stories of what transpired inside of the fever sheds are narrated by the female religious who administered them. Yet because they were unpublished and written in French, the annals remain largely unknown.[116] Indeed, the Grey Nuns' Famine annals have been only recently digitized, transcribed and translated into English prior to their publication in this volume.[117] They are accompanied in the section that follows with other eyewitness testimonies about what befell Famine emigrants in North America, and particularly the fate of orphaned children.

Since Marguerite d'Youville had founded the order in 1738, the Grey Nuns had been led by a succession of strong women, including their Mother Superior Elizabeth McMullen in 1847. Under her leadership, they first entered Montreal's fever sheds on 9 June 1847. According to their annals:

> What a spectacle unravelled in the eyes of this good mother and her company! Hundreds of people were laying there, most of them on bare planks, pell-mell, men, women and children. The moribund and cadavers are crowded in the same shelter, while there are those that lie on the quays or on pieces of wood thrown here and there along the river.[118]

The Grey Nuns' harrowing first impression is of dead and dying Irish emigrants lying haphazardly and unattended in makeshift sheds at the water's edge, the 'moribund and cadavers . . . crowded in the same shelter'. The sight of numerous Irish cadavers 'was a spectacle that should have discouraged Mother McMullen and her generous companions', records the annal. Yet, 'on the contrary, they felt their souls lifted to the heights of the mission that the heavens were preparing for them'.[119] Indeed, the annals repeatedly emphasize that the Grey Nuns offered themselves of their own volition to care for the fever victims.

INTRODUCTION

The Grey Nuns were, in fact, one of three orders of French-Canadian female religious who cared for Famine emigrants in Montreal during the summer of 1847. Two weeks after they entered the fever sheds, the Grey Nuns were forced to withdraw on 24 June 1847 because of illness and fatalities within their ranks. They were replaced by the Sisters of Providence, a female religious community founded only three years earlier by Émilie Tavernier Gamelin (1800–1851). Like the Grey Nuns, the Sisters of Providence were struck by the spectacle of Irish suffering in their midst. As their annals recount:

> From hundreds of the sick, couched upon straw, in the wrestlings of their agony came forth dolorous cries; little children, who were still clasped in the arms of mothers who had died during the night, wept and cried; corpses lying here and there, already exhaled the odor of death; women who were scarcely able to drag themselves about, sought in that frightful chaos, for a husband or child of whose fate they were ignorant. Such was the dismal picture presented by that field of suffering.
>
> The Sisters set to work at once, causing the dead to be removed, and lavishing their care upon the sick.[120]

Like the Grey Nuns, the Sisters of Providence would soon provide homes for Irish orphans when the children were evacuated from the fever sheds on 11 July 1847 to their shelter in the heart of the city.[121] They also kept copious records of their experiences.[122]

The third order of nuns to care for the Famine Irish, in turn, was the cloistered Religious Hospitallers of St Joseph who replaced the Sisters of Providence after they too succumbed to the epidemic. Their annals recall the moment of their arrival in the fever sheds:

> We were in the presence of the most pitiful and touching spectacle. About fifteen hundred of these suffering and abandoned persons were lying helpless on miserable pallets, lacking everything because of their great number; nevertheless the majority showed a patience and submission that were truly admirable.
>
> We were more than once touched to tears in seeing young persons, who seemed to have been reared delicately, shudder with horror and to groan at the idea of lying on these straw pallets to die where everything was revolting to nature.[123]

The release of the sisters from their cloister was vividly recalled decades later by the novelist Mary Anne Sadlier in 'The Plague of 1847'. She recollects how they

> petitioned the Bishop to dispense them their vows of long seclusion, that they might go to the aid of their dear sister communities in the pestilential atmosphere of the fever sheds.

> The permission was freely given, and the strange sight was seen day by day in the streets of our ancient city, of the close carriage that conveyed the Sisters of the Hôtel Dieu from their quiet old-time convent to the lazar-house. . . . People pointed it out to each other with solemn wonder, as the writer well remembers, and spoke with bated breath of the awful visitation that had brought the cloistered nuns from their convent into the outer world, in obedience to the call of charity.[124]

Sadlier's recollection of the release of the Hôtel Dieu 'cloistered nuns from their convent' actually occurred in the first week of July 1847. The image of the uncloistered nun with the Irish orphan became deeply imprinted in popular memory.[125]

The Grey Nuns were the first of these female religious orders to care for Famine emigrants and they returned to the fever sheds in September of 1847 after they had recuperated and been replaced by their sisters. From the moment of their arrival in the sheds, their annals repeatedly emphasize the bodily suffering and mass mortality of Irish fever victims. In their own words:

> Words are lacking to express the hideous state in which the sick found themselves, up to three of them in the same bed, or cots to be more exact, that had been hastily fashioned and gave the impression that they were caskets. When touring the SHEDS, we would find cadavers exhaling an insufferable infection, lying in the same bed as those that still breathed; the number of sick was so considerable, that we at some point counted 1100 of them, some of whom had been dead for a few hours before we had noticed. One day, a Sister, passing one of those sheds, saw a poor afflicted that appeared restless; she came near his cot and saw that he was attempting to push off two dead bodies between which he was lying down. In spite of the delirium that deprived him of some of his faculties, the sight of those cadavers, one black as coal, the other, in contrast, yellow like saffron, caused him such fright that it momentarily brought him back to his senses; once delivered from his two companions, he fell back in his previous state of insensibility, and the next day, it was his turn to join the ranks of the dead . . . we could cite a thousand traits of this kind; but it is impossible to report all of them.[126]

The spectacle of helpless Irish infants being removed by the sisters from the breasts of their stricken mothers also recurs throughout the annals. They record:

> What is even more heart wrenching is to see little children, only a few months old, abandoned due to the death of their mothers . . . During these visits, we found more than one young child lying with mothers who no longer existed, suckling their breasts, to find some nourishment.[127]

These mortuary scenes of stricken parents and oblivious children continue on a daily basis:

> The priests, the nuns linger in these scenes of desolation to temper the bitterness with words of peace and resignation. Sister MONTGOLFIER traversing the enclosure met a little girl of 11 or 12 years old who was looking for her mother; she had been transported to Montreal before her. The good Sister took her affectionately by the hand and went with her from bedside to bedside. All anxious, the little one looked left and right, her little heart beating with fear and hope. All of a sudden she heard a most tender exclamation 'O Mother!' but in embracing her mother, her little arms held a moribund on her last breaths. Another morning, Sister MONTGOLFIER was completing her usual visits when she noticed that young children had entered the enclosure where their dead father lay; these poor little ones were calling him caressing him and playing amongst themselves.
>
> Worried about the fatigue that this illness could cause, the vigilant sister hastened to make the young children back away, but, what pain! Their father was but a cadaver! Such force did she need to take these children away while hearing their heart breaking cries; she guided them to the SHEDS designated for children and a few days later, she placed them happily with a family.[128]

The annals thus capture the very moment in which Irish families were torn asunder. They provide an unrivalled sense of the immediacy and intimacy of death and suffering within the sheds. Consider, for example, their account of a grieving husband cradling his dead wife:

> One day came a man from GROSSE ILE, where he had remained upon his arrival, being too sick to be transported to Montreal, where his wife, who was in good health, was sent with everyone else who had yet to be infected with the contagion. This poor man was looking everywhere for his wife without being able to find her; finally, he enters the SHEDS and looks on every cot to no avail. Finally, he goes out to pursue his search; while crossing the courtyard, he sees a great number of dead bodies. He comes nearer to examine them more closely. What does he see? . . . The inanimate body of his wife whom he was looking for all this time. He takes her in his arms, seeming to doubt that she is in fact dead; he wants to bring her back to life, talks to her, calls her by her name, kisses her tenderly; but for all these demonstrations, the only answer he receives is death's silence. Once he is convinced that she no longer exists, he abandons himself to his pain, the air is filled with his cries and sobs, the spectacle was most heart wrenching. Scenes of this nature occur several times a day.[129]

INTRODUCTION

The same spectacle is recorded more fleetingly in the *Montreal Transcript*: 'Many cases of extreme distress came to our knowledge during a recent visit to the sheds. We met with one poor heart-broken man, whose children were in the hospital at Grosse Isle, and whose wife was uttering her last sighs in our shed'.[130] It is these vignettes, these fleeting glimpses of families torn apart, these individual catastrophes in which husbands, wives, parents and children were irrevocably separated from one another, that have left their imprint on the memory of the Famine migration; but it is only through cross-referencing between primary sources and contemporary press accounts that the spectacle of the grieving husband can be traced to its historical moment of origin.

Despite these harrowing scenes, the Grey Nuns also recorded remarkable stories of Irish resilience and survival. They recount how a Galway widow named Suzanne Brown became separated from her youngest daughter, Rose, in Montreal's fever sheds after she had nearly succumbed to typhus, only to recover from her illness having lost contact with her child. While convalescing under the care of the Grey Nuns, Rose's mother, Suzanne Brown, helped educate some of the other orphans they had taken in. According to the annal:

> When she found herself surrounded by the orphans who absorbed her teachings like thirsty earth absorbs the dew, she thought of her little Rose: 'If I had her here with me, she said, I would teach her with all the others.' With this weighing on her mind, one March evening, she attended a . . . Holy Sacrament in St Patrick's church. In the silence of the ceremony, she was disturbed from her contemplation by the sound of a marble rolling on the floor which came to rest in the folds of her clothes. She had barely raised her eyes when she saw a little girl aged three or four running to collect it. 'Is this not my little Rose', she said trembling with emotion. Indeed, it was this child who she mourned and thought she had lost forever, now returned to her at this moment by our Lord, and by instinct, she reached out. However, her adoptive mother who had missed nothing of what happened, intervened and protested. Before the ceremony had even finished both women went to the sacristy to submit the case to Father Dowd. He did not delay in resolving the issue, and that very evening, Madame Brown triumphed, coming back to the refuge with little Rose.[131]

This reunification of Suzanne Brown with her daughter Rose attests to the broader role that the Grey Nuns played in caring for Irish emigrants and keeping their families together.

Implicit in their accounts of compassion and suffering, however, is also intense anxiety of proselytization. While there is limited evidence of actual religious conversions taking place within the fever sheds, the fear of them was intense. The Grey Nuns' *Typhus of 1847* annal recounts that Sister Collins 'in seeing Protestant ministers circulating in the shelters, she made a good guard against those that wished to indoctrinate'.[132] Likewise, Father Richards, the first English language priest for Irish Catholics in Montreal, who ultimately succumbed to typhus, is recorded taking charge of Famine orphans and insisting that 'a shed specifically [be] designated for children . . . in the fear that the Protestants would seize these poor little ones'.[133] On 16 July 1847, Sister Collins is also recalled 'having absented herself for a few moments from the bedside of her patients, a Protestant minister exerted his propaganda and by consequence argued for the alleged reform. But the Sister entered suddenly, her patients screaming'.[134] The Grey Nuns' annals recount an increasing sense of tension in late summer when 'a great number of Protestants circulated in the shelters, and saw with an envious eye the happy catch that the charity and selflessness of our sisters and priests were making daily. A great number converted to Catholicism. Children especially were collected with care to be placed in good families'.[135] Conversely, the plight of Protestant orphans inspired a strong press reaction and the publication of *The Emigrant Ship: Written for the Protestant Orphan Bazaar*, which is reproduced in this volume, to raise funds on their behalf.[136] The compression of ethno-religious and social tension into these confined settings led to an escalating sense of conflict. Like the coffin ships, the fever sheds became a contested cultural space.

The Grey Nuns' annals also attest to their spirit of female fellowship. They are written from the viewpoint of the entire community, and often collapse any distinction between past and present or individual and collective endeavours. In inscribing and reciting the annals, the Grey Nuns do not merely summon to memory the deeds of their fellow sisters and predecessors, but seek to relive their experiences. The names of individual sisters become subsumed within the entire community under the auspices of the pronoun 'we'. Thus, their recollection of their arrival in the fever sheds is recounted in the present tense:

> Despite the mud and other inconveniences, the sisters made their journey within twenty minutes, already hearing the groans of the ill and the wails of the dying . . . We disperse ourselves in this unfamiliar maze . . . Could we imagine for a moment the spectacle this multitude of men and women piled pell-mell offered, up to three or four in the same bed, indifferent to everything, groaning, however, heartbreakingly? We were running here, running there . . . supporting a poor, dying woman, ripping away from her the poor infant she clung to so close to her heart . . . We point out the heavens to another while wiping away his agonizing sweat. We have the cadavers taken away from those still breathing, and we took a look around us . . . We step outside the shelter only to find more of the miserable poor, recumbent without salvation, we eagerly go to their aid, multiplying our steps without counting. What misery! Who could describe them? This is not just a family, or one hundred that are ill, but almost an entire nation feeling the anxieties of this agony.[137]

INTRODUCTION

In recounting their experiences, the Grey Nuns largely eschew individual deeds to emphasize the actions of the entire community. Their narrative is focalized from the perspective of a present tense, collective voice that conveys the nuns' sense of disorientation and the intensity of Irish suffering when they first arrived in the sheds. The sheer scale of Irish misery is also intimated in the figure of the 'poor infant' ripped away from the 'dying woman' who becomes a synecdoche for the family and the 'entire nation feeling the anxieties of this agony'.

Moreover, when the annals do focus on the deeds of individual sisters they appear representative of the community as a whole. Impressions of individual nuns flash briefly into view and then quickly recede. Consider how the narrative perspective oscillates between the third person 'we' and first person 'I' as well as past and present in the following passage:

> The odour that these cadavers produced and the horror they naturally caused add to the distressing picture of this situation. We, nevertheless, see the sisters calmly patrolling around the diverse enclosures; they take charge of the department Mother McMullen trusted them with. Sister BRAULT expends energy, as well as showing remarkable strength to gently care for her beloved sick . . .
>
> Sister Desjardins appears to us as an unchanged, flowering figure. Oh! If she had in this moment her brushes and a canvas, she would faithfully reproduce the gloomy scenes of our sad shelters. But it is to these poor sick individuals that she presently gives all her time.
>
> Over there, at the end of the dark corridor, I see the silhouette of Sister Marie [Barbeau]. She strives to find the most miserable.[138]

In fact, Sister Marie Barbeau perished on 21 July 1847, as a result of caring for Famine emigrants, but with each retelling of her story she is summoned to memory for alleviating their misery. Her silhouette marks her liminal position between past and present, individual action and communal recollection, life and death. She hovers in the shadows of the sheds, a borderer of the dead.

The death zones at Grosse Isle and Montreal were also documented in other primary sources. One of the few eyewitnesses who wrote about both locations over several decades was the reverend Bernard O'Reilly.[139] In 1847, he had been stationed as a missionary priest in the village of Sherbrooke, where he had arrived a year earlier from a much larger urban parish in Quebec City. As a missionary priest, he served a mixed and largely impoverished congregation of French-Canadian and Irish Catholic parishioners who were scattered over a vast area. O'Reilly was summoned from Sherbrooke to serve on Grosse Isle from 6 to 14 July 1847, and then a week later he testified about his experiences, on 23 July, before a commission of inquiry instituted by Montreal's Board of Health. On 11 July 1847, O'Reilly sent a letter from Grosse Isle that exclaimed: 'this is strong language, but the language of a priest and an Irishman . . . who writes

27

INTRODUCTION

on the coffins of the hecatombs slaughtered by legislative neglect, much more than by the hands of sickness'. Because of the difficulty of communicating from the quarantine station, O'Reilly's letter was published only sixteen days later in the *Quebec Mercury* on 27 July 1847.[140] Shortly thereafter when called to testify before Montreal's Board of Health, O'Reilly insisted that 'many thousands of my fellow-creatures, my fellow countrymen, and subjects of this empire, . . . have been sacrificed to *neglect* and *improvidence*'. Such negligence could be construed, he suggested, as 'consent to the wholesale murder of thousands who are just now on the ocean, or preparing to leave home for Canada', unless conditions improved.[141]

It was after he left Grosse Isle and was travelling en route to Montreal that O'Reilly had a profoundly formative experience. On 18 July in the town of Trois Rivières, he presided over the mass-adoption of a party of Famine orphans, whom he had escorted from quarantine, into French-Canadian families. As described in a letter by Father Thomas Cook, 'Messrs Harper and O'Reilly went through here this morning, in great spirits. Charitable people everywhere are arguing over who is to have the orphans whom they have brought from Quebec'.[142] Their procession was also reported in *The Gazette* and *The Pilot*, both of which noted that 'in less than hour [they] found worthy *habitants* with either small families, or who had no children, to adopt these poor little destitute orphans, and to secure for them the comforts of a home, and the care of parents, under [their] immediate eye'. According to *The Pilot*, such adoptions attest to 'the humane and Christian dispositions of our [French-] Canadian brethren' in spite 'of the calumny which imputes to them hostility to the Irish race'.[143]

The memory of this generosity engendered a heightened sense of empathy in O'Reilly for his French-Canadian parishioners. In a lecture that he delivered in New York in 1852, he specifically paid tribute to the 'Bishops, Priests, Nuns, and people of Canada, in 1847', but most especially

> the *French Canadian people*: for, . . . so strongly were their sympathies aroused towards the emigrant – that although most parishes already wept for their dead, or feared for their sick Pastor, and that it appeared certain death to take an emigrant under one's roof: still, as each Parish Priest returned from Quarantine, or from Montreal, the parishioners came forward to meet them at the landing places with long trains of carriages, to escort the Priest and his numerous orphans home. And touching was the meeting of those French mothers with the little children misfortune gave them.[144]

As a parish priest himself who escorted Famine orphans from quarantine into the arms of the 'charitable people' of Quebec, O'Reilly provided one of the first documented Irish expressions of gratitude for French-Canadian generosity in 1847. His reminiscences of 'the meeting of those French mothers with the little children misfortune gave them' became increasingly elaborate in later years. Indeed,

28

INTRODUCTION

O'Reilly expounds upon his experiences in *The Mirror of True Womanhood;*
A Book of Instruction for Women in the World that was first published in 1877 and
then reprinted in sixteen editions by 1883. In *The Mirror of True Womanhood*, he
claims to 'remember returning from quarantine, in the second week of July, with
the Rev. John Harper', after having

> spent a fortnight among the fever-sheds, and [having] had, at the urgent
> request of their parishioners, brought home with them a large number of
> orphans . . . We had been delayed, . . . and on our arrival about midnight
> at Three Rivers, we found a crowd of eager and excited women, mothers
> of families all of them, waiting and watching for us . . . It was a spectacle
> worthy of the admiration of angels, which was beheld that sultry mid-
> night in July, these farmers' wives, weeping every one of them with that
> holy emotion which the sweetest charity creates, pressing around their
> pastor and choosing, when they could, in the uncertain light, the child
> that pleased them best, or accepting joyously and folding in a motherly
> embrace the little orphan allotted to them.[145]

Thirty years later, O'Reilly vividly remembered delivering Irish children into the
arms of French-Canadian mothers who waited so steadfastly to receive them. In
both O'Reilly's and popular memory, their adoptions were recollected as a form
of religious devotion.

Such French-Canadian compassion inspired him to conjure the memory of their
fallen parents to pledge support for their benefactors as a sacred responsibility.
To his Irish brethren, O'Reilly declared that he would not be worthy of his collar

> if I attempted to stir up strife between the Irish exile on the banks of the
> St. Lawrence and his Canadian brother, when I cannot pass a thresh-
> old in town or country where I may not see some fatherless, motherless
> orphan from Ireland, seated at the fire-side, and enjoying the sunshine
> and warmth of French Canadian sympathy and protection . . . The noble
> Canadian Clergymen who descended to an early grave, the victims
> of their devotedness to my poor stricken countrymen, would they not
> raise their voices from the tomb to accuse me of unnatural, unparalleled
> ingratitude? How could I visit Montreal where I saw those heroic nuns
> attending by night and by day the death bed of the emigrant; and, day
> after day, laying down their lives in the performance of the work of Char-
> ity? It is only a week ago, that I heard the death-knell of another of these
> angels of earth, who caught the contagion whilst attending upon our poor
> orphans . . . How many more of that devoted French Canadian Clergy
> will be torn from their flocks and their heart-broken parents by the hand
> of pestilence? And all this for the sake of the Irish emigrant! Could there
> be a pulse in my heart that would not throb for such a people? No! If
> I loved them not, praised them not, blessed them not, you would spurn

me from you to some other shore where I could no longer see the emigrant's unhonoured grave, and beside it the grave of the Canadian priest and the Canadian nun, who cheered the lonely exile's last hour . . . But the scenes of Grosse Isle and Montreal would follow me thither; the spectacle I beheld at Three Rivers and in the neighbouring parishes, would come back to my mind's eye; – those Canadian women as I landed on the wharf, with my orphan charge, craving them from me, unappalled by their squalor and the dread sickness that spoke through every wan feature, pressing them to their bosoms with more than maternal fondness and heroism, and bedewing them with tears of sympathy![146]

If the Irish were the beneficiaries of French-Canadian compassion, then they were beholden to reciprocate in kind. In the midst of continued French-Canadian and Irish suffering, O'Reilly sought to raise the ghosts of the Famine dead and to swear on the 'emigrant's grave and . . . grave of the Canadian Priest and the Canadian nun' that it was his sacred duty to honour the sacrifice made by the French-Canadian people to better establish them on their native soil. He conjures a spectacle of reproach from the dead should he 'stir up strife between the Irish exile . . . and his Canadian brother' to sunder the bonds of his brethren, their fraternal ties having been sanctified by suffering in the fever sheds and incarnated in Famine orphans. Should he break faith with either side of his congregation, they 'would come back to [his] mind's eye' in silent condemnation.

Thus, the myth of the Famine orphans was created.[147] It was not until a generation later, however, that it became popularized in texts such as O'Reilly's *Mirror of True Womanhood* (1877) and especially John Francis Maguire's *The Irish in America* (1868)[148] which is partially reproduced in this volume. There has been relatively little research on the construction and transmission of Famine memory in North America in the decades after 1847, although both Mark McGowan and James Donnelly have examined its dissemination in the writing of Irish nationalists such as John Mitchel, Thomas D'Arcy McGee and Maguire in the 1860s in particular.[149] Unlike Mitchel or McGee, however, Maguire's interpretation of Famine memory was based on the interviews he conducted with people who actually lived through the experience in Canada and the United States. His tour of North America in 1866 was motivated by his desire to find evidence that the Irish fared better abroad than under British rule at home. He also emphasized their resilience and upward mobility rather than sense of grievance and anti-English hostility to distance himself from Mitchel's brand of revolutionary nationalism and Fenian sentiment following the failed invasion of Canada at the Battle of Ridgeway in June 1866 and Irish rising in March 1867. Whereas Mitchel styled himself in *Jail Journal; or, Five Years in British Prisons* (1854) as the definitive Famine exile, Maguire sought to discover the stories of the steerage class. The importance of *The Irish in America* lies in the facts both that he came to North America to converse with Famine emigrants and those who ministered to them, and that it found a mass readership on both sides of the Atlantic. Because he was editor of the *Cork Examiner*, the paper reported in detail on Maguire's travels and reprinted the numerous reviews his book received. The extensive publicity generated by these reviews and sales provided the conduit through which the memory of the Famine orphans was popularized, in both an Irish and international context.

More importantly, Maguire's evocation of the Famine orphans is the first to combine all three core motifs that recur in popular memory: (i) the posthumous fulfilment of a maternal pledge to maintain their Catholic identity, (ii) the children's procession from the fever sheds into nearby communities and (iii) the retention of their Irish surnames after their adoption into French-Canadian families. He repeatedly emphasizes the spectacle of the dying Irish mother bequeathing her children to the care of Catholic clergy who preside over their adoption into French-Canadian households. As the Irish beneficiaries of French-Canadian compassion, the orphans appeared to be, in a cultural sense, immaculately conceived, effortlessly integrated into French-Canadian society without the anxieties of assimilation or of losing their Irish identity. They were summoned to memory as reminders of the instinctive good will that the French and Irish should have felt towards one another in the decades after 1847 when they increasingly came into conflict.[150] Communal tensions and ethnic rivalries were set aside by the symbol of the Famine orphans. Indeed, their memory was often compensatory for the varying degrees of tension that existed between Irish Catholics and French-Canadians in the latter nineteenth century.

The myth of the Famine orphans was also embodied in children who not only survived the calamity but were adopted, educated and ordained as priests fully capable of shaping their own stories. Two of their accounts by Thomas Quinn and Robert Walsh are included at the end of this volume. Thomas (6) and his elder brother Patrick (12) had been left orphans on Grosse Isle in August 1847 after having been forced to emigrate from the Strokestown Park House estate of Major Denis Mahon on the *Naomi*, one of the worst of the coffin ships. During the *Naomi*'s voyage from Liverpool to Quebec, 196 out of 421 passengers perished; a further 267 of 467 passengers died on the *Virginius* which also transported Mahon's tenants. Denis Mahon was assassinated in November 1847 after their horrific fate became widely known. The Quinn brothers were orphaned and adopted by a French-Canadian family in rural Quebec. They were well educated, entered the seminary and became priests who ministered to joint French-Canadian and Irish Catholic congregations. As they rose through the ranks of the clergy, the Quinn brothers endeavoured to create institutions that would bring together their French and Irish parishioners. 'Through their teaching, both brothers ensured that their parishioners . . . did not forget the lessons of the Famine'.[151]

Perhaps the most poignant expression of Irish gratitude for French-Canadian generosity came from the Famine orphan Father Thomas Quinn himself.[152] On 25 June 1912, he delivered a speech entitled 'Une Voix d'Irlande' – 'A Voice of

INTRODUCTION

Ireland' – in Quebec City at the First Congress of the French Language in Canada. Speaking in French, he recalled:

> It was in 1847. A famine, even worse than the one which had preceded it, threatened the Irish people with total extinction. The most astonishing part of the awful spectacle was, not to see the people die, but to see them live through such great distress. Like walking skeletons they went, in tears, seeking hospitality from more favoured lands. Stirred with compassion, French-Canadian priests, braving the epidemic, contended for the glory of rushing to their relief. I still remember one of these admirable clergymen who led us to the bedside of my dying father. As he saw us, my father with his failing voice repeated the old Irish adage, 'Remember your soul and your liberty'.[153]

In his remembrance of his father's dying utterance, Father Quinn identified his French parishioners' vulnerability with his own. Just as he was taken in as a helpless orphan by the French-Canadian people, he would now champion their linguistic and religious freedom in turn. He implored his audience to 'struggle without fear, like O'Connell and Redmond, because your cause is right and just'. Father Quinn equated Ireland's demand for Home Rule with the French-Canadian struggle for cultural survival. In travelling from Famine Ireland to Quebec, he found his voice in French Canada.

The other orphan, Robert Walsh, had lost his voice as a result of the Famine migration. In *The Irish in America*, John Francis Maguire recounts the story of an unnamed child who was so traumatized by his experiences that he had lost the power to speak:

> A decent couple had sailed in one of the ships, bringing with them two girls and a boy, the elder of the former being about thirteen, the boy not more than seven or eight. The father died first, the mother next. As the affrighted children knelt by their dying mother, . . . she invoked a blessing upon him and his weeping sisters. Thus the pious mother died in the fever-shed of Grosse Isle. The children were taken care of, and sent to the same district, so as not to be separated from each other. The boy was received into the home of a French Canadian; his sisters were adopted by another family in the neighbourhood. For two weeks the boy never uttered a word, never smiled, never appeared conscious of the presence of those around him, or of the attention lavished on him by his generous protectors, who had almost come to believe that they had adopted a little mute, or that he had momentarily lost the power of speech through fright or starvation. But at the end of the fortnight he relieved them of their fears by uttering some words of, to them, an unknown language; and from that moment the spell, wrought, as it were, by the cold hand of his dying mother, passed from the spirit of the boy, and he thenceforth clung

with the fondness of youth to his second parents. The Irish orphan soon spoke the language of his new home, though he never lost the memory of the fever-sheds and the awful death-bed, or of his weeping sisters ... Of his Irish name, which he was able to retain, he is very proud; and though his tongue is more that of a French Canadian, his feelings and sympathies are with the people and the country of his birth.[154]

In finding his voice and then becoming a priest, the Famine orphan's ordination represents the posthumous fulfilment of a maternal pledge. 'The spirit of the boy' epitomizes an ideal of adaptability and linguistic facility as well as a remarkable story of escape from adversity. The formative experience 'of the fever sheds and the awful death-beds' takes on the qualities of a fable in Maguire's prose.

Yet the Famine orphan's story does not end happily. Recent research has revealed him to be Robert Walsh.[155] It is most likely that his family sailed on the *Avon* from Cork which arrived at Grosse Isle on 13 July 1847, after fifty-four days at sea, where it was detained in quarantine for thirteen days. It was also one of the worst of the coffin ships, with a total death toll of 246, including 136 at sea, twenty-six on board ship at Grosse Isle and thirty-six in the fever sheds on the island. More importantly, records exist for Robert and his sisters Anne and Mary's evacuation from the island under the care of Reverends Bernard O'Reilly and Jean Harper of St Grégoire on 14 July in the 'Emigration Agent Returns of Emigrant Orphans, 1847'.[156] O'Reilly testified before Montreal's Board of Health on 23 July that 'I only visited two ships, the *Avon* and the *Triton* [on Grosse Isle] ... We administered the last rites of religion to about two hundred on board these two ships, and many others were in a state of great debility'.[157] He added:

So long as they are sent away from the ports of Great Britain and Ireland crammed up by hundreds in the hold of a ship, without air, food, or the necessary means of procuring cleanliness and ventilation, as on board the *Avon* and the *Triton*, they must die by hundreds; disease must seize on the strongest frames and soon consume them.[158]

Among the children rescued from the hold of the *Avon* and then escorted from Grosse Isle by O'Reilly and Harper to be adopted by the people of St Grégoire were Anne, Mary and Robert Walsh, whose names also appear in the town's orphan register.[159]

As he grew older, Robert Walsh's most earnest desire was to trace his family history and establish contact with living relatives in Ireland. In 1857, he naively wrote a letter to 'an unnamed Irish bishop' in which he recalls that:

In the horrendous emigration of 1847, my father, David Walsh, and my mother, Honora O'Donnell resolved to go with their family to [the New World] where they had relatives. They had five children; but they left in Ireland with relatives or acquaintances a little girl, aged roughly five to six months, if I remember well. She could have been more or less, for I then was but seven years old and had experienced a long voyage so my misfortunes made me lose the exact memory of these things. My oldest sister was ten and called Mary, the youngest was eight and is called Anny; I had a younger brother called Patrick; I think he was only four years old.

We all arrived in Quebec on the St. Lawrence at the end of June or beginning of July 1847. There, my father, my mother, and my brother Patrick died. They were sick of the typhus which caused so much devastation in this year in Canada. We were three, my two sisters and me, without any support in a foreign country.[160]

In his letter, Robert Walsh goes on to request information about his younger sister who had been left behind in Ireland after the family emigrated. He contends:

We were of Kilkenny, if I am right, and there must still be some of our relations there. My father was the intendant of the lord Montgomery who lived very near Kilkenny then I believe. It was he who conveyed labourers in the lord's service. I was then an infant and I remember that I would go sometimes with my mother and sisters and the lord to a magnificent orchard near his estate. How I love to recall these memories which are for me like a fair dream! Yes, I had a father, a mother, and now they are no more. If only I learned one day that we have relations who think of us, who know the details of our misfortune, and who would write to me, then I would be a little comforted . . . My sister, my dear sister, if she exists, when she would learn that she has a brother and sisters in Canada who are thinking of her she would write to them, although she does not know them! Oh! how much these words would mean in our hearts! We will see then we are not alone in the world, and it is this thought that will give us courage to endure our separation here.[161]

Unfortunately, there is no evidence that Robert Walsh ever received a reply to his letter. He did, however, embark on his own voyage to Ireland in 1872 to find his younger sister, but was sorely disappointed because nobody remembered his family or where they had lived. He returned to Canada and died soon thereafter on 31 January 1873, at the age of 33. He never found that 'little comfort' of lasting kinship in Ireland. His profound desire to rediscover his infant sister they had left behind as proof that 'we are not alone in the world', to provide 'courage to endure our separation here', ultimately came to nothing.

Yet despite his failure, Robert Walsh's voice has been preserved from oblivion as an ephemeral archival remain. It attests that first person primary sources exist for even the most vulnerable of Famine emigrants, such as orphaned children. Records in the vernacular of the steerage class like the former tenants from Lissadell are comparatively rare; but eyewitness impressions of them and their caregivers abound in this volume. It brings together major newly discovered primary sources such as the journals of Stephen De Vere and the Grey Nuns' annals that are published here for the first time, along with numerous accounts of those who sailed across the Atlantic in 1847 and witnessed the arrival of Famine emigrants in the fever sheds of Grosse Isle, Montreal, and in the United States. Whether it is the testimony of benefactors like Bernard O'Reilly who escorted Irish children to safety from the sheds, or the voices of orphans themselves, these records provide first person accounts of the Famine migration from the perspective of those who endured, suffered and survived. They range from full length annals and narratives to hastily scrawled letters and journal entries, but all give voice to Famine emigrants themselves and their caregivers. These primary sources have remained undiscovered and overlooked to the detriment of scholarship on the Irish Famine migration. Their recovery provides an opportunity to create fuller histories of the Famine exodus from the first-hand perspectives of those who witnessed it.

Jason King

Notes

1 This *Times* editorial was republished by Robert Whyte in his introduction to *The Ocean Plague: A Voyage to Quebec in an Irish Emigrant Vessel* (Boston, MA: Coolidge and Wiley, 1848), pp. 14–16.

2 K. A. Miller, 'Emigration to North America in the era of the Great Famine, 1845–5', in J. Crowley, W. J. Smyth and M. Murphy (eds), *Atlas of the Great Irish Famine* (Cork: Cork University Press, 2012), pp. 214–227, on pp. 214–215.

3 D. Wilson, *Thomas D'Arcy McGee: Passion, Reason, and Politics – 1825–1857* (Montreal & Kingston: McGill-Queens University Press, 2008), vol. 1, p. 192.

4 G. Moran, *Sending Out Ireland's Poor: Assisted Emigration to North America in the Nineteenth Century* (Dublin: Four Courts, 2004); P. Gray, ' "Shovelling out your paupers": The British state and Irish Famine migration, 1846–50', *Patterns of Prejudice*, 33.4 (1999), pp. 47–65.

5 P. O'Neill, *Famine Irish and the American Racial State* (London: Routledge, 2017); M. Corporaal and J. King, 'Irish Global Migration and Memory: Transnational Perspectives on Ireland's Great Hunger and Exodus', *Atlantic Studies: Global Currents*, 11.3 (2014), pp. 301–320.

6 M. J. Gallman, *Receiving Erin's Children. Philadelphia, Liverpool, and the Irish Famine Migration, 1845–1855* (Chapel Hill, NC: University of North Carolina Press, 2000); D. Horner, ' "If The Evil Now Growing Around Us Be Not Staid": Montreal and Liverpool Confront the Irish Famine Migration as a Transnational Crisis in Urban Governance', *Histoire Sociale / Social History* 46.92 (2013), pp. 349–366; J. King, 'Une Voix d'Irlande: Integration, Migration, and Travelling Nationalism Between Famine Ireland and Quebec in the Long Nineteenth Century', in C. Reilly (ed.), *The Famine Irish: Emigration and the Great Hunger* (Dublin: History Press, 2016), pp. 193–208; J. King, 'The Famine Irish, the Grey Nuns, and the fever sheds of Montreal: Prostitution and female religious institution building', in C. Kinealy, J. King and C. Reilly, (eds.), Women and the Great Hunger (Hamden, CT: Quinnipiac University Press, 2016), pp. 95–108; M. McGowan, *Death or Canada: The Irish Famine Migration to Toronto, 1847* (Montreal and Toronto: Novalis Publishing, 2009).

7 H. Hirota, *Expelling the Poor: American Seaboard States & the 19th Century Origins of American Immigration Policy* (Oxford: Oxford University Press, 2017).

INTRODUCTION

8 M. Corporaal, *Relocated Memories: The Great Famine in Irish and Diaspora Fiction, 1846–1870* (Syracuse, New York: Syracuse University Press, 2017); M. Corporaal and C. Cusack, 'Rites of passage: The coffin ship as a site of immigrants' identity formation in Irish and Irish American fiction, 1855–85, *Atlantic Studies*, 8.3 (2011), pp. 343–359; E. Mark-Fitzgerald, *Commemorating the Irish Famine: Memory and the Monument* (Liverpool: Liverpool University Press, 2013); J. King, 'Remembering Famine orphans: The transmission of Famine memory between Ireland and Québec', in C. Noack, L. Janssen,and V. Comerford (eds), Holodomor and Gorta Mór: Histories, Memories, and Representations of Famine in Ukraine and Ireland (New York: Anthem Press, 2012), pp. 115–144; J. King, 'The remembrance of Irish Famine migrants in the fever sheds of Montreal', in M. Corporaal, C. Cusack, L. Janssen and R. van den Beuken (eds), *Global Legacies of the Great Irish Famine: Transnational and Interdisciplinary Perspectives* (Brussels: Peter Lang, 2014), pp. 245–266; M. McGowan, *Creating Canadian Historical Memory: The Case of the Famine Migration of 1847* (Ottawa: Canadian Historical Association, 2006); C. McMahon, 'Recrimination and reconciliation: Great Famine memory in Liverpool and Montreal at the turn of the twentieth century', *Atlantic Studies*, 11.3 (2014), pp. 344–364.

9 J. King, 'The genealogy of *Famine Diary* in Ireland and Quebec: Ireland's Famine migration in historical fiction, historiography, and memory', *Éire-Ireland*, 47 (2012), pp. 45–69; M. McGowan, 'Famine, facts, and fabrication: An examination of diaries from the Irish Famine migration to Canada', *The Canadian Journal of Irish Studies*, 33. 2 (2007), pp. 48–55.

10 See J. King, 'The Famine Irish migration to Canada in 1847–1848: Assisted emigration, colonisation, and the unpublished Famine diaries of Stephen De Vere', in P. Fitzgerald and A. Russell (eds), *John Mitchel, Ulster, and the Great Irish Famine* (Dublin: Irish Academic Press, 2017), pp. 30–45.

11 N. van Hear, *New Diasporas: The Mass Exodus, Dispersal and Regrouping of Migrant Communities* (Seattle: University of Washington Press, 1998), p. 8.

12 Hirota, *Expelling the Poor*, pp. 41–69.

13 Ibid., p. 58.

14 Ibid., p. 208.

15 C. J. Houston and W. J. Smyth, *Irish Emigration and Canadian Settlement: Patterns, Links, and Letters* (Toronto: University of Toronto Press, 1990), pp. 27–29.

16 Ibid., p. 28.

17 Eyewitness accounts and newspaper coverage of the Famine Irish in 1847 at Grosse Isle quarantine station can also be found in M. O'Gallagher and R. M. Dompierre (eds), *Eyewitness: Grosse Isle, 1847* (Sainte-Foy, Quebec: Carraig Books, 1995), and A. Charbonneau and A. Sévigny (eds), *1847, Grosse Île: A Record of Daily Events* (Ottawa: Parks Canada, 1997).

18 S. De Vere, *Minutes of Evidence Before Select Committee on Colonisation from Ireland, Letter to the Select Committee* (30 November 1847) in *British Parliamentary Papers, Emigration*, vol. 5 (Shannon: Irish University Press, 1968), pp. 45–48; 1847–1848 America Journals, vols. I-II. Trinity College Library Dublin. Manuscripts Department, MSS 5061–5062 (hereafter, De Vere, MSS 5061–5062); 1847–1848 Letter-book. Trinity College Library Dublin. Manuscripts Department, MS 5075a (hereafter, De Vere, MS 5075a).

19 MS John Burke, *Reminiscences* (New York: New York Historical Society Library).

20 John Young, unpublished *'Diary of John Young'* in Nancy Mallett Archive and Museum of St. James' Cathedral, Courtesy of Nancy Mallett (St. James Cathedral, Toronto: Cathedral).

21 R. Whyte, *The Ocean Plague, or a Voyage to Quebec in an Irish Emigrant Vessel by 'A Cabin Passenger'* (Boston, MA: Coolidge and Wiley, 1848).

INTRODUCTION

22 H. Melville, *Redburn: His First Voyage* (New York: Russell & Russell, 1963 [1849]). Also see W. Gilman, *Melville's Early Life and Redburn* (London: Oxford University Press, 1951), p. 204.

23 Gore-Booth letters, appendix x, *Minutes of Evidence before Select Committee on Colonisation from Ireland, British Parliamentary Papers, Emigration*, vol. 5 (Shannon: Irish University Press, 1968), pp. 122–132.

24 Henry Johnson letter from Hamilton, Canada West, to Jane Johnson, Dungonnell, Antrim, 18 September 1848. McConnell MS. Metropolitan Toronto Central Library, Toronto, Ontario. Reprinted in L.Wyatt (ed.), 'The Johnson letters', *Ontario History* (1948), pp. 7–52.

25 J. White, letter from 'Grosse Island to Eleanor Wallace, Newtownards', 29 June, 1849. Public Record Office, Northern Ireland, document 1195/3/5. Reprinted in Houston and Smyth, *Irish Emigration and Canadian Settlement*, pp. 290–292.

26 W. Smith, *An Emigrant's Narrative, or, a Voice from the Steerage: Being a Brief Account of the Sufferings of the Emigrants in the Ship 'India,' on Her Voyage from Liverpool to New-York, in the Winter of 1847–8, Together with a Statement of the Cruelties Practiced Upon the Emigrants in the Staten Island Hospital* (New York: Published by the Author, 1850).

27 K. A. Miller, *Emigrants and Exiles: Ireland and the Irish Exodus to North America* (Oxford: Oxford University Press, 1985), p. 295.

28 Miller, *Emigrants and Exiles*, pp. 294, 314, 292, 326.

29 C. Kinealy, *This Great Calamity: The Irish Famine, 1845–52* (Boulder, CO: Roberts Rinehart, 1995), p. 299.

30 Whyte, *The Ocean Plague*, p. 10.

31 C. Woodham-Smith, *The Great Hunger: Ireland, 1845–1849* (Harmondsworth: Penguin, 1962), p. 267.

32 Gore-Booth letters, p. 130.

33 Ibid.

34 Ibid, p. 131.

35 Young, 'Diary', p. 2.

36 Houston and Smyth, *Irish Emigration and Canadian Settlement*, p. 289.

37 Johnson, 'Johnson letters', p. 35.

38 Whyte, *Ocean Plague*, p. 31.

39 Ibid., p. 29.

40 Melville, *Redburn*, p. 250.

41 Smith, *A Voice from the Steerage*, p. 5.

42 Corporaal and Cusack, 'Rites of passage', p. 345.

43 M. M. Bakhtin, *The Dialogic Imagination*. Ed. Michael Holquist. Translated by Caryl Emerson and Michael Holquist (Austin, TX: University of Texas Press, 1981), pp. 70, 77–79.

44 See King, 'The remembrance of Irish Famine migrants in the fever sheds of Montreal', pp. 245–266.

45 Whyte, *Ocean Plague*, p. 34.

46 Young, 'Diary', p. 6.

47 Smith, *A Voice from the Steerage*, pp. 16–17.

48 Melville, pp. 244–245; Smith, p. 16.

49 S. H. Craigy, 'Journal of a passage from Belfast to New York', Public Record Office, Northern Ireland, reference number: T 3258/66, pp. 6–7.

50 Craigy, 'Journal', pp. 9–10.

51 Melville, *Redburn*, p. 254.

52 When his vessel was threatened with imminent destruction during an ocean gale, Johnson records how he 'took the matter cooly enough' (35), setting a standard for

INTRODUCTION

courageous resignation and equanimity that few of his Catholic fellow passengers –
most of whom were gathered on deck 'like sheep in a pen', 'praying and crossing
themselves' and 'crying on the Captain to save them' (34) – could hope to match. John
Burke too stresses his personal bravery and the leadership role he played under adverse
conditions, when his vessel entered seas that were 'always very squally [–] and ours
was no exception no picknic – [where] I'm free to say I acted as Cap'n between decks
and a most uncomfortable and trying position it turned out to be' (24).

53 E. Burke, *A Philosophical Enquiry Into the Origin of Our Ideas of the Sublime and
    Beautiful* (1759). Ed. James T. Boulton (London: University of Notre Dame Press,
    1958), p. 58.
54 Smith, *A Voice from the Steerage*, pp. 9–10.
55 Craigy, 'Journal', pp. 2–3, 9.
56 Johnson, 'Johnson letters', p. 35.
57 Whyte, *Ocean Plague*, p. 60.
58 Ibid., p. 22.
59 Young, 'Diary', p. 12.
60 Melville, *Redburn*, p. 287.
61 William Smith records a similarly favourable impression of the pilot as the *India*
    approaches New York harbour: 'about nine o'clock next morning', he writes, 'the pilot
    came on board amid the huzzas of those who were able to shout for joy. Early in the
    afternoon, the exciting cry of "Land" "Land!" "Land!" ran through the ship like a wild
    fire. A number of passengers came down from the deck to tell their sick relatives and
    friends that they had seen it, and yet such were my feelings, vacillating between hope
    and fear, that I could scarcely believe it. The effect it had on some of the passengers,
    baffles all description. Some fell on their knees and thanked God for his mercy to them,
    some wept for joy, others capered about, exhibiting extravagant demonstrations of joy'
    (23). 'Early on the morning of the 27th May we sighted land', writes John Burke, also
    destined for New York City, 'and to the weary, Emaciated, forlorn Emigrants [it] is
    about the happiest moment of his life no words can describe it. Thanking the lord for
    our deliverance and full of hope in the future' (28).
62 Craigy, 'Journal', pp. 28–29.
63 H. D. Thoreau, *The Shipwreck*, *Putnam's Monthly*, 5.30 (1855), pp. 632–637, on
    p. 637.
64 J. Pugliese, 'Crisis heterotopias and border zones of the dead', *Continuum*, 23.5 (2009),
    pp. 663–679.
65 Whyte, *Ocean Plague*, p. 92. Also see J. King, 'Mortuary spectacles: The genealogy
    of the images of the Famine Irish coffin ships and Montreal's fever sheds', in M. Cor-
    poraal, O. Frawley and E. Mark-FitzGerald (eds), *The Great Irish Famine: Visual and
    Material Cultures* (Liverpool: Liverpool University Press, 2018), pp. 88–109.
66 Whyte, *Ocean Plague*, p. 80.
67 Ibid., p. 74.
68 Houston and Smyth, *Irish Emigration and Canadian Settlement*, p. 290.
69 Ibid., p. 292.
70 Ibid., p. 291.
71 Anon. 'Notes of a trip to Canada East', *The Globe* (1 September, 1847).
72 Whyte, *Ocean Plague*, pp. 74, 71.
73 Ibid., pp. 80–81.
74 See King, 'The Famine Irish migration to Canada in 1847–1848', pp. 24–37.
75 De Vere, MS 5061, pp. 2–3.
76 Ibid.
77 De Vere, *Minutes of Evidence*, p. 45.
78 Ibid., pp. 45–48.

INTRODUCTION

79 A year after his arrival in British North America, De Vere reiterated in a letter to Sir G. Wilder how unsanitary the steamers serving the emigrants were when he first travelled upon them. 'I have frequently travelled upon them since', he writes, '+ I found them comfortable; but I do most strongly maintain that they were small, ill-ventilated, + incommodious if considered with reference to the numbers + conditions of those whom they carried, those squalid masses of filth and disease whom they disgorged daily'. 'The effect of ill ventilation and infected air upon those in health', he adds, 'was distinctly visible. I saw one poor fellow beginning to droop, took a cabin passage for him at once, put him into a clean airy berth, + had the pleasure of seeing him land at Toronto in perfect health' (De Vere, MS 5075a, pp. 178–179).

80 De Vere, *Minutes of Evidence*, p. 48.

81 O. MacDonagh, *A Pattern of Government Growth: Passenger Acts and Their Enforcement, 1800–1860* (London: MacGibbon & Gee, 1961), pp. 194–199.

82 A. De Vere, *Recollections of Aubrey De Vere* (London: Edward Arnold, 1897), p. 253.

83 MacDonagh, *A Pattern of Government Growth*, p. 191.

84 De Vere, MS 5061, p. 4.

85 Ibid., p. 7.

86 Ibid., pp. 14–15.

87 Ibid., p. 16.

88 De Vere, MS 5062, pp. 48–50.

89 Ibid., p. 4.

90 Ibid., p. 4.

91 De Vere, MS 5061, p. 55; De Vere, MS 5062, pp. 5, 12, 14, 24.

92 De Vere, MS 5075a, pp. 81–82.

93 De Vere, MS 5061, p. 55.

94 De Vere, MS 5075a, p. 133.

95 De Vere MS 5061, p. 14.

96 Limerick City Archive, Aubrey De Vere Letters: P221/396.

97 De Vere, MS 5075a, pp. 135, 163.

98 Ibid., p. 152.

99 Also see King, 'Remembering and forgetting the Famine Irish in Quebec', pp. 20–41, 31–34.

100 De Vere, MS. 5061, p. 54.

101 De Vere, MS 5062, p. 8. Also see De Vere, MS 5061, p. 54.

102 De Vere, MS 5061, p. 22.

103 Ibid.

104 De Vere, MS 5062, p. 16.

105 De Vere, MS 5053, pp. 1–10.

106 MacDonagh, *A Pattern of Government Growth*, pp. 185–187; Moran, *Sending Out Ireland's Poor*, pp. 101–116.

107 Smith, *A Voice from the Steerage*, p. 28.

108 Ibid., p. 34.

109 Melville, *Redburn*, p. 282. 'What ordinance', Redburn asks, 'makes it obligatory upon the captain of a ship, to supply the steerage passengers with decent lodgings, and give them light and air in that foul den, where they are immured, during a long voyage across the Atlantic? What ordinance necessitates him to place the *galley*, or steerage-passengers' stove, in a dry place of shelter, where the emigrants can do their cooking during a storm, or wet weather? What ordinance obliges him to give them more room on deck, and let them have an occasional run fore and aft? – There is no law concerning these things. And if there was, who but some Howard in office would see it enforced? and how seldom is there a Howard in office!' (282). Nevertheless, despite his scepticism about legislation designed for the protection of emigrants at

INTRODUCTION

sea, Redburn does feel that at least limited steps should be taken for the prevention of loss of life. 'To be sure', he writes, 'no vessel full of emigrants, by any possible precautions, could in case of a fatal disaster at sea, hope to save the tenth part of the souls on board; yet provision should certainly be made for a handful of survivors, to carry home the tidings of her loss; for even in the worst of the calamities that befell patient Job, some *one* at least of his servants escaped to report it' (285).

110 Melville, *Redburn*, pp. 282–283.

111 'Besides that natural tendency, which hurries into oblivion the last woes of the poor', Redburn writes of his ill-fated voyage on the *Highlander*, 'other causes combine to suppress the detailed circumstances of disasters like these. Such things, if widely known, operate unfavourably to the ship, and make her a bad name; and to avoid detection at quarantine, a captain will state the case in the most palliating light, and strive to hush it up, as much as he can' (281).

112 Melville, *Redburn*, p. 283.

113 Ibid.

114 Thoreau, *The Shipwreck*, pp. 232–233.

115 Ibid.

116 But see King, 'The Famine Irish, the Grey Nuns, and the fever sheds of Montreal', pp. 95–107; and King, 'The remembrance of Irish Famine migrants'. The points developed here are taken from these works.

117 J. King (ed.), *Irish Famine Archive*, http://faminearchive.nuigalway.ie. Also see J. King, 'Remembering Famine orphans: The transmission of Famine memory between Ireland and Quebec', p. 141.

118 Grey Nuns Famine Annal, *The Typhus of 1847*, *Ancien Journal*, Volume II, p. 16. http://faminearchive.nuigalway.ie/docs/grey-nuns/TheTyphusof1847.pdf. (hereafter, *The Typhus of 1847*).

119 Ibid., p. 1.

120 A. T. Sadlier, *Life of Mother Gamelin: Foundress and First Superior of the Sisters of Charity of Providence* (Montreal: Mother House of Providence, 1912), pp. 191–192. Sadlier translated this text from French into English. She was the daughter of the prolific author Mary Anne Sadlier who wrote several novels about the Famine Irish in Canada and the United States, including *Willy Burke; or, the Irish Orphan in America* (1850); *New Lights; or, Life in Galway* (1853); *The Blakes and Flanagans* (1855); *Con O'Regan; or, Emigrant Life in the New World* (1856); *Elinor Preston; or, Scenes at Home and Abroad* (1857); and *Bessy Conway; or, The Irish Girl in America* (1861).

121 Sadlier, *Life of Mother Gamelin*, p. 193.

122 These records are held in the Providence Archives Montreal: *Mother House of Montreal Chronicles, 1828–1864*, (May 1847– March 1848), pp. 72–85; *Notes Historiques des Souers de la Providence 1799–1893*, pp. 46–62; Positio *of Mother Emilie Tavernier-Gamelin*, pp. 168–172, 201; *The Institute of Providence*, tome II, pp. 111–163, 170–171; *Institute of Providence*, tome IV, pp. 145–161, 165–176; 'Typhus Orphans Register'; 'St-Jérôme-Émilien/Saint Patrick Hospital Chronicles (M6)'; *Activités Hospitalières des Soeurs de Charité de la Providence (au Canada et en pays des missions*, pp. 18–23 (D2259.H2.2 (775) – AG-Cb1.1).

123 M. E-L. Couanier de Launay, *History of the Religious Hospitallers of Saint Joseph*, vol. II, 3rd edition (Paris: Société Générale De Librairie Catholique, 1889). Translated and revised by Sister F.C. Kerr (1949), LIB2000.607. Reference library, St. Joseph Region Archives of the Religious Hospitallers of St. Joseph, Kingston, Ontario, p. 219.

124 M. A. Sadlier, 'The Plague of 1847', *Messenger of the Sacred Heart* (Montreal: League of the Sacred Heart, 1891), pp. 204–208, on pp. 207–208.

INTRODUCTION

125 J. King, 'Remembering and forgetting the Famine Irish in Quebec: Genuine and false memoirs, communal memory and migration', *Irish Review* 44 (2012), pp. 20–41, on pp. 26–31.

126 Grey Nuns Famine Annal, *Ancien Journal*, vol. I. pp. 6–7. http://faminearchive.nuigalway.ie/docs/greynuns/GreyNunsFamineAnnalAncienJournalVolumeI.1847.pdf (hereafter, Grey Nuns, *Ancien Journal*).

127 Ibid., pp. 7–8.

128 Grey Nuns, *The Typhus of 1847*, p. 27.

129 Grey Nuns, *Ancien Journal*, p. 7.

130 *Montreal Transcript* (19 June 1847).

131 Grey Nuns Famine Annal, *Foundation of St. Patrick's Asylum*, pp. 10–11. http://faminearchive.nuigalway.ie/docs/grey-nuns/GreyNunsFamineAnnalFoundationofStPatricksOrphanAsylum.pdf (hereafter, Grey Nuns, *Foundation of St. Patrick's Asylum*).

132 Grey Nuns, *The Typhus of 1847*, p. 26.

133 Ibid., p. 28.

134 Ibid., p. 41.

135 Ibid., p. 84.

136 See King, 'The Remembrance of Irish Famine migrants', pp. 255–260; anon. 'The emigrant ship: Written for the protestant orphan bazaar,' in *The Literary Garland, and the British North American Magazine* (Montreal: Lowell and Gibson, 1850).

137 Grey Nuns, *The Typhus of 1847*, pp. 18–19.

138 Ibid., p. 22.

139 See King, 'The Genealogy of *Famine Diary*' for a more detailed discussion.

140 *Quebec Mercury* (27 July, 1847).

141 O'Gallagher and Dompierre, *Eyewitness: Grosse Isle*, p. 194.

142 Ibid., p. 106. Fr. Jean Harper (1801–1869) accompanied Fr. Bernard O'Reilly to Grosse Isle from 8–14 July, 1847.

143 *The Gazette* (July 20, 1847); *Pilot* (July 22, 1847).

144 *True Witness* (17 December, 1852).

145 B. O'Reilly, *The Mirror of True Womanhood; a Book of Instruction for Women in the World* (New York: P. J. Kennedy, Excelsior Publishing House, 1877), p. 98.

146 *Quebec Mercury* (30 March, 1848).

147 See King, 'Remembering Famine orphans' for a more detailed discussion.

148 J. F. Maguire, *The Irish in America* (New York: D & J Sadlier and Co., 1868).

149 McGowan, *Creating Canadian Historical Memory*, p. 6; J. S. Donnelly Jr., 'The construction of the memory of the Famine in Ireland and the Irish diaspora, 1850–1900', *Éire-Ireland*, 31.1–2 (1996), pp. 26–61, on pp. 42–43, 48.

150 J. King, 'L'historiographie irlando-québécoise: Conflits et conciliations entre Canadiens français et Irlandais'. Translated by S. Jolivet, *Bulletin d'histoire politique du Québec* 18.3 (2010), pp. 13–36.

151 P. Southam, *Irish Settlement and National Identity in the Lower St. Francis Valley* (Richmond, Quebec: Richmond St. Patrick Society, 2012), pp. 94–95.

152 For a more detailed discussion, see King, 'Une Voix d'Irlande', pp. 193–208.

153 T. Quinn, 'Une Voix d'Irlande', in *Premier Congrès de La Langue Français au Canada. Québec 24–30 Juin 1912*. Translated by J. King. (Québec: Imprimerie de l'Action Sociale Limitée, 1913), pp. 227–232.

154 Maguire, *The Irish in America*, p. 43.

155 See J. King, 'Finding a Voice: Irish Famine orphan Robert Walsh's search for his younger sister', in C. Kinealy, J. King and G. Moran (eds), *Children and the Great Hunger* (Cork and Hamden, CT: Cork University Press and Quinnipiac University Press, 2018), pp. 123–138.

INTRODUCTION

156 Names of Orphan Children, 1847. Ottawa, Ontario, Canada: Library and Archives Canada, n.d. RG 4, C1, vol. 204, file 3036. Microfilm Reel H-2487.
157 O'Gallagher and Dompierre, *Eyewitness*: *Grosse Isle,* p. 194.
158 Ibid., p. 194.
159 Fonds d'archives Fabrique Saint-Grégoire, F356/A14/5.
160 Archives du Séminaire de Nicolet, F091/B1/5/2 & F091/B1/5/3, transcribed and translated by J. King.
161 Ibid.

Part I

IRISH FAMINE MIGRATION NARRATIVES

1

STEPHEN DE VERE TO T. F. ELLIOT, 30 NOVEMBER, 1847, *MINUTES OF EVIDENCE BEFORE SELECT COMMITTEE ON COLONISATION FROM IRELAND, BRITISH PARLIAMENTARY PAPERS, EMIGRATION, V 5, PP. 45–48*

In April 1847, Stephen De Vere (1812–1904) risked his life travelling steerage and accompanying former tenants from his estate Curragh Chase, County Limerick, to provide an eyewitness account of the hardships of the trans-Atlantic voyage. 'Prior to his departure he told an audience in Pallaskenry, Co. Limerick, that his aim was to see a movement on an extensive scale that would benefit both countries.'[1] Unlike other proponents of assisted emigration, De Vere personally escorted former tenants to British North America in order to put his ideas into practice.

Stephen De Vere was the second son of Sir Aubrey De Vere and Mary Spring Rice, and older brother of the Victorian poet Aubrey De Vere. His other siblings were Elinor, Horatio, William, and Vere Edmond De Vere, whom Stephen succeeded to become 4th Baronet of Curragh in 1880 after his older brother died without an heir. After he returned to Ireland from Canada in 1848, he was elected Liberal Party MP for Limerick County from 1854 to 1859, and was appointed High Sheriff of County Limerick in 1870; he also suffered from terrible nightmares which led him to 'lamentable howls' on a nightly basis.[2] He relocated from Curragh Chase to the island of Monare, Foynes, Co. Limerick where he spent his later years living as a notable eccentric in a laborer's cottage. De Vere had converted to Catholicism while in Canada in 1847, defended Irish Catholic institutions upon his return, and built a Gothic church in Foynes, County Limerick, where he is buried. Like his brother Aubrey, De Vere never married and died childless in 1904, when the baronetcy became extinct. The Hunt/De Vere family estate is now publicly owned, the Curragh Chase National Forest Park, though the estate house was accidentally destroyed by fire in 1941.

Ultimately, Stephen De Vere's legacy was to help safeguard Irish emigrants at sea *and* to inadvertently stymie the passenger trade he had sought to promote. He is at once the most influential and least understood eyewitness of the Irish Famine migration of 1847. After accompanying former tenants from his estate at Curragh Chase to British North America in April 1847 to bear witness to the hardships of the transatlantic crossing, De Vere wrote a letter in Toronto to Thomas Frederick Elliot that is reproduced below. His account provides the most widely cited description of the Famine voyage. He also wrote extensively in his 'America journals' and letters that remain unpublished and almost completely unknown, yet represent some of the most compelling and vivid Canadian travel narratives in the mid-Victorian period. They are partly reproduced here for the first time in print. The journal is comprised of two volumes, from April 29 – December 1, 1847 (MS. 5061, 67 pages), and Dec 1. 1847 – June 23 1848 (MS 5062, 57 pages). *Irish Famine Migration Narratives* publishes De Vere's first journal and beginning of his second one to the date of 9 January, 1848, covering the period until he dispatched his influential letter to T. F. Elliot.

These documents reveal that De Vere's attempt to establish a model colonial settlement failed because he sought to recreate Ireland's hierarchical, semi-feudal class relations on Canadian soil, whereas his former tenants often preferred waged labour, moved to the United States, or were emboldened by the Young Ireland uprising.[3] More broadly, De Vere's personal failure to resettle Famine emigrants had policy implications in compounding the lack of political will to fund colonization schemes, even when it seemed a distinct possibility[4] and his recommendations for Passenger Act reform were accepted in 1848. Ultimately, De Vere was dismayed that the very legislation he inspired to safeguard emigrants at sea increased Canadian immigration levies and thereby stymied the passenger trade he had sought to promote. Nevertheless, his letter to T. F. Elliot and unpublished 'America Journals' remain the most important eyewitness accounts of the Irish Famine migration.

London, Canada, West.
November 30, 1847.
My dear sir,
I HAVE to thank you for sending me the Report of the Colonisation Committee of last year, the evidence contained in which (though I have not yet had time fully to go through it) proves to one the value of emigration at home, and confirms the opinions I had already formed of the benefit likely to result to the colonies from it.

The emigration of the past year was enormous, though deriving no assistance from Government until its arrival here. The mortality also was very great. During the next year, the number of emigrants will probably be still larger; and I fear we shall have a repetition of the mortality if the errors which experience has detected be not promptly and liberally corrected.

I shall not regret the disasters of the last two years if their warning voice shall have stimulated and enabled us to effect a system of emigration *leading to future colonisation*, which shall gradually heal the diseased and otherwise incurable state of society at home, and, at the same time, infuse a spirit into the colonies, which shall render them the ornament, the wealth, and the bulwark of the parent country.

We have no right to cure the evil of over-population by a process of decimation, nor can emigration be serviceable in Canada unless the emigrants arrive in a sound state, both of body and mind. I say 'both of body and mind,' because clamour in Canada has been equally directed against the diseased condition and the listless indolence of this year's emigrants; but, while I admit the Justice of that clamour to a certain extent, I must protest against the injustice of those here who complain that the young and vigorous should be accompanied by the more helpless members of their families whom they are bound to protect; and I cannot but remember that famine and fever were a divine dispensation inflicted last year upon nearly the whole world, and that the colony could not reasonably expect to be wholly exempt from the misfortunes of the parent state.

The fearful state of disease and debility in which the Irish emigrants have reached Canada must undoubtedly be attributed in a great degree to the destitution and consequent sickness prevailing in Ireland; but has been much aggravated by the neglect of cleanliness, ventilation and a generally good state of social economy during the passage, and has been afterwards increased, and disseminated throughout the whole country by the mal-arrangements of the Government system of emigrant relief. Having myself submitted to the privations of a steerage passage in an emigrant ship for nearly two months, in order to make myself acquainted with the condition of the emigrant from the beginning, I can state from experience that the present regulations for ensuring health and comparative comfort to passengers are wholly insufficient, and that they are not, and cannot be enforced, notwithstanding the great zeal and high abilities of the Government agents.

Before the emigrant has been a week at sea he is an altered man. How can it be otherwise? Hundreds of poor people, men, women, and children of all ages, from the drivelling idiot of ninety to the babe just born, huddled together without light, without air, wallowing in filth, and breathing a fetid atmosphere, sick in body and despair at heart, the fevered patients lying between the sound in sleeping places so narrow as almost to deny them the power of indulging, by a change of position, the natural restlessness of the disease, by their agonized ravings disturbing those around them and predisposing them, through the effects of the imagination, to imbibe the contagion; living without food or medicine except as administered by the hand of casual charity, dying without the voice of spiritual consolation and buried in the deep without the rites of the Church.

The food is generally unselected and seldom sufficiently cooked. The supply of water, hardly enough for cooking and drinking, does not allow washing. In many ships the filthy beds, teeming with all abominations, are never required to be brought on deck and aired. The narrow space between the sleeping berths and the piles of boxes is never washed or scraped, but breathes up a damp fetid stench, until the day before arrival at quarantine, when all hands are required to 'scrub up' and put on a fair face for the doctor and government inspector. No moral restraint is attempted. The voice of prayer is never heard. Drunkenness, with its consequent train of ruffianly debasement, is not discouraged, because it is profitable to the captain who traffics in the grog.

In the ship which brought me out from London last April, the passengers were found in provisions by the owners, according to a contract, and furnished scale of dietary. The meat was of the worst quality. The supply of water shipped on board was abundant, but the quantity served out to the passengers was so scanty that they were frequently obliged to throw overboard their salt provisions and rice (a most important article of their food), because they had not water enough both for the necessary cooking, and the satisfying of their raging thirst afterwards.

They could only afford water for washing by withdrawing it from the cooking of their food. I have known persons to remain for days together in their dark close berths, because they thus suffered less from hunger, though compelled, at the same time, by want of water to heave overboard their salt provisions and rice. No cleanliness was enforced; the beds never aired; the master during the whole voyage never entered the steerage, and would listen to no complaints; the dietary contracted for was, with some exceptions, nominally supplied, though at irregular periods; but false measures were used (in which the water and several articles of dry food were served), the gallon measure containing but three quarts, which fact I proved in Quebec, and had the captain fined for; once or twice a week ardent spirits were sold indiscriminately to the passengers, producing scenes of unchecked blackguardism beyond description; and lights were prohibited, because the ship, with her open fire-grates upon deck, with lucifer matches and lighted pipes used secretly in the sleeping berths, was freighted with Government powder for the garrison of Quebec.

The case of this ship was not one of peculiar misconduct, on the contrary, I have the strongest reason to know from information which I have received from very many emigrants well-known to me who came over this year in different vessels, that this ship was better regulated and more comfortable than many that reached Canada.

Some of these evils might be prevented by a more careful inspection of the ship and her stores, before leaving port; but the provisions of the Passenger Act are insufficient to procure cleanliness and ventilation, and the machinery of the emigration agencies at the landing ports is insufficient to enforce those provisions, and to detect frauds. It is true that a clerk sometimes comes on board at the ship's arrival in port; questions the captain or mate, and ends by asking whether any passenger means to make a complaint; but this is a mere farce, for the captain takes care to 'keep away the crowd from the gentleman.' Even were all to hear the question, few would venture to commence a prosecution; ignorant, friendless, penny less, disheartened, and anxious to proceed to the place of their ultimate destination.

Disease and death among the emigrants; nay, the propagation of infection throughout Canada, are not the worst consequences of this atrocious system of neglect and ill-usage. A result far worse is to be found in the utter demoralization of the passengers, both male and female, by the filth, debasement, and disease of two or three months so passed. The emigrant, enfeebled in body, and degraded in mind, even though he should have the physical power, has not the *heart*, has not the *will* to exert himself. He has lost his self-respect, his elasticity of spirit – he no longer stands erect – he throws himself listlessly upon the daily dole of Government, and, in order to earn it, carelessly lies for weeks upon the contaminated straw of a fever lazaretto.

I am aware that the Passengers' Act has been amended during the last Session, but I have not been yet able to see the amendments. They are probably of a nature calculated to meet the cases I have detailed; but I would earnestly suggest the arrangement of every passenger ship into separate dimensions for the married, for single men, and for single women; and the appointment, from amongst themselves, of 'monitors' for each ward; the appropriation of an hospital ward for the sick; the providing of commodious cooking stoves and utensils, and the erection of decent privies; and the appointment, to each ship carrying more than 50 passengers, of a surgeon paid by the Government, who should be invested during the voyage with the authority of a Government emigration agent, with power to investigate all complaints at sea on the spot, and at the time of their occurrence to direct and enforce temporary redress, and to institute proceedings on arrival in port in concert with the resident emigration agent. He ought, for this purpose, to have authority to detain witnesses, and to support them during the prosecution at Government expense. I would also suggest the payment of a chaplain of the religion professed by the majority of the passengers.

The sale of spirituous liquors should be prohibited except for medicinal purposes, &c., the minimum supply of water enlarged from three to four quarts.

I believe that if these precautions were adopted, the human cargoes would be landed in a moral and physical condition far superior to what they now exhibit, and that the additional expense incurred would be more than compensated by the saving effected in hospital expenses and emigrant relief.

The arrangements adopted by the Government during the past season, for the assistance of pauper emigrants after their arrival in Canada, were of three sorts, hospitals, temporary sheds, and transmission. These measures were undertaken in a spirit of liberality deserving our best gratitude; and much allowance ought to be made for imperfections of detail, which it was not easy to avoid under the peculiar and unexpected exigencies of the case; but I think I can demonstrate that much of the mortality which has desolated as well the old residents as the emigrants, may be attributed to the errors of those arrangements.

In the quarantine establishment at Grosse Isle, when I was there in June, the medical attendance and hospital accommodations were quite inadequate. The medical inspections on board were slight and hasty – hardly any questions were asked – but as the doctor walked down the file on deck, he selected those for hospital who did not look well, and, after a very slight examination, ordered them ashore. The ill-effect of this haste was two-fold: some were detained in danger who were not ill, and many were allowed to proceed who were actually in fever.

The sheds were very miserable, so slightly built as to exclude neither the heat nor the cold. No sufficient care was taken to remove the sick from the sound, or to disinfect and clean the bedding after the removal of the sick to hospitals. The very straw upon which they had lain was often allowed to become a bed for their successor; and I have known many poor families prefer to burrow under heaps of loose stones which happened to pile up near the shore rather than accept the shelter of the infected sheds.

It would, I am aware, have been difficult to have provided a more substantial shelter for the amount of destitution produced by the peculiar circumstances of the past year; but I hope that, in future, even though the number of emigrants should greatly exceed that of last year, so large an extent of pauper temporary accommodation may not be necessary, and that a better built, and better regulated house of refuge, may be provided.

Of the administration of temporary relief by food to the inmates of the sheds, I must speak in terms of the highest praise. It was a harassing and dangerous duty, and one requiring much judgment on the part of the agent, and it was performed with zeal, humanity, and good sense.

I must now advert to what has been the great blot upon the Government arrangements – the steam transmission up the country. The great principle, that the due regulation of passenger ships is a duty of the State, is admitted by the Passengers' Act. The Government itself enforces the heaviest penalties for the infringement of its provisions; but yet, when the Government itself undertakes to transmit emigrants from Quebec to Montreal, Kingston, and Toronto, how has it acted? I state, upon the authority of Mr. McElderry, the able and indefatigable emigrant agent at Toronto, who has fallen a victim to his zeal and humanity, that the Government made an exclusive contract with one individual for the steam transmission of all emigrants forwarded by the State, at a certain price per head, without any restrictive regulations. The consequences were frightful. I have seen small, incommodious, and ill-ventilated steamers arriving at the quay in Toronto, after a forty-eight hours passage from Montreal, freighted with fetid cargoes of 1,100 and 1,200 Government emigrants of all ages and sexes. The healthy who had just arrived from Europe, mixed with the half-recovered convalescents of the hospitals, unable, during that time, to lie down, almost to sit. In almost every boat were clearly marked cases of actual fever – in some were deaths – the dead and the living huddled together. Sometimes the crowds were stowed in open barges, and towed after the steamer, standing like pigs upon the deck of a Cork and Bristol packet. A poor woman died in the hospital here, in consequence of having been trodden down when weak and fainting in one of those barges. I have, myself, when accompanying the emigrant agent on his visit to inspect the steamer on her arrival, seen him stagger back like one struck, when first meeting the current of fetid infection, exhaled from between her decks. It is the unhesitating opinion of every man I have spoken to, including Government officers and medical men, that a large proportion of the fever throughout the country has been actually generated in the river steamers. Surely – surely this may be avoided for the future. If the entire steam navigation should be, as I am informed it was this year, in the hands of one unopposed individual, and that he should refuse to accept a contract upon *reasonable* terms, and with the conditions necessary for securing ventilation, comfort, and health, the Government might easily take the transmission into their own hands, put on steamers, and forward the emigrants at half of this year's charges, not to mention the saving which would certainly be effected in hospital expenses.

The causes which produced the immense emigration of the past year still exist, and the numbers next year will probably be still larger, and we shall have a repetition of the same scenes of misery, if prompt measures be not taken for their prevention. But Government must not stop there; something must be done for the profitable employment of the emigrants. To support them is but a temporary shift; they must be enabled to become valuable Citizens to the colony.

Notes

1 G. Moran, *Sending Out Ireland's Poor: Assisted Emigration to North America in the Nineteenth Century* (Dublin: Four Courts, 2004), p. 72.
2 J. Gwynn Jones, *The Abiding Enchantment of Curragh Chase: The Big House Remembered* (Cork: Clo Duanaire, 1983), p. 28.
3 J. King, 'The Famine Irish Migration to Canada in 1847–1848: Assisted Emigration, Colonisation, and the Unpublished Famine Diaries of Stephen De Vere', in P. Fitzgerald and A. Russell (eds.), *John Mitchel, Ulster, and the Great Irish Famine*, (Dublin: Irish Academic Press, 2017), pp. 30–45.
4 P. Gray, "Shovelling out your paupers': the British state and Irish famine migration, 1846–50', *Patterns of Prejudice*, 33:4 (1999), pp. 47–65, on pp. 63–65; Moran, *Sending Out Ireland's Poor*, pp. 83–90.

2

STEPHEN DE VERE, UNPUBLISHED 'AMERICA JOURNALS' 1847–1848 (TRINITY COLLEGE DUBLIN MANUSCRIPTS DEPARTMENT, MSS 5061–5062)

Thursday evening, April 29, 1847.
We arrived in London for railway from Bristol, & embarked in Bark Birman. Hopped down that night to Gravesend. Hanly ill.

Friday
Gravesend. Taking in powder. Dined on shore with Stephen S. Rice.[1] Hanly still ill.

Saturday May 1st
Sailed.

Wednesday June 9
Off Cape Breton in sight of land. Having reached banks of Newfoundland June 3rd

Saturday June 12 1847
West of Cape Gaspe. About 250 miles from Quebec. Dead calm. Thick & incessant fog. Sudden tremendous squalls from north – lasted about 5 minutes. Ship in great danger. Main royal & all studding sails set. Gradually righted.

Sunday June 13.
Took pilot on board in the morning. River narrows – vast woods from mountain tops to the shore with white rocks & gleams of snow between – crowds of ships taking out cargoes of corn for Europe.

Wednesday 16th June
Arrived at Grosse isle quarantine about 7 am. Detained waiting for dr till evening, when he inspected & gave us clean bill of health – abt. 40 ships detained there – villages of white tents on shore for the sick. Daily mortality about 150. One ship, Sisters of Liverpool, in with all passengers & crew in fever. Of this

ship, all but the Cap'n and one girl died. Laid alongside of 'Jessy' in which many ill. Water covered with beds cooking utensils refuse of the dead. Ghastly appearance of boats full of sick going ashore never to return. Several died between ship and shore. Wives separated from husbands, children from parents. Ascertained by subsequent enquiry that funds in agents hands altogether insufficient for care. Medical attendance bad. Exemplary conduct of Catholic clergy.

Thursday 17th June
Towed by steamer arrived in Quebec. Remain on board till Saturday when engaged lodgings at the O'Connells, Champlain Street 5[?] per day. For each.. beef & mutton 6 per lb—Lower town principally Canadian. Streets dirty, crooked, narrow, hot. All under guns of fortress – immense flight of steps to Upper Town where stone buildings & good shops – cheating Canadians. Fortifications of great strength admirable state of repair, two regiments insufficient to man guns – Irish population well affected to England. Irish & Canadians dislike one another. Two companies of firemen by voluntary enrolment. Occasional drill. Exempt from juries. Entitled to protection in case of war for families within fortress.
Country round Quebec very poor. No corn. Picturesque scenery. Rolling ground. Soft perfumed soil, of short poor grass. Lawns with occasional thickets of dwarf spruce firs. Like a most beautiful pleasure ground of vast extent. Canadian country houses beautifully neat – do not use beds but sleep on the floor in summer. Canadian horses small but very hardy & kind generally. Stallions. Fast trotters. Admirable drivers.
Lodged complaint before Buchanan[2] agst. Capt. Guthrie for false measures of water. Capt. wants to compromise. I refused except in presence of Buchanan – accompanied Capt. before him – made him pay £10 which I handed to Revd. McMahon PP.[3] for the use of destitute Emigrants. Revd Acknowledged in newspapers.
Admitted to news room – English papers – Limerick Chronicles. Wrote to my mother, Mick, Stephen, Aubrey – saw many persons who had been working under my orders last winter. All employed at about 5/ per day. Enormous wages offered for loading infected ships. 8 to 10/ per day. Price of provisions very high. No money laid by – no work in winter, when people go up the country for work.
Left letter of directions for Mick at Buchanan's office. He related his plan which he had proposed to Gov. General for colonisation. Govt. to take charge of emigrants, capital & provide cheap and well regulated passage – when assisted out, give them the worth of the balance in a plain log house and a quantity of land. States that £50 will send out a man with wife & 3 children. Give provisions for 15 months, utensils, 50 acres land and seed.
I suggested that to emigrants capital should be required in addition. A certain contribution from the landlords & that in place of giving wild land & a stock of

provisions, that a portion of the money should be advanced by the government & employed a year before in cultivating a few acres, round each log house, to be built along the Halifax railroad or elsewhere. Thus affording employment to labourers now, and giving the settler his supply of food not in his store room but on his own ground & immediate employment to reap his own harvest. Buchanan spoke more favorably of the project of the Halifax railway. P. neill wife ill.

Thursday 24th June 5pm. 1847.
Left Quebec by John Mann steamer. Magnificent American river steamers. Great comfort for deck passengers. Rapid pace. Reached Montreal at 6am. 180 miles – Rafts going down river with shanties built upon them great improvement of cultivation as we ascend the river. Took two rooms in Quebec suburb at £1 per week. Room for self at Daley's hotel. Presented letters of introduction to Viger,.[4] . . McGill[5] visits in return. Provisions somewhat cheaper than Quebec.
Frightful mortality. Emigrant sheds hospitals & generally throughout the town.
Pat Neill's wife still ill. Medical attendance cheap 2/ English per visit, a few pence for medicine attendance, careful & respectable. Clothes washing 60 or 70 shirts.

Monday, 28th June
Accompanied by Roger and Hanley. Started to visit friends at Troy NY. Lake Champlain by steamer, passing Burlington to Whitehall (ferry steamer to railroad to St. John's rough & slow) . . . thence by canal to Troy . . . left Montreal 12 noon. Arrived at Whitehall 6am. Troy 10am. Lower part of Lake Champlain very fine & full wooded – banks very low . . .
Thursday 1st July
Visit paper factory & start by canal on return at 11pm. Comfortable night on board canal boat.

Friday 2nd July breakfast
Whitehall – Friday night on Lake Champlain chill & heavy. J Hanly complains of a chill – breakfast at St. John's. Reach Montreal at 12 noon. Saturday determined to start for Toronto. Monday. L'homme propose, mais Dieu dispose.

Tuesday 6th July.
Send off my party to Toronto remaining myself to take care of patient. Help Roger to inform the rest in case it should take the fever, but do not allow him to see the patient – wrote a codicil to my will, addressed to Samuel [?] Gerrard, an old Gentleman of great intelligence & kindness. Thermometer in shade 100. In sun 125.

Wednesday, 7th July.
Hanly rather better. Hottest day yet. Thermometer in sun at noon up to the top of the tube at 135 & then rapidly rising – no air.

Thursday 8th July

Hanly almost recovered. Recd a letter from Mary Suey mentioning the happy news of Mick's wife having had a daughter. Both thriving well. Heat greater than yesterday. Therm up to 125 shade.

Saturday 10th July

Hanly better again. Write to Michael Ma. Go with Roger at night to the circus. Intense heat there.

Sunday 11th July

Hanly up recovered. Peter Bridgeman arrived here yesterday. Attended Divine service at St. Patrick's Church. Sermon by Bishop Phelan Of Toronto [sic][6] who attributed misfortunes of Ireland to the atrocious avarice of the landlords. . .
Say they never knew such unmitigated heat.

Monday 12 July

Engage place to Toronto . . . Stage to Lachine – long and lumbering shore. Railroad in progress. Beauhornois canal looks admirable. Work and machinery. Steamer going down the rapids. Cornwall canal by night. Much larger and finer work – cannot bear heat of the fur cloak. Sleeping on deck. Thence up to Prescott. Can stem the rapids. Numerous wooded islands deeply indented. Can make you think of a series of beautiful lakes but that the rapidity of the current preserves the river character. Narrow channel of expansive lakes . . . wooded particularly at American side which in the advantage over ours in picturesque beauty because less culti-vated. Lombardy poplars, weeping elms, summach underwood general want of fine timber, which it appears was cut as here or there bare clad and half scorched stems of great height remain giving to the deepest woods a desolate appearance.
Everything in America speaks a land of timber – roads, struts, pavements, bridges. Houses, long ranges of wharved roofs of shingles balconied cottages etc . . . And yet firewood is at Montreal one of the most expensive articles of household economy.

July 13th, Tuesday

From Brockville to Kingston. This an archipelago of islands. Perfect labyrinth. The larger ones with large trees, the smaller ones with brushwood & dwarf pines. Landed in one. Beautiful andromeda. Narrow channels where hardly room for steamers. Suddenly spreading out great inland seas, & then as suddenly contracted. Lavish profusion of vegetation. The most barren rock has its tree – tree arboretum. At Kingston change steamers. New fortifications Kingston. In a great scale for the protection of harbour. Immense crowd of German and Irish emigrants on board of the worst description. Great apparent disease. Pay difference for cabin passage to Toronto. $6.
Pass Cobourg and Port Hope at night.

Wednesday July 14th

Arrive at Toronto at 11am after long search succeed in finding Neil. They have engaged 2 unfurnished rooms in an airy country situation at $2 ½ per month.

Magnificent Catholic Cathedral. New building brick with cut stone door-ways etc . . .

Friday July 16, 1847.

Start by stage with P. Neill at 10am for Bradford . . .

Beautiful butterflies. Brilliant bird with blacklaps to casing bright scarlet head and neck.

The country from Toronto northwards to Holland Landing where the stage stops, exhibits the back country in every stage of improvement. You have the wild forest – trees of enormous height & girth, but furnished with few & short branches – groves of the graceful hemlock and balsam spruce, a rich thicket underwood of hemlock and aborite, here called the cedar – occasional elms as tall and straight as the pines – Ash, walnut, beech, sugar maple, thickets of sumach with leaves of great size, crowned with spikes of crimson flowers. Then the past stages of improvement where the underwood has been cut down and lucent[?] round the stems of the giant pines, now dead & blackened – all around the scene of smoking desolation. Great trees lying over the ground – then, the rich crops of corn growing amongst the bare trunks. In the next stage the trees have been cut down to within about 3 feet of the surface with luxuriant drops of meadow between the logs piled into burned fences & for log huts or shanties – lastly the rich & highly cultivated farms (always however backed by the eternal forest) with its neat farm house framed, whitewashed, & its flourishing orchard – government are making a great road from Toronto to Holland Landing – the Engineers' object appearing to be to make it as straight as possible in defiance of the difficulties presented by a varied surface. The cuttings & fillings are as great as upon an English railroad line. It is a remarkable fact that not one 20th of the laborers who might be profitably employed are at work upon it. It would be better and cheaper to employ the poor emigrants than to forward them from hospital to hospital.

Dine at Holland Landing and walked over to Bradford 21 miles, through clouds of musquitoes. Arrived 9 pm. Sleep there.

Saturday July 17

Start on foot in search of Mr. John Rose, Col. licensed militia. Great difficulty in finding out where he lives. At last a man points out to me some pines overlapping the surrounding forest, near which he tells me I will find his house. No road or . . . path. I explore the wood and at last reach the pines. See a little boy. Hut smaller than any Irish hovel. A dirty stockingless capless old woman is washing at the door.

Enquire for Col. Ross's house. She tells me I am in it and that [she is] his wife. Blown a horn calls him in. His son is at work today with a neighbouring farmer for a patch of meadow.

The coll. is in possession of 200 acres here of which he has cleared about 30 – he & his wife & son have been down with fever and ague – no wonder in the thick of a swampy forest with a broad fat marsh almost always covered with water separating him from the sluggish Holland river.

I return to Bradford. Walked on to Holland Landing. Between those places the road winds through the forest, crossing Holland river . . . by a rough plank bridge nearly a mile long. The underwood is cut & the trees dead and scorched at both sides of the road, so that there is no shelter from the rays of the burning sun which are inflected by the knee deep hot white sand which formed the road – not a breath of air can penetrate this forest, the swampy soil of which is completely covered with beds of the red epilobium. Beautiful little pink Andromeda.

Delay under such a sun would be fatal – I rush . . . on into Holland Landing & recover myself with 3 or 4 cups of Holland tea, the best drink in great heat – at 2 oc 6pm get into the stage – tremendous rain, thunders & lightning.

At 12 at night reach Toronto. Tired but in perfect health. The present state of the road is clearly shown by it having taken a four horse stage with 6 passengers 10 hours to go 32 miles.

Monday July 19th

Wrote a paper describing the treatment of passengers on board emigrant ships with sundry suggestions for ensuring better arrangements. Gave to Frank [?] Widder, Commissioner of Canada West[7] who was much pleased with it & took it up warmly. Drank tea at Mr. O'Briens – found out.

Wednesday July 21st

Toronto. Tremendous storm of thunder and lightning. Great fire in town.

Friday July 23rd

Received of the Emigration office an old letter from MM dated May 20th. Received a letter from S. Gerrard acknowledging receipt of £26. & advising me to invest capital in Montreal Bank stock. Determined to leave for London U.C. on Monday, Please God.

Saturday, July 24th

Roger not well. Send for Dr. in the evening who says it is an attack of lake fever. Not much chance of starting on Monday. From all the accounts I have been able to gather in the last two days, it seems to me that Guelph will be a better temporary look out residence than London. Healthier, cheaper, easier. . .

Sunday July 25th

My birthday. My only pleasure writing a long letter to my mother, Roger's fever heavy.

Wednesday July 28th
Roger had a good night & is better, pulse slower less heat of the skin & restful. An offer is made to some angry people to engage them by a rich farmer. They refer the matter to me. I explain to them that if on my arrival at my ultimate destination I cannot employ them myself it will be necessary for them to provide temporary employment for themselves that in case of their doing so & my being afterwards able to employ them would cheerfully do so – That it is very uncertain whether I can this year procure land to employ them upon – but that I left the adoption or rejection of the present offer to themselves. They refused to accept it.

Friday August 6th
Attended divine service at 7am. Roger going on favorably. Hanly rather better. Finished Tom Jones.[8] How infinitely superior the humour of Fielding to that of Sterne! Of the one natural; of the other laboured and affected.

Saturday, August 7th
Morning service. Roger recovering fast. Hanly better. During the whole day expected with intense anxiety the arrival of the English mail which I hoped would bring a letter from Mick to announce his departure. Mail arrived late in the evening. Alas; no letters.

Saturday Aug. 21st
No morning service. Gave Mr. Elmsly [?] a subscription of $4 for the organ of Toronto cathedral.

Tuesday August 24th
No morning service. Clergy all sick but the Bishop who has to attend the hospital and emigrant sheds. 10 deaths in hospital yesterday. Anxiously expecting arrival of English mail. Arrives Alas! Alas! No letters.

Friday August 27th
No morning service. Alas, no letters. Mme. Pindar arrives, having left home 15th June. Gave her 2 dollars & a letter to McElderry[9] asking him to procure work for her little boys.

Thursday, Sept. 2nd
Morning serv. Roger much better. At ½ past 11 board . . . Steamer American for Rochester US . . . for Troy. My principal object being to see Mick's letter to J. Burns, hoping it may give me some means of gauging the time of his sailing . . . The captain tells me that an engineers party of 13 men went out lately to survey and value the lands in the neighbour of a govt. canal near Peterboro. In one week the party returned the officer of the men dangerously ill, leaving two corpses, and having buried two. This is a canal made by flooding, not excavation.

Friday Sept 3rd

At 4pm, stop in [?] river, close under the magnificent falls. Custom house officer at ½ 4 at 5 reach Rochester . . . I eat enormous table d'hote breakfast.

My impressions hitherto of the Americans is that they are the hungriest, the dirtiest, the most dishonest & altogether the meanest people I have ever seen. They are so entirely absorbed in the pursuit of wealth that they have no time for the courtesies, the decencies of life. They cry 'O my ducats'! without 'O my daughter'! They seem to rely wholly on themselves, never brushing with their neighbours. Their dishonesty is audacious, because they are too vain to attempt to conceal it; & whilst they are cheating you, they do not even pay you the poor compliment of trying to deceive you. Proud of their country, (because she belongs to themselves) they are most proud of her meanest vices. An expert windbag is honoured and as a smart man. Their dress is exaggerated, uncouth & ill matched; . . . they poke about with their long hair breathing necks, like a cur seeking for a bone, & if they catch your eye, right themselves into a swagger; they peer through you with their hungry eyes, but would fain have you believe that they do not care to look at you, they combine the contemplative chicanery of a Jewish shop seller with the shameful roguery of roulette bully – They do not even deserve credit for the boldness of their commercial speculations because the great stake, character, never depends upon the issue of language, the noblest gift of God, they use but for a boast, and sneer, or a lie . . .

Monday Sept. 6th

Receive a note from Pat Neill today that there is a home letter for me at Toronto. I start on my return at 7pm. By railway – 6 miles out of Troy. . . . At last another engine arrives – we get in to Schenectady at 11pm. The western train from Albany being long passed, I remain here, miserable quarters at small inn, which I prefer to a room at the grand hotel, to be there with 4 yankees.

Thursday Sept 9

Thank God, I have at last received most satisfactory letters. My mother is well . . . at home. Her letter is dated July 26th. Another from my dear Mick dated Aug 4th, in which he says that he is to sail in Anne of Limerick on 7th of August. May God grant him a happy voyage – I find Roger much recovered, but John Hanly again sick, since Sunday, of a [?] attack.

I write, as the English mail goes out tomorrow, to my mother. I write also to John Burns . . .

In the evening, unexpectedly, a long print letter from Mary Suey and my mother dated August 15th mentioning that Mick & Stephen had sailed on Monday 9th august in the Anne.

Thursday Sept 16th

Morning service. Hanly passed the night decidedly better . . . McElderry tells me that he proposes to build permanent barrack buildings instead of sheds. Also that next year there will be a steamboat opposition on the river, consequently lower terms and less crowding. Admits that Govt. this year is in the hands of one person for river transmission. I ask why did not government put on emigrant steamers of their own.

He says that were it not for the fear of disease, the supplying of ordinary labour market here would absorb emigration double this year.

Saturday Sept. 18th

Morning service. Hanly passed a bad night. Much trouble with very violent cough and suppression pulse 100 profuse perspiration all night. He improved during the day watch . . . McElderry mentions that the farmers in the country are raising subscriptions to send back the emigrants into Toronto.

Sunday, Sept. 26th

Morning service. J.H. not quite so well. A slight attack of dysentery during the night. The weather for the last fortnight has been becoming very cool. Hear with great concern that Buchanan is very ill of fever at Quebec. Also that Bishop Power[10] has taken fever here. English mail in the evening. Tremendous storm of thunder and lightning which continued all night. Never did I witness such a storm. The forked lightning every minute dancing from heaven to earth, illumining the darkness with a red glare, the way the lightning ladders from heaven to earth were seen, of all colours, sometimes golden yellow, sometimes violet, sometimes purple blue, sometimes intense vermillion, and then the thunder simultaneously with the lightning, bursting, crashing rending . . . shaking the whole city with its metallic danger, and sometimes succeeded at certain distances by single explosions. Like the successive firing of some enormous artillery. The mere sound of the rain was frightful, bewildering.

Wednesday Sept. 29th

52nd day

Morning service. Bishop Power very ill of typhus fever. Kingston boat 2pm no account of my dear brothers. Give $25 to John Hanly and J. Fiztgerald for their journey to be accountable for.

Thursday Sept. 30th

Morning service. No other man present being capable I am obliged to act as clerk. John Hanly & J. Fitzgerald start for Hamilton on their way to London by steamer at 8am. Fare to Hamilton 3/9 each.

Had the irrepressible relief from the Emigration office Quebec to announce the arrival of the Anne.

Friday October 1st

54th day

Morning service. Rev. Michael Power DD. Cath bishop of Toronto died this morning.

He was a man of great generosity and nobleness, most kindly and charitable in a true and most extended kindly sense, a humble Christian. By his example, his justice, his unfailing attention to the duties of his high station, & the strictness of his discipline, he brought into perfect order a diocese which he found almost in anarchy. His death is attributable, under providence, to the noble and devoted zeal with which, since the illness of so many of his clergy, he has visited the beds of every sick and dying emigrant. He did not spare himself, but God has spared him a longer sojourn on earth. He was a man of no political party, of no religious bigotry. He was too strong-minded to be a bigot, & too wise to be a partisan. He was therefore respected and beloved by men of all creeds and parties. May Almighty God have Mercy on his soul.

Saturday Oct. 2nd 1847
Morning service. Rec. 2 letters from J. Hanly and J. Fitzgerald. Have arrived in London at 10am Friday. Safe.
Happiness of happiness! At 4pm dear Michael and Stephen with little Catharine Biddy and baby arrived safe and well for which I humbly thank the Almighty God. They bring me letters from my death mother, Ellen and Aubrey, of rather old date, of numerous little gifts and tokens of love. Oh, could they but know with what a heart, glowing with unchanged love, I received them. One most valuable gift was my dear father's 'Mary Tudor'.

Thursday Oct. 7th
Make some purchases of furniture. Excellent French seats . . . large parlour table of black walnut . . . Weather very dark. Land stands high on a sandy plane. The river divided the plan from the woodland.

Wednesday Oct. 13th
Went out shooting a long expedition through the bush – met or shot only a few black squirrels. Will make a capital pie. One my return find little Catharine ill. Very feverish. . .

Saturday Oct. 16th
Bought 24 bushels of oats at 10s = $4
My dear brother Mick is feverish and generally unwell. May the almighty God be the guardian and protector of the finest fellow that ever drew breath in this world – of one with whom I feel my fate to be inseparably bound. The dr declares his illness emigrant fever.

Saturday Oct. 23rd
Catherine better. Mick in great nervous despondency & suffering much from cough with bloody expectoration. Dr. however does not think him worse. Great meeting for raising first sod of Western railway which is done by Col. Talbot. Up all night.

Tuesday Oct. 26th

Priest visits dear Mick in the morning, after which he becomes rapidly better. Pulse falling from 116 to 104 in two hours, & his intellect greatly cleared. Dr. declared the crisis to be over and that he considers him out of danger. Orders wine and other stimulants. I thank God for his great mercy. I care not what may be my own fate, if my dear brother be spared. Up all night.

Sunday Oct. 31st, 1847.

Divine service. Both patients going on very well.

Pat Neill J Hanly & J Fitzgerald went to work at railroad on Friday and Roger commenced on Saturday at 3/? per day. I inform them that I shall expect a payment from each of one dollar a week towards household expenses which they admit to be most moderate.

Monday Nov. 1st

Patients recovering. I invite the priest to open a subscription for building a new church, the present one being quite insufficient and scandalously bad. I subscribe $10 and each of my men $1.

Friday Nov. 5th

I pay the Dr. in full for his attendance and medicine. $30. I have been much pleased with his skill and attendance. He informs me that the Board of Health here has been closed by the government and that no new cases can be admitted into the hospital. [Rate of payment] from govt. $5 per day for attending dying in the hospital. Poor Dr. Lee died of typhus fever last week.

Saturday Nov. 6th.

I drive to St. Thomas with Mr. O'Dwyer. Country flat, poor, & undrained & half civilized. St. Thomas is a stand still of a settled place. Capital inn. Pleasant evening. Mr. O'Dwyer recounts his dispute with the Cath. Bishop Power who seems to have treated him in a haughty and impolite manner. He forbade him to accept a salary of $30 from the Govt. for attending the military hospital. O'Dwyer therefore allowed the money to accumulate in the payment for lands and some claim of it. He says what use are those bishops – they are only tyrants – one can do the business of the diocese very well without them. I have heard nearly the same language and found the same feeling amongst the Irish clergy. I regret to hear of poor McElderry's death of fever at Toronto.

Sunday Nov. 7th

Divine service at St. Thomas. Ill feeling between priest and flock in consequence of nonpayment of any dues. A meeting is held after mass where it is agreed that the collection of clergy's dues shall be vested in trustees who are to assess the congregation individually. Pews to be thrown open and pew rents abandoned. Strong expectation expressed that the priest shall never again find it necessary to speak of money matters from the altar. All right.

Thursday Nov. 11th
The Indian Summer appeared ended, the thermometer having suddenly fallen from 70 in the shade to below the freezing point. People in this climate seem remarkably free from colds – not a cough in a congregation. Letters from my mother and Aubrey.

Friday Nov. 12th
Letters again from home. Oct. 12th. Receive report from Emigration committee. Very cold. Warm weather again.

Saturday Nov. 13th
Mr. O'Dwyer acting on my earnest suggestions publicly renounced the present building of his own house and devoted the funds already subscribed for that purpose of the building of the new Church.

Sunday Nov. 14th
Divine service. Wrote a long letter to my mother describing the physical and moral state of Canada.

Tuesday Nov. 16th
Fine warm weather. Visit railroad superintendent and Yankee Boston. . . [Building?] of railroads has greatly increased the western emigration which . . . had enormously increased commerce. Many people thought the Erie canal would have been replaced by the western railway, far from it its traffic has doubled. It is now choked with western produce and is required to be doubled in width. The colonisation of wild land through which railways progress very remarkable and value of land greatly enhanced. System of wooded rails bad. Better to lay down iron at once. If Canadian people do not take stock of railway Yankees will.

Wed Nov. 17th
Went to visit a farm offered for sale within 3 miles of London. It consists of 50 acres, of which about 10 cleared and about 10 more partially cleared. A very small . . . wooden house. Soil very poor wet low sandy ill fenced – not one acre really arable. This farm will feed some 5 or 6 head of cattle during the summer, but give no hay. Price £300.
Near it is a farm belonging to Mr. Wright, a Quaker, well laid out, about 4 excellent houses & offices. Land sandy, subsoil shallow, but fine. I was told he was rich and asked had he made his money by his land. Answered with a laugh, no by building his money at 20 percent.

Saturday, Nov. 20th

Hard frost. Therm. 22 at 9am.

At 10am it has risen again to 36.

Mr. O'Dwyer tells anecdote of Tipperary man who came out here and bought 100 acres of remote wild land on which he built a miserable hut. He wrote to his sisters comfortably off at home to come out here where they can find him like another Count Dallen. Upon arriving this year they proceeded on the wings of hope to his estate, which they found to consist of the hut only, he having sold the land again to procure the bread of idleness.

They spent a week 'Scorching' and roaring about the shanty and returned to London. They are very glad to enter into service with two farmers at $4 per month.

A family from Mayo came out this year apparently in the most abject poverty. They consisted of a father mother uncle a little boy about 12 years old. There were transmitted to Toronto at the govt. expense. The mother was there taken into hospital suffering from a rapid cancer in the breast. She soon died. The father, uncle, little boy took a poor lodging close to me. I frequently met them and the father complaining to me of dysentery. I recommended him to send for a doctor, but he said he was too poor. He at last went into hospital, and died, from want of care in the early stage of the disease, leaving his little son in possession of 300 sovereigns tied up in an old rag, which had, during the voyage, been tied under the mother's breast and had produced the cancer of which she died.

Tuesday Nov. 23rd.

Dr. attends. Mick's wife unwell. Dr. fears fever. Bought a very handsome sleigh, with bear skin for £8 & a good set of harnesses for £3.10.

In the evening P. Neill informs me that he has hired himself to a farmer for driving his teams and to reside in his house for $10 per month, and that he is to go to him tomorrow morning. I tell him that I consider his conduct and sudden leaving the house as altering my domestic arrangements without previously consulting me, most disrespectful. He replies with cool impertinence. For some time back the manner of P. O'Neill J Hanly & R Kennedy has been most disrespectful to me, and they have announced to others their determination never to work for me except at $10 a month, to provide for themselves as soon as they have earned enough money to leave this. It is fortunate for me that I did not purchase a farm in the expectation of their performing their contract.

Wednesday Nov. 24th

Mick and his wife much better.

P. Neill goes to his new master. Went out to shoot . . . a woodpecker and a grouse. Seen the process of burning charcoal. Enormous logs being piled up into a huge cone and then covered with sandy earth and set on fire. The priest has a number of free labourers employed in taking up stone for the new church on a plot of 10 acres appropriated by govt. about 2 miles from the town to the Cath. Church. Amongst them were about 30 soldiers allowed by the Coll. to work. N.B. He allows soldiers to work for hire after parade.

Friday Nov. 26th
Heavy snow showers all day. Therm 25. I put a frame of glass in my window. Shelves into my presses, and build a shed for my sleigh. Roger J Hanly & J Fitzgerald were discharged tonight from the railroad. The number of men being reduced for the winter. I fear the opening of this work was but a demonstration to get the stock broker.
My dear mother's birthday.

Sunday Nov. 28th
Heavy snow. Therm. 26. I inform P. Neill that it is very doubtful whether I will take land at all it being so high, that I shall certainly take none this winter, that . . . the other boys, if they cannot get day work, must engage with the farmers as I cannot afford to keep them idle and pay.

Tuesday Nov 30th
I inform the boys that they must look out for employment. P. Neill asks me to keep his wife here, he paying $1 per week for her board. I decline.
Preparing dispatch for Elliot.[11] During the night it begins to thaw.

Wednesday Dec. 1st.
Dispatch my letter to Elliot, and a copy to my mother. . . . Therm. 42

End of journal

MS 5062. Vol. 2. Dec 1. 1847 – June 23 1848.
. . .

Friday Dec. 10th
Took out my gun and walked 6 or 8 miles through the woods down the river. Shot two American 'Pheasants' a bird about the size and shape of a grouse with plumage more than a partridge. Shot 2 squirrels, a specimen of the large scarlet headed woodpecker.
. . .

Sunday Dec. 12th
Divine service. Therm. 50 Long ride.

IRISH FAMINE MIGRATION NARRATIVES

Monday Dec. 13th
Went out shooting accompanied by Mick, Stephen, & Tommy. Overwhelmed by heavy snow. Lost our way in forest. Shot a brace of pheasants a brace of large quails here called partridges and a magnificent owl.

Wednesday Dec. 15.
Out shooting again, but got no shots although I walked over 20 miles . . . snow disappeared towards evening and sudden hard frost. Night exceeding cold.

Thursday Dec. 16th.
Painfully cold. Strong east wind and severe frost. Therm. However much below 20 though infinitely colder than where it stood at 7.
. . .

Saturday Dec 18th
Dispatched a copy of my letter to Elliot to Revd J. Foley. & 2 newspapers. I went out shooting walked about 25 miles. I shot only a brace of quails. . .

Sunday Dec. 19th
Divine service being at St. Thomas. I read prayers to my family. Small snow falling. Therm. 30.

Monday Dec. 20.
Therm. 20 to 13. Write part of my letter on colonisation.

Tuesday Dec 21
Harsh frost. Light covering snow. Therm. 12. English mail rec. Letter from my mother.. and my uncle dated Nov. 12. Giving but bad accounts of the state of prospects at home.

Wednesday December 22.
Wrote a long letter to my uncle on colonisation. Heavy snow showers all day. Therm 15. 20.
. . .

Friday December 24th.
Beautiful sunny day. Therm. 20. Drive out in my sleigh 10 ½ miles on the Woodstock road and back in 2 hours.

Saturday Dec. 25th
Christmas Day. Bright clear frost . . . It is not in the least cold. I stroll about in a light cloth frock, without great coat. Gay sleighs, glancing about in all directions, covered before and behind with 'robes' of comfy furs generally trimmed with . . . scarlet cloth. Every horse wearing his collar of bells, and tossing his head as if

he enjoyed their sweet and merry sound. In consequence of the noiselessness of the sleigh there is a regulation enjoining the use of bells. There is something very delirious in the silent smooth motion of the sleigh under a warm sun, and breathing the dry, bracing and frosty air. I have felt colder at home with the therm. at 40, than in Canada at 10, but where there is a high wind with the frost, it is fiendishly cold.

Sunday Dec. 26th
Divine service. Frost continues. . . . Post letters for L. Monteagle Aubrey J. Gould[?]
. . .

Wednesday Dec. 29th
Snow recently gone. Very warm. Therm. 52. . .
Mr. O'Dwyer proffers [?] me to buy his farm in Biddulph, 22 miles from London on the Goderich Road. 200 acres – 75 cleared – for £500. If I do not wish to buy at present I can have a lease about £30 a year. I will allow out of such to pay the excess of any money laid out on building a house or any permanent improvement. . . .

Saturday, Jan 1 1848.
Newyears day. Heavy rain. Mr. Widder states that the expenditure of the Board of health for Kingston workhouse exceeds £30,000, of that, there are survivors of great misfortune. . .

Tuesday January 4th
Therm. 30. Frost commencing.
Nominations for candidates for the Co. of Middlesex. Two rivals . . . the former Conservative, the latter one of the Baldwin Lafontaine and Reform party. About the usual quality of coarse personalities, frothy declamations and specious profferings. Most slothful though drunk enough, I have some fun in them. It is expected that the Irishman will succeed because his opponent at the last election offended the Scotch by an uncivil allusion to their lice. Courthouse good and commodious. . . .

Thursday January 6th
Letters from my mother, Mary, Lucy, & S. Spring Rice about the state of the country more and more gloomy. . .

Sunday January 9th
Tremendous thick snow, drifting with a high wind like thick vapours over the surface of a lake. Start at 8am with Stephen McDonough in my sleigh for St. Thomas, where divine service. Reach it at 10. 18 miles. Proceed in afternoon to Port

Stanley – 10 miles. This day was so cold that few of the old inhabitants stirred out from fear of being frozen. The thermometer was 5 below zero, but the high winds and drifting snow make it worse. Warmly wrapped up in furs. . ., I slipped along without a sensation of cold. My pony was covered with congealed perspiration – at particular exposed parts of the road I sometimes felt a little inconvenienced . . . froze into ice. Port Stanley seems a thriving little port, carrying on a large export trade in corn, pork, flour. . .

There are two large inns. I stopped at Thompson's, an American's, & found him civil and communicative. He mentioned an affecting circumstance that happened last year. One of the Irish emigrants who landed at Port Stanley was an elderly man with his wife and 3 daughters. They moved a little inland and obtained a house. Shortly afterwards Mr Thompson met a beggar in a lonely part of the bush heading towards an old burial ground. It bore three coffins – an old man drove the oxen, & a weak and sickly woman toiled alongside. The coffins were those of the three young women who had all died together of fever. So great was the fear of infection that none of the neighbours would attend the funeral. The old father with difficulty obtained a team of oxen & 2 wagons, & with the assistance of his wife, herself in fever, dug his daughters graves & buried their remains. In a few days the wife died, & the old man still survives, the last of his race.

Notes

1   Stephen Edmund Spring Rice (1814–1865), was an Anglo-Irish civil servant and philanthropist from the Mount Trenchard estate in County Limerick who served as the Secretary of the British Relief Association between 1847 and 1848.
2   Alexander Carlisle Buchanan (1808–1868), chief Emigration Agent in Quebec City.
3   Reverend Patrick McMahon (1796–1851), parish priest of St. Patrick's Church, Quebec City.
4   Jacques Viger (1787–1858) was the first mayor of Montreal.
5   Peter McGill (1789–1860) was the second mayor of Montreal and a member of the Legislative Council of the United Provinces from 1841 to 1860.
6   Patrick Phelan (1795–1857), Bishops of Kingston (1843–1857).
7   Frederick Widder (1801–1865), *Canada Company Commissioner*.
8   Henry Fielding, *The History of Tom Jones, a Foundling*, or *Tom Jones* (1749). De Vere contrasts Fielding (1707–1754)) with Lawrence Sterne (1713–1768), author of *The Life and Opinions of Tristram Shandy, Gentleman* (1759–1767).
9   Edward McElderry, Toronto Emigrant Agent, died on 29 October, 1847.
10 Bishop Michael Power (1804–1847), of Toronto, died 1 October 1847.
11 Thomas Frederick Elliot (1808–1880), assistant-under-secretary for the colonies in 1847. De Vere's dispatch was published in the *Minutes of Evidence before Select Committee on Colonisation from Ireland* which is reproduced in this volume.

3

JOHN BURKE, 'REMINISCENCES', OR 'MIGRATION OF SEVEN BROTHERS' (MS JOHN BURKE, 'REMINISCENCES', NEW YORK HISTORICAL SOCIETY LIBRARY, NEW YORK, 1891)

John Burke's (1818 or 1819–1891) unpublished 'Reminiscences' or 'Migration of seven brothers' (dated August 11, 1891), describe his migration along with his six brothers from Ireland to New York during the Famine migration of 1847, after which he established a shoe business in New York City. The manuscript is held in the New York Historical Society Library (MS 2958.1483). Little is known about John Burke, but his 'Reminiscences' offer a compressed version of the genre of the Irish Famine migration narrative that attests to his experiences of an ocean storm, sense of deliverance at the end of his voyage, and complex motives for emigration. Thus, he recollects how in '1847 [I] made up my mind to Emigrate to America . . . and try [my] fortunes in the Grand Republic, . . . as the thinking portion of the country gave up hope of any improvement in their condition'. 'I left the country in disgust,' he stresses, for 'after the year of the famine I came to the conclusion the country had the day of [reckoning?] . . . and the sooner she was left to her own fate the better for those who had enterprise enough to leave'.[1] In this short passage, Burke contends that he left Ireland for reasons of economic opportunity and of his personal volition yet nevertheless regards himself as an exile. In his own words: "if population is wealth' than England must have cost a good [deal of it?], in oppressing her Irish subjects and forcing them to migrate[,] and losing her part of pesantry their national pride where ever distress can never be supplied.'[2] Like many Famine emigrants, Burke conflates notions of personal agency, economic opportunity, political banishment, and enforced expulsion into a highly over-determined self-image of the emigrant as exile.

I left the country in disgust after the year of the famine I came to the conclusion the country had the day of [reckoning?] . . . and the sooner she was left to her own fate the better for those who had enterprise enough to leave. If 'population is wealth' than England must have cost a good [deal of it?] in oppressing her Irish subjects and forcing them to migrate and losing her part of pesantry their national pride where ever distress can never be supplied.

In 1847 [I] made up my mind to Emigrate to America . . . and try [my] fortunes in the Grand Republic, . . . as the thinking portion of the country gave up hope of any improvement in their condition.

Took my chance in the good ship Symitry. Captain M. Kennelly. Genuine sea dog! A good navigator and sailor at heart – strong as a lion . . . during a long and stormy voyage.

Before we reached the end of the voyage and never was an admonition more true than on this occasion we all stashed on the hope for a 30 day passage but alas for human expectations we were sadly disappointed.

First week and fair wind we made good headway. . . [followed by] the Horrors of the storms which overtook the good old craft – everytime [during] her creaking and stead[ying] I felt she would [get] into some more terrible strain [and] tear apart.

During the raging of the storm from the n.w. the captain ordered all of the sails to be furled . . . After the storm subsided found we had been driven back near the coast of Cork in two days.

Rested for some time. Ship turns her head again towards the great west and began again our voyage which was this time always very squally[, –] and ours was no exception no picknic – I'm free to say I acted as Cap'n between decks and a most uncomfortable and trying position it turned out to be. Some I felt must enforce order and cleanliness or we were at the mercy of typhus or some disorder which was at any moment likely to break out from lack of food and all its consequences. Kept the good old ship fully up to his work and after 20 days came among the 40th again tacking much of the way arriving in fog around the banks of Newfoundland. We were very near having run into a steamer . . . a close call I thought to myself when the danger passed. In such weather foghorn should be continually blown to avoid collision in such dreary fog.

On a fine May morning I rose early to witness what the Captain said the previous night would be the grandest sight of my life and true it was as the sun rose above the horizon it fell on a sight to inspire awe! Delight! Wonder! And magnificence! For there as if anchored, quietly and majestically moving was an immense ice burgh, bright as a mirror, reflecting the golden rays of the rising sun. Such a sight is not often seen by man to such good advantage as we were treated to this morning. Suffice it was grand beyond description.

There is no mistaking the proximity of an iceberg as the air in the vicinity becomes so much cooler and the thermometer drops immediately. . .

After a few days we experienced a burial at sea and a sad sight it is to look upon. A few boards and sails together with the body placed in a box with a few old chains and scraps from the ship and placed upon a plank. The captain reads the burial service and overboard [the] body is sent.

Early on the morning of the 27th May we sighted land, and to the weary, emaciated, forlorn Emigrants [it] is about the happiest moment of his life no words can describe it. Thanking the lord for our deliverance and full of hope in the future.

Notes

1 MS John Burke, 'Reminiscences', New York Historical Society Library, New York, pp. 20, 19.
2 Burke, 'Reminiscences', pp. 20, 19.

4

JOHN YOUNG, 'DIARY OF JOHN YOUNG' (NANCY MALLETT ARCHIVE AND MUSEUM OF ST. JAMES' CATHEDRAL, TORONTO)

John Young (1827–1904) was born in Glasgow, Scotland, on May 10, 1827, and emigrated to Ancaster, Ontario in 1847. In 1849, he moved to Toronto where he married in 1862. He became the Comptroller of the Upper Canada Bible and Tract Societies and his family lived on the premises of the Society House in Toronto, where he died in 1904. Although he was not an Irish emigrant himself, Young's unpublished diary contains an eyewitness account the Famine voyage on a transatlantic vessel to Grosse Isle and then upriver by steamer to Montreal, Kingston, and Toronto. The unpublished diary is held in the Nancy Mallett Archive and Museum, St. James Cathedral in Toronto, which is named for archivist Nancy Mallett who is a descendant of John Young. His diary is published here for the first time.

Glasgow, Wednesday, 23rd June, 1847.
Rose at 20 minutes to 4 o'clock, and at 5, with the assistance of the Smiths, my father's man, carried the greater part of our luggage down to the close mouth to be in readiness for the cart, which came shortly after six. Got it safely deposited in the shed at the quay, along with some that had been left the night before. Watched it all forenoon till it could be slung down the hold, during which time two burrows loads more came down making in all, 2 good cart loads. During the afternoon got them all safe on board, and received visits from all our friends, Hugh Miller of Irvine included. Mother, Eliza, and all the children then went to sleep, some in Maxwell St. with Aunt Nanny and some in Russell St. while the rest of us slept in the boat with our clothes on. The beds having been flung in any way, we did not sleep much, and were up by half past 3 o'clock.

Thursday, 24th June, 1847.
Employed our time till six in wandering through Tradeston, where we met Uncle John. Went to the post office with two letters for Hugh. Expected the vessel to sail this morning, but it did not. Were mustered at 10 o'clock, and one woman turned out who had tried to get away without paying, and another family who were suspected of being infected with fever. We then heard a Gaelic sermon and prayer . . . All the passengers having been got on board we were at last taken out

by the Gulliver Tug, about 8 o'clock p.m., and without a stop floated down the river, amid the cheers of a crowd of spectators, many of whom followed us down to Govan and further. About 9 o'clock the women were ordered to bed out of the road, and within half an hour afterwards, and we all got in, when a little past Renfrew, and I soon fell asleep.

Friday 25th

Rose about 5 o'clock, and found the sailors washing the decks. Were ordered down out of the way, and found ourselves at the tail of the bank opposite Greenock, having arrived about 1 o'clock, a.m. when the tug left us. We lay all that day, at the tail of the bank. Oh! Wearying and wondering when we would get away. No water or biscuits or stores are yet served out. Took a last look of all the well-known places from Dunbarton Rock down by Nolenburgh Roseneath, Loch Long, Holy Lock, Gourock, Greenock, and Fort Glasgow, and watched the arrival and departure of steamers and sailing vessels. The 'Marchioness of Ailsa' is advertised to sail the same day as us, was tugged down this morning, and there was some speculation as to which should arrive at Quebec first. The pilot has been on board several times today, fuming and prating about the delay and we are all equally anxious to get off.

Saturday 26th

On rising this morning found ourselves in the same spot, but active preparations making for the voyage. The captain came down and ordered half of the passengers' provisions chests into the hold. Some things that we intended to use during the voyage went down with the rest, however we came on better than many, of whom father was one. About 10 o'clock the Conqueror Steam Tug came out from Greenock, and took us in tow, the wind not being very favourable, and as it is a very powerful tug, we went down very rapidly, passing Greenock, Dimoon, Toward Point, Rothsay bay and between Bute and the two Cunibraes, past Arran till were were getting near Ailsa Craig, when the tug left us to our own resources. A pretty brisk wind had by this time sprung up, so that we went on as fast as ever, till we had passed Ailsa, at a considerable distance from it, however. We also saw the Ayrshire coast indistinctly.

Sabbath, 27th

We found we had not made much progress during the night; on our right hand was Cantire and on the left the Ayrshire coast, near Loch Ryan. I omitted to mention yesterday that we got our first allowance of water and biscuit, three days allowances of the latter. This being Sabbath we had a chapter of the Bible, and a sermon read to us by the captain, who had the capstan for a desk, and there was also a service in Gaelic in the fore part of vessel, where they also sung a Psalm. We have got into favour with the cook by lending him a can full of water now and then, and have twice got something tasty from him. The cook is a black man and rather an original; he talks Gaelic to the Highlanders, which divert them much, and makes them draw water for him, in return for which he sometimes gives them hot water. The captain and mate are both very attentive to the passengers. Towards the afternoon we came in sight of Ireland, and the Mull of Cantire . . . We also saw an island off the coast of Ireland which I think is Rathlin. Making little progress towards night, there being no wind, and a swell which made the vessel heave up and down considerably. Several were vomiting. Felt rather queer myself and was in bed for a while. All went to bed about half past 9 o'clock.

Monday 28th

When we rose this morning found that we had made no progress during the night, lying between the same mull and the same part of Ireland. A child fell down one of the hatches today and has been hurt. Mother and Eliza both a little sick, but Mother vomited and has been better since. Was not quite right myself in the forenoon, but in the afternoon had a good vomit and have been quite well since. I omitted to mention yesterday that the captain distributed both Gaelic and English tracts among the passengers. All the officers of the vessel are very attentive inquiring after the sick and giving them medicines. This afternoon we got a sight at distance of Londonderry Loch on the one hand and Islay on the other.

Tuesday 29th

Opposite Derry Loch, with a little more wind. The girl that got hurt is worse today and is not expected to live. Got the fire kindled shortly after 6 o'clock. Put the kettle on shortly after. Took breakfast at 8, consisting of bread and ham or butter and tea. We have all had porridge only once and that was on Sabbath and then neither Jane nor Agnes would take any. Elizabeth, Martha and James got them almost every morning. Took dinner about one o'clock of anything handiest. Supper about 5 of tea and bread as in the morning and an egg. The above is repeated with little variation every day. Go to our beds about 9 o'clock lying heads and tails like herring in a barrel. Were going about 41/2 knots an hour tonight.

Wednesday 30th

Rose this morning before 5 o'clock and immediately after, the body of the child before mentioned was brought up on deck, having died last night about one o'clock. It was wrapped in a sack and laid above the galley. Could not see land on either hand but that was on account of the fog. Happened to be down stairs when the body was consigned to the deep, so that I did not see the ceremony. It was very simple I understand. After a prayer in Gaelic the corpse was laid on a plank, with one end over side and then slid into the water. A piece of pig iron, part of our cargo, was used for a weight to take the body down. After the fog had cleared away found ourselves still in sight of Ireland. Had light wind, which took us only about two or three knots per hour through the water. We pass great numbers of sea-fowl which, on our approaching them, dive down, and can remain a long time under water. They have a black head and black and white under the wings and on the belly. All the land we have seen since leaving the Clyde has been most barren and mountainous. The part of Ireland we have seen consists of precipices sheer down to the water. The Mull of Cantyre is similar, and Ayrshire little better. Waited up last night to see the sun set. It was very pretty from the many changes of shape it underwent, from a rail-pot to a punch bowl.

July 1st 1847 Thursday

One week today since we left Glasgow, and the scenes we have passed through are rather different, I guess, from those we expected, within the vessel that is to say. If we were hailed by any ship and asked what our cargo was I would answer, 'Highlanders, tin-pots, and porridge' of all which there is great abundance. Had a fair wind this morning, and had made good progress during the night. Got a last glimpse of Ireland, at least I hope so, for this voyage at all events. By noon we were quite out of sight of land. We have got bagpipes on board which have been played out several times, but this night we had a dance as well, when about a dozen couples footed it upon the deck, the captain approving and enjoying the sport as well as any. A shoal of porpoises passed about mid-day, which I did not see, being unfortunately down below. They were about 50 in number, passing us towards the east, one the starboard side of the vessel. Again watched the sunset, but it kept its own shape to the last this time. We have had beautifully calm weather as yet, all except one wet day.

Friday July 2nd

Did not rise till nearly 7 o'clock. Little wind and plenty of fog, which continued all day. Could not see very far from the vessel's side. Our rations today were served out, part biscuit and part flour, which was an improvement, as the biscuits were very hard and coarse, and we can make scones or anything we like with the flour. We have already gathered a donkey's load of biscuits, and in a short time will not know where to put them. Last night I omitted to mention there was almost a mutiny among the sailors because they had to work overtime. It passed away, however, with some grumbling and we have heard no more about it except the threats of some of the sailors that they would desert at Quebec, though they are engaged for the whole voyage. Of course that does not concern us. Another dance tonight, but I did not see it, being early in bed.

Saturday 3rd

A brisk and favourable wind all night, which continued this morning. Each day is like another so that there is almost nothing for a faithful chronicler like me to record. Sometimes a quarrel between two or more of the passengers diverts us a little. There is a man and women on board named Love, who, it is reported, were both married to other persons at home but eloped with each other. It is perhaps not true, but they are rather queer customers whatever they are. There is sometimes a rumpus between them when she kicks him and he kicks her, and then she roars, 'murder'. Even when on good terms she watches him like a cat with a mouse and follows him wherever he goes. A dance again.

Sabbath, 4th

On walking found ourselves rolling about in bed as much as one foot in breadth would let us. The good wind we had yesterday had freshened and the vessel was scudding along at the rate of nearly ten knots an hour. The sea was of course pretty rough and the vessel rolled from side to side making people stagger about as if they were drunk. There was no public service on deck today on account of the heaving, I suppose, there being fewer people on deck than usual. Some more porpoises or some such animal passed us this morning. They were going the same way as us and yet shot ahead of us like arrows, they were going with such speed. It is singular that though they have been seen four times now, I have not them once yet, always being out of the way some place or other. There was worship in Gaelic below, twice, among a few; the rest, us included, passed our time in reading what fit books we could lay hands on. The wind slackening a little in the evening, but we still went on at a good rate, about seven knots an hour.

Monday, 5th

My first job in the mornings this week back has been making sand for one floor. Everyone has to sweep, scrape, sand and scrub opposite their own berth. The next job is washing my face, and it is no very easy affair. First you have to look for a basin, then the water, then the soap, then the towel, then the comb, every one of which things are locked up or put by too well some way. Then finally the fire when it is our turn. Then breakfast, then waiting our turn for water, after which nothing to do till dinner, unless is the day for biscuit, which is served out twice a week. This day had a fair wind and got on pretty well. In the afternoon saw several jets of steam or smoke rising from the sea, and was told it was a whale blowing. It appeared to be two or three miles distant, and did not come nearer. A dance as usual.

Tuesday 6th

A north-east wind today which sent us on at a fine pace, viz 9 knots an hour, the vessel was lying over a good deal to the starboard side, and there was some good fun with people strolling about the deck. Saw a shoal of porpoises. The sailors call them blackfish. They are black or brown on the back and greyish white on the belly, with a horny fin sticking out of their back, which cuts the water like a knife when they rise to the surface.

Wednesday 7th

Little or no wind today, taking in the morning 3 knots an hour and at night not so much. There was a general turn out today of all the passengers that the tween decks might be thoroughly scraped. Everyone was sent up on deck even the sick had to take up their bed and walk. We were kept up about three hours.

Thursday 8th

The wind increased a little before we went to bed last night and continued favourable during the night and this morning; but towards the afternoon it veered round

JOHN YOUNG, 'DIARY OF JOHN YOUNG'

to the opposite direction, gradually becoming stronger. As a rough night was expected, everything loose was secured. By 6 o'clock the vessel was pitching and lying over so much that very few people were on deck. We lay down with our heads to the outside of the berths, as the vessel was inclined more to our side at the time. N.B. No dancing tonight.

Friday 9th

We had not long lain down last night when the order was given 'About ship', now inclined as much to the other side, and of course our heads were lower than our feet. What with this, and every now and then the noise of falling pots and pans, the ship heaving, folk groaning and the sailors trampling overhead, there was little sleep that night. I rose about 4 o'clock, and got up on deck, but could not stand without holding on. There were two vessels in sight at the time; the first we have seen since losing the sight of land. Several signals were hoisted to the nearest one, but there was no reply. The mate said it was a Dutch ship. The wind was calming down considerably by this time, but a swell was on the water all day. We saw 4 other vessels throughout the day, making in all 6 vessels today. It is likely that they were all destined by the same wind that brought us on so well, and now when it is against us, it is in their favour. Numbers of birds have been seen yesterday and today which makes us think we are coming near some land. No dancing for several days past.

Saturday 10th

A child of the name of Watson died this morning. He had been ill for more than a week of dysentery. The burial took place about 2 o'clock. A sailor stood in the chains and the body laid on a board was handed out to him; while resting on the bulwarks a short prayer in Gaelic was said by the same man as formerly and then the sailor took the board in his hands and sloped it down to the water. A plunge, and nothing more was seen. The wind still continued contrary and blew pretty hard. I forgot to say yesterday that a temporary sort of hospital was erected on deck under the starboard side of the longboat for the accommodation of a child who has got the small pox, so that it may not spread among the rest.

Sabbath 11th

The water rough today and the vessel lying much to one side. Father met with an accident by slipping on the wet deck and his feet going under a spar, so that he almost broke his legs. The waves often broke over the side of the vessel, giving those upon the deck a ducking. Did not see a vessel today, although we saw 6 or 7 on Saturday (except one at a very great distance in the evening). No service on deck.

Monday 12th

These three days back have made very little progress on account having to tack so much; for example, on Saturday gained only about 10 miles although I suppose we ran about 100. A great shoal of porpoises played about the ship for a while today. The mate came with a harpoon to catch one if possible but was too late, they were all gone. All on deck today again but were sent down in a hurry by a heavy shower. The wind has changed again so that we are making something today, 6 knots reported.

Tuesday 13th
Still light winds and variable. Have not seen a ship for several days. The dancing continues every night, though some people are complaining of it, both on account of the sin and of the noise. The captains says he cannot hinder it, suppose he was willing, as it is in his instructions to permit every recreation to the passengers conducive to their health. Great preparations making for fishing for cod on the banks of Newfoundland which we expect to reach soon.

Wednesday 14th
A favourable wind today takes us on finely. The Captain has given out a number of hooks to those that have none, or rather to those that are most importunate and greediest.

Thursday 15th
Still keeping up a good pace, about 8 knots an hour, but the weather is very foggy and damp, so that a lookout has to be kept at the bow in case of collision with any vessel. Numbers of weeds, both sea and land ones floated by. Cannot see above a boat's length on any side.

Friday 16th
The wind had abated by the morning and died away altogether by noon. Saw three vessels at a distance. Lay all day in the Captain's boat reading. The temperature of the water was tried today by a thermometer in a case being lowered down, and it was found by the coldness of the water that we were getting near the banks. Saw some porpoises at a distance.

Saturday 17th
A little wind this morning. Soundings were taken about 7 o'clock and the bottom found at 50 fathoms. On the banks at last, but no fishing vessels seen. A few had out their lines but on account of the motion of the vessel nothing was got. The banks of fog seen at a distance looks so very like land, that I do not wonder at shipwrecked mariners being often deceived by it. The wind increased towards night and led us to expect a rough morning.

Sabbath 18th
Had as usual on Sabbath, a rough forenoon. The wind contrary so that we had to tack about and did not make much way. We are now on a fishing station, vessels on all sides of us, none of them nearer than 3 or 4 miles except one

JOHN YOUNG, 'DIARY OF JOHN YOUNG'

which came within half a mile of us. I saw no less than 15 at one time. Still no fishing.

Monday 19th

No vessels in sight and little wind, about midday none at all, when a number of lines were put out and two cod caught. Of the fortunate passengers, one sold his to the steward I believe, the other prepared a piece of his for dinner. The wind rising a little however in the afternoon put a stop to the fishing for a day.

Tuesday 20th

On this day, the 26th from Glasgow, 24th from Greenock and 20th since we saw land, we got our first sight of the new world. In the morning it was known that we were near Newfoundland and, after the fog had cleared away saw it right ahead of us. It being a westerly wind, we had to tack towards the north otherwise we would not have seen it. We neared it rapidly having a smart breeze, and run in till we were about 2 miles from the shore, then we stood on the opposite tack. The part we saw was between Cape Pine on the north east, and Cape Race on the south west, a rugged coast, without any appearance of human habitation. Saw several small vessels coasting. When upon the opposite tack we saw a large steamer in the distance, homeward bound. It was the North American Mall Packet from Halifax to Liverpool, and was in sight for about two hours but did not come nearer than 2 or 3 miles. It had sails up as well, and will likely reach Liverpool before we are at Quebec. By this time we had tacked again, being out of sight of Newfoundland and starting north west speedily sighted it further to the west than before. We then coasted along several miles from shore, passing through a whole fleet of fishing vessels, mostly at anchor, hauling up cod as quickly as they could, others scudding before the wind away home. Three or four came very close upon us and hailed us crying out, 'Good luck to you, boys'. They were the first that had come so close that we could see faces. We would have been glad to have bought some fresh fish from the time we passed them it was getting dark and we were crossing the mouth of a large deep bay which I could not ascertain the name of and were still in sight of land when we went to bed.

Wednesday 21st

Slept but very so-so last night, the ship heaving and tumbling so much, the wind besides was blowing in shore and the water rough so that many were afraid of being cast ashore. About 12 o'clock at night they tacked about and in the morning we were again out of sight of land. There are rats in the ship, which seem to be increasing, and have been seen on the deck twice or thrice. They don't disturb me at night but Eliza is terribly frightened about them, and thinks she sees them in bed, which costs her many a night's sleep.

Thursday 22nd

During the night a man was seen lighting a piece of paper at the lantern, which is against the rules, he was therefore informed against and the captain condemned

IRISH FAMINE MIGRATION NARRATIVES

him to kindle the fire and sweep the decks three days. Another child has taken the small pox and has got a cot erected beside the former one, which is progressing favourably. Some small whales have been seen playing about the ship. We have still contrary winds and have enough adv(?) to keep ourselves from losing ground instead of gaining any. We have had to buy 2 pounds more of tea from the ship, the former being done. We have little left now but oatmeal and butter, so that porridge and tea is our only food now.

Friday 23rd
Another child died this morning and was buried during the day. It had been delicate ever since it came on board, having never quite recovered from the measles. We are still baffled by contrary winds but expect a change soon. See vessels now and then, but none come very near us.

Saturday 24th
A calm, warm day. Our neighbours in the next bed to us, are called Sinclair. Mr. Sinclair's mother, brother and sister are along with them. The mother has not been very well for 2 or 3 days, but before that was as well for her age, as any on board. This morning she was very ill, but we did not think her near so near, so we were affected on hearing of her death when everybody that was able had to be put up on deck, it being a cleaning day. This is the fourth death, but very hearty before her illness. A number of whales were seen playing about the ship today, and it was supposed by the superstitious that they knew a dead body was on board. The sailors foretell a fair wind tonight.

Sabbath 25th
The wind has not yet risen, we are going about 2 knots an hour. The body was brought up last night and lain in the long boat, and in there yet, being the first that has lain overnight. I omitted to say on Saturday that the stores were taken out of the long boat to make it the hospital, 2 more children having taken the small pox. Our speed is increasing rapidly, at 10 it was about 4 knots, at 1 about 6 knots and in the afternoon 8 knots an hour. Another child died tonight about 10 o'clock.

Monday 26th
Scudding before the wind at the rate of 9 ½ knots an hour. Very foggy in the forenoon which made sail be shortened a little, as we are nearing land again. The anchors also got ready. About noon it cleared and about 2 o'clock the cry was heard, 'land upon the weather bow'. It was St. Paul's Island and part of Cape Breton, from which we were distant yesterday at 12 exactly 200 miles. Before this time the two bodies had been committed to the deep, both at once, after prayers had been read by the Captain. Mrs. McTavish's corpse had been kept so long, out of respect to the feelings of her relatives, who wished if possible to keep her for burial on land, but it was found impractical. Got our nearest view of America

about 4 o'clock, both island and mainland consisting of barren hills as far as we could see, but we were at least 5 miles distant from St. Paul's and nearly 20 miles from the mainland. There is a lighthouse on St. Paul's. About 9 o'clock passed Bird Rocks at a distance, after we had lost sight of the former.

Tuesday 27th
Fair winds continued. Passed Magdalen Islands in the afternoon, which was all we saw today. They were at a distance, but appeared to be formed of rocks rising nearly perpendicular from the water for a little, and quite flat upon the top. We much puzzled by an appearance we saw about sunset. First what appeared to be a vessel appeared upon the horizon, then it widened till we supposed it to be a rock. Then a smaller one appeared on one side, after which they split into 6 or 7, when they looked like a fleet. After about half of an hour they disappeared all of a sudden and in about 5 minutes one again showed itself then went out of sight again. The only thing it could be would be a cloud, but such a strange one I never saw before.

Wednesday 28th
Today had our first view of the American continent in the shape of Cape Gaspe. Still rocks, rocks, all the world over. After passing the precipitous part, the hills receding back a little, left room for houses which now showed themselves for the first time. They were all white and glistened very nicely in the sun. Likewise I saw a considerable town called Great Fox River. All that the inhabitants depend on is fishing, the soil appearing very barren and rocky. The hills behind the town are in many places covered with trees, but we were not near enough to see what they were like. An old man died today. I have not learned exactly what was the matter with him, he was very infirm at any rate, and slept along with one of the children that had the small pox. He was not kept above two hours before the body was buried in the waters.

Thursday 29th
The wind having veered about the west, we had a day of tacking about and came pretty close upon the Island of Anticosti and some small rocky islands near it called Seven Islands. We did not make 6 miles altogether. I think Anticosti is like all the land we have seen, viz., hilly and barren (about Great Fox River expected) and it is said to be 100 miles long.

Friday 30th
Made a little progress today, the wind not being so directly in our face, but keep so near the centre of the river that we cannot see anything very plain. I do not think that a person on one side could see the other, although they are both very hilly. The St. Lawrence here has very little current, only about 2 knots an hour and the breadth I have not heard, but think it must be about 40 miles.

Saturday 31st

These last days a gum boil has been gathering on my right cheek, and today it is so much swelled that I cannot show myself on deck, but have kept in bed all day. Luckily for me, there was nothing to be seen above at any rate, on account of a dense fog, and as we were now coming into shallow waters and will not see a ship's length before us, the anchor was dropped in 16 fathoms of water. There was also heavy rain all day. The anchor fell foul at first and dragged, but was taken up and dropped again and we were all snug. The pilot is expected to come on board about this place and if we had one, we would not most likely have anchored at all. A large ship came very close to us, which appeared to be an emigrant one like ourselves, but it soon disappeared in the fog. Land was also seen upon the starboard bow, only about 1 mile distant, during a partial clearing away of the fog.

Sunday 1st August, 1847

Managed to get up this morning with a napkin up my jowls, the boil having broken during the night. Still at anchor waiting on a pilot. The fog is clearing away, giving us views of the scenery. The houses are all white-washed and have a pretty look. We have passed several small islands in the fog and others lie before us. The river is getting perceptibly narrower. In the forenoon, the pilot came on board, a man in a light frock coat and military cap, and altogether not very like a sailor. He is a French Canadian. Shortly after, the anchor was weighed and although the wind was still contrary, what with tide and tacking, we made a little way before going to bed. In the morning there was another death, the brother of him who died last. He has left a wife and family. It was his child which first caught the small pox and he was much exposed to the weather in tending it, not being very strong at any rate.

Monday 2nd

The anchor was dropped last night about 9 o'clock and weighed early this morning again, but the wind most obstinately continued to drive us back. After 'Jumping Jim Crow' for some hours we quietly sat down a little, below Green Island. This is the largest of many islands in sight and is covered every foot with the original forest, except a small spot cleared about the lighthouse which stands on one side of it. As it was a beautiful day and the wind had lulled, the captain took a trip in his gig to the island, along with the lady passenger and four steerage passengers as rowers. It was about 3 miles distant and they were away about 2 hours. They found the trees and underwood so thick and luxuriant that they could hardly move a step. The trees were principally spruce, but were very small, none being as thick in the trunk as a man's body. There was abundance of berries of different kinds, raspberries, gooseberries, and others, but none were ripe. There was also seen some deserted Indian wigwams. They brought away as trophies some flowers which were in great request on board after so long a voyage. While we lay at anchor, 2 boats came alongside with some provisions and speedily got them disposed of, they consisting of butter for which they charged 1/- currency p. pound, eggs and 1 loaf. It was black, but we relished it very much after our hard biscuit. We had quite a feast today! Weighed anchor again, when we saw a passenger schooner, the 'Jessie' of Limerick to which we spoke, it had been out 35 days. Spoke also with a brig from which we learned that there has been a great mortality among emigrants this season, some ships about half of them died and the quarantine station is so bad, they are dying every day. We had been fortunate both in health and speed, for some had taken 8 and 9 weeks upon the road. This news is alarming some of us lest we be put among the infected at the quarantine station, but we are all thankful that we have come safe so far.

Tuesday 3rd
The same routine goes on, anchoring at the ebb tide and weighing anchor when it favours us, passed the Pilgrim Islands and Hare Island today and the 'Argo' a new ship belonging to Robert Gilmour and Co. going on its first voyage laden with timber. We both lay to and spoke, when she confirmed what we heard yesterday. After wishing each other good passage they went on. The banks of the river are becoming thickly peopled, but only on the south side yet, on the north side the mountains are close upon the water.

Wednesday 4th
There being little wind today and that little unfavourable we lay at anchor all day. We are surrounded by beautiful scenery, islands being scattered all over the river, so that though it is many miles broad it sometimes appears not a mile.

Thursday 5th
A fine breeze springing up today we started as soon as the tided turned, and were soon going at the rate of 10 miles an hour. The river soon got more confined with many rocky islets on its surface, some with lighthouses and other buildings upon them and in about 3 hours we arrived at Grosse Island where many vessels were lying at the time.

Friday 6th
Grosse Island, where is quarantine, is about 33 miles from Quebec on the right side going up the river. It is covered all over with low trees except where it is cleared for the hospital and a few small houses. On account of the great sickness this season there was not enough of accommodation for the patients, so that they have erected several hundred small tents for those who are well. It looks like the encampment of an army. Between this island and one opposite, lie the vessels who are either waiting for inspection or else for their passengers. This forenoon the Doctor came on board and the passengers were passed in review before him, just like counting a flock of sheep, and were pronounced clean all except 2 who were ailing. There were several steamers taking up passengers out of the passed

vessels and one came alongside ours to take us also, but the Highlanders stuck out like bricks for a steamer for themselves and gained their point, so we had to lie another night.

Saturday 7th

Early this forenoon, the Rowland Hill steamer came alongside with a custom-house officer. All the luggage was hauled up from below, the beds had been emptied 2 days before. The officer examined each box as it was put into the steamer, and we had to open all our boxes though many of them were clasped with iron. He was rather suspicious of the lot of books we had with us and turned them over a good deal, but at last we were passed and got on board the steamer. It was built in the Yankee fashion with promenade deck and walking beam and appeared very strange to us who had never been in anything like it before. It was about 12 o'clock before all were on board and then we started getting three cheers from the sailors, which we returned. We now passed up the river very rapidly the tide being in our favour. The banks were lined on both sides with one continuous line of houses, which being all whitewashed and the numerous churches having all tin steeples glistened beautifully in the sun. Now the large island of Orleans divided the river, and shortly Quebec burst upon us with castle on the height, the steep descent, and the high wooden houses at the bottom and hundreds of vessels lying in the smooth water. But before coming near enough to distinguish one house from another our attention was called to another object. After passing the island of Orleans the falls of Montmorency, hitherto concealed by it, came in sight. We were several miles from it and at that distance it looked just like a white sheet hung over the rock. When opposite Quebec the steamer went close to the wharf, but did not touch at any, and then without stopping, up we went past the plains of Abraham, Wolfe's Cove and other places famed in history. Wolfe's Cove is now part of Pollock Gilmour and Co.'s ship building yard. The river at Quebec suddenly narrows to about half a mile wide and continued so long as it was light. When it got dark we each tried to get as good a place as we could to get a little sleep, but we had little success, for it became rather blowy and on account of the boat being top heavy we had to keep running from one side to the other to keep the vessel from capsizing.

Sabbath 8th

During the night we passed through Lake St. Peter which is a wider part of the St. Lawrence. The banks near Quebec are high and steep, but near Montreal they are quite low and many low islands divide the river. About 8 o'clock we saw Montreal. It has not so impressive an appearance as Quebec, lying upon the bank, with a mountain from which the town is named behind it. It is on a large island, and like Quebec, is on the right side going up. We passed all the wharfs to the last one which is the one for emigrants and where the sheds are. The sheds being full of sick emigrants, them in our vessel were advised to keep on board all day till the others could be removed, which they did. During the day Father tried to get lodgings in some hotel for the women, but they were all so afraid of the fever that they would not admit them. Passed the day as well as we could looking about the town. There is a great many fine stone buildings in it, particularly the market facing the river and the French Church which was the largest church I ever saw. There is no slates to be seen nor tiles, only shingles or tin upon the roofs. There was not a great many vessels at the wharfs as the most do not come above Quebec. Some Indians prowling about the quay tried to come on board to spy out the land, but they were prevented, partly for fear of infection and partly to prevent theft and there was almost a battle about it. I omitted to mention before that the boatmen were French Canadians and we heard some songs from them. We had again to lie down on deck to get a little sleep.

Monday 9th
Had very little sleep on account of the noise and fighting made by some drunken passengers. Early in the morning began to take ashore our luggage and place it in the shed where if we did not get lodgings we would have to remain all day as Father had some business to transact before leaving Montreal. Made search through the town for Mark MacFarlane and after some time found him. Some of us had to take care of the luggage, but the rest took dinner in Mark's house. After making arrangements for going to Lachine next day, in the meantime Robert and a lad called John Wilson a fellow traveller were sent on with the luggage by two trucks. What is called a truck is just like a long ladder laid between two wheels, it is so very narrow and long being made for taking flour in barrels. We had intended to go by the Rideau Canal but as it was shut up for repairs we had to go by the Mail Steamer and it was well we did so for though they are dearer they go in less than half the time. We then took up our quarters for the night in Mark's house and were very hospitably treated, Mark leaving off work in honor of his old boss.

Tuesday 10th
Started about 10 o'clock in the stage for Lachine, having taken our passages in the Passport Steamer for Kingston. When we got to Lachine found the vessel packed full of soldiers going up so that there was no room for us. Father complained of being thus treated and the agent gave us the use of a large store for ourselves alone to wait for the next day upon another steamer. As we had no alternative we settled down as comfortably as we could. Robert and John Wilson we found all safe, having to a night's lodging after some trouble. When night came on we spread our beds on the floor and lay down and got as good a sleep as we had done since we left home.

Wednesday 11th
This morning the steamer Henry Gildersleeve came in and we got our boxes on board. The other emigrants who had come out with us had mostly taken the

government passage and a while before starting we saw them passing up the river in barges, exposed without shade to a burning sun, with a steamer tugging them at a snail's pace. After we started we soon passed and shortly arrived at the Beauharnois Canal, made to avoid rapids in the river. The vessel was here detained for some time going through several locks, during which time many country people stepped on board selling different commodities. We saw a steamer going down the rapids at a tremendous rate, for though they are so violent that a steamer cannot stem them going up, yet they may be gone through on the way down. We now found ourselves in a narrow canal hardly as wide as the promenade deck of the steamer, through which they had to steer cautiously. After the rapids were passed it joins the river again, but the current is still very rapid and continued so all the way up to Kingston. We were ploughing our way among islands of all sizes when it became dark.

Thursday 12th

Went through the Cornwall and other canals during the night to avoid other rapids and in the morning found ourselves in the lake of a thousand islands, threading our way as through the streets of a large town. The scenery was most beautiful the islands being richly wooded and we touched at several to take in wood where little wharfs were erected for the purpose. These steamers consume a tremendous quantity of wood, the hold is filled when they start and it has to be replenished six or seven times each voyage. We saw Yankeeland today in the town of Ogdensburgh, but did not go near it. Early in the forenoon we reached Kingston at entrance to Lake Ontario. It appears to be strongly fortified and 2 new forts are building out in the water facing the town. The end of the Rideau Canal is here and if we had come by it we would have been a week later. We had not to land at all but just went alongside the steamer for Toronto the Princess Royal which was lying at a wharf, and transferred ourselves to it. It soon pushed out and we thought we were off but it went again to another wharf where there were some thousands of Irish emigrants and proceeded to pack them on board. We were rather alarmed at this as many of them were sick and so many were packed that we had not room to stir. Father complained to the Captain and offered to pay cabin fare to get out of such a squad but got nothing but impudence from him, Captain Twohey. We had all to squat down in a corner keeping back from the rest as well as we could. Bread was then distributed among them and we started. We soon lost sight of land on one side and when it got dark we could see none. We were now on Ontario. The night was very cold and we being on the promenade deck got a good share, so one of the sailors taking compassion on us flung a tarpaulin over us to cover us, which the upstart Captain no sooner saw than he ordered it off. We had some shivers so we huddled all together in a corner to keep each other warm and tried to sleep. I got about 2 hours sleep but some of us got none.

Friday 13th

We kept along the north shore of the lake touching at 1 or 2 places till we arrived at Toronto. There is a long strip of land juts out for a mile or two then turns round to the west enclosing a first rate harbour. Toronto lies on the mainland within the bay, upon a gentle slope with many handsome hotels facing the water with their tin roofs glittering in the sun. There is a lighthouse on the extremity of the tongue of land. We here got rid of the most of our living cargo, whom they treated just like cattle driving them about, and tried to do the same with us, but we rebelled. They were all turned out and kept back with sticks till their luggage would be tumbled out after them. Father, William and Robert looked after ours and managed to get it laid all in one place and then got it put on board the Eclipse Steamer for Hamilton and soon after we were all safe on board. After two or three hours sail we came in sight of Burlington Bay and soon went through the canal into it and got our first sight of Hamilton. When we got up the wharf Hugh and William Wright were there waiting for us and we had a happy meeting after all our troubles.

5

ROBERT WHYTE, *THE OCEAN PLAGUE: A VOYAGE TO QUEBEC IN AN IRISH EMIGRANT VESSEL, EMBRACING A QUARANTINE AT GROSSE ISLE IN 1847. WITH NOTES ILLUSTRATIVE OF THE SHIP-PESTILENCE OF THAT FATAL YEAR. BY A CABIN PASSENGER* (BOSTON: COOLIDGE AND WILEY, 1848)

Robert Whyte's *The Ocean Plague: A Voyage to Quebec in an Irish Emigrant Vessel* (1848) is one of the most compelling and controversial examples of the Irish Famine migration genre. There is some debate about whether it is a genuine Famine journal or work of historical fiction. The fact that James J. Mangan, editor of the spurious *Famine Diary: Journey to a New World* (1991), republished *The Ocean Plague* under the title *Robert Whyte's 1847 Famine Ship Diary: The Journey of an Irish Coffin Ship* (1994),[1] has heightened suspicions of the text.

What remains beyond dispute, however, is that *The Ocean Plague* was published in Boston in 1848 when the Irish Famine migration was still occurring. According to André Charbonneau and André Sévigny, it is an

> Eyewitness account by Robert Whyte, an Irish emigrant who left the port of Dublin on May 30 and arrived at Grosse Île in the evening of July 27. He was a cabin passenger, probably on the *George*, a ship commanded by Captain Sheridan whose arrival at the quarantine station was registered on July 28. Whyte stayed at Grosse Île until August 2.[2]

Mark McGowan agrees that the vessel in question is most likely the *George*, but he offers a more probing critique of *The Ocean Plague's* authorship and provenance. He notes the text's endemic 'lack of clarity' in which 'Whyte never makes mention of the name of the 'brig' upon which he is sailing, nor the full names of the captain, crew or any of the passengers'.[3] McGowan does concede that 'only one ship, the *George* could pass for Whyte's, based on its size, passengers, port of departure, and time of arrival, but even here there are problems: Whyte's ship arrived on 2 August, the *George* on 3 August; Whyte's ship had 110 passengers, eight deaths at sea, and two deaths at Grosse Île for its five days in quarantine, while the *George* had 107 passengers, seven deaths at sea and four in hospital, spending only one day in quarantine'.[4] Indeed, McGowan contends that these and other 'serious inconsistencies place the authenticity of Whyte's diary in some doubt'. Ultimately, McGowan concludes:

> The numerous contradictions between Whyte's record and the routinely generated records of his era, the circumstantial evidence that suggests his ship may have been the *George*, the author's perspicacity in providing rich historical, statistical, and geographic details within his prose, and the questions of authorship, collectively identify this journal as bearing a complexity that defies simple explanation. What seems plausible is that the author, perhaps Robert White the physician [who was an Irish resident of Boston], used fragments of a diary not his own, but from a passenger on the *George*, as the heart of a pamphlet designed to expose the horrors of the Famine migration of the 'Black '47'.[5]

On the other hand, Occam's Razor would suggest that the author undertook the Famine voyage himself and then augmented his narrative afterwards, rather than basing his account on 'fragments of a diary not his own, but from a passenger on the *George*'. The supposition that *The Ocean Plague* is 'based loosely on a real voyage' and fragments of another emigrant's diary involves even more assumptions about the authorship of the text than that Robert Whyte wrote it himself. The more plausible hypothesis remains that the author documents his own voyage.

CHAPTER I

30 May 1847

Many and deep are the wounds that the sensitive heart inflicts upon its possessor, as he journeys through life's pilgrimage but on few occasions are they so acutely felt as when one is about to part from those who formed a portion of his existence; deeper still pierces the pang as the idea presents itself that the separation may be forever, but when one feels a father's nervous grasp, a dear sister's tender, sobbing embrace and the eye wanders around the apartment, drinking in each familiar object, until it rests upon the vacant chair which she who nursed his helpless infancy was wont to occupy, then the agony he wishes to conceal becomes insupportable. But as the skilful surgeon tears off the bandage which the hand of affection gently withdraws from the wound, thereby unconsciously inflicting greater pain, so it is better not to linger upon the affecting scene but rush suddenly away.

It was a charming morning on which I left dear old Ireland. The balmy new-born day in all the freshness of early summer was gladdened by the beams of the sun which rose above the towers of the city, sunk in undisturbed repose. It was a morning calculated to inspire the drooping soul with hope auguring future happiness.

Too soon I arrived at the quay and left my last footprint on my native land. The boat pushed off and in a few minutes I was on board the brig that was to waft me across the wide Atlantic.

There was not a soul on deck but presently the grizzled head of the captain was protruded from the cabin and from the uninviting aspect of his face I feared that he would prove an unsocial companion for a long voyage. He received me as kindly as his stubborn nature would allow and I was forced to admire the manly dignity of the rude tar when, from the bent attitude he was obliged to assume while ascending the companion ladder, he stood upright on the deck. The sailors now issued from the forecastle and the mate came up and introduced himself to me.

The captain having given the word to weigh anchor, a bustle immediately arose throughout the vessel; the seamen promptly proceeded to their work with apparent pleasure although (being the Sabbath) they did not accompany the action with the usual chant. The chain having become entangled in the cables of some fishing boats, it was a considerable while before the anchor was hoisted. At length the top-sails were unreefed and our bark glided through the beauteous bay.

In a short time we rounded the promontory of Howth having taken the north channel as the wind was southerly.

The captain then led me down to the cabin for breakfast and introduced me to his wife who he informed me always accompanied him to sea and whom I shall for the future designate as the mistress, as by that term she was known to both crew and passengers. Feeling an inclination towards squeamishness and being much more sick at heart, I retired to my stateroom and lying down upon the berth, fell into a dreamy slumber, in which I remained until aroused when I found it was late in the afternoon and tea was ready. I felt somewhat revived by the grateful beverage and accompanied the captain on deck. We were off Carlingford and the mountains of Mourne. The passengers were cooking their evening meal at their fires upon the foredeck and the sailors discussing their coffee in the forecastle. I endeavoured to enter into conversation with the captain but he was provokingly taciturn; however, we were soon joined by the mistress, who was not unwilling to make up for her husband's deficiency. The sun set and twilight subsided into darkness. A cold night breeze also told that it was time to go below.

Monday, 31 May

I rose early and inhaled the fresh morning air. We made good progress during the night and the bold cliffs of the coast of Antrim were visible on one hand, the Scotch shore on the other. At 8 a.m. the bell rang for breakfast and I took my seat opposite the captain. The mistress sat in an armchair and the mate on a stool next to me, completing the cabin circle. We were attended by Simon the cabin boy whom at first sight I took to be a 'Darky'.

His face was coated with smoke and soot, streaked by the perspiration that trickled from his brow which was surmounted by a thicket of short, wiry black hair standing on end, his lustreless brown eyes I cannot better describe than by borrowing a Yankee illustration: they were Dike two glass balls lighted by weak rush lights; his lips were thick, straight and colourless; his complexion (when unveiled) was a grimy yellow and the expression of his wide flat face, idiotic. He wore a red flannel shirt and loose blue pilot trousers but neither shoes nor stockings. His movements were slow, except at meals, when he seemed to regain his suspended animation and it was a goodly sight to see him gulping coffee, bolting dodges of fat pork and crunching hard biscuit as ravenously as a hungry bear.

No two specimens of human nature could possibly present more striking contrasts than Simon and his fellow apprentice, Jack. The latter was about 15 years of age, remarkably small and active. Squirrel never climbed a tree more nimbly than Jack could go aloft, and in the accomplishment of chewing and smoking he might compete with the oldest man aboard. His fair skin was set off by rosy cheeks and his sparkling blue eyes beamed with devilment. He was a favourite of everyone – except the mistress, with whom his pranks did not pass – being therefore exempt from the menial offices of cabin boy which devolved upon Simon. His principal amusement consisted in persecuting that genius.

The mate was a very little man not more than five feet high but in excellent condition, as seamen generally are. He was lame in one leg which deformity he took great pains to hide, causing a constrained limp that was extremely ludicrous. He was well-looking and sported a capacious pair of black whiskers, the outline of which he frequently altered. He had been a 'Captain' but unfortunately, loving the bottle, he lost his 'cast'. There existed little confidence between him and the captain and, both being of a warm temperament, there were occasional symptoms of collision but they were prevented from ending in open rapture by the timely interference of the mistress, on whom the captain would let loose his wrath, which though expressed in no gentle terms she bore with exemplary patience.

The mistress was small, ruddy and sun-burnt, having seen some sixty winters, forty of which she had spent at sea, generally in the home trade but varied occasionally by voyage to Russia or to America. She was in the habit of keeping a private log, in which she noted the incidents of her travels. I was allowed to look into this interesting production, which amused me no less by the originality of the orthography, than its elegance of diction. Being a native of Cumberland her pronunciation was not particularly euphonious. She also, when addressing her husband, the mate and all familiar acquaintances, used the terms 'Thee' and 'Thou' invariably reversing their grammatical order.

Tuesday, 1 June
After breakfast, the mate invited me to see the depot of provisions. I accordingly followed him, descending by a ladder into an apartment partitioned off from the hold, and dividing it from the cabin.

By the light from the lantern I perceived a number of sacks, which were filled with oatmeal and biscuit. The mate having proceeded to prepare the passengers' rations for distribution, I sat down upon one of the sacks, from beneath which suddenly issued a groan. I jumped up, quite at a loss to account for the strange sound and looked at the mate in order to discover what he thought of it. He seemed somewhat surprised but in a moment removed two or three sacks and lo! there was a man crouched up in a corner. As he had not seen him before, the mate at once concluded that he was a 'Stowaway', so giving him a shake to make him stand upright, he ordered him to mount the ladder, bestowing a kick upon the poor wretch to accelerate his tardy ascent.

The captain was summoned from below and a council immediately held for the trial of the prisoner, who confessed that, not having enough of money to pay for his passage, he bribed the watchman employed to prevent the possibility of such an occurrence. He had been concealed for three days but at night made his way into the hold, through a breach in the partition; his presence was therefore known to some of the passengers. He had no clothes but the rags he wore nor had he any provisions. To decide what was to be done with him was now the consideration, but the captain hastily terminated the deliberation by swearing that he should be thrown overboard. The wretched creature was quite discomfited by the captain's wrath and earnestly begged for forgiveness. It was eventually settled that he should be landed upon the first island at which we should touch, with which decision he appeared to be quite satisfied. He said that he was willing to work for his support but the captain swore determinedly that he should not taste one pound of the ship's provision. He was therefore left to the tender mercies of his fellow passengers.

In consequence of this discovery, there was a general muster in the afternoon, affording me an opportunity of seeing all the emigrants – and a more motley crowd I never beheld; of all ages, from the infant to the feeble grandsire and withered crone.

While they were on deck, the hold was searched, but without any further discovery, no one having been found below but a boy who was unable to leave his berth from debility. Many of them appeared to me to be quite unfit to undergo the hardship of a long voyage, but they were inspected and passed by a doctor, although the captain protested against taking some of them. One old man was so infirm that he seemed to me to be in the last stage of consumption.

The next matter to be accomplished was to regulate the allowance of provisions to which each family was entitled, one pound of meal or of bread being allowed for each adult, half a pound for each individual under fourteen years of age, and one-third of a pound for each child under seven years. Thus, although there were 110 souls, great and small, they counted as 84 adults. That was, therefore, the number of pounds to be issued daily. On coming on board, provisions for a week were distributed but as they wasted them most improvidently, they had to be served again today. The mate consequently determined to give out the day's rations every morning.

Wednesday, 2 June

We made but little progress during the night and were still in the channel, within sight of the Mull of Kintyre and the northern shore of Ireland.

Having but a few books with me, I seized upon a greasy old volume of sundry magazines, which I found in the cabin. I also commenced the study of a book of navigation. These, varied with the Book of books, Shakespeare and Maunder's Treasuries, kept me free from ennui. When tired of reading, I had ample scope for observation.

The mistress spent the forenoon fishing, and the afternoon in curing the mackerel and gurnet she caught. We had some at tea when I met with a deprivation I had not anticipated – there was no milk! and I did not at all relish my tea without it. One cup was quite enough for me, but I soon became habituated to it. Having rounded the long promontory of Donegal, the outline of the shore became indistinct and, making our calculations not to see land again for some time, the mate took his 'departure' from Malin Head.

CHAPTER II

Roll on, thou dark and deep blue blue ocean, roll!
Byron

Thursday, 3 June

When I came on deck this morning I found that we were sailing upon the bosom of the broad Atlantic, no object being visible to relieve the vast expanse of water and sky, except the glorious sun and as I turned my eyes from the survey of the distant horizon and fixed them upon the little bark that wafted us, a sensation akin to that of the 'Ancient Mariner' possessed my mind.

Alone, alone, all, all alone
Alone on a wide, wide sea.

As the boy who was unable to attend the muster still continued ill, and was reported to be feverish, the mistress and I reviewed the medicine chest. We found it to contain a jar of castor oil, Epsom salts, laudanum, hartshorn, etc; also a book of directions, which were by no means explicit, and they so perplexed the mistress, even with the aid of her spectacles, that as she was nothing the wiser of the study she resolved to trust to her own experience in the concoction of a dose. The mate took his first observation at noon and as he stood peering through the eye-hole of the quadrant, he reminded me forcibly of poor old Uncle Sol's little midshipman.

The passengers' fireplaces, upon either side of the foredeck furnished endless scenes, sometimes of noisy merriment, at others of quarrels. The fire was contained in a large wooden case lined with bricks and shaped something like an old-fashioned settee – the coals being confined by two or three iron bars in front. From morning till evening they were surrounded by groups of men, women and children; some making stirabout in all kinds of vessels, and others baking cakes upon extemporary griddles. These cakes were generally about two inches thick, and when baked were encased in a burnt crust coated with smoke, being actually raw in the centre. Such was the unvaried food of the greater number of these poor creatures. A few of them, who seemed to be better off, had herrings or bacon. The meal with which they were provided was of very bad quality – this they had five days and biscuit, which was good, two days in the week.

Friday, 4 June
The sailors and apprentices were (as the mate expressed it in his log) variously employed mending sails, tarring ropes, spinning yarns, etc. Sailors sit and sew very differently from tailors; instead of doubling up their legs under them they stretch them out straight before them as they sit upon the deck. Their thimble is also peculiar, not being worn on the top of the finger, but upon the ball of the thumb, to which it is fastened by a leather strap, buckled round the wrist. I was surprised at the expedition and neatness with which they sewed with their coarse needles and long threads.

Jack created some diversion by daubing a gossoon's face with tar, and shaving him with a rusty knife. It was exhilarating to hear the children's merry laughter – poor little things, they seemed quite reconciled with their situation! I learned that many of these emigrants had never seen the sea nor a ship until they were on board. They were chiefly from the County Meath, and sent out at the expense of their landlord without any knowledge of the country to which they were going, or means of livelihood except the labour of the father of each family. All they knew concerning Canada was that they were to land in Quebec and to go up the country; moreover they had a settled conviction that the voyage was to last exactly three weeks. In addition to these, there were a few who were going to try their fortunes on their own account. One of the latter was a Connaught 'Boy', who having lived upon the coast and spent his time partly in fishing, made himself useful about the brig and thereby ingratiated himself into favour with the captain and won the consequent jealousy of his fellow passengers, who, thinking him rather soft, took pleasure in teasing him. Two young men from Kilkenny and one from the County Clare completed the list. The former used to astonish the Meathmen with the triple wonders of their native city.

Saturday, 5 June
As the passengers had a great inclination to infringe upon the after-deck, the captain drew a line, the penalty for crossing which was the stoppage of a day's water.

I observed the sea to be crowded with myriads of slimy looking objects, which the sailors called 'Slobbs'. They varied in size, form, and colour, some of them resembling a lemon cut in half. How beautiful also was the luminous appearance of the water at night, which I delighted to watch, as we glided through the liquid fire.

Nor was it less pleasing to observe the 'Portuguese men of war', with their tiny sails set to the breeze, and surmounting the crests of the rolling billows. I had a rummage through the charts and enjoyed a practical lecture upon them, with illustrative lectures by the mistress, enlivened by way of episode with occasional contradictions by the captain who with rule and compass traced our progress daily upon the great chart of the North Atlantic ocean. We had two ships in company with us all the day; they were too distant to distinguish their names. One of the passengers having thrown the Connaughtman's hat overboard, the captain gave him a blue and white striped night-cap, with which on his head he strutted about, much to the amusement of the youngsters, one of whom attached a rope to the tail of his coat; this he dragged after him for some time, until Jack changed the scene by cutting the tail off. When Paddy discovered his loss, he was outraged and made a grievous complaint to the mate who doctored the coat by abstracting the other tail, thereby transforming the garment into a jacket. When the matter came to the captain's ears he presented Paddy with an old pilot jacket, which made a great coat for him; he was, therefore, no loser by the affair.

Sunday, 6 June
The favourable breeze that carried us out of the channel having forsaken us, the little progress we made was gained by tacking, which kept the sailors constantly employed. The passengers were dressed in their best clothes and presented a better appearance then I expected. The sailors also donned their holiday toggery in the afternoon.

A group of young men, being at a loss for amusement, began to wrestle and play 'pitch and toss' but the mate soon put a stop to their diversions at which they grumbled, saying that they 'didn't think that Mr Mate would be so hard'.

Very few of them could read; neither did they seem to have any regard for the sanctity of the Sabbath. In the evening they had prayers in the hold and were divided into two parties – those who spoke Irish, and those who did not; each section having a leader who gabbled in his respective language a number of 'Paters and Aves', as quickly as the devotees could count their beads.

After these religious exercises they came upon deck and spent the remainder of the day jesting, laughing and singing.

We had a clear and beautiful sunset from which the captain prognosticated an easterly wind.

CHAPTER III

Thou shalt not be afraid for any terror by night, nor for the arrow that flieth by day; for the pestilence that walketh in darkness, nor for the sickness that destroyeth in the noon-day.
Psalms of David

Monday, 7 June
The passengers elected four men to govern their commonwealth, the principal of whom had the title of 'head committee'. The other three being inactive, the sole

authority was wielded by him much to the terror of the little boys who were often uproarious and to keep whom in order he frequently administered the 'cat'. The other duties of this functionary consisted in seeing that the hold was kept clean, in preventing smoking below, settling differences, etc. He was also the medium of communication with the 'other house' – he and Paddy alone being permitted to go aft.

Tuesday, 8 June
We steered southward course but gained very little longitude.

The two ships were again in sight, one was the *Tamerlane* of Aberystwyth, the other the *Virginius* of Liverpool; both fine vessels with passengers.

The head committee reported that two women were ill. They were therefore dosed according to the best skills of the mistress, who was desirous of going into the hold to see them, but the captain peremptorily desired her upon no account to do so and kept a sharp lookout that she might not visit them unknown to him. The boy, whom nothing ailed but seasickness and fatigue, had recovered. I saw him upon deck – miserable looking little animal, with a huge misshapen head, sallow, lantern-jaws and glassy eyes – apparently about twelve years of age; but his father said that he was twenty. I could scarcely credit him but was assured of the fact by his neighbours who said that he always had the same emaciated appearance, although he never before complained of illness. He went by the name of 'The little shoemaker'.

Wednesday, 9 June
As we were seated at dinner in the cabin discussing a savoury dish of lobscouse made by the mistress, we were alarmed by the shouting of men and screaming of women. We hurried on deck, thinking that someone was overboard and judge of our terror when we saw the fore part of the brig in a blaze. All hands having assisted, a plentiful supply of water in a short time subdued the fire which extended no further than the caboose; it arose from the negligence of Simon who fell asleep leaving a lighted candle stuck against the boards. This was the only brilliant act of which he was guilty during the voyage and as a reward for which the mate bestowed upon him a rope's end.

Thursday, 10 June
The only incidents of the day were breakfast, dinner and supper – and the meridional observation and the temporary stir consequent on the captain coming upon deck after a snooze, and shouting, 'bout ship'. Some more cases of illness were reported and the mistress was kept busy mixing medicine and making drinks, hoping that by early attention the sickness might be prevented from spreading.

As I was pacing the deck in the afternoon I observed one of the passengers – a well-looking man with fine brown eyes – timidly approach me. After looking about him to assure himself that the captain was below, he doffed his hat and addressed me as follows: 'I beg your honour's pardon, but I hope it's no offence.' Having told him that he had given me none, he proceeded – 'Well then, Master, isn't it mighty quare intirely and how can the likes of us know the differ; but I hope your honour it's all right?'

I replied that I was not aware of anything being wrong and desired him to say what was the danger he feared which caused him to ask: 'Aragh! Why thin are we goin' back to ould Ireland?' I demanded his reason for such a supposition when, after scratching his head and casting a glance towards the cabin, looking rather perplexed, he went on. 'That little gossoon of mine, your honour – a mighty smart chap he is too and a great scholar entirely, he tould us – but faith! I dunno how to believe him though he got his larnin' at the national school[6] and can cast up figures equal to the agent and can read the whole side of a book without stoppin'. He says, sir, that the sun, God bless it, sets in the wist. . .'

Here he paused and looked earnestly at me, as if for confirmation of the fact. I therefore said that the boy's knowledge was pretty accurate.

Seeming encouraged, he continued – 'Moreover than that, he says that Ameriky, where we are goin' to, if the Almighty God spares us. (Here he crossed himself.) Glory be to his name! it's in the wist of the world too.' He again paused and looked enquiringly.

'Well,' said I, 'He is pretty right there also, America is west from Ireland.' 'Then, Master, here's what we want to come at, you see. If Ameriky is in the wist, mustn't the sun set in it? Then why is it your honour, that instead of followin' it, we're runnin' away from it as hard as we can lick?'

Such was the fact – a fresh northerly breeze compelling us to bear to the south-east. I now saw the nature of the problem he wished to have solved and explained the matter as explicitly as I possibly could but it was some time before he comprehended me. At length he seemed to become enlightened on the subject, for, giving his thigh a slap of his open palm, he exclaimed: 'Och! By the powers, I see it all now, it's as plain as a pike-start and I'm sure I'm obleeged to your honour and so is the gossoon too. Oh, that divil's clip Jack – wait till I ketch him. If I don't murder him it's not matter. What do you think, your honour, he tould the little chap, when he axed him all about it? 'Why,' says he, 'Sure we're goin' back again for the mistress' knittin' needles that she forgot.' 'So as he wouldn't tell him, nor none of the sailors, I made bould to ax your honour as the little chap is loath to make so free.'

On the conclusion of the dialogue, Jack, who was over our heads in the shrouds, burst into a hearty fit of laughter, in which I could not but participate when I noticed the comicality of the arch sailor-boy's appearance and the simplicity of my interlocutor, who, hearing the captain's heavy step coming up the ladder, hastily retired, vowing vengeance upon Jack.

Saturday, 12 June

I amused myself taking a sketch of the cabin 'interior'. It was about ten feet square and so low that the only part of it in which the captain could stand upright was under the skylight. At either side was a berth, both of which were filled with the mistress' boxes, the captain's old clothes, old sails and sundry other articles, which were there stowed away and concealed from view by chintz curtains trimmed with white cotton fringe.

The ceiling was garnished with numerous charts rolled up and confined by tapes running from beam to beam, from one of which – carefully covered by a cotton handkerchief was suspended the captain's new hat.

A small recess above the table contained a couple of wine glasses, one of them minus the shank; also an antique decanter resting upon an old quarto prayer book and guarded by a dangerous looking blunderbuss, which was supported by two brass hooks, from one of which hung a small bag containing the captain's spectacles, rule, pencil and compass. At each side of this recess was a locker, one of them containing a crock of butter and another of effects besides tobacco and soap; the other held a fine Cheshire cheese, a little keg of sprats and other articles too numerous to mention.

An unhappy canary, perched within a rusty cage, formed a pendant from the centre of the skylight, but a much more pleasing picture decorated one of the panels a still life admirably delineating an enormous flitch of bacon which daily grew less.

A small door led into the captain's state-room the ceiling of which was tastefully ornamented by several bunches of dipped candles, while the narrow shelves groaned under the weight of jars of sugar, preserves, bottled porter, spices and the other usual necessaries for a long voyage. I was disturbed in the progress of my portraiture by the mistress who came down to warm a drink at the stove for some of the sick folks. The two women who first became ill were said to show symptoms of bad fever and additional cases of illness were reported by the head committee. The patients begged for an increased allowance of water, which could not be granted as the supply was very scanty, two casks having leaked.

Sunday, 13 June
The reports from the hold became very alarming and the mistress was occupied all day attending the numerous calls upon her. She already regretted having come on the voyage, but her kind heart did not allow her to consult her case. When she appeared upon deck she was beset by a crowd of poor creatures, each having some request to make, often of a most inconsiderate kind and few of which it was in her power to comply with. The day was cold and cheerless and I occupied myself reading in the cabin.

Monday, 14 June
The head committee brought a can of water to show it to the captain; it was quite foul, muddy and bitter from having been in a wine cask. When allowed to settle it became clear, leaving considerable sediment in the bottom of the vessel but it retained its bad taste. The mate endeavoured to improve it by trying the effect of charcoal and of alum but some of the casks were beyond remedy and the contents,

when pumped out, resembles nauseous ditch water. There were now eight cases of serious illness – six of them being fever and two dysentery. The former appeared to be of a peculiar character and very alarming, the latter disease did not seem to be so violent in degree.

Tuesday, 15 June
The reports this morning were very afflicting and I felt much that I was unable to render any assistance to my poor fellow passengers. The captain desired the mistress to give them everything out of his own stores that she considered would be of service to any of them. He felt much alarmed; nor was it to be wondered at that contagious fever – which under the most advantageous circumstances and under the watchful eyes of the most skilful physicians, baffles the highest ability – should terrify one having the charge of so many human beings likely to fall a prey to the unchecked progress of the dreadful disease; for once having shown itself in the unventilated hold of a small brig, containing one hundred and ten living creatures, how could it possibly be stayed without medicines, medical skill or even pure water to slake the patients' burning thirst? The prospect before us was indeed an awful one and there was no hope for us but in the mercy of God.

Wednesday, 16 June
The past night was very rough and I enjoyed little rest. No additional cases of sickness were reported, but there were apparent signs of insubordination amongst the healthy men, who complained of starvation and the want of water to make drinks for their sick wives and children. A deputation came aft to acquaint the captain with their grievances but he ordered them away and would not listen to a word from them. When he went below the ringleader threatened that they would break into the provision store.

The mate did not take any notice of the threat but repeated to me, in their hearing, an anecdote of his own experience, of a captain, showing with what determination he suppressed an outbreak in his vessel. He concluded by alluding to cut-lasses and the firearms in the cabin. And in order to make a deeper impression on their minds he brought up the old blunderbuss from which he fired a shot, the report of which was equal to that of a small cannon. The deputation slunk away muttering complaints.

If they were resolute they might easily have seized upon the provisions. In fact, I was surprised how famished men could so patiently bear with their own and their starved children's sufferings, but the captain would willingly have listened to them if it were in his power to relieve their distress.

Thursday, 17 June
Two new cases of fever were announced and, from the representation of the mate, the poor creatures in the hold were in a shocking state. The men who suffered from dysentery were better; the mistress' prescription – flour porridge with a few drops of laudanum – having given them relief. The requests of the friends of the

fever patients were most preposterous, some asking for beef, others wine. They were all desirous of laudanum being administered to them in order to procure sleep but we were afraid to dispense so dangerous a remedy except with extreme caution. Our progress was almost imperceptible and the captain began to grow very uneasy, there being at the rate of the already miserable allowance of food, but provisions for 50 days. It also now became necessary to reduce the complement of water and to urge the necessity of using sea water in cookery.

Friday, 18 June

The fireplaces were the scenes of endless contentions. The sufferings they endured appeared to embitter the wretched emigrants one against another. Their quarrels were only ended when the fires were extinguished at 7 p.m. at which time they were surrounded by squabbling groups preparing their miserable evening meal. They would not leave until Jack mounted the shrouds of the foremast and precipitated a bucket full of water on each fire – when they snatched up their pots and pans and, half blinded by the steam, descended into the hold with their half-cooked suppers. Although Jack delighted in teasing them, they never complained of his pranks, however annoying.

CHAPTER IV

I saw the seven angels which stood before God; and to them were given seven trumpets . . .
And the seven angels which had the seven trumpets prepared themselves to sound . . .
And the seventh angel sounded
And the sea gave up the dead which were in it; and death and hell delivered up the dead which were in them and they were judged every man
– Revelations

Saturday, 19 June

A shark followed us all the day and the mate said it was a certain forerunner of death. The cabin was like an apothecary's shop and the mistress a perfect slave. I endeavoured to render her every assistance in my power. The mate also was indefatigable in his exertions to alleviate the miserable lot of our helpless human cargo. Not having seen the stowaway on deck for some time, upon inquiring after him, I learned that he was amongst the sick and was very bad but he was kindly attended by the young man from the County Clare who devoted himself to attending the afflicted, some of whom the members of their own families neglected to take care of.

Sunday, 20 June

Having hinted to the captain the propriety of having divine service read upon the Sabbath, he said that it could not be done. Indeed the sailors seldom had a spare moment and as to the mate, I often wondered how he got through so much work. This day, therefore, had no mark to distinguish it from any other. The poor emigrants were in their usual squalid attire, neither did the crew rig themselves out as on former Sundays.

All were dispirited and a cloud of melancholy hung over us. The poor mistress deplored that she could not get an opportunity of reading her Bible. I pitied her from my heart knowing how much she felt the distress that surrounded us and her anxiety to lighten the affliction of the passengers.

Monday, 21 June
I was surprised at the large allowance of food served out to the sailors. They had each 1–2lbs of beef or pork daily, besides coffee and as much biscuit as they pleased, but it being a temperance vessel, they had no grog, in lieu of which they got lime-juice. However, there was a little cask of brandy in a corner of the cabin but the captain was afraid to broach it, knowing the mate's propensity. I noticed the latter often casting a wistful glance at it as he rose from dinner and he did not fail to tell me that it was the best possible preventive against the fever.

Tuesday, 22 June
One of the sailors was unable for duty and the mate feared he had the fever. The reports from the hold were growing even more alarming and some of the patients who were mending, had relapsed. One of the women was every moment expected to breathe her last and her friends – an aunt and cousins were inconsolable about her as they had persuaded her to leave her father and mother and come with them. The mate said that her feet were swollen to double their natural size and covered with black putrid spots. I spent a considerable part of the day watching a shark that followed in our wake with great constancy.

Wednesday, 23 June
At breakfast, I inquired of the mate after the young woman who was so ill yesterday, when he told me that she was dead and when I remarked that I feared her burial could cause great consternation, I learned that the sad ordeal was over, her remains having been consigned to the deep within an hour after she expired. When I went on deck I heard the moans of her poor aunt who continued to gaze upon the ocean as if she could mark the spot where the waters opened for their prey. The majority of the wretched passengers who were not themselves ill were absorbed in grief for their relatives, but some of them, it astonished me to perceive, had no feeling whatever, either for their fellow creatures' woe or in the contemplation of being themselves overtaken by the dreadful disease. There was further addition to the sick list which now amounted to twenty.

Thursday 24 June
Being the festival of St John and a Catholic holiday, some young men and women got up a dance in the evening regardless of the moans and cries of those who

were tortured by the fiery fever. When the mate spoke to them of the impropriety of such conduct, they desisted and retired to the bow where they sat down and spent the remainder of the evening singing. The monotonous howling they kept up was quite in unison with the scene of desolation within and the dreary expanse of ocean without.

Friday 25 June

This morning there was a further accession to the names upon the sick roll. It was awful how suddenly some were stricken. A little child who was playing with its companions, suddenly fell down and for some time was sunk in a death like torpor from which, when she awoke, she commenced to scream violently and writhed in convulsive agony. A poor woman, who was warming a drink at the fire for her husband, also dropped down quite senseless and was borne to her berth. I found it very difficult to acquire precise information respecting the progressive symptoms of the disease, the different parties of whom I inquired disagreeing in some particulars, but I inferred that the first symptom was generally a reeling in the head, followed by swelling pain, as if the head were going to burst. Next came excruciating pains in the bones and then swelling of the limbs commencing with the feet, in some cases ascending the body and again descending before it reached the head, stopping at the throat. The period of each stage varied in different patients, some of whom were covered with yellow, watery pimples and others with red and purple spots that turned into putrid sores.

Saturday, 26 June

Some of those who the other day appeared to bid defiance to the fever, were seized in its relentless grasp and a few who were on the recovery, relapsed. It seemed miraculous to me that such subjects could struggle with so violent a disease without any effective aid.

Sunday, 27 June

The moaning and raving of the patients kept me awake nearly all the night and I could hear the mistress stirring about until a late hour. It made my heart bleed to listen to the cries for 'Water, for God's sake some water'. Oh! it was horrifying, yet strange to say I had no fear of taking the fever, which, perhaps, under the merciful providence of the Almighty was a preventive cause. The mate, who spent much of his time among the patients, described to me some revolting scenes he witnessed in the hold but they were too disgusting to be repeated. He became very much frightened and often looked quite bewildered.

Monday 28 June

The number of patients upon the list now amounted to thirty and the effluvium of the hold was shocking. The passengers suffered much for want of pure water and the mate tried the quality of all the casks. Fortunately he discovered a few which were better and the circumstance was rather cheering.

Tuesday 29 June

The wind kept us to the south but though occasionally becalmed, we were slowly gaining longitude. I could not keep my mind fixed upon a book so I was obliged to give over reading and spent the day watching the rolling of the dolphin, the aerial darts of the flying-fish with the gambols of numbers of porpoises that danced in the waters around the prow. It being the mate's watch, I remained upon deck until midnight, listening to his yarns. Some of them were rather incredible and, upon expressing such to my opinion, he was inclined to take offence. Being the hero of some of his stories himself, I could not doubt the veracity of them, though they were not the least marvellous. Although a well informed and intelligent man, he was very superstitious. But it is not uncommon for sailors to be so.

Wednesday 30 June

Passing the main hatch, I got a glimpse of one of the most awful sights I ever beheld. A poor female patient was lying in one of the upper berths – dying. Her head and face were swollen to almost unnatural size, the latter being hideously deformed. I recollected remarking the clearness of her complexion when I saw her in health, shortly after we sailed. She then was a picture of good humour and contentment, now how sadly altered! Her cheeks retained their ruddy hue but the rest of her distorted countenance was of a leprous whiteness. She had been nearly three weeks ill and suffered exceedingly until the swelling set in, commencing in her feet and creeping up her body to her head. Her afflicted husband stood by her holding a 'blessed candle' in his hand and awaiting the departure of her spirit. Death put a period to her existence shortly after I saw her. And as the sun was setting, the bereaved husband muttered a prayer over her enshrouded corpse which, as he said Amen, was lowered into the ocean.

Thursday 1 July

The wind was still unfavourable but we gained a little by constantly tacking and were approaching the banks of Newfoundland. Some new cases were announced making thirty-seven now lying. A convalescent was assisted on deck and seemed revived by the fresh air. He was a miserable object. His face, being yellow and withered, was rendered ghastly by the black streak that encircled his sunken eyes.

CHAPTER V

Friday 2 July

We were enveloped in a dense fog and had a horn sounding constantly. One of the patients, who was represented to be dying, sent for the mate and, giving him the key of his box in which there was a small sum of money, requested him to take charge of it and, upon his return to Ireland, send it to his (the sick man's) mother. The mate promised to do so but did not consider the poor fellow as bad as he himself feared he was.

Saturday, 3 July

Any idea I ever formed of complete horror was excelled by the stern reality of the frightful picture which the past night presented. The gloom spread around by the impenetrable fog was heightened by the dismal tone of the foghorn, between each sound of which might be heard the cries and ravings of the delirious patients and occasionally the tolling of a bell, warning us of the vicinity of some fishing-boat, numbers of which were scattered over the banks. The mate being unable to make an observation, we were obliged to depend upon his 'dead reckoning'.

Sunday, 4 July

We enjoyed a favourable breeze, and the fog having cleared off at noon, the mate made an observation, by which we were in 45*11' N lat. 51*10' W lon. No new cases of sickness were reported but some of the patients were said to be very bad.

We spoke to a bark and a brig, both homeward bound and differed but little in longitude. There was something exciting in listening to the friendly voice from the deep toned speaking trumpet and in beholding the board marked with the longitude. In a few moments the ensigns were lowered and each pursued its course. The day was exceedingly cold, so much so that the captain supposed that we were in the neighbourhood of icebergs and I hoped to see one of these castellated floating masses, lifting its pinnacles on high and glittering in the rays of the sun.

Monday, 5 July

The morning was foggy and we were near running into a French fishing boat. The captain having given orders for sounding, Jack was sent to find the reel and line, which he brought up from the depths of the lazaretto. This receptacle for all sorts of commodities was situated below the cabin and it afforded me some amusement to see the boy, by the faint light of the lantern, groping among beef casks, pork barrels, paint and tar pots, spars and rusty irons. The sails having been put aback so that the brig stood motionless upon the bosom of the water, the reel was held by a man at the stern and the line being uncoiled was drawn outside the ropes of the rigging, until it reached the bow. The lead was then attached and carried by a seaman to the point of bowsprit, where the sailor sat swinging the weight like a pendulum until, upon the order to heave, he cast it forth upon its mission. Bottom having been found at thirty-four fathoms, the line was placed upon a pulley and drawn up when there was found imbedded in the grease with which the lead was filled, fine white sand, as laid down in the chart. The sails were again set to the breeze and we were once more gliding through the water, the momentary commotion soon settling down into the usual inanity.

Tuesday 6 July

During the past night there was a heavy fall of rain which left the atmosphere clear and cool. Two men (brothers) died of dysentery and I was awakened by the noise made by the mate, who was searching for an old sail to cover the remains with. In about an hour after, they were consigned to the deep, a remaining brother being the solitary mourner. He continued long to gaze upon the ocean, while a tear that dropped from his moistened eye told the grief he did not otherwise express. I learned in the afternoon that he was suffering from the same complaint that carried off his brothers.

Wednesday 7 July

The phosphorescent appearance of the ocean at night was very beautiful. We seemed to be gliding through a sea of liquid fire. We passed a great number of fishing boats, chiefly French, from the isles St Pierre and Miquelon. They were anchored at regular intervals for the purpose of catching cod-fish, which, allured by the vast numbers of worms found upon the bottom, abound upon the banks. The vessels generally are large sloops and have a platform all round with an awning over the deck. When a fish is taken, it is immediately split and cleaned, then it is thrown into the hold and, when the latter is full, the fishermen return home and land their cargo to be dried and saved. Owing to these processes being sometimes too long deferred, the bank fish, though larger, is considered inferior to that taken along the coast of Newfoundland. Great variety of opinion exists respecting the nature and origin of these submarine banks but none of them appears to me so natural as this. The stream which issues from the Gulf of Mexico, commonly called the 'Florida gulf stream', being checked in its progress by the southern coast of Newfoundland, deposits the vast amount of matter held in suspension. This, by accumulation, formed the banks which are still increasing in extent. The temperature of the water upon the banks is higher than that of the Gulf of St Lawrence and of the ocean and its evaporation causes the fog that almost perpetually prevails. The afternoon was clear with a gentle breeze which formed a ripple on the surface of the water and gave a beautiful appearance to the reflection of the declining sun, looking like jets of gas bursting from the deep.

Thursday 8 July

Another of the crew was taken ill, thereby reducing our hands when they were most required. The captain had a great dread of the coast of Newfoundland which, being broken into deep bays divided from each other by rocky capes, is rendered exceedingly perilous, more especially, as the powerful currents set towards this inhospitable shore. We kept a lookout for some vessel coming from the gulf, in order to learn the bearings of land but did not perceive one during the day.

Friday 9 July

A few convalescents appeared upon deck. The appearance of the poor creatures was miserable in the extreme. We now had fifty sick, being nearly one half the whole number of passengers. Some entire families, being prostrated, were dependent on the charity of their neighbours, many of whom were very kind, but others seemed to be possessed of no feeling. Among the former, the head committee was conspicuous. The brother of the two men who died on the sixth instant followed them today. He was seized with dismay from the time of their death, which no doubt hurried on the malady to its fatal termination. The old sails being all used up, his remains were placed in two meal-sacks and a weight being fastened at foot, the body was placed upon one of the hatch battens from which, when raised over the bulwark, it fell into the deep and was no more seen. He left two little orphans, one of whom – a boy, seven years of age – I noticed in the evening wearing his deceased father's coat. Poor little fellow! He seemed quite unconscious of his loss and proud of the accession to his scanty covering. The remainder of the man's clothes were sold by auction by a friend of his who promised to take care of the children. There was great competition and the 'cant', as they called it, occasioned jibing and jesting, which it was painful to listen to surrounded as were the actors (some of whom had just risen from a bed of sickness), by famine, pestilence and death.

CHAPTER VI

The floods are risen. O Lord, the floods have lifted up their voice: the floods lift up their waves. The waves of the sea are mighty and rage horribly: but yet the Lord who dwelleth on high is mightier.
– David

Saturday 10 July
We spoke to a ferry which was conveying cattle from Nova Scotia to Newfoundland and learned from the steersman the bearings of St Paul's Island. We shortly afterwards passed a large fleet coming from the gulf and in the afternoon descried Cape North.

The passengers expressed great delight at seeing land and were under the impression that they were near their destination, little knowing the extent of the gulf they had to pass and the great river to ascend. Early in the evening we saw Isle St Paul and indistinctly the point of Cape Ray, between which and Cape North is the passage into the Gulf of St Lawrence. St Paul's Island lies about ten miles to the north of the latter cape, in latitude 47* 14' North and longitude 60* 11' 17' West. It is a huge rock, dividing at top into three conical peaks. Rising boldly from the sea there is a great depth of water all round it and vessels may pass at either side of it. It has been the site of numerous shipwrecks; many vessels carried out of their reckoning by the currents, having been dashed against it when concealed by fog and instantly shattered to atoms.

Human bones and other memorials of these disasters are strewn around its base. We passed the light of this dangerous island at 10 p.m. entering into the 'Goodly great gulf full of islands, passages and entrances towards what wind so ever you please to bend'.

This gulf was first explored by John Cabot[7] in 1497, who called the coast of Labrador Primarista. The Portuguese afterwards changed the name of that desert region to Terra Coterealis and the gulf they designated as that of the 'Two Brothers' in memory of Gaspar and Michael Cotereal, the first named of whom not having returned from the second expedition he commanded, the latter went in search of him, but neither of them was afterwards heard of. Jaques Cartier,[8] having entered it upon the festival of St Lawrence, gave to the gulf and the river flowing into it the name they still retain.

Sunday, 11 July

We had a fair wind and were going full sail at 7 knots an hour. At noon we passed the Bird Islands which are low ledges of rocks and swarm with gannets, numbers of which were flying about. They were as large as geese and pure white with the exception of the tips of the wings which were jet black. Some of Mother Carey's chickens were following in our wake and it was highly amusing to watch the contentions of the little creatures for bits of fat thrown to them.

We had a distant view of the Magdalen Islands which, although lying nearer to Nova Scotia, are considered as belonging to Canada and form a portion of the circuit within the district of Gaspe, court being held at Amherst harbour annually from 1 to 10 July. The largest of the group are Bryon, Deadman's, Amherst, Entry and Wolf islands which are inhabited by a hardy race of fishermen. The huge walrus may at times be seen upon their shores.

12 July

In the morning we were becalmed, the water being smooth as glass and of a beautifully clear, green hue. A breeze sprung up at 12 o'clock and, the captain having provided himself and me with lines, we spent the afternoon fishing for mackerel, which were so plentiful that I caught seventy in about two hours, when I had to give over, my hands being cut by the line. The captain continued and had a barrel full by evening. They were the finest mackerel I ever saw and we had some at tea which we all enjoyed as a delicious treat after six weeks of salt beef and biscuit diet. Many of the passengers, having noticed our success, followed our example and lines were out from every quarter; all the twine, thread, etc. that could be made out being put into requisition, with padlocks and bolts for weights and wire hooks. Even with such rude gear they caught a great number, but their recreation was suddenly terminated, a young man who was drawing in a fish having dropped upon the deck quite senseless and apparently dead. He was carried below and put into his berth, there to pass through the successive stages of the fever.

Tuesday 13 July

We were again becalmed during the forenoon, but a breeze that soon became a gale arose about 1 p.m. and lasted until evening, being accompanied by thunder and lightning and followed by a heavy shower of rain. The clouds cleared away at sunset when we were within 10 or 12 miles of the eastern point of the island of Anticosti which, when the captain perceived, he gave the order to sheer off on the other tack. This island is particularly dangerous, being surrounded by sunken reefs. It is of considerable extent, being 130 miles in length from east to west and 30 miles across its greatest breadth. Its surface is low and level and covered with a pristine forest, through which prowls the bear undisturbed, except when hunted by Indians who periodically resort hither for that purpose.

The sterility of its soil offering no inducement to the white man, it is uninhabited except by the keepers of the lighthouses to which are attached small establishments for the purpose of affording relief to shipwrecked mariners. The name 'Anticosti' is probably a corruption of Natiscotee, which it is called by the aborigines. Cartier named it L'isle de L' Assumption.

Wednesday, 14 July
We had the bold headlands of Capes Gaspe and Rosier on our left and had entered the majestic river St Lawrence which here, through a mouth 90 miles in width, after a course of upwards of 2,000 miles, disgorges the accumulated waters of the great lakes swollen by the accession of hundreds of tributaries (some of them noble rivers) draining an almost boundless region.

The reports of the suffering in the hold were heartrending. Simon and Jack were both taken ill.

Last night I was suddenly wakened by the captain shouting 'Get up! Get up and come on deck quickly!' Somewhat alarmed I obeyed the summons as speedily as possible and was well recompensed for the start by the magnificence of the glorious scene I beheld. The northern portion of the firmament was vividly illuminated with a clear though subdued light, while across it shot fiery meteors from different directions, now rushing against each other as if engaged in deadly warfare, again gliding about in wanton playfulness.

Disappearing for a while and leaving behind a faintly luminous trail, they would again burst forth upon their stage, lighted up by a sudden flash for the igneous performers. I watched with delight until the lustrous picture was finally enshrouded in darkness when I returned to bed.

There was birth on board this morning and two or three deaths were momentarily expected. The mate's account of the state of the hold was harrowing. It required the greatest coercion to enforce anything like cleanliness or decency and the head committee had no sinecure office. I spent the greater part of the day upon deck, admiring the numberless jets dread of the bottlenose whales that plunged about in the water. The poor mistress was greatly grieved about Jack and Simon and the captain was savage for lack of assistance.

Friday 16 July
We were tacking about all day which, though tedious I enjoyed, as it afforded an opportunity of seeing both shores of the noble river. That to the north is indescribably grand, rugged mountains rising precipitously from out of the water, and indented by sweeping bays, in which are numerous islets. Towards evening we were in view of Seven Islands Bay, lovely though desolate. No human eyes behold

this region of unbroken solitude, save now and then those which can but lightly appreciate its grandeur. I cannot describe the effect produced by the mist that sometimes completely hides the mountains, rolling up their sides and resembling gracefully festooned drapery.

The sailors who could work were greatly harassed by being obliged to tack repeatedly. The mate especially was one moment down in the hold waiting on some dying fellow creature; the next perhaps stretched across a yard, reefing a top-sail. Although lame, he was surprisingly active and used to astonish the emigrants, one of whom said to me 'Och! your honour, isn't Mr Mate a great bit of a man?'

Saturday, 17 July
The morning was fine and shortly after breakfast I was upon deck admiring the beauty of the pine-clad hills upon the southern shore of the river, when the captain came up from the cabin and after looking about gave the word to 'double reef top-sail and make all snug'. Not long after, the sky, which had been quite clear, became black and a violent gale arose, lashing the water into tremendous waves which tossed us mercilessly about, one moment borne up by an angry billow, the next plunging into a deep abyss. The roaring wind was drowned by the tremendous noise of successive peals of thunder, while the forked lightning played about in zigzag lines and the rain descended in torrents.

At 5 p.m. the wind abated and the waves began to subside. About an hour after, the leaden clouds parted and, as if in defiance of the contending elements, the sun set in gorgeous splendour. The poor passengers were greatly terrified by the storm and suffered exceedingly. They were so buffeted about that the sick could not be tended and after calm was restored a woman was found dead in her berth.

CHAPTER VII

So frequent death
Sorrow he more than causes, but confounds
For human sighs, his rival strokes contend
And make distress, distraction.
– Young

Sunday 18 July
I was enchanted with the extraordinary beauty of the scenery I beheld this morning when I came on deck. The early beams of the sun played upon the placid surface of the river, here 40 miles wide, the banks on either hand being moderately elevated and covered with firs. On the north was Cape des Monts, terminating in a low point on which stood a lighthouse and diminutive cottage. On the south Cape Chat rose to a considerable height, the outline of its summit being broken by sudden gaps, giving to it a character that to me was unique.

An unbroken stillness reigned around as if nature were at rest after the storm of the previous day and our brig lay almost motionless upon the water.

I occupied myself again and again noting, so as to impress upon my mind, the peerless beauty I am unable to portray and in reading the Acts of the Apostles. I felt a renewed interest in the account of St Paul's voyages as I could now appreciate by experience the force and accuracy of their description. We made no way and it was with difficulty we retained our position against the current.

Another death and burial. A few who had been ill again appeared on deck, weak and weary. The want of pure water was sensibly felt by the afflicted creatures and we were yet a long way from where the river loses its saltiness. In the morning there came alongside of us a beautiful little schooner, from which we took a pilot on board. When he found that we had emigrants and so much sickness he seemed to be frightened and disappointed as he had avoided a large ship, thinking we had not passengers. However, he could not dare retreat. The first thing he did was to open his huge trunk and take from it a pamphlet which proved to be the quarantine regulations. He handed it to the captain who spent a long time poring over it. When he had read it I got a look at it, one side was printed in French, the other in English. The rules were very stringent and the penalties for their infringement exceedingly severe, the sole control being vested in the head physician, the power given to whom was most arbitrary. We feared that we should undergo a long detention in quarantine and learned that we could hold no communication whatever with the shore until our arrival at Grosse Isle.

The pilot was a heavy, stupid fellow, a Canadian, speaking a horrible patois and broken English. He was accompanied by his nephew and apprentice, Pierre – a fine lad.

The wind favoured us for some hours and towards evening we saw Mount Camille upon the southern bank, rising above the surrounding hills to a height of 2,036 feet.

Tuesday, 20 July
Our course lying more to the southern bank of the river, I could observe minutely the principal objects upon that side. Many charming tributary streams rolled along sweet valleys, enfolded in the swelling hills, whose sides were clothed with verdure. I would fain explore each of these enchanting vales but too soon we passed them and some jutting cape would hide from view the little settlements at each embouchure. The most considerable of these was that upon Point aux Snellez, near the mouth of the river Metis, about 200 miles from Quebec. Here commences the Kempt road which terminates at Cross Point on the river Restigouche, a distance of 98 miles. A new road, connecting this with Grande Nouvelle on the Bay des Chaleur, completes the communication with Halifax.

Wednesday 21 July
A thick fog concealed every object from view, at times so low as only to hide the hulls of vessels by whose rigging we could perceive them tacking like ourselves,

the sky being unclouded. A strong wind blew down the river, which, together with the forcible current kept us back. One of the sick sailors reappeared upon deck but was too weak to resume duty. The other man was still very bad as were also Simon and Jack.

Simon got up from his berth in a delirious fit and ran down to the cabin, where his wild appearance nearly frightened the life out of the mistress. It was with difficulty he was laid hold of and he resisted violently while he was carried back to his hammock in the forecastle where he was strapped down.

Thursday 22 July

Soon after retiring to my berth last night I heard a grating noise accompanied by a tremulous motion of the brig and felt alarmed, fearing that we had grounded upon some bank, but my anxiety was relieved by learning that it was caused by the dropping of the anchor, it being useless to contend against both wind and current, the latter here being strengthened by the vast body of water discharged from the river Saguenay. When I came on deck this morning I found that we were anchored off the village of Trois Pistolles, with Cape L'Original to the east, and Basque Isle on the west. Being the first Canadian village I had seen, I was delighted by the rural aspect of the pretty white cottages with red roofs, scattered over the sloping bank, each surrounded by a small garden. The captain was impatient and though the pilot said it would only tend to harass the sailors, we weighed anchor at noon and, after beating about all the day, again came to, near the same spot as before. A child – one of the orphans – died and was buried in the evening, no friend being by to see the frail body committed to its watery grave. The water could not be used by the wretched emigrants and but half a cask of that provided for the cabin and crew remained. They were therefore obliged to use the saline water of the river.

Friday, 23 July

We remained at anchor all day, a fresh breeze blowing down the river. Some of the recovered patients who were slowly regaining strength had relapsed into the most violent stages and three new cases were announced, showing exceedingly virulent symptoms.

The wind abated at noon and it was quite calm for about an hour. During this period I was up on deck and on looking across the river was greatly astonished at perceiving something resembling an island which I had not before noticed. It was circular and quite black. I spent some time in conjecturing what it could be. The captain could not tell and the pilot was asleep. At length, two vessels sailing down the river, when they came near this object, assumed a similar appearance – from which I immediately inferred that it was a ship at anchor, transformed by mirage.

As the vessels sailed along they underwent extraordinary metamorphoses – sometimes the bow and stern were turned up like those of a Chinese junk. At others the hulls were up in the air and the masts seemingly in the water; the latter being twisted and curved. A cottage upon the north bank stood apparently upon the surface of the river and the lighthouse on Big Island had a duplicate of itself perched upon it, the copy being inverted, lantern down and base up. The illusions occurred only within certain limits which were defined by an appearance distinct from the surrounding atmosphere. The difference being something like that presented by clear water and the empty space within a half filled vial.

CHAPTER VIII

These are miracles, which men
Cag'd in the bounds of Europe's pigmy plan
Can scarcely dream of; which his eye must see
To know how beautiful this world can be.
– Moore

Saturday 24 July

We once more weighed anchor this morning and beat about all the day between Trois Pistoles and the mouth of the river Escamin which discharges itself nearly opposite, upon the north shore. We had a large fleet of ships, barques and brigs in company, two of which were transports with troops. It was a pleasing sight to see: such a number of vessels continually passing each other and each evidently endeavouring to gain upon the rest, every tack.

In the afternoon, a brig hoisted her ensign as a signal of recognition and upon the next tack we passed near enough to speak. When the captain turned out to be a particular friend of our captain and the mistress, they kept up a regular conversation the rest of the day every time we met, which was pretty often, each inquiring of the other: the number of deaths? what sickness? how many days out? from what port? etc. We learned – much to our surprise – that she had a greater number of deaths than we and this news was very consoling to the mistress. Towards evening the wind abated and we were in hope that it was about to change. It died away altogether and the vessels that before shot past one another were now almost motionless and scattered over the surface of the river, which here is 25 miles wide.

At sunset we lay at the north side and could almost reach the trees covering the bank. I have seen many a beautiful sunset but all fade before the exquisite beauty of that which I witnessed this evening. The glorious luminary sunk behind the dark blue hills upon the summits of which seemed to rest the border of heaven's canopy, dyed in crimson sheen, softening down to a light orange tint that imperceptibly blended with the azure sky, which was here and there hid by fleecy vermilion clouds. Cape L'Orignal was clothed in a vesture of purple of every shade from violet to that of the deepest hue, overshadowing the village of Trois Pistolles. There was not a ripple upon the water but gentle undulations heaved its bosom, decked in a tissue of carmine, ultramarine and gold. Such vividness and variety of colours I never before conceived or since experienced. Oh! thought I, why is not Danby[9] here to fix them upon imperishable canvas? As night came on, the pilot grew uneasy, there not being good anchorage at that side. However, a slight breeze from the old quarter wafted us across to the very spot where we before lay and where we again dropped anchor in the midst of our consorts.

Sunday 25 July

We lay at anchor all day, the wind blowing strongly against us. It was exceedingly trying to be detained here within a few miles of the tidal influence, having once gained which, we would be independent of the wind. The poor patients, too, were anxiously looking out for the quarantine station where they hoped to find some alleviation of their sufferings. The mistress and mate were uneasy, as the cabin water was nearly out and they feared to let the captain know of it.

I was obliged to remain below, the effluvia from the hold being quite overpowering. I could hear the tolling of the village church-bell and its sweet tone induced me to go on decks for a few moments where I was charmed with the appearance of the showily dressed Canadians, some standing in groups talking, others seated upon benches while caleshes were momentarily arriving with habitants from distant settlements who, after tying up their horses under a shed close by the presbytery joined the chatting parties until the bell ceased, when all retired within the church.

Monday 26 July

The wind was not so strong and the effluvia not quite so unpleasant. I was therefore not so much confined to the cabin. The captain was desirous of sailing but the pilot would not consent and the latter proved to be right, as two of the vessels weighed anchor in the morning and after beating about for a couple of hours were obliged to come to. A pretty stream- the mingled waters of the Abawisquash and Trois Pistolles rivers flows into the St Lawrence adjacent to the village. Like all the tributaries upon the southern side, it is of inconsiderable length, the hills in which they have their sources lying at no great distance from the bank. But many of those which empty themselves at the north side as the, Manicouagan, Bustard, Belsiamites, Portneuf, etc. are fine rivers rising in the elevated ridge that divides Canada from the Hudson's Bay territory and, in their courses through the untrodden forests, expanding into large lakes.

After dinner, the mistress carried down to the cabin the baby that was born on board. The captain at first was very angry but a smile upon the face of the little innocent softened his heart and he soon caressed it with all the endearments he was in the habit of lavishing upon the canary. When tired of which amusement, he opened the locker and took there from an egg, which he held up to the light and looked through to see if it were good. Not being satisfied on that point he tried another and then another, until he got one to please him. He next got some salt and, opening the infant's little hand, placed it upon the palm and gently closed the tiny fingers upon it. He then performed a similar operation upon the other, enclosing a shilling in lieu of salt. The egg he handed to the mistress to send to the mother and acquaint her that he wished the child to be called 'Ellen', after her.

The mistress, kind to all, was particularly so to the little children about twenty of whom we had aboard. One poor infant whose father and mother (neither of whom was twenty years of age) were both ill and unable to take care of it, she paid a woman for nursing and I could not believe it to be the same child when I saw it clean and comfortably covered with clothes she made for it.

Jack came upon deck. Poor fellow! He was sadly altered. Simon also was reported to be better but unable to leave his hammock. The mate began to complain and the brandy cask (which had been broached) supplied his remedy.

Monday 26 July

The wind veered about 5 o'clock last evening and the vessels one by one sailed away. Our pilot, saying that it would again change in a short time, was not inclined to weigh anchor but the captain insisted upon doing so. At 6 p.m. we were once more in motion and in a few minutes were in full sail going 7 knots an hour. Basque Island was soon left behind and, stemming the dark waters discharged by the Saguenay, as day was fading, we were before Tadoussac, a settlement at the mouth of that grand river.

The Saguenay ranks second amongst the tributaries of the St Lawrence. Indeed, although its course is not so long it is supposed to convey a larger body of water than the Ottawa. At its juncture with the St Lawrence it is about a mile wide but in some parts it expands to three. At a distance of 140 miles it receives the waters of Lake St John which is the reservoir of numerous rivers, some of which are precipitated into it by magnificent rapids and falls. This lake, which is about 100 miles in circumference, is remarkable for its shallowness from which cause the navigation of it is frequently dangerous, as the least wind produces a ground swell and breakers. Its water is said to be tepid and it abounds with a variety of fish, great quantities of which are taken at the mouth of the Ouiatchouan river where there is a station at which they are salted and packed for traffic. The climate is very salubrious and the soil of the great valley that borders the lake is susceptible of the highest culture. A few Indians wander over this fine tract of country which it is the intention of the provincial government to open to French Canadians whose laws acknowledging no right of primogeniture, they have overpopulated many of the old settlements. The Indians call this fine sheet of water 'Piegongamis,' signifying 'the flat lake'. First-class ships can ascend the Saguenay to Chicoutimi, a distance of 68 miles. There is a small settlement here, the communication between which and the lake, being broken by rapids, can only be overcome by experienced voyageurs in canoes. At Ha-Ha Bay, 18 miles below Chicoutimi, there is a pretty large settlement and here the river assumes its grand and romantic feature, passing for the remainder of its course between almost perpendicular cliffs from 1,000 to 1,500 feet in height. Its great depth is another characteristic, bottom not being found near the mouth with a line of 330 fathoms, while the depth of the

St Lawrence at the junction is but 240 feet. However, its great rapidity renders it impossible accurately to learn its soundings.

CHAPTER IX

But soft! the tinges of the west decline
And night falls dewy o'er these banks of pine.
Among the reeds in which our idle host
Is rocked to rest, the wind's complaining note
Dies like a half breath'd whispering of flutes.
Along the waves the gleaming porpoise shoots.
And I can trace him like a wat'r star
Down the steep current, till he fades afar
Amid the foaming breakers' silver light
Where yon rough rapids sparkle through the night
– Moore

Tuesday

Feeling somewhat excited by the sudden acceleration of our progress, I determined to remain on deck until the turn of the tide would compel us to come to an anchor. There was something also most enchanting in being wafted by both wind and tide at the rate of 10 knots an hour, watching the lights upon the different islands and the myriads of bright stars that studded the firmament and were reflected in the darkened surface of the broad river, which upon the north side was overshadowed by the mountainous banks, while the southern shore might be traced by a continuous line of flickering lamps within the cottages upon its border.

We soon left Green Island behind us, then Hare Island and Riviere du Loup, upon which is a large settlement with a population of about 1,500. There are some large sawmills here and a portage leading through Madawaska to the lower provinces. After passing The Pilgrims, a group of rocky islets, I went below and had not long turned in when I heard and felt the dropping of the anchor.

In the morning I found that we lay off Kamouraska which is charmingly situated in a rich district at the base of a chain of hills that rise behind the village and stretch far beyond it. This lovely spot, being one of the healthiest places in Lower Canada, attracts many visitors during the summer season. It is also enriched by the fisheries established upon the numerous islands that lie immediately in front supplying abundance of shad, salmon, herrings, etc. Directly opposite upon the other side of the river is Murray Bay, into which flows the Malbaie River, upon whose banks reside the descendants of Wolfe's highlanders[10] many of whom settled there after the campaign. The bay is environed by an amphitheatre of majestic hills cultivated to the very summits, their sloping sides being dotted over with comfortable abodes.

We weighed anchor at noon and gently glided through a scene of indescribable loveliness. The noble river here unbroken by islands presented a lake-like expanse bounded by the lofty Cap Diable and Goose Cape. Village succeeded village upon the south shore and the gigantic hills upon the north were adorned by sweet alpine cots surrounded by cleared patches of land, embosomed by the dark green pines. The weather was very warm and nature basked in uninterrupted sunshine.

Oh! what a contrast to this magic beauty was presented within our floating pest-house, not that matters were worse than they had been, there was rather an abatement in the violence of the fever and I perceived some faces that I with difficulty recognised, so changed were they since I saw them before their illness. Simon and Jack were both on deck, the former being deprived of memory and partially deranged in his mind. Poor fellow having the previous voyage fallen from the top-sail yard and injured his head, his intellect was thereby impaired and the fever confirmed the insanity which had not left him when I quitted the brig some three weeks after.

Being now in fresh water the passengers were relieved of one calamity and the women who were able were busy washing. Two or three men were also similarly engaged, their wives being unable and we endeavoured to impress upon them the fact that the length of our detention in quarantine would greatly depend on the cleanliness of their persons and of the hold. There were still some very bad cases and the poor head committee was in great trouble about his wife who was dying. The mate still kept up being afraid of going to hospital but it was quite evident that he was very ill indeed.

We passed two steamers that were going down the river to tow up ships. We also had a Scotch brig, the Delta, in company.

At 6 p.m. the tide being on the ebb, we once more anchored opposite to the Isle aux Coudres which lies in front of St Paul's Bay. This beautiful island was so named by Cartier who found upon it a profusion of filberts. A smaller island lies inside of it, whose origin is thus accounted for in a manuscript belonging to the Jesuit college of Quebec which relates the effects of the earthquake felt throughout Canada in 1663:

Near St Paul's Bay (fifty miles below Quebec on the north side) a mountain about a quarter of a league in circumference, situated on the shore of the St Lawrence, was precipitated into the river but, as if it had only made a plunge, it rose from the bottom and became a small island forming with the shore a convenient harbour, well sheltered from all winds.

The same authority says:

Lower down the river towards Point Alouette an entire forest of considerable extent was loosened from the main bank and slid into the river St Lawrence where the trees took fresh root.

The rivers Du Gouffre and Des Marees empty themselves into St Paul's Bay flowing through luxuriant valleys intervening between the detached mountains.

Delightfully located upon an eminence on the south bank stands the village of St Anne at the head of a bay of the same name into which flows the river Ouelle. It is large and has a Catholic college and some handsome churches. The surrounding country is highly cultivated, presenting every feature of softness and beauty that can adorn a landscape.

The evening was a charming one, clear and still. The water smooth as a mirror in which gleamed the reflection of the tin covered roofs and spires that glittered in the rays of the setting sun while occasionally a huge snow-white porpoise rose above the surface, plunging again beneath the water which, closing, formed circles becoming larger and larger until the unwieldy creature again appeared and formed them anew. I remained on deck long after all had retired to rest and watched the grey twilight creeping over day until it was illumined by the pale moon which soon smiled upon one of earth's most beauteous pictures.

I retired to my berth and took a short repose which was broken shortly after midnight by the weighing of the anchor. As I wished not to lose the sight of the least part of the river (which I loved to look upon by night as well as by day) I hurried on deck.

We passed through the Traverse, an intricate channel, marked by floating lights and by the Pillars, a group of dangerous rocks on one of which is a revolving light. At daybreak we were passing Goose Island which at low water is connected with Crane Island on the northern extremity of which is the handsome residence of the seigneur. The southern bank presented the same charming features and in the distance I discerned the chain of hills claimed by the United States as the boundary of the State of Maine. In a short time we arrived before the village of St Thomas picturesquely situated on the banks of Riviere du Sud in which were anchored some vessels which were being freighted with lumber from the several saw-mills. The soil in this neighbourhood is exceedingly productive and is well cultivated – on which account it is called the granary of the lower province. The village is of considerable extent and is composed of white houses clustering around a pretty church. A few miles further sail brought us among a number of beautiful islets, so beautiful that they seemed like a fairy scene. Their verdant turf was almost level with the blue water that wound amongst them, submerging not a few so that the first that grew upon them appeared to rise from the river. A vast fleet of vessels lying at anchor told that we had arrived at Grosse Isle, and after wending our way amongst isles and ships, we dropped anchor in the ground allotted for vessels upon arrival and hoisted our ensign at the peak as a signal for the inspecting physician to board us.

CHAPTER X

And when I looked,
behold, a hand was sent unto me,
and, lo, a roll of a book was therein:

And he spread it before me:
and it was written within and without:
and there was written therein
lamentations and mourning, and woe.
– Ezekiel

Grosse Isle, Tuesday, 28 July

By 6 a.m. we were settled in our new position before the quarantine station. The passengers that were able to be up were all busy clearing and washing, some clearing the hold of filth, others assisting the sailors in swabbing the deck. The mistress herself washed out the cabin last evening and put everything in order.

The captain commenced shaving himself at 7 and completed the operation in about an hour and a half. The mate was unable to do anything but kept repeatedly calling to the mistress for brandy and requested that his illness should be kept from the doctor as he was sure he had not fever. Breakfast was speedily despatched and anxiety was depicted on every countenance. At 9 o'clock a boat was perceived pulling towards us with four oars and a steersman with broad-leafed straw hat and leather coat who, the pilot told us, was the inspecting physician. In a few minutes the boat was alongside and the doctor on deck. He hastily enquired for the captain and before he could be answered was down in the cabin where the mistress was finishing her toilet. Having introduced himself he enquired: if we had sickness aboard? Its nature? How many patients at present? These questions being answered and the replies noted upon his table, he snatched up his hat ran up the ladder along the deck and down into the hold. Arrived there, 'Ha!' said he sagaciously, 'there is fever here.' He stopped beside the first berth in which a patient was lying, felt his pulse, examined his tongue and ran up the ladder again. As he passed by me he handed me some papers to be filled up by the captain and to have ready 'tomorrow or next day'. In an instant he was in his boat from which, while the men were taking up their oars, he shouted out to me that I was not obliged to remain in quarantine and might go up to Quebec when I pleased.

I brought the papers to the captain who remained in the cabin, supposing that the doctor would return thither, in order to give directions for our guidance, and when he learned that that gentleman had gone, he was desperately enraged. The mistress endeavoured to pacify him by suggesting that it was likely he would visit us again in the course of the day or at least that he would send a message to us. When I acquainted the mistress that I was at liberty to leave the brig she looked at me most pitifully as if she would say, 'are you too going to desert us?' But I had no such intention and was determined to remain with them at all events until they reached Quebec.

The poor passengers, expecting that they would be all reviewed, were dressed in their best clothes and were clean, though haggard and weak. They were greatly disappointed in their expectations as they were under the impression that the sick would be immediately admitted to the hospital and the healthy landed upon the island, there to remain until taken to Quebec by a steamer. Indeed, such was the procedure to be inferred from the book of directions given to the captain by the pilot when he came aboard.

When the mistress appeared on deck I scarcely knew her. She usually wore a black stuff gown, a red worsted 'bosom friend', which she told me (at least once a day) was knit for her by her niece, with a cap, having three full borders which projected beyond the leaf of the little straw bonnet, covered with the accumulated stains and smoke of many a voyage. Now she had on a new fancy striped calico dress as showy as deep reds, yellows, blues and greens could make it; a black satin bonnet with no lack of red ribands and a little conservatory of artificials around her good natured face, not forgetting her silver spectacles. All day long we kept looking out for a message from shore and in watching the doctor's boat going from vessel to vessel. His visit to each occupying about the same as to us – which was exactly five minutes. We sometimes fancied that he was making for us but the boat the next moment would be concealed by some large ship. Then we were sure we would be the next but no, the rowers poled for shore. The day wore away before we gave up hope.

I could not believe it possible that here, within reach of help, we should be left as neglected as when upon the ocean. That after a voyage of two months' duration we were to be left still enveloped by reeking pestilence, the sick without medicine, medical skill, nourishment or so much as a drop of pure water – for the river, although not saline here, was polluted by the most disgusting objects thrown overboard from the several vessels. In short, it was a floating mass of filthy straw, the refuse of foul beds, barrels containing the vilest matter, old rags and tattered clothes, etc.

The head committee was greatly grieved for his wife whose death he momentarily expected. He had looked anxiously forward to the time when we should arrive here, hoping that at least the doctor would see her, but his hopes – as well as those of others – were suddenly blasted. The brig that arrived with us sailed for Quebec immediately after the doctor's visit, possibly not having had any sickness. Five other vessels also were discharged. How long they were detained we could not tell but the captain was so provoked that he vowed he would sail without permission. The pilot, who did not well understand his hasty disposition, ventured to remonstrate with him and fell in for a hurricane of curses and abuse to which, though ignorant of many of the expressions, he replied in French, not finding himself sufficiently eloquent in the English tongue.

Four vessels arrived with the evening tide and hoisted their signals but were not visited. Several sailed by us without stopping, not having passengers, and a vast number went down the river during the day.

Two huge steamers also arrived and in the afternoon brought off hundreds of human beings from the island.

Thursday, 29 July
This morning, a boat was perceived making towards us which at first was thought to be the doctor's but when it approached nearer there appeared but two persons in it, both of whom were rowing. In a few minutes more the boat was alongside and from the cassocks and bands of the two gentlemen we learned that they were Canadian priests. They came on deck, each carrying a large black bag. They

inquired for the captain who received them courteously and introduced them to the mistress and to me, after which they conversed a while in French with the pilot whom they knew. When having put on their vestments, they descended into the hold. They there spent a few minutes with each of the sick and administered the last rites to the dying woman and an old man, terminating their duties by baptising the infant. They remained in the hold for about an hour and, when they returned, complimented the captain on the cleanliness of the vessel.

They stayed a short time talking to us upon deck and the account they gave of the horrid condition of many of the ships in quarantine was frightful. In the holds of some of them they said that they were up to their ankles in filth. The wretched emigrants crowded together like cattle and corpses remaining long unburied – the sailors being ill and the passengers unwilling to touch them. They also told us of the vast numbers of sick in the hospitals and in tents upon the island and that many nuns, clergymen and doctors were lying in typhus fever, taken from the patients.

They were exceedingly intelligent and gentlemanly men and, telling us that we had great case of thankfulness in having escaped much better than so many others, they politely bowed and got into their little boat, amid the blessings of the passengers who watched them until they arrived beside a distant ship.

The head committee expressed himself satisfied that his wife saw a priest before her death which occurred about an hour after, and as the pilot said that the remains should not be thrown into the river – there being a burial ground upon the island – the corpse lay in the hold until the next day.

The mate continued to grow worse and the mistress was unceasing in her attention to him. The day was exceedingly hot and sultry and I could not have remained on deck but the captain spread an awning over it which kept the cabin cool. We lay at some distance from the island, the distant view of which was exceedingly beautiful. At the far end were rows of white tents and marquees, resembling the encampment of an army. Somewhat nearer was the little fort and residence of the superintendent physician and nearer still the chapel, seaman's hospital and little village with its wharf and a few sail boats, the most adjacent extremity being rugged rocks, among which grew beautiful fir trees. At high water this portion was detached from the main island and formed a most picturesque islet.

However, this scene of natural beauty was sadly deformed by the dismal display of human suffering that it presented – helpless creatures being carried by sailors over the rocks on their way to the hospital, boats arriving with patients some of whom died in their transmission from their ships. Another, and still more awful sight, was a continuous line of boats, each carrying its freight of dead to the burial ground and forming an endless funeral procession. Some had several corpses so tied up in canvas that the stiff, sharp outline of death was easily traceable. Others had rude coffins constructed by the sailors from the boards of their berths, or I should rather say, cribs. In a few, a solitary mourner attended the remains but the majority contained no living beings save the rowers. I would not remove my eyes until boat after boat was hid by the projecting point of the island, round which they steered their gloomy way. From one ship a boat proceeded four times during the day, each time laden with a cargo of dead. I ventured to count the number of boats that passed but had to give up the sickening task.

The inspecting doctor went about from vessel to vessel, six of which came in each tide and as many sailed. We expected him to visit us every moment but he did not come near us.

In the afternoon a boat made for our brig and the mistress, who was on deck, was greatly delighted to find that it contained two 'Captains', one of whom was her nephew. One arrived the day before we came, the other a day previous. They were as ignorant of the course of proceeding as we and before they went away it was agreed on that they, our captain and I should wait on the superintendent physician the next day.

CHAPTER XI

As from the wing no scar the sky retains,
The parted wave no farrow from the keel,
So dies in human hearts the thought of death.
E'en with the tears which nature shed
O'er those we love, we drop it in their graves.
– Young

Friday 30 July

This morning when I came on deck, a sailor was busily employed constructing a coffin for the remains of the head committee's wife and it was afflicting to hear the husband's groans and sobs accompanying each sound of the saw and hammer, while, with his motherless infant in his arms, he looked on. About an hour after, the boat was lowered and the bereaved husband, with four rowers, proceeded to the burial ground to inter the corpse, and they were followed by many a tearful eye until the boat disappeared behind the rocky point.

At 10 a.m. we descried the doctor making for us, his boatmen pulling lustily through the heavy sea. A few minutes brought him alongside and on board, when he ran down to the cabin and demanded: if the papers were filled up with a return of the number of deaths at sea? How many cases of sickness? etc. He was handed them by the captain, when he enquired how many patients we then had. He was told there were twelve, when he wrote an order to admit six to hospital, saying that the rest should be admitted when there was room – there being 2,500 at that time upon the island and hundreds lying in the various vessels before it. The order written, he returned to his boat and then boarded a ship lying close to us, which lowered her signal when he approached. Several other vessels that arrived in the morning had their ensigns flying at the peak until each was visited in turn.

Immediately after the doctor left us, the captain gave orders to have the patients in readiness. Shortly after, our second boat was launched and four of the passengers volunteered to row – the sailors that were able to work, being with the other. O God! May I never again witness such a scene as that which followed: the husband, the only support of an emaciated wife and helpless family, torn away forcibly from them in a strange land; the mother dragged from her orphan children that clung to her until she was lifted over the bulwarks, rending the air with their shrieks; children snatched from their bereaved parents who were perhaps ever to remain ignorant of their recovery, or death. The screams pierced my brain and the excessive agony so rent my heart that I was obliged to retire to the cabin where the mistress sat weeping bitterly.

The captain went in the boat and returned in about an hour, giving us a frightful account of what he witnessed upon the island.

The steamers returned and all the afternoon were engaged taking the healthy passengers out of some of the vessels. They went alongside several until their cargo was complete when they sailed for Montreal, their decks thickly crowded with human beings and – most extraordinary to relate – each of them had a fiddler and a dancing party in the prow.

Early in the evening the captain's nephew came to take us in his boat, on shore. After a long pull through a heavy swell, we landed upon the Isle of Pestilence and, climbing over the rocks, passed through the little town and by the hospitals, behind which were piles upon piles of unsightly coffins. A little further on, at the edge of a beautiful sandy beach, were several tents, into one of which I looked but had no desire to see the interior of any others. We pursued our way by a road cut through a romantic grove of firs, birch, beech and ash, beneath the shade of which grew and blossomed charming wild flowers, while the most curious fungi vegetated upon odd, decayed stumps. The path led us into a cleared lawn, passing through which we arrived in front of the superintendent physician's cottage, placed upon a sloping bank at the river's side, on which were mounted two pieces of ordnance guarded by a sentinel. The view from this spot was exquisitely beautiful; upon the distant bank of the broad river were the smiling, happy-looking Canadian villages backed by deep blue hills, while the agitated water in front tossed the noble vessels that lay at anchor and which were being swung round by the turning tide.

The doctor not being within, we walked about until his return when he invited us into his cottage and heard what the captains had to say, after which he promised to discharge our friend the next day and that he would send a steamer to take our passengers. He also gave the captain an order for the admission of the mate to the seaman's hospital. Our mission having been so successful, we thanked the doctor and departed. Upon our return we called at the store licensed to sell provisions upon the island. It was well stocked with various commodities among which were carrion beef and cattish mutton, bread, flour, cheese, etc. Although the captain wished to treat the mistress to fresh meat, he declined purchasing what we saw and merely bought some flour. The storekeeper did not lack better customers, however, for there was a vast concourse of mates, stewards, seamen and boys buying his different articles and stowing them away in their boats. The demand for bread was very great and several batches were yielded from a large oven while we remained.

Hearing the music of a fiddle accompanied by the stamping of feet in time with the tune, I walked up to the shed from which it issued. There were two men dancing a jig, one of them a Canadian, the other a sailor – both fine fellows who were evidently pitted against each other in a trial of skill. The former wore huge boots coming above the knees and, drawn over his grey trousers composed of 'Etoile du pays', a light blue flannel shirt confined at the waist by a scarlet scarf whose parti coloured ends hung at one side. On his head was a woollen bonnet rouge whose tassel jumped about with the wearer's movements. His brilliant black eyes lighted up his swallow visage and his arms were as busily engaged as his legs. The sailor was rigged out in pumps, white trousers, blue jacket and straw hat with streaming black ribands, his ruddy face glowing with the exercise. The fiddler's costume was similar to that of his brother Canadian except that his bonnet was blue. He stood upon a barrel and around the dancers was a circle of habitants and sailors who encouraged them by repeated 'bravo's'. I did not remain long nor could I enjoy the amusement in such a place and therefore joined my companions in the boat where we were detained a few moments while one of the men returned for lime which the captain had forgotten to procure. He soon returned and, again ploughing through the waves, we shortly arrived beneath the 'Leander', after examining which noble ship, the captain and I returned to the brig and acquainted the mistress with the issue of our adventure.

Our boat returned just at the same time, the men having been away all the day. It appeared that they could not find the burial ground and consequently dug a grave upon an island when as they were depositing the remains they were discovered and obliged to decamp. They were returning to the brig when they perceived several boats proceeding in another direction and, having joined them, were conducted to the right place. The wretched husband was a very picture of desperation and misery that increased the ugliness of his countenance, for he was sadly disfigured by the marks of small pox and was blind of an eye. He walked moodily along the deck, snatched his child from a woman's arms and went down into the hold without speaking a word. Shortly after, one of the sailors who was with the boat told me that after the grave was filled up he took the shovels and placing them cross-wise upon it, calling heaven to witness said, 'By that cross, Mary, I swear to revenge your death – as soon as I earn the price of my passage home, I'll go back and shoot the man that murdered you and that's the landlord.'

Saturday, 31 July
It was with great reluctance that the mate consented to go to hospital, and as he went into the boat he charged the captain, the mistress and me with cruelty. The captain went with him and gave him in charge of a doctor.

In consequence of the superintendent's promise to send a steamer to take our passengers and give us clean bills if the vessel were well whitewashed between decks, the passengers' berths were all knocked away and the filthy boards thrown into the river, after which four men worked away cleaning and whitening all the day - but no steamer arrived that day. One which lay overnight took 250 passengers from the captain's nephew who sailed not long after.

Vessels were arriving with every tide; two ships from Bremen came in the morning and were discharged at once, having no sickness. Some others sailed up with the evening tide, after which there were more than 30 in quarantine. Boats were plying all day long between the several vessels and the island and, the sea being high, the miserable patients were drenched by the spray, after which they had to clamber over the slimy rocks or were carried by sailors. There was also an almost unbroken line of boats carrying the dead for interment. Then there was the doctor's boat, unceasingly shooting about, besides several others containing captains of ships, many of whom had handsome gigs with six oars and uniformly dressed rowers. It was indeed a busy scene of life and death. To complete the picture, the rigging of the vessels was covered over with the passengers' linen hanging out to dry - by the character of which as they fluttered in the breeze, I could tell with accuracy from what country they came; alas! the wretched rags of the majority told but too plainly that they were Irish.

CHAPTER XII

O the tender ties
Close twisted with the fibres of the heart
Which broken break them, and drain off the soul
Of human joy; and make it pain to live.
– Young

Sunday 1 August

The passengers passed a miserable night, huddled up as they were without room to stretch their weary limbs. I pitied them from my soul and it was sickening to see them drink the filthy water. I could not refuse to give one or two of them a mouthful from the cask upon the quarter deck which fortunately was filled lower down the river. They asked for it so pitifully and were so thankful – but I could not satisfy all and regretted the disappointment of many.

They had on their best clothes and were all clean, with the exception of one incorrigible family. The doctor came on board in the forenoon to inspect the passengers, who were all called on deck but those who were unable. Placing himself at a barrier, he allowed each to pass, one by one, making those he suspected of being feverish show their tongues. This proceeding lasted about a quarter of an hour when the doctor went into the hold to examine those below and to see if it were clean. He then wrote out the order to admit the six patients to hospital and promised to send the steamer to take the remainder, after which we should have clean bills. When he had gone, the patients were lowered into the boat amid a renewal of the indescribable woe that followed the previous separations. Two of them were orphan sisters who were sent for by a brother in Upper Canada. Another was a mother who had tended all her family through illness, now care-worn and heart-broken, she became herself a prey.

In the early part of the voyage I observed the un-filial conduct of a boy who frequently abused and even cursed his mother, following the example set by his wretched father. On one occasion his hand was raised to strike her when his arm was arrested by a bystander, but the poor woman begged of the man not to punish him and wept for the depravity of her son. It was she who was now being carried to the boat while the boy who cursed and would have stricken her, clung to her, crying and imploring her blessing and forgiveness but she was unable to utter a word and, by an effort, raised her arm feebly and looked sadly upon the afflicted boy who seized her hand and bathed it with his tears until he was torn away and she dropped into the boat which, a moment after, rowed off. I felt much for the poor fellow who was conscious that he should never again see his mother for there was no hope of her recovery and I little thought that any one could be so heartless as to aggravate his sufferings as did two or three women who surrounded him, one of them saying, 'Ha! You villain there's the mother you abused and cursed, you rascal! You may now take your last look at her.' He followed the boat with his eyes until it reached the shore when he beheld the inanimate figure borne to the hospital. It was evident from the poignancy of his sorrow that his heart was not depraved but that his conduct arose from education.

The morning was fine, clear and warm and many of the vessels were decorated with their flags giving a cheerful aspect to the scene which, alas, was marred by the ensigns of two ships (one on either side of us) which were hoisted halfmast high, the captain of one and the chief mate of the other, being dead. While the captain was away with the boat, the steamer came alongside of us to take our passengers. It did not take very long to tranship them as few of them had any luggage. Many of them were sadly disappointed when they learned that they were to be carried on to Montreal, as those who had left their relatives upon Grosse Isle hoped, that as Quebec was not far distant, they would be enabled by some means to hear of them, by staying there. Each of them shook hands with the mistress, and all heaped blessings upon her head; and as to the captain, one of them remarked that 'though he was a divil, he was a gintleman.'

The steamer pushed off, amid the cheers of her motley freight, and was soon out of sight. The mistress was quite overcome by the expressions of the poor creatures' gratitude for her unceasing, and otherwise unrequited attention, and benevolence. The captain returned, and after dinner he and I went ashore for our clean bills of health. We saw Dr. Douglass,[11] who informed us that the inspecting physician, Dr. Jaques, had them, and that he was going his rounds among the vessels; with the intention of calling at the brig. But as we considered that it would probably be late before he would reach her, we pulled for a barque, beside which we descried the well known boat. Before we were half way, it was gone and making for a ship some distance off; however, we still followed, and again were disappointed. We determined not to give up the chase, and at length caught the doctor on board a German emigrant vessel. He was inspecting the passengers, of whom there were 500,—all of them (without a single exception,) comfortably and neatly clad, clean, and happy. There was no sickness amongst them, and each comely fair haired girl laughed as she passed the doctor, to join the group of robust young men who had undergone the ordeal.

Although it was pleasing to see so many joyous beings, it made me sad when I thought of the very, very different state of my unfortunate compatriots; and I had become so habituated to misery, disease, and death, that the happiness that now surrounded me was quite discordant with my feelings. The doctor having completed his task, countersigned our clean bills, and handed them to the captain; we therefore thanked him and took our leave. Before returning to the brig, we called to see the mate, who was lying with his clothes on, upon a bed; the next one to which contained a figure writhing in torture, and, as the face was turned towards me, I recognized to my great surprise and dismay, the sailor, who, but the evening but one before, was dancing with the Canadian. When the mate perceived us, he rose from the bed, and taking the captain by one arm, and me by the other, walked us both out of the hospital, to the porch; saying that we had no business there, as there was fever upon all sides of us. The hospital was a large chapel, transformed to its present use, and was exceedingly clean and well ventilated, the large windows were all open, causing a draught of air that was agreeable; the evening being very sultry.

We did not remain long with the mate, who raved considerably in his conversation, though he said he was quite well; so, the captain giving him in charge of the attendant, with pressing injunctions to have every attention paid to him, and saying that he hoped he would be able to join the brig upon his return, we departed. As we got into the boat, we made a signal to the pilot (who was desired to be on the lookout,) to weigh anchor, so as not to lose the tide by any unnecessary delay. As we repassed the German ship, the deck was covered with emigrants, who were singing a charming hymn, in whose beautiful harmony all took part; spreading the music of their five hundred voices upon the calm, still air, that wafted it round. The vessel being discharged, began to move almost imperceptibly, so that we quickly passed her; but she gradually gained speed, and was ahead of us by the time we reached the brig, and as the distance between us increased, the anthem died away, until it became inaudible. It was the finest chorus I ever heard,—performed in a theatre of unrivalled magnificence.

The mistress was delighted when she learned that we were free, and all were glad to leave behind the Isle of Death, though we regretted leaving the mate there. The sailors that had been ill, still continuing very weak, the captain induced two

ROBERT WHYTE, *THE OCEAN PLAGUE*

young men to remain, in order to assist in working the vessel. At 7 p.m. the anchor was weighed, the sails unreefed and we glided slowly along.

CHAPTER XIII

Sail on, sail on, thou fearless bark,
Wherever blows the welcome wind;
It cannot lead to scenes more dark
More sad than those we leave behind.
– Moore

Monday, 2 August

It was indeed with gratefulness to the Almighty for having preserved me scatheless in the midst of the dread pestilence that I left Grosse Isle, and a more beautiful panorama I never beheld than the country through which we passed – the churches of St Thomas and St Pierre's, surrounded by handsome cottages and beautiful fields. On our right, Isle Madame, the largest of the numerous islands that clustered in the centre of the river, embosomed in the mighty stream beyond which rose Cap Tourment with the village of St Joachim at its base. And Mount St Anne, sheltering its village also – both of these lofty hills being of a deep purple hue. At sunset, we had reached the eastern extremity of the Isle of Orleans and an hour after, dropped anchor before St Francois, a sweet village composed of quaint looking cottages whose walls were as white as snow with red roofs, bright yellow doors and green Venetian window blinds. Such was the universal style, all of them appearing as if they had been newly painted.

We again set sail soon after daybreak this morning with a breeze against us which compelled us to tack about. I did not regret this as I had many near views of the southern bank of the river and of the beautiful shore of Orleans Island with its luxuriant orchards and well cultivated farms flopping down to the water's edge, and dark forest upon the crest of its elevated interior. This fine island, which is 20 miles in length and 5 in width, is divided into five parishes and has a population of 5,000 Canadians. While it is an object of the greatest beauty, it is at the same time of great usefulness – affording shelter to the harbour of Quebec on the east side and producing large supplies of fruits and vegetables of the finest description. The northern shore consists of low and marshy beaches that abound with game. It is surprising that there is no regular communication between the island and the city during the summer season, but in winter it is easy of access over the frozen river when the inhabitants convey their produce to market. When Cartier visited it in the year 1535, the island was covered with vines, on which account he called it the Isle of Bacchus. It was on it also that Wolfe took up his quarters previous to the attack upon Quebec. At 8 a.m. we passed St Vallier and St John's; the latter upon the island consisting of entirely white cottages which are chiefly inhabited by the branch pilots upwards of 250 of whom find lucrative employment in the river navigation during the season, enabling them and their families to live comfortably through the long winter in which they are unemployed.

At noon, we dropped anchor again before St Michel's, where we lay until 6 p.m. when we once more renewed our tacks, passing the sheltered cove called Patrick's hole, in which a fine ship rode previous to leaving port for sea.

This little natural harbour is very valuable as it securely shelters vessels that arrive before the winter's ice is sufficiently broken up to allow them to gain the city.

At Anseau Maraud which is adjacent, there were launched, in the year 1824, two enormous ships- the *Columbus* and the *Baron* of Renfrew – which were built with the intention of being broken up in England, the projectors thinking thereby to save the duty on the timber of which they were constructed. But their object was frustrated by the decision that a voyage should previously be made out of an English port. The *Columbus* traversed the Atlantic and returned in safety but was wrecked upon her second voyage. The *Baron*, in whose construction 6,000 tons of timber were consumed, was 309 feet long and of proportionate breadth. She sailed for London on 25 August 1825 with a cargo (it is said of 10,000 tons) of lumber, her four masts crowded with sails, and followed down the river by a fleet of steamers and pleasure yachts. After a voyage of 50 days she arrived at Dover where she took on board both deal and river pilots but, her draft of water being 30 feet, she could not be taken through the queen's channel which is safe for ships of war. She was therefore obliged to remain outside of the Goodwin sands, near the entrance of the king's channel. Having encountered a violent gale, she grounded upon the Long sands but was got off on the following day. She safely rode out a second gale upon 19 October but successive storms and strong northerly winds eventually drove her upon the Flemish banks and, after being buffeted for several weeks by the waves, she was shattered to atoms; the fragments of the wreck and her cargo being wafted along the coast from Calais to Ostend.

Such was the history of these monster ships whose ill fortune deterred Canadian builders from again constructing such unwieldy vessels.

We next passed Beaumont where the south bank becomes elevated, increasing in height to Point Levi, the tin spire of whose church was visible, and on Orleans Island, St Famille.

The magnificent fall of Montmorenci then was revealed to view, in a sheet of tumbling snow-white foam, set between the dark green banks covered with fir and other trees. As we approached nearer, the low thundering sound of the 'many waters' broke on the ear, which died away as we sailed upon the other tack, and night spread its curtain over the splendid picture when we reached the mouth of the St Charles River where we dropped anchor.

Tuesday 3 August

I was charmed with the splendid prospect I enjoyed this morning when I came on deck.

The harbour was thickly covered with vessels, many of them noble ships of the largest class.

The city upon the side of Cape Diamond, with its tin covered dome and spires sparkling in the morning sun and surrounded by its walls and batteries bristling with cannon, was crowned by the impregnable citadel, while a line of villages spread along the northern shore reaching to Beauport and Montmorenci. The lofty Mount St Anne bounding the view upon the east. Opposite the city lay Point Levi with the village of D'Aubigne. Crossing the river were steam ferryboats, horse-boats and canoes and up the stream, far as the eye could reach, the banks were lined by wharves and timber ponds while the breeze wafted along a fleet of bateaux with great white sails, and numberless pilot boats were in constant motion.

We could not go ashore, neither dare any one come on board until we were discharged from quarantine by the harbour master and medical inspector. These functionaries approached us in a long six-oared boat with the Union Jack flying in her stern. When they came on board they demanded the ship's papers and clean bills of health which the captain gave them, in return for which he received a release from quarantine. Soon after they left us, a butcher brought us fresh meat, milk, eggs and vegetables to which we did ample justice at breakfast, when I went with the captain on shore. I remained with the brig during her stay in Quebec harbour and sailed in her for Montreal on the evening of Thursday, 5 August. We were towed up the river by a steamboat and by daylight the following morning were passing the mouth of the river Batiscan.

The sail during the day was extremely pleasing; true the St Lawrence did not present the same grand features as below Quebec but there was something of exceeding interest or beauty to be seen every moment. The banks varied in height but did not gain any great elevation and were lined by an almost unbroken chain of settlements, with villages upon either side at intervals of about 10 miles. At noon we sailed by Trois Rivieres upon the River St Maurice which divides into three branches before it empties itself into the St Lawrence, forming two pretty islands connected with each other and the mainland by three handsome bridges. A couple of hours brought us into Lake St Peter which is an extension of the river and of intricate navigation, affording but a narrow channel which is marked out by buoys and beacons. Towards its western extremity it is full of low, marshy islands surrounded by rushes, between which lies the winding passage. At sunset we had a charming view of Sorel upon the eastern bank of the Richelieu which discharges the waters of lakes George and Champlain.

The river again narrowed and presented similar features as below the expansion. We anchored for the night and early next morning were forcing our way through the rapids called current St Mary, passing the village of Longueil and the charming isle St Helens. Montreal then opened to our view, and by 8 a.m. we were moored to its fine quay.

The brig, having completed her cargo, sailed for London on 19 August when I bade the captain and the mistress adieu and followed them some distance down the river until the favourable breeze that filled her sails wafted the brig out of sight.

I have represented these worthy people just as they appeared to me, and if I have spoken too plainly, I would crave their pardon should they ever recognise their lineaments in these sheets (which I do not think probable). Indeed, I should much regret causing their displeasure, having received from them every attention, their conduct towards me extending even to unwonted kindness and for which I shall never cease to feel grateful.

I was anxious to learn if the mate recovered and, in compliance with my desire, the captain wrote to me from Quebec and also from Green Island. The first of these letters was dated 23 August, and the following is an extract from it:

'I got doun hear on satterday and saled all the way down which was a great saving to me it was bubful sale we Ankered all night and saled in the day which gave hus opertunety of seeinz every Curisitv we went on Shore and got Eags and milk and sead a little of the Contry this Mornning I am gowing on Shore if there be any Letters for you I will forward them to you I have not heard of my Mate Ariving hear yet which Disapoints me Greatly I wish you had bean with hus Yeasterday we had a Drive in the Countrey 9 Miles which was a plesent drive and toke tea in the Countrey a long with Cpt –. I will sale on Tuesday Morning My Wlfe Joyns me in Cinde Regards to you.'

In justice I must also quote the postscript: 'You must Excuse this as I am in a hury'. The second letter was written on 27 August. In it the captain says:

'I am sorey to inform you of my Mate being so hill I coled at Gruss Ile for him and went on shore and it would have hurt you much to have sean him he was mostly but a Skellitan but though as hill as he was, I should have brought him on Boord if the Docter would Aload me, I have not any hopes of him, he got nerely well, and mite have come up to the ship but as I told you made two frea with is self putting Bottel to is head Docter to my Wife and we are all well at present which I hope you cape you Helth, my Wife Joyns me in Cind regards to you.'

I learned with satisfaction that the brig arrived at her destination in safety, but of the mate's fate I still remain ignorant. Of the passengers I never afterwards saw but two, both of them young men who got employment upon the Lachine Canal. The rest wandered over the country, carrying nothing with them but disease, and that but few of them survived the severity of the succeeding winter (ruined as their constitutions were) I am quite confident.

CHAPTER XIV

Of comfort not man seek.
Let's talk of graves, orworms and epitaphs
Make dust our paper, and with rainy eyes
Write sorrow on the bosom of the earth.

Let's choose executors and talk of walls
And yet not so - for what can we bequeath
Save our deposed bodies to the ground.
– Shakespeare

That the system of quarantine pursued at Grosse Isle afforded but a very slight protection to the people of Canada is too evident from the awful amount of sickness and the vast number of deaths that occurred amongst them during the navigable season of 1847. From the plan that was adopted of sending the majority of the emigrants from the island directly up to Montreal, Quebec did not suffer so much as that city. However, during the three days I was there in the month of August too many signs of death were visible and upon a second and more prolonged visit, later in the season, it presented an aspect of universal gloom – the churches being hung in mourning, the citizens clothed in weeds and the newspapers recording daily deaths by fever contracted from the emigrants. To their honour and praise be it spoken, these alarming consequences did not deter either clergymen or physicians from the most unremitting zeal in performing their duty, and it is to be lamented that so many valuable lives were sacrificed. A paper of the month of September contained the following paragraph:

'QUARANTINE STATION, GROSSE ISLE. The Rev. J. Butler, missionary at Kingsey, went down on Tuesday morning to make his turn in attendance upon the sick at the quarantine station.

The Rev. Richard Anderson and Rev. N. Gueront came up on the evening of the same day. The former felt indisposed and thought it prudent to remain in town for the benefit of medical advice. If he should have an attack of fever the precaution thus 85 early taken will, it is hoped, prevent its proving severe. We regret to say that the Rev. C.J. Morris recently returned from the station, is now seriously ill with Typhus Fever.'

The death of the last gentleman is recorded as follows:

'Died this morning at the private hospital at Beauport of typhus fever, the Rev. Charles J. Morris A.M. missionary of the Church of England, at Portneuf in this district. Mr Morris contracted the disease which has thus proved fatal to him, in his ministrations to the sick at Grosse Isle. The funeral will take place in the Cathedral church, tomorrow afternoon, at 3 o'clock.'

The Rev. Mr Anderson also died within a few days of the same period, and that the mortality continued to a late part of the season appears by the following from the Boston Journal of 1 December:

'We learn from Quebec that Drs Painchaud and Jackson and seven or eight nuns of the Hotel Dieu were sick with the ship fever. One of the Quebec physicians says that mortality among the physicians during the past season has been greater than it was during the Cholera.' On Sunday, 10 October, I had the pleasure of listening to a discourse delivered in St Patrick's chapel by Rev. Mr McMahon before he commenced which he read a list of the names of several persons (emigrants) who were separated from their families and who took this method of endeavouring to find them out. The Rev. gentleman also acknowledged having received several sums of money remitted from parties in Ireland to friends in Canada, amongst which he said were some without signatures, and one of these was directed 'to my Aunt Biddy', upon which his Reverence remarked that people should be more particular where money was concerned.

Although (as I have already stated) the great body of emigrants were sent out to Montreal by steamers, all of them could not be so transferred and many were detained in Quebec where the Marine and Emigrant Hospital contained during the season several hundreds – the number that remained upon 2 October being 113, of whom 93 were admitted during the week previous, and in which time there were discharged 132 and 46 died.

One of the first objects that appeared to my view upon my arrival in Montreal was the Emigrant Hospital upon Point St Charles, a low tract of ground cut off from the city by the Lachine Canal and on which the Indians were in the habit of encamping every summer before it was turned to its present purpose. On the day I arrived, 7 August, it contained 907 patients, 16 having died during the last 21 hours. An official return of burials in the city was furnished up to the same day, by which it appeared that during the previous nine weeks the number was 1,730, of which 924 were residents and 806 were emigrants. Exclusive of these, there died in the sheds 1,519 emigrants making a total of 3,240 - being 2,752 more than occurred during the corresponding period of the preceding year. Upon 23 August, the emigrant sheds contained 1,330—27 having died during twenty-four hours and so late as 11 October, there remained 746 patients in them.

Montreal lost many of her most valuable citizens in consequence of the contagion, among whom were Dr Cushing and the mayor. Neither was the pestilence stayed here, for the inhabitants of Kingston, Bytown, Toronto and other places were infected and a great number died of the fever, amongst whom was the Rev. Dr Power, RC Bishop of Toronto who contracted the disease in the discharge of his sacred functions among the sick. The following extract taken from the *Toronto Standard* serves to the manner in which the people of Canada suffered, and their sympathy for those who brought so much woe amongst them: 'The health of the city remains in much the same state as it did several weeks ago. The individual cases of fever have abated nothing of their violence and several families have caught the infection from having admitted emigrants into their houses. The greatest caution should be observed in this respect as it does not require contact alone, to infect a healthy person with the deadly virus of the fever. Breathing the same atmosphere with the infected or coming under the influence of the effluvia rising from their clothes is, in some states of the healthy body perfectly sufficient for effecting a lodgement of the disease m the human frame. On Monday evening last the report of the Finance Committee on the subject of erecting a House of Refuge for the destitute persons who have sought refuge in our City, was received by the Council. This committee report in favour of erecting immediately such a building as would shield those from the securities of winter and recommend that a sum not exceeding $5,000 should be expended for that purpose and that this sum should be put under the joint superintendence of the Board of Works and the Finance Committee so that now we have from the praiseworthy benevolence and alacrity of the Council, an assured hope that the emigrants will not be exposed to any hardships which it is in the power of the city authorities to ward off.'

The reader will bear in mind that the above relates in the city of Toronto, in Western Canada, at a distance of upwards of 500 miles from the Quarantine station whose stringent regulations were intended to protect the country from contagion. It now only remains for me to say a few words respecting the people that endured and reproduced so much tribulation.

The vast number of persons who quitted Europe to seek new homes in the western hemisphere in the year 1847, is without a precedent in history. Of the aggregate I cannot definitely speak but to be within the limits of truth, they exceeded 350,000. More than one half of these emigrants were from Ireland and to this portion was confined the devouring pestilence. It is a painful task to trace the causes that led to such fatal consequences—some of them may perhaps be hidden but many are too plainly visible. These wretched people were flying from known misery into unknown and tenfold aggravated misfortune. That famine which compelled so many to emigrate became itself a cause of the pestilence. But that the principal causes were produced by injustice and neglect, is plainly proven.

Many, as I have already stated, were sent out at the expense of their landlords. These were consequently the poorest and most abject of the whole and suffered the most. No doubt the motives of some landlords were benevolent but all they did was to pay for the emigrants' passage—this done, these gentlemen washed their hands of all accountability transferring them to the shipping agent whose object was to stow away the greatest possible number between the decks of the vessels chartered for the purpose. That unwarrantable inducements were held out to many I am aware, causing some to leave their homes who would not otherwise have done so. They were given to understand that they would be abundantly provided for during the voyage and that they were certain of finding immediate employment upon their arrival at a dollar per day.

Another serious injury was done to many families who had previously experienced the blessings of temperance from being, upon their arrival at the different ports where they were to embark, obliged to lodge in public houses of the worst description whose proprietors, knowing that they possessed a little stock of money, seduced them to violate their 'pledge' under the specious pretext that they were no longer bound by its obligations and that whiskey was the very best preventive of seasickness.

After a detention, often of many days, the vessel at length ready for sea, numbers were shipped that were quite unfit for a long voyage. True they were inspected and so were the ships but from the limited number of officers appointed for the purpose, many oversights occurred. In Liverpool, for instance, if I am rightly informed, there was staff of but five or six men to inspect the mass of emigrants and survey the ships in which there sailed from that port 107,474.

An additional heavy infliction was their sufferings on ship-board from famine - the legal allowance for an adult being one pound of food in twenty-four hours. But perhaps the most cruel wrong was in allowing crowds of already infected beings to be huddled up together in the confined holds, there to propagate the distemper which there was no physician to stay. The sufferings consequent upon such treatment I have endeavoured to portray in the previous narrative which—alas!—is but a feeble picture of the unmitigated trials endured by these most unhappy beings. Nor were their sufferings ended with the voyage. Oh, no! far from it. Would that I could represent the afflictions I witnessed at Grosse Isle! I would not be supposed to think that the medical officers situated there did not exercise the greatest humanity in administering their disagreeable duties which consisted not in relieving the distress of the emigrants but in protecting their country from contamination. Still, it was most afflicting that after combating the dangers of the sea, enduring famine, drought and sickness, the wretched survivors should still have to lie as uncared for as when in the centre of the Atlantic Ocean.

The inefficacy of the quarantine system is so apparent that it is needless to particularize its defects, neither need I repeat the details of the grievous aggravations of their trials heaped by it upon the already tortured emigrants. My heart bleeds when I think of the agony of the poor families - who, as yet undivided, had patiently borne their trials, ministering to each other's wants – when torn from each other. Painful as it was to behold the bodies of those who died at sea committed to the deep, yet the separation of families was fraught with much greater misery. And as if to reach the climax of endurance, the relatives and friends of those landed upon the island were at once carried away from them to a distance of 200 miles. On their way to Montreal many died on board the steamers. There, those who sickened in their progress were received into the hospital and the survivors of this second sifting were sent on to Kingston, 180 miles further, from thence to Toronto and so on, every city and town being anxious to be rid of them. Nor were there wanting, villains who preyed upon these stricken people. The *Montreal Herald* of 13 October thus writes:

'The rapid closing of the season of course diminishes the number of arrivals of emigrants and thus the hospitals and asylums are less crowded than they have been at an earlier period of the year. The statements are, however, still extremely distressing. An assertion has been made in the Common Council and is generally believed to be true that considerable sums have been brought here by some of these people and consigned by them in their last moments, to persons who have in many instances appropriated the money to their own use. An Alderman named Tully who is known to have the means of information, calculates the average of the sums brought to Canada by emigrants at £10 each, we suppose heads of families.'

In a tour which I made through Upper Canada I met in every quarter some of my poor wandering fellow-country people. Travelling from Prescott to Bytown by stage, I saw a poor woman with an infant in her arms and a child pulling at her skirt and crying as they went along. The driver compassionately took them up and the wayfarer wept her thanks. She had lost her husband upon the voyage and was going to Bytown to her brother who came out the previous year and, having made some money by lumbering in the woods, remitted to her the means of joining him. She told her sad tale most plaintively and the passengers all sympathised with her. The road being of that description called 'Corduroy' and the machine very crazy, the latter broke down within 5 miles of our destination and as she was unable to carry her two children, the poor creature was obliged to remain upon the road all the night. She came into Bytown the following morning and I had the satisfaction to learn that she found her brother.

A large proportion of the emigrants who arrived in Canada, crossed the frontiers in order to settle in the United States, so that they were to be seen in the most remote places. At St Catherine's upon the Welland Canal, 600 miles from Quebec, I saw a family who were on their way to the western part of the state of New York. One of them was taken ill and they were obliged to remain by the wayside with nothing but a few boards to protect them from the weather. There is no means of learning how many of the survivors of so many ordeals were cut off by the inclemency of a Canadian winter so that the grand total of the human sacrifice will never be known but by 'Him who knoweth all things'.

As I cannot so well convey my sentiments in my own language I will conclude with the following quotation from England's most popular writer, and would that his suggestions uttered five years before the commencement of the tragic drama had been attended to in time: if they had, much evil had been spared humanity.

'The whole system of shipping and conveying these unfortunate persons is one that stands in need of thorough revision. If any class deserve to be protected and assisted by the government, it is that class who are banished from their native land in search of the bare means of subsistence. All that could be done for those poor people by the great compassion and humanity of the captain and officers, was done but they require much more. The law is bound, at least upon the English side, to see that too many of them are not put on board one ship and that their accommodations are decent, not demoralising and profligate. It is bound too, in common humanity to declare that no man shall be taken on board without his stock of provisions being previously inspected by some proper officer and pronounced moderately sufficient for his support upon the voyage. It is bound to provide or to require that there be provided a medical attendant; whereas in these ships there are none, though sickness of adults and deaths of children on the passage are matters of the very commonest occurrence. Above all it is the duty of any government, be it monarchy or republic, to interpose and put an end to that system by which a firm of traders in emigrants purchase of the owners the whole 'tween decks of a ship and send on board as many wretched people as they can get hold of on any terms they can get, without the smallest reference to the conveniences of the steerage, the number of berths, the slightest separation of sexes, or anything but their own immediate profit. Nor is this the worst of the vicious system, for certain crimping agents of these houses, who have a percentage of all the passengers they inveigle, are constantly travelling about those districts where poverty and discontent are rife and tempting the credulous into more misery, by holding out monstrous inducements to emigration which never can be realised.

Dickens, American Notes.[12]

Notes

1 James J. Mangan (ed.), *Robert Whyte's 1847 Famine Ship Diary: The Journey of an Irish Coffin Ship* (Cork: Mercier Press, 1994).
2 A. Charbonneau and A. Sévigny, (eds.), *1847, Grosse Île: A Record of Daily Events* (Ottawa: Parks Canada, 1997), p. 164.
3 M. McGowan, 'Famine, Facts, and Fabrication: An Examination of Diaries from the Irish Famine Migration to Canada', *The Canadian Journal of Irish Studies*, 33, 2 (2007), pp. 48–55, on p. 52.
4 McGowan, 'Famine, Facts, and Fabrication', p. 52.
5 McGowan, 'Famine, Facts, and Fabrication', p. 53.
6 The National School system was established in Ireland in 1831.
7 John Cabot (c. 1450 – c. 1500), Venetian navigator who discovered the coast of North America in 1497.
8 Jacques Cartier (1491–1557), French explorer who sailed up the St. Lawrence river on his second voyage of discovery in 1535–6, leading to the establishment of the colony of New France.
9 Francis Danby (1793–1861) was a Romantic era Irish painter.

10 Scottish Highlanders who fought with General James Wolfe and conquered the French in Quebec City in 1759, claiming New France as a British colony.
11 Dr George Mellis Douglas (1809–1864), medical superintendant of Grosse Isle in 1847.
12 Charles Dickens, *American Notes for General Circulation* 2 vols. (London: Chapman and Hall, 1842), vol. 2, pp. 235–237

6

HERMAN MELVILLE, *REDBURN: HIS FIRST VOYAGE* (NEW YORK: HARPER AND BROTHERS, 1849)

Herman Melville's (1819–1891) *Redburn: His First Voyage* (1849) was his fourth novel after *Typee* (1846), *Omoo* (1847), and *Mardi* (1849), as well as forerunner of classic *Moby Dick; or, The Whale* (1851). *Redburn* is a semi-autobiographical work of fiction, a sea-borne *bildungsroman*, that recounts the adventures of a middle class youth who takes to the sea with coarse sailors on a voyage from New York to Liverpool and back. Like his protagonist Wellingborough Redburn in the novel, Melville himself was born into a genteel New England family that suffered a series of economic setbacks until his father went bankrupt. Also like Redburn, Melville himself also took to sea on the *St Lawrence* in 1839, when he was aged 20, the experience of which he revisited in his fictional works. Although Melville did not sail on the *Highlander*, he did encounter Famine Irish emigrants while returning by canal boat from his honeymoon in Quebec in mid-August 1847. According to his new bride, Elizabeth Shaw, 'Herman preferred to remain on deck all night to being in the crowd',[1] an experience which helped to furnish the aloof self-image for his protagonist in *Redburn*.[2]

The chapters excepted here are taken from the final third of the novel when Redburn observes a large group of Irish emigrants stricken with typhus on board the *Highlander's* return journey from Liverpool to New York at the height of the Famine migration. This section is not based on Melville's own experiences, but rather is cobbled together from newspaper accounts, travelogues, and maritime journals which gives it a composite and sweeping account of the Famine exodus. According to William Gilman, Melville's sources include – perhaps ironically given the questions about its own authenticity – Robert Whyte's *The Ocean Plague: or A Voyage to Quebec in an Irish Emigrant Vessel* as well as 'Nathaniel Ames's *A Mariner's Sketches* (1830)'.[3] 'This literary pilfering, however, is trivial,' Gilman suggests, 'in comparison with the large-scale appropriation which, unless Melville relied entirely upon his imagination, he must have committed to gather details of immigrant life on the 'Highlander'. He was probably struck by newspaper or magazine accounts of immigrant ships, which in 1849 were bringing to America hundreds of thousands of refugees from the Irish famine under exactly the same conditions he described'.[4] Indeed, what makes the novel so important

THE EMIGRANTS

After the first miserable weather we experienced at sea, we had intervals of foul and fair, mostly the former, however, attended with head winds, till at last, after a three days' fog and rain, the sun rose cheerily one morning, and showed us Cape Clear. Thank heaven, we were out of the weather emphatically called *'Channel weather,'* and the last we should see of the eastern hemisphere was now in plain sight, and all the rest was broad ocean.[5]

Land ho! was cried, as the dark purple headland grew out of the north. At the cry, the Irish emigrants came rushing up the hatchway, thinking America itself was at hand.

'Where is it?' cried one of them, running out a little way on the bowsprit. 'Is *that* it?'

'Aye, it doesn't look much like *ould* Ireland, does it?' said Jackson.

'Not a bit, honey: – and how long before we get there? to-night?'

Nothing could exceed the disappointment and grief of the emigrants, when they were at last informed, that the land to the north was their own native island, which, after leaving three or four weeks previous in a steamboat for Liverpool, was now close to them again; and that, after newly voyaging so many days from the Mersey, the *Highlander* was only bringing them in view of the original home whence they started.

They were the most simple people I had ever seen. They seemed to have no adequate idea of distances; and to them, America must have seemed as a place just over a river. Every morning some of them came on deck, to see how much nearer we were: and one old man would stand for hours together, looking straight off from the bows, as if he expected to see New York city every minute, when, perhaps, we were yet two thousand miles distant, and steering, moreover, against a head wind.

The only thing that ever diverted this poor old man from his earnest search for land, was the occasional appearance of porpoises under the bows; when he would cry out at the top of his voice—'Look, look, ye divils! look at the great pigs of the sea!'

At last, the emigrants began to think, that the ship had played them false; and that she was bound for the East Indies, or some other remote place; and one night, Jackson set a report going among them, that [Captain] Riga purposed taking them to Barbary, and selling them all for slaves; but though some of the old women almost believed it, and a great weeping ensued among the children, yet the men knew better than to believe such a ridiculous tale. . .

Now, whenever we discover a dislike in us, toward any one, we should ever be a little suspicious of ourselves. It may be, therefore, that the natural antipathy with which almost all seamen and steerage-passengers, regard the inmates of the cabin, was one cause at least, of my not feeling very charitably disposed toward them, myself.

Yes: that might have been; but nevertheless, I will let nature have her own way for once; and here declare roundly, that, however it was, I cherished a feeling toward these cabin-passengers, akin to contempt. Not because they happened to be cabin-passengers: not at all: but only because they seemed the most finical, miserly, mean men and women, that ever stepped over the Atlantic.

One of them was an old fellow in a robust looking coat, with broad skirts; he had a nose like a bottle of port-wine; and would stand for a whole hour, with his legs straddling apart, and his hands deep down in his breeches pockets, as if he had two mints at work there, coining guineas. He was an abominable looking old fellow, with cold, fat, jelly-like eyes; and avarice, heartlessness, and sensuality stamped all over him. He seemed all the time going through some process of mental arithmetic; doing sums with dollars and cents: his very mouth, wrinkled and drawn up at the corners, looked like a purse. When he dies, his skull ought to be turned into a savings box, with the till-hole between his teeth.

Another of the cabin inmates was a middle-aged Londoner, in a comical Cockney-cut coat, with a pair of semicircular tails: so that he looked as if he were sitting in a swing. He wore a spotted neckerchief; a short, little, fiery-red vest; and striped pants, very thin in the calf, but very full about the waist. There was nothing describable about him but his dress; for he had such a meaningless face, I cannot remember it; though I have a vague impression, that it looked at the time, as if its owner was laboring under the mumps.

Then there were two or three buckish looking young fellows, among the rest; who were all the time playing at cards on the poop, under the lee of the *spanker;* or smoking cigars on the taffrail; or sat quizzing the emigrant women with opera-glasses, leveled through the windows of the upper cabin. These sparks frequently called for the steward to help them to brandy and water, and talked about going on to Washington, to see Niagara Falls.

There was also an old gentleman, who had brought with him three or four heavy files of the *London Times*, and other papers; and he spent all his hours in reading them, on the shady side of the deck, with one leg crossed over the other; and without crossed legs, he never read at all. That was indispensable to the proper understanding of what he studied. He growled terribly, when disturbed by the sailors, who now and then were obliged to move him to get at the ropes.

As for the ladies, I have nothing to say concerning them; for ladies are like creeds; if you cannot speak well of them, say nothing.

THE EMIGRANTS' KITCHEN

I have made some mention of the 'Galley,' or great stove for the steerage passengers, which was planted over the main hatches.

HERMAN MELVILLE, *REDBURN*

During the outward-bound passage, there were so few occupants of the steer-age, that they had abundant room to do their cooking at this galley. But it was otherwise now; for we had four or five hundred in the steerage; and all their cooking was to be done by one fire; a pretty large one, to be sure, but, nevertheless, small enough, considering the number to be accommodated, and the fact that the fire was only to be kindled at certain hours.

For the emigrants in these ships are under a sort of martial-law; and in all their affairs are regulated by the despotic ordinances of the captain. And though it is evident, that to a certain extent this is necessary, and even indispensable; yet, as at sea no appeal lies beyond the captain, he too often makes unscrupulous use of his power. And as for going to law with him at the end of the voyage, you might as well go to law with the Czar of Russia.

At making the fire, the emigrants take turns; as it is often very disagreeable work, owing to the pitching of the ship, and the heaving of the spray over the uncovered 'galley.'

Whenever I had the morning watch, from four to eight, I was sure to see some poor fellow crawling up from below about daybreak, and go to groping over the deck after bits of rope-yarn, or tarred canvas, for kindling-stuff. And no sooner would the fire be fairly made, than up came the old women, and men, and children; each armed with an iron pot or saucepan; and invariably a great tumult ensued, as to whose turn to cook came next; sometimes the more quarrelsome would fight, and upset each other's pots and pans.

Once, an English lad came up with a little coffee-pot, which he managed to crowd in between two pans. This done, he went below. Soon after a great strapping Irishman, in knee-breeches and bare calves, made his appearance; and eying the row of things on the fire, asked whose coffee-pot that was; upon being told, he removed it, and put his own in its place; saying something about that individual place belonging to him; and with that, he turned aside.

Not long after, the boy came along again; and seeing his pot removed, made a violent exclamation, and replaced it; which the Irishman no sooner perceived, than he rushed at him, with his fists doubled. The boy snatched up the boiling coffee, and spirted its contents all about the fellow's bare legs; which incontinently began to dance involuntary hornpipes and fandangoes, as a preliminary to giving chase to the boy, who by this time, however, had decamped.

Many similar scenes occurred every day; nor did a single day pass, but scores of the poor people got no chance whatever to do their cooking.

This was bad enough; but it was a still more miserable thing, to see these poor emigrants wrangling and fighting together for the want of the most ordinary accommodations. But thus it is, that the very hardships to which such beings are subjected, instead of uniting them, only tends, by imbittering their tempers, to set them against each other; and thus they themselves drive the strongest rivet into the chain, by which their social superiors hold them subject.

It was with a most reluctant hand, that every evening in the second dog-watch, at the mate's command, I would march up to the fire, and giving notice to the assembled crowd, that the time was come to extinguish it, would dash it out with my bucket of salt water; though many, who had long waited for a chance to cook, had now to go away disappointed.

The staple food of the Irish emigrants was oatmeal and water, boiled into what is sometimes called *mush;* by the Dutch is known as *supaan;* by sailors *burgoo;* by the New Englanders *hasty-pudding;* in which hasty-pudding, by the way, the poet Barlow found the materials for a sort of epic.

Some of the steerage passengers, however, were provided with sea-biscuit, and other perennial food, that was eatable all the year round, fire or no fire.

There were several, moreover, who seemed better to do in the world than the rest; who were well furnished with hams, cheese, Bologna sausages, Dutch herrings, alewives, and other delicacies adapted to the contingencies of a voyager in the steerage.

There was a little old Englishman on board, who had been a grocer ashore, whose greasy trunks seemed all pantries; and he was constantly using himself for a cupboard, by transferring their contents into his own interior. He was a little light of head, I always thought. He particularly doated on his long strings of sausages; and would sometimes take them out, and play with them, wreathing them round him, like an Indian juggler with charmed snakes. What with this diversion, and eating his cheese, and helping himself from an inexhaustible junk bottle, and smoking his pipe, and meditating, this crack-pated grocer made time jog along with him at a tolerably easy pace.

But by far the most considerable man in the steerage, in point of pecuniary circumstances at least, was a slender little pale-faced English tailor, who it seemed had engaged a passage for himself and wife in some imaginary section of the ship, called the *second cabin*, which was feigned to combine the comforts of the first cabin with the cheapness of the steerage. But it turned out that this second cabin was comprised in the after part of the steerage itself, with nothing intervening but a name. So to his no small disgust, he found himself herding with the rabble; and his complaints to the captain were unheeded.

This luckless tailor was tormented the whole voyage by his wife, who was young and handsome; just such a beauty as farmers'-boys fall in love with; she had bright eyes, and red cheeks, and looked plump and happy.

She was a sad coquette; and did not turn away, as she was bound to do, from the dandy glances of the cabin bucks, who ogled her through their double-barreled opera glasses.

This enraged the tailor past telling; he would remonstrate with his wife, and scold her; and lay his matrimonial commands upon her, to go below instantly, out of sight. But the lady was not to be tyrannized over; and so she told him. Meantime, the bucks would be still framing her in their lenses, mightily enjoying the fun. The last resources of the poor tailor would be, to start up, and make a dash at the rogues, with clenched fists; but upon getting as far as the mainmast, the mate would accost him from over the rope that divided them, and beg leave to communicate the fact, that he could come no further. This unfortunate tailor was also a fiddler; and when fairly baited into desperation, would rush for his instrument, and try to get rid of his wrath by playing the most savage, remorseless airs he could think of.

While thus employed, perhaps his wife would accost him—

'Billy, my dear;' and lay her soft hand on his shoulder.

But Billy, he only fiddled harder.

'Billy, my love!'

The bow went faster and faster.

'Come, now, Billy, my dear little fellow, let's make it all up;' and she bent over his knees, looking bewitchingly up at him, with her irresistible eyes.

Down went fiddle and bow; and the couple would sit together for an hour or two, as pleasant and affectionate as possible.

But the next day, the chances were, that the old feud would be renewed, which was certain to be the case at the first glimpse of an opera-glass from the cabin.

ALMOST A FAMINE

'Mammy! mammy! come and see the sailors eating out of little troughs, just like our pigs at home.' Thus exclaimed one of the steerage children, who at dinner-time was peeping down into the forecastle, where the crew were assembled, helping themselves from the 'kids,' which, indeed, resemble hog-troughs not a little.

'Pigs, is it?' coughed Jackson, from his bunk, where he sat presiding over the banquet, but not partaking, like a devil who had lost his appetite by chewing sulphur.—'Pigs, is it?—and the day is close by, ye spalpeens, when you'll want to be after taking a sup at our troughs!'

This malicious prophecy proved true.

As day followed day without glimpse of shore or reef, and head winds drove the ship back, as hounds a deer; the improvidence and short sightedness of the passengers in the steerage, with regard to their outfits for the voyage, began to be followed by the inevitable results.

Many of them at last went aft to the mate, saying that they had nothing to eat, their provisions were expended, and they must be supplied from the ship's stores, or starve.

This was told to the captain, who was obliged to issue a ukase from the cabin, that every steerage passenger, whose destitution was demonstrable, should be given one sea-biscuit and two potatoes a day; a sort of substitute for a muffin and a brace of poached eggs.

But this scanty ration was quite insufficient to satisfy their hunger: hardly enough to satisfy the necessities of a healthy adult. The consequence was, that all day long, and all through the night, scores of the emigrants went about the decks, seeking what they might devour. They plundered the chicken-coop; and disguising the fowls, cooked them at the public galley. They made inroads upon the pig-pen in the boat, and carried off a promising young shoat: *him* they devoured raw, not venturing to make an incognito of his carcass; they prowled about the cook's caboose, till he threatened them with a ladle of scalding water; they waylaid the steward on his regular excursions from the cook to the cabin; they hung round the forecastle, to rob the bread-barge; they beset the sailors, like beggars in the streets, craving a mouthful in the name of the Church.

At length, to such excesses were they driven, that the Grand Russian, Captain Riga, issued another ukase, and to this effect: Whatsoever emigrant is found guilty of stealing, the same shall be tied into the rigging and flogged.

Upon this, there were secret movements in the steerage, which almost alarmed me for the safety of the ship; but nothing serious took place, after all; and they even acquiesced in, or did not resent, a singular punishment which the captain caused to be inflicted upon a culprit of their clan, as a substitute for a flogging. For no doubt he thought that such rigorous discipline as *that* might exasperate five hundred emigrants into an insurrection.

A head was fitted to one of the large deck-tubs—the half of a cask; and into this head a hole was cut; also, two smaller holes in the bottom of the tub. The head— divided in the middle, across the diameter of the orifice—was now fitted round the culprit's neck; and he was forthwith coopered up into the tub, which rested on his shoulders, while his legs protruded through the holes in the bottom.

It was a burden to carry; but the man could walk with it; and so ridiculous was his appearance, that in spite of the indignity, he himself laughed with the rest at the figure he cut.

'Now, Pat, my boy,' said the mate, 'fill that big wooden belly of yours, if you can.' Compassionating his situation, our old 'Doctor' used to give him alms of food, placing it upon the cask-head before him; till at last, when the time for deliverance came, Pat protested against mercy, and would fain have continued playing Diogenes in the tub for the rest of this starving voyage.

THOUGH THE *HIGHLANDER* PUTS INTO NO HARBOR AS YET; SHE HERE AND THERE LEAVES MANY OF HER PASSENGERS BEHIND

Although fast-sailing ships, blest with prosperous breezes, have frequently made the run across the Atlantic in eighteen days; yet, it is not uncommon for other vessels to be forty, or fifty, and even sixty, seventy, eighty, and ninety days, in making the same passage. Though in the latter cases, some signal calamity or incapacity must occasion so great a detention. It is also true, that generally the passage out from America is shorter than the return; which is to be ascribed to the prevalence of westerly winds.

We had been outside of Cape Clear upward of twenty days, still harassed by head-winds, though with pleasant weather upon the whole, when we were visited by a succession of rain storms, which lasted the greater part of a week.

During the interval, the emigrants were obliged to remain below; but this was nothing strange to some of them; who, not recovering, while at sea, from their first attack of seasickness, seldom or never made their appearance on deck, during the entire passage.

During the week, now in question, fire was only once made in the public galley. This occasioned a good deal of domestic work to be done in the steerage, which otherwise would have been done in the open air. When the lulls of the rain-storms would intervene, some unusually cleanly emigrant would climb to the deck, with a bucket of slops, to toss into the sea. No experience seemed sufficient to instruct some of these ignorant people in the simplest, and most elemental principles of ocean-life. Spite of all lectures on the subject, several would continue to shun the leeward side of the vessel, with their slops. One morning, when it was blowing very fresh, a simple fellow pitched over a gallon or two of something to windward. Instantly it flew back in his face; and also, in the face of the chief mate, who happened to be standing by at the time. The offender was collared, and shaken on the spot; and ironically commanded, never, for the future, to throw anything to windward at sea, but fine ashes and scalding hot water.

During the frequent *hard blows* we experienced, the hatchways on the steerage were, at intervals, hermetically closed; sealing down in their noisome den, those scores of human beings. It was something to be marveled at, that the shocking fate, which, but a short time ago, overtook the poor passengers in a Liverpool steamer in the Channel, during similar stormy weather, and under similar treatment, did not overtake some of the emigrants of the *Highlander*.

Nevertheless, it was, beyond question, this noisome confinement in so close, unventilated, and crowded a den: joined to the deprivation of sufficient food, from which many were suffering; which, helped by their personal uncleanliness, brought on a malignant fever.

The first report was that two persons were affected. No sooner was it known, than the mate promptly repaired to the medicine-chest in the cabin: and with the remedies deemed suitable, descended into the steerage. But the medicines proved of no avail; the invalids rapidly grew worse; and two more of the emigrants became infected.

Upon this, the captain himself went to see them; and returning, sought out a certain alleged physician among the cabin-passengers; begging him to wait upon the sufferers; hinting that, thereby, he might prevent the disease from extending into the cabin itself. But this person denied being a physician; and from fear of contagion—though he did not confess that to be the motive—refused even to enter the steerage. The cases increased: the utmost alarm spread through the ship: and scenes ensued, over which, for the most part, a veil must be drawn; for such is the fastidiousness of some readers, that, many times, they must lose the most striking incidents in a narrative like mine.

Many of the panic-stricken emigrants would fain now have domiciled on deck; but being so scantily clothed, the wretched weather—wet, cold, and tempestuous— drove the best part of them again below. Yet any other human beings, perhaps, would rather have faced the most outrageous storm, than continued to breathe the pestilent air of the steerage. But some of these poor people must have been so used to the most abasing calamities, that the atmosphere of a lazar-house almost seemed their natural air.

The first four cases happened to be in adjoining bunks; and the emigrants who slept in the farther part of the steerage, threw up a barricade in front of those bunks; so as to cut off communication. But this was no sooner reported to the captain, than he ordered it to be thrown down; since it could be of no possible benefit; but would only make still worse, what was already direful enough.

It was not till after a good deal of mingled threatening and coaxing, that the mate succeeded in getting the sailors below, to accomplish the captain's order.

The sight that greeted us, upon entering, was wretched indeed. It was like entering a crowded jail. From the rows of rude bunks, hundreds of meager, begrimed faces were turned upon us; while seated upon the chests, were scores of unshaven men, smoking tea-leaves, and creating a suffocating vapor. But this vapor was better than the native air of the place, which from almost unbelievable causes, was fetid in the extreme. In every corner, the females were huddled together, weeping and lamenting; children were asking bread from their mothers, who had none to give; and old men, seated upon the floor, were leaning back against the heads of the water-casks, with closed eyes and fetching their breath with a gasp.

At one end of the place was seen the barricade, hiding the invalids; while— notwithstanding the crowd—in front of it was a clear area, which the fear of contagion had left open.

'That bulkhead must come down,' cried the mate, in a voice that rose above the din.

'Take hold of it, boys.'

But hardly had we touched the chests composing it, when a crowd of pale-faced, infuriated men rushed up; and with terrific howls, swore they would slay us, if we did not desist.

'Haul it down!' roared the mate.

But the sailors fell back, murmuring something about merchant seamen having no pensions in case of being maimed, and they had not shipped to fight fifty to one. Further efforts were made by the mate, who at last had recourse to entreaty; but it would not do; and we were obliged to depart, without achieving our object.

About four o'clock that morning, the first four died. They were all men; and the scenes which ensued were frantic in the extreme. Certainly, the bottomless profound of the sea, over which we were sailing, concealed nothing more frightful.

Orders were at once passed to bury the dead. But this was unnecessary. By their own countrymen, they were torn from the clasp of their wives, rolled in their own bedding, with ballast-stones, and with hurried rites, were dropped into the ocean.

At this time, ten more men had caught the disease; and with a degree of devotion worthy all praise, the mate attended them with his medicines; but the captain did not again go down to them.

It was all-important now that the steerage should be purified; and had it not been for the rains and squalls, which would have made it madness to turn such a number of women and children upon the wet and unsheltered decks, the steerage passengers would have been ordered above, and their den have been given a thorough cleansing. But, for the present, this was out of the question. The sailors peremptorily refused to go among the defilements to remove them; and so besotted were the greater part of the emigrants themselves, that though the necessity of the case was forcibly painted to them, they would not lift a hand to assist in what seemed their own salvation.

The panic in the cabin was now very great; and for fear of contagion to themselves, the cabin passengers would fain have made a prisoner of the captain, to prevent him from going forward beyond the mainmast. Their clamors at last induced him to tell the two mates, that for the present they must sleep and take their meals elsewhere than in their old quarters, which communicated with the cabin.

On land, a pestilence is fearful enough; but there, many can flee from an infected city; whereas, in a ship, you are locked and bolted in the very hospital itself. Nor is there any possibility of escape from it; and in so small and crowded a place, no precaution can effectually guard against contagion.

Horrible as the sights of the steerage now were, the cabin, perhaps, presented a scene equally despairing. Many, who had seldom prayed before, now implored the merciful heavens, night and day, for fair winds and fine weather. Trunks were opened for Bibles; and at last, even prayer-meetings were held over the very table across which the loud jest had been so often heard.

Strange, though almost universal, that the seemingly nearer prospect of that death which anybody at any time may die, should produce these spasmodic devotions, when an everlasting Asiatic Cholera is forever thinning our ranks; and die by death we all must at last.

On the second day, seven died, one of whom was the little tailor; on the third, four; on the fourth, six, of whom one was the Greenland sailor, and another, a woman in the cabin, whose death, however, was afterward supposed to have been purely induced by her fears.

These last deaths brought the panic to its height; and sailors, officers, cabin-passengers, and emigrants—all looked upon each other like lepers. All but the only true leper among us—the mariner Jackson, who seemed elated with the thought, that for *him*—already in the deadly clutches of another disease—no danger was to be apprehended from a fever which only swept off the comparatively healthy. Thus, in the midst of the despair of the healthful, this incurable invalid was not cast down; not, at least, by the same considerations that appalled the rest.

And still, beneath a gray, gloomy sky, the doomed craft beat on; now on this tack, now on that; battling against hostile blasts, and drenched in rain and spray; scarcely making an inch of progress toward her port.

On the sixth morning, the weather merged into a gale, to which we stripped our ship to a storm-stay-sail. In ten hours' time, the waves ran in mountains; and the *Highlander* rose and fell like some vast buoy on the water. Shrieks and lamentations were driven to leeward, and drowned in the roar of the wind among the cordage; while we gave to the gale the blackened bodies of five more of the dead.

But as the dying departed, the places of two of them were filled in the rolls of humanity, by the birth of two infants, whom the plague, panic, and gale had hurried into the world before their time. The first cry of one of these infants was almost simultaneous with the splash of its father's body in the sea. Thus we come and we go. But, surrounded by death, both mothers and babes survived.

At midnight, the wind went down; leaving a long, rolling sea; and, for the first time in a week, a clear, starry sky.

In the first morning-watch, I sat with Harry on the windlass, watching the billows; which, seen in the night, seemed real hills, upon which fortresses might have been built; and real valleys, in which villages, and groves, and gardens, might have nestled. It was like a landscape in Switzerland; for down into those dark, purple glens, often tumbled the white foam of the wave-crests, like avalanches; while the seething and boiling that ensued, seemed the swallowing up of human beings.

By the afternoon of the next day this heavy sea subsided; and we bore down on the waves, with all our canvas set; stun'-sails a low and aloft; and our best steersman at the helm; the captain himself at his elbow;—bowling along, with a fair, cheering breeze over the taffrail.

The decks were cleared, and swabbed bone-dry; and then, all the emigrants who were not invalids, poured themselves out on deck, snuffing the delightful air, spreading their damp bedding in the sun, and regaling themselves with the generous charity of the captain, who of late had seen fit to increase their allowance of food. A detachment of them now joined a band of the crew, who proceeding into the steerage, with buckets and brooms, gave it a thorough cleansing, sending on deck, I know not how many bucketsful of defilements. It was more like cleaning out a stable, than a retreat for men and women. This day we buried three; the next day one, and then the pestilence left us, with seven convalescents; who, placed near the opening of the hatchway, soon rallied under the skillful treatment, and even tender care of the mate.

But even under this favorable turn of affairs, much apprehension was still entertained, lest in crossing the Grand Banks of Newfoundland, the fogs, so generally encountered there, might bring on a return of the fever. But, to the joy of all hands, our fair wind still held on; and we made a rapid run across these dreaded shoals, and southward steered for New York.

Our days were now fair and mild, and though the wind abated, yet we still ran our course over a pleasant sea. The steerage-passengers—at least by far the greater number—wore a still, subdued aspect, though a little cheered by the genial air, and the hopeful thought of soon reaching their port. But those who had lost fathers, husbands, wives, or children, needed no crape, to reveal to others, who they were. Hard and bitter indeed was their lot; for with the poor and desolate, grief is no indulgence of mere sentiment, however sincere, but a gnawing reality, that eats into their vital beings; they have no kind condolers, and bland physicians, and troops of sympathizing friends; and they must toil, though to-morrow be the burial, and their pallbearers throw down the hammer to lift up the coffin.

How, then, with these emigrants, who, three thousand miles from home, suddenly found themselves deprived of brothers and husbands, with but a few pounds, or perhaps but a few shillings, to buy food in a strange land?

As for the passengers in the cabin, who now so jocund as they? drawing nigh, with their long purses and goodly portmanteaus to the promised land, without fear of fate. One and all were generous and gay, the jelly-eyed old gentleman, before spoken of, gave a shilling to the steward.

The lady who had died was an elderly person, an American, returning from a visit to an only brother in London. She had no friend or relative on board, hence, as there is little mourning for a stranger dying among strangers, her memory had been buried with her body.

But the thing most worthy of note among these now light-hearted people in feathers, was the gay way in which some of them bantered others, upon the panic into which nearly all had been thrown. . .

And since, if the extremest fear of a crowd in a panic of peril proves grounded on causes sufficient, they must then indeed come to perish;—therefore it is, that at such times they must make up their minds either to die, or else survive to be taunted by their fellow-men with their fear. For except in extraordinary instances of exposure, there are few living men, who, at bottom, are not very slow to admit that any other living men have ever been very much nearer death than themselves. Accordingly, *craven* is the phrase too often applied to anyone who, with however good reason, has been appalled at the prospect of sudden death, and yet lived to escape it. Though, should he have perished in conformity with his fears, not a syllable of *craven* would you hear . . .

The cabin passenger who had used to read prayers while the rest kneeled against the transoms and settees, was one of the merry young sparks, who had occasioned such agonies of jealousy to the poor tailor, now no more. In his rakish vest, and dangling watch-chain, this same youth, with all the awfulness of fear, had led the earnest petitions of his companions; supplicating mercy, where before he had never solicited the slightest favor. More than once had he been seen thus engaged by the observant steersman at the helm: who looked through the little glass in the cabin bulk-head.

But this youth was an April man; the storm had departed; and now he shone in the sun, none braver than he.

One of his jovial companions ironically advised him to enter into holy orders upon his arrival in New York.

'Why so?' said the other, 'Have I such an orotund voice?'

'No;' profanely returned his friend—'But you are a coward—just the man to be a parson, and pray.'

However this narrative of the circumstances attending the fever among the emigrants on the *Highlander* may appear; and though these things happened so long ago; yet just such events, nevertheless, are perhaps taking place to-day. But the only account you obtain of such events, is generally contained in a newspaper paragraph, under the shipping-head. *There* is the obituary of the destitute dead, who die on the sea. They die, like the billows that break on the shore, and no more are heard or seen. But in the events, thus merely initialized in the catalogue of passing occurrences, and but glanced at by the readers of news, who are more taken up with paragraphs of fuller flavor; what a world of life and death, what a world of humanity and its woes, lies shrunk into a three-worded sentence!

You see no plague-ship driving through a stormy sea; you hear no groans of despair; you see no corpses thrown over the bulwarks; you mark not the wringing hands and torn hair of widows and orphans:—all is a blank. And one of these blanks I have but filled up, in recounting the details of the *Highlander's* calamity.

Besides that natural tendency, which hurries into oblivion the last woes of the poor; other causes combine to suppress the detailed circumstances of disasters like these. Such things, if widely known, operate unfavorably to the ship, and make her a bad name; and to avoid detention at quarantine, a captain will state the case in the most palliating light, and strive to hush it up, as much as he can.

In no better place than this, perhaps, can a few words be said, concerning emigrant ships in general.

Let us waive that agitated national topic, as to whether such multitudes of foreign poor should be landed on our American shores; let us waive it, with the one only thought, that if they can get here, they have God's right to come; though they bring all Ireland and her miseries with them. For the whole world is the patrimony of the whole world; there is no telling who does not own a stone in the Great Wall of China. But we waive all this; and will only consider, how best the emigrants can come hither, since come they do, and come they must and will.

Of late, a law has been passed in Congress, restricting ships to a certain number of emigrants, according to a certain rate. If this law were enforced, much good might be done; and so also might much good be done, were the English law likewise enforced, concerning the fixed supply of food for every emigrant embarking from Liverpool. But it is hardly to be believed, that either of these laws is observed.

But in all respects, no legislation, even nominally, reaches the hard lot of the emigrant. What ordinance makes it obligatory upon the captain of a ship, to supply the steerage-passengers with decent lodgings, and give them light and air in that foul den, where they are immured, during a long voyage across the Atlantic? What ordinance necessitates him to place the *galley*, or steerage-passengers' stove, in a dry place of shelter, where the emigrants can do their cooking during a storm, or wet weather? What ordinance obliges him to give them more room on deck, and let them have an occasional run fore and aft?—There is no law concerning these things. And if there was, who but some Howard in office would see it enforced? and how seldom is there a Howard in office!

We talk of the Turks, and abhor the cannibals; but may not some of *them*, go to heaven, before some of *us*? We may have civilized bodies and yet barbarous souls. We are blind to the real sights of this world; deaf to its voice; and dead to its death. And not till we know, that one grief outweighs ten thousand joys, will we become what Christianity is striving to make us.

Notes

1 J. Leda, *The Melville Log: A Documentary Life of Herman Melville 1819–1891* (New York: Gordian Press, 1969), 256.
2 H. Melville, *Redburn: His First Voyage* (New York: Harper Brothers, 1863), 26.
3 W. Gilman, *Melville's Early Life and* Redburn (London: Oxford University Press, 1951), pp. 351, 200.
4 Gilman, *Melville's Early Life*, p. 201.
5 Joel Barlow (1754–1812), an American poet known for the epic *Vision of Columbus* (1807) and *The Hasty Pudding* (1793).

7

WILLIAM SMITH, *AN EMIGRANT'S NARRATIVE, OR, A VOICE FROM THE STEERAGE: BEING A BRIEF ACCOUNT OF THE SUFFERINGS OF THE EMIGRANTS IN THE SHIP 'INDIA,' ON HER VOYAGE FROM LIVERPOOL TO NEW-YORK, IN THE WINTER OF 1847–8, TOGETHER WITH A STATEMENT OF THE CRUELTIES PRACTICED UPON THE EMIGRANTS IN THE STATEN ISLAND HOSPITAL* (NEW YORK: PUBLISHED BY THE AUTHOR, 1850)

William Smith was power-loom weaver from Manchester who emigrated from Liverpool to New York on board the *India* amongst Famine Irish emigrants in November, 1847. Little else is known about him. The *India* set sail from Liverpool on 26 November 1847 with 270 passengers and arrived in New York on 21 January, 1848; 39 emigrants, as well as Captain Thompson, and his successor, Captain Connor, perished during the voyage. William Smith's *Emigrant's Narrative, Or, A Voice from the Steerage*, offers a rare and vivid account of suffering 'Ship fever' or typhus, and the abuses and hardships suffered by Famine migrants in New York's Staten Island Hospital.

PREFACE.

As I have been often requested by my relatives in England, and a few friends in New York, to give them a comprehensive account of my sufferings, and my relatives and friends frequently asking me many questions concerning the voyage and subsequent events, has induced me to give them the gratification they desire.

In doing so, however, I can promise them nothing more than a plain narrative of the prominent events of the voyage, interspersed with such remarks as suggested themselves to my mind.

In consequence of my limited education, I have not that talent in recording facts, that I otherwise might have possessed; I must therefore beg the kind indulgence of my well informed friends for the incorrect manner in which I have put together few facts selected from so many. Whatever may be its defects it shall have one merit, at least, namely: a truthful statement of a few out of many events that came under my own observation.

I am well aware that my hair-breadth escapes and severe sufferings have affected those whom I love and esteem, and I know that the following narrative will be read with interest by them. Let me hope that though separated from them by a world of waters, they still cherish an affectionate remembrance of me, and though we may never meet again in this vale of tears, I hope to meet them in a better world. 'May we all lay up our treasures there.'
—Matt. vi. 20.

NARRATIVE.

I left Manchester, and arrived in Liverpool on Tuesday, the ninth of November. On the following day, I engaged passage in the steerage of the ship *India*, belonging to H--n & Co.

The day advertised for sailing was the 12th of that month, but in consequence of not having got in the cargo, which consisted of pig iron and earthen-ware, we were detained ten days for that purpose, and one day to stop a leak, which sprung as the ship was leaving the dock; the immigrants being thus detained eleven days, and as they were of the very poorest class, and most of them having families, with only a small stock of provisions, and that too of the coarsest description, most of them having left Ireland a week, some a fortnight, before the day fixed for sailing, this detention of eleven days was severely felt by those poor creatures, many of them having consumed half of their provisions, without the means of obtaining more. Under these circumstances, the immigrants applied at the office of H--n for the sum of eleven shillings, which was due to each adult immigrant, as the law allowed one shilling per day to each adult passenger from the day advertised to sail to the day of sailing; but as they refused to comply with the request, the immigrants selected six persons to go and state their case to the Government agent. We went to him and stated our grievances; he came with us to the office of H--n, and ordered them to obey the law by paying the amount due to each person. They promised him that they would do so. He then left us, telling us to call upon him again if we did not receive the sum already stated. The ship owners ordered us to go immediately on board, where we would be paid the amount due us. Believing that they would do so, we all went on board the *India*, when we were paid two shillings, and two pounds of sea-biscuit. No sooner had we received this trifle, than a steamboat towed us down the river, in order to prevent us from again complaining to the agent of their base conduct. There we remained two days, anchored, during which time there was great confusion and uproar on board, from the above cause. On the next morning, Friday, November 26, 1847, we set sail. The crew numbered twenty-four good seamen, exclusive of the captain and first mate. I had wished many times during my stay in Liverpool that the ship would set sail, but when the hour came, and a fine breeze wafted me from the shores of my native land, when I saw it gradually receding from my view, the tears, unreproved, chased each other down my cheeks, as I began to reflect that I had left my wife and child behind me. I had also left an aged father, and three affectionate sisters, and a few friends to whom I was bound in the strongest ties of friendship. I had left my native land, which I loved, though I detested her tyrants. I had voluntarily exiled myself from all that was near and dear to me in my native country, to seek for that remuneration for my labor in a foreign land, which I could not obtain in my own. The bitter thought too, that if I should arrive safe in America, in a few days I should be penniless, perhaps without employment and without food, among strangers, without a friend to do me a single act of kindness, or to take any interest in my welfare. For several years I had vainly endeavored to raise myself from the state of poverty and the consequent degradation which the small remuneration I received for my labors [I was a Power-Loom Weaver], forced me into. If, in the *free* and *happy land* to which I was going, my last and only hope should be destroyed, my wife and child would then suffer by my absence.

As these thoughts were preying upon my mind, I began to grow sea-sick. I cannot describe the sensations I felt, but I shall not easily forget them. It reduced me so much that I could not walk without assistance, for I felt as weak as an infant. On the third day, feeling much better, I went on deck, and, for the first time, beheld a boundless expanse of ocean. In the distance appeared ships under full sail; above was a clear blue sky; the water seemed to be of a blue tint and the ship was running like a race-horse, coursing over the waters with a speed that promised to bring us quickly to our journey's end. All was new to me: the scene was one of sublimity, magnificence and grandeur. Who, possessing a reflective mind, can look above, and not exclaim, with the inspired psalmist, 'The Heavens declare the glory of God, and the Earth showeth his handy-work?'—Ps. xix. 1. Who can look upon the mighty ocean, and behold the wonders thereof, and not acknowledge the hand of God? 'O, Lord, how manifold are thy works! In wisdom hast thou made them all: the earth is full of thy riches.'—Ps. civ. 24.

When we had been at sea three weeks, during which time we had made slow progress, having to contend with head and contrary winds most of that time, a storm arose, which continued four days and five nights. The day on which this storm commenced it rained so heavily the whole day we could not make a fire on deck to cook our victuals with. About three o'clock in the afternoon, the rain began to fall in torrents, the clouds were black, and moved rapidly, and the wind gradually increased in force till eight o'clock, when the roaring of the tempest was truly appalling. I heard the mate order the hatchways to be fastened down, (an order indispensably necessary to the safety of the ship.) The order was quickly obeyed, and from that time commenced our sufferings. The increasing violence of the storm, the moaning and creaking of the ship, the howling of the wind, and the roaring of the waves, was horrible to those not accustomed to such scenes; and every few minutes a wave would strike the ship with such force as to make it tremble beneath us, causing a shock so great that at every blow we expected to see the bow stave in and the ship sink.

About midnight, a number of boxes and barrels broke loose and rolled from side to side, according to the motion of the ship, breaking the water cans and destroying everything capable of being destroyed by them; to fasten them was almost impossible, for we could not keep ourselves from sliding down without grasping something. In a few minutes the boxes and barrels broke to atoms, scattering the contents in all directions—tea, coffee, sugar, potatoes, pork, shirts, trowsers vests, coats, handkerchiefs, &c., &c, were mingled in one confused mass. The cries of the women and children was heart-rending; some praying, others weeping bitterly, as they saw their provisions and clothes (the only property they possessed) destroyed. The passengers being sea-sick, were vomiting in all parts of the vessel; the heat became intense in consequence of the hatchways being closed down, and the passengers, 300 in number, being thus kept below, we were unable to breathe the pure air or see the light of heaven but a few hours at a time. The scent arising from the matter vomited up, and from other causes, became intolerable. Things continued in this way until the fourth day, when the storm abated, and the hatchways were opened. Most of the passengers were so eager to get on deck that they pushed each other off the ladder; several were severely hurt, and I expected that loss of life would be the consequence of this confusion; however, I am happy to say, my expectations were not realized. As an apology for such conduct on the part of the passengers, let me remind you of the horrors of our situation. We had been five nights and nearly four days with only one hatchway (the after hatchway) open for a few hours at a time, and 300 souls confined below, breathing the close, polluted, and unhealthy atmosphere constantly in all ships, especially immigrant ships, where large numbers of human beings are crowded together in a small space: in this case rendered doubly sickening and intolerable from the causes before alluded to. So oppressive was the atmosphere we were compelled to inhale, that it was proposed to break open the hatchways when both were closed upon us, and were only dissuaded from it by being told that the captain would again open it as soon as he could do so with safety to the vessel. Had they broke open the hatchways during the storm, the ship would inevitably have sunk, as it was constantly shipping a sea. Ever and anon, we heard the waves rushing over the forecastle upon the deck with terrible impetuosity. On the other hand, to remain much longer below would be certain death. We all felt a sense of suffocation, and a difficulty of breathing which plainly indicated that the air so necessary to our existence was wanting, and unless speedily renewed, death would soon ensue. You will not wonder then at their eagerness to get upon deck. It is impossible to keep men in a state of discipline under such circumstances. For my part I was as eager as anyone, but by waiting a few moments till the rush and confusion had subsided, I was enabled to get upon deck without risk of life or limb. I forgot to state that we had nothing but cold water to our biscuit, for, having no means of cooking our food, such provisions as could not be eaten without cooking, could not be eaten at all. However, I did not feel the loss of a fire much, as I soon lost my appetite when confined below—cold water and biscuit being all I could eat during the two last days of the storm.

We were startled about three o'clock in the morning by a loud crash, caused by the breaking of the fore-mast, which a sudden gust of wind had shivered to atoms. The women and children were screaming in despair, believing we had struck a rock. Nearly one half of the crew had a providential escape from a watery grave, as they had been aloft reefing and just got down upon deck the moment it broke. A portion of the bulwarks were also destroyed. The scene which met my eye upon reaching the deck was awful. Broken fragments of the fore-mast, rigging, chains, &c, were strewn from one end to the other. We assisted the sailors at the pumps, but soon got wet through with spray caused by the waves dashing against the bows of the ship. Cold, hungry and exhausted, I went below to change my wet clothes for dry ones, and recruit myself with sea-biscuit and cold water, which was all I could get without fire. I have said that the scene on deck was awful. The following description of 'A Storm at Sea;' written, I believe, by a missionary, is such a faithful statement of facts, that when you have read it, you will be able to form some idea of a storm. The writer says:

'On deck the scene is truly grand. The sky is black, rugged, and shifting; the wind is terrible, with alternate gust, 'seugh' and lull; the sea heaped up into a ridge of low hills on either side. The ship lies wriggling in the gale like a winter tree; the masts stripped of all their clothing, the storm staysail being the only stitch of canvass left. A billow is rushing forward with its white cress shaking like a lion's mane, nearing the bow—it looks so lofty hat she must be overwhelmed—but, with mingled delight and apprehension, you see her rear herself on its base; then, as if rejoicing in her escape, at that moment a cross sea strikes on the weather bow with a dull sound, like the shake of a battering-ram. The noble bark shudders like a child in a thunder clap; and while you are quivering with sympathy, a fierce surge sweeps along the deck, making your firmest grasp needful to prevent being borne away. When you emerge, the ship is resting on the top of another wave, as if to shake off the moisture of the last immersion; and just as this passes from under her, it strikes fiercely on the counter, in seeming anger at its being foiled in its assault. While staggering from the effects of this after-blow, a broken sea, like an enemy in ambush attacking the flank, dashes suddenly on the weather-beam. Instantly the top-masts seem nearly touching the water, and the strongest hold of a rope or bulwark can scarcely save you from sliding down the almost vertical deck; it seems impossible the ship can right. Volumes of water rushing over you, confirm the impression that the moment of danger is come; but a counter swing restores you to your footing, and shows the bow plunging into another billow.

'The whole scene is sufficiently awful, and if one but give way to fear or fancy, it is easy enough to make the waves mountains, the gusts artillery, and to crowd the whole with gigantic forms of horror. The lesson of a storm is humility. Each cloud may be the engine of destruction, each sea may capsize or overwhelm your ark; you cannot lighten its stroke by a single drop. Surrounded by objects, all potent to destroy, there is nought on which your skill can work the least amelioration. The sky, the wind, the waves, are eloquent with the announcement, 'God is all in all;' you can do nought but meekly crave his compassion, or humbly await his will, and when the danger is past, man has had no hand in averting it. It came upon you, pressed you on every side, brought you to your 'wit's end,' showed human help to be vain, and then disappeared. You are safe again: that safety is sealed with the hand of God. You see his agency through no obstructive instrument, you have been dealing directly with your Maker; therefore, being glad they are quiet, they praise God for his goodness.'

Anyone who has been in a ship on the stormy ocean, and beheld the forked lightning dart, and hear the thunder roll, and seen the mountainous waves dashing against the vessel, each wave seeming the one commissioned to engulf him in the bowels of the deep, will, then have realized my feelings at this time. Such was the sight I beheld on being released from the horrors of confinement below. After I had put on dry clothes, I had been in the steerage about two hours, when I heard the cry of 'a man overboard!' which ran like fire through the ship. I hurried upon deck, and saw the sailors throwing ropes over; all were looking upon the maddened waters with a hope to see him rise to the surface. But alas, alas, vain hope; he sank to rise no more 'Till the last trumpet shall sound,' 'and the sea give up its dead.' (Cor. xv. 52, and Rev. xx. 13.) Upon inquiry, I found it was a sailor who had fallen from the yard-arm. He was a fine young man, a native of Germany, of a quiet, inoffensive disposition. I had several conversations with him during the first part of the voyage, and as he was fond of reading, I lent him a copy of Southey's[1] poems, and other works, with which he seemed much pleased. An intimacy sprung up between us, and any one may imagine the shock I received on learning that it was he who was drowned. This sad accident caused a general gloom among the passengers, but I was sorry to see the heartless indifference manifested by the sailors at the loss of their ship-mate.

On the following day, hearing the sailors pumping, I went upon deck, and having filled a bucket with water, I washed myself, when, with my overcoat on my arm, I went to the hatch-way for the purpose of going below. Just as I got on the second step, the ladder being wet and slippery, my foot slipped, and I fell, my head coming in contact with the lid of a box at the foot of the ladder, three quarters of an inch thick, which was broken by the concussion. The violence of the blow stunned me, and I was taken up senseless and carried to bed. Upon returning to consciousness I saw the captain, first mate and several sailors around me, with my head bandaged, and my shirt collar and bosom covered with blood from a wound in my left temple, the mark of which I shall carry to my grave. I was in great agony from the pains in my head and sides. When the captain and sailors left me, I was informed by the passengers, that, upon seeing me fall and lie motionless, covered with blood, they thought I was dead, and it was rumored that a man was killed in the steerage. The captain and sailors came down to test the truth of the rumor, and finding me not dead, tied a bandage around my head to stop the blood. In the afternoon the captain came again to see me, and gave me some medicine. The passengers told me that my overcoat fell under my side, and broke the force of the blow, which saved my ribs from being broken. I was confined to my bed for several days, during which time a fearful accident happened to a boy, fourteen years old. It appears that he was lying down on the forecastle, with the rope of the jib (the foremost sail) lying near him, when a gust of wind instantly filled the jib, which straightened the rope suddenly, hitting him with such force as to nearly take off his scalp; it was cut nearly around, and resembled the cut of an Indian's scalping knife. The captain held him, while the first mate sewed up the wound; during which painful operation, the boy did not utter a scream or even a murmur. The captain, in admiration of his courage, said if the boy lived, he would make him a present of a good pair of boots when he got in New York, as he was bare-foot.

We had been at sea four weeks, and being one day upon deck, I was looking at the unruffled ocean as we lay upon its bosom. There was not wind enough to move a feather. The ship lay motionless, and did not seem to move upon the water the weather was quite warm, which surprised me, as it was near Christmas, and I was emigrating to a colder climate, (the winters being much colder in North America than in England) I naturally expected to find the weather gradually becoming colder as we neared New York; but finding it was warmer instead of colder, I inquired the cause from one of the sailors, who told me that the captain was taking a southerly passage in order to avoid the inclement weather as much as possible, and not disable the seamen by the frost: also to avoid the ice-bergs so numerous and dangerous to ships. Some of the sailors said that the captain had done right in so doing, others said he had done wrong. The same difference of opinion also existed among the passengers. One thing, however, I felt sure of, which was, that however good the motives were which induced the captain to take a southerly passage, that that dreadful scourge, the ship fever, (which was already on board our ship) would be increased by it; an opinion which facts soon verified by the number of cases and deaths increasing. As it may be interesting to some, I will give a description of a Funeral at Sea:

When a death occurs, the body is enveloped in canvass, and sewed up with about forty or fifty pounds of stone, which are fastened at the feet, for the purpose of causing the body to sink deep in the ocean. The corpse is then brought on deck and extended upon a plank; the Union Jack flag is then spread over the body, and the plank is put on the rail at the gang-way; all hands are called to witness the solemn scene: and every head is uncovered. The captain then reads the funeral service; and as he reads the words 'We commit the body to the deep,' the plank is raised, and the body is launched into the bosom of the ocean. I expected to see the body thrown over in a careless, unceremonious manner, but was glad to find myself mistaken. The funeral was far more impressive than those that take place on land. To hear the earth thrown upon a coffin in a church-yard is sufficiently appalling, but not as bad as this awful plunge into the deep. The first time I saw this sight, it so shocked my feelings that I felt the blood run cold through my veins. Little did I think that I should see this scene so often that I should view it with so little emotion. Up to the fifth week, we had buried fifteen passengers who had died by the ship-fever, besides forty-two confined to bed. The fever was raging through the whole ship. A cabin passenger, a sailor, and two of the steerage passengers died in one day, and thus the deaths increased from one to four a day. Mr. Thompson, our captain, and Mr. Connor, first mate, from the commencement, did all they could to alleviate the sufferings of the sick. Two kinder-hearted men never walked a ship's deck, and as we had no doctor on board, they went round and administered medicine, and otherwise assisted the sick. Every day the fever was increasing to a fearful extent. At the end of the fifth week the captain was taken sick, and after an illness of three days, died. After Captain Thompson was dead, the carpenter made a coffin for his body; and having run melted pitch down the seams, his remains were put in, and the coffin secured upon the roof of the cabin, outside, and his boat put over it to keep the rain off. In this way he was brought to Staten Island, but whether he was buried there or not, I do not know. Woes came in clusters; our provisions and water began to be scarce, and we were only allowed a pint of water a day, and half of our usual provisions. We spoke a ship from the East Indies, bound for Dublin, Ireland, with a cargo of rum. The captain told Mr. Connor, (then our captain,) that half of his sailors were sick with the ship fever, and that more than half of his passengers had died by that disease; that he had been sixty days at sea; that he had a long voyage before him, and but few men to work the ship; consequently he could not spare either. Bidding the other ship adieu, we parted company. I remained on deck as long as I could see the ship.

It had been twenty-two days since we had before seen a ship, which was a great disappointment to us, as we expected to get some relief. The death of Captain Thompson was severely felt by the sick, as Captain Connor had little time to spare, but when he had an opportunity, he went among them, doing all that lay in his power for their assistance. Three days after, a sailor at the mast-head, called aloud to the captain that he saw a sail, and pointed out the direction of the ship. The captain took the telescope, but said he could not see any. The sailor still persisted that he saw a ship, and we looked anxiously over the dark blue sea, but could discern no ship. In a few moments, however, the captain announced the ship, which he said was on the star-board bow, and ordered signals of distress to be instantly made. The sailors obeyed with alacrity, and in half an hour after, we could see the ship with the naked eye. It looked like a small speck on the wide ocean. In an hour more we saw the ship distinctly. The joyful news ran through the ship that the strange vessel had discovered our signal, and was bearing down toward us. Oh, how my heart was agitated with conflicting emotions. At one moment I was lifting up my heart in gratitude to God for the prospect of relief we had before us; in the next moment the thought that perhaps the vessel might be in the same situation as the one we had met the night before, almost drove me to despair. Thus, for two hours we were in painful suspense until the ship came along side of ours. She was a merchant ship from South America, with a cargo of cotton, bound for

Liverpool. Our captain took his speaking trumpet, and informed the American captain of our awful situation, and asked him for relief. He told Captain Connor that he would have most willingly have given him the desired assistance if it had been in his power; as it was, he could not spare any. He had lost the mizen mast of his ship in a storm, and like us, he was sailing with a jury mast. He said his stock of provisions was rather scant at first, and that he had been three weeks at sea, but in consequence of bad weather, he had not made more than a week's sail; he also said that he had seen two ships the day before, and if we were so fortunate as to meet either of them he had no doubt we should get some relief. The two captains bid each other adieu, unfurled their sails, and continued their course. Thus was my worst fears realized. Oh, how this bitter disappointment pierced the hearts of all on board; our situation was truly deplorable; the bitter thought that unless we soon got relief we must perish for the want of water, while we were surrounded by a sea of it. Nearly every misfortune that could happen, had befallen us; everything seemed to conspire against us; even the two ships, the only ones that we had met since our great misfortunes, seemed as though they only came to mock us in our distress. Our forlorn hope being thus nearly destroyed, the passengers gave themselves up to despair, and gloomy, sullen silence pervaded the captain and sailors. Never did the death knell fall more dismally on the heart of a condemned criminal, than did the refusal of relief from the last ship fall upon me.

I gave up all as lost, and wished I never had been born; the scenes I witnessed daily were indeed awful; to hear the heart rending cries of wives at the loss of their husbands, the agonies of husbands at the sight of the corpse of their wives, and the lamentations of fatherless and motherless children; brothers and sisters dying, leaving their aged parents without means of support in their declining years. These were sights to melt a heart of stone. I saw the tear of sympathy run down the cheek of many a hardened sailor. Most of those who died of ship-fever were delirious, some a day, others only a few hours previous to death. One day there were three men walking about the ship raving mad; one fancied himself a priest, and told the passengers they would all die and go to hell, unless they permitted him to make the sign of the cross and baptize them; at daylight, next morning, he was found dead in his berth. The second one imagined himself in New York; this man had an intimate friend who kept watch of him, but while absent a moment, the lunatic ran up on deck, and before any one was aware of his intentions, threw himself into the sea and was drowned. Hearing an alarm on deck, I hastened to learn the cause, hoping it was a ship coming in sight, but beheld the man struggling in the water. Before Captain Connor was told of it, the man was nearly out of sight, and he declared that it was too late to save him, as he would sink before a boat could reach him. This unfortunate man's wife was already in New York, some friends or relatives having sent for her; she had taken with her her youngest child, and he was bringing the other. Oh, how my heart bled for the poor child that was weeping for hours, asking for its father. The other lunatic, having attempted to stab his wife, had to be tied down to his berth. His wife said he was a kind and affectionate husband until seized with the fever. Three days after I was glad to see him so far recovered as to be able to walk about the steerage, leaning upon his wife—he finally recovered. In consequence of these last occurrences, the captain had every delirious person tied down who evinced a disposition to injure themselves or others. The captain then placed a guard at each hatchway, with strict orders not to permit any delirious person to come on deck, thus preventing, in future, any danger of their drowning themselves.

I will give a few instances of the selfishness, hard-heartedness, and depravity of human nature, which, if I had not seen, I could not have believed. One day a little girl about ten years old, came to the fire to cook some gruel for her dying mother; as she was putting her can on for that purpose, a monster in human form, came up just as she had got it on, took it off, and put on his; I remonstrated with him on the cruelty of such a proceeding, telling him the gruel was for her mother, who was not expected to live many hours—her father was recovering from sickness, but unable to leave his bed—he replied that everyone must take care of themselves, and that he would cook his meal in spite of any one. A man who had seen this, told him that the girl should have her gruel cooked first, as she came to the fire first; a quarrel then ensued, when the captain, who happened to be passing by, inquired the cause of it. On being informed of the man's conduct, he instantly threw the villain's pan off and put the girl's can on the fire; he also ordered the steward to deduct his pint of water the next day—the greatest punishment the captain could inflict upon him. In two days after, he was seized with the ship-fever, and after an illness of twelve hours, died in great agony, his eyes wide open, and no one to close them, his friends having all deserted him the moment they found he had the ship-fever. He was nicknamed 'Big Roger,' from the South of Ireland, (as were most of the passengers) and was the largest man I ever saw; yet, in twelve short hours, sickness had snapped the thread of life, and left his remains a horrid spectacle to behold. How little did he think, when he drove the poor child from the fire, that in three days he should be summoned to the judgment bar of God, with all his imperfections on his head. How fearfully true is the proverb of Solomon: 'Boast not thyself of to-morrow, for thou knowest not what a day may bring forth' (Prov. xxvii, 1.) I have seen husbands desert their wives when they were attacked by fever, and sleep with a friend. They would cook food for their family, but would not go near them, generally sending the food by their children. But when the fever spread over the ship from stem to stern, they were compelled, to keep to their own berths. Although I saw several instances of such selfishness on the part of husbands and fathers in their fear of the epidemic, I never saw a wife desert her husband, a sister her brother, a daughter her father or mother. In the hour of affliction, how much greater is the fortitude of woman than man; the sacrifices they make, the noble devotion they evince in the hour of trial, is beyond all praise. A French author has very applicably observed, 'Without woman, the two extremities of life would be helpless, and the middle of it joyless.' Mr. Ledyard[2] also says, 'To a woman I never addressed myself in the language of decency and friendship without receiving a decent and friendly answer; if I were hungry or thirsty, wet or sick, they did not hesitate, like men, to perform a generous action. In so free and kind a manner did they contribute to my relief, that if I were dry I drank the sweetest draught, and if I were hungry, I ate the coarsest meal with a double relish.'

My experience of the kindness of woman is the same; when my hour of sickness came, if I asked a man to go for my allowance of water, he would say he had no time; a second would say he was ill, and could not; a third said he was sorry he could not go, but would if he could. Such were the answers I received from men for whom I had done many a kind action. Who, in my time of need, sympathised with my sufferings? To none (Captain Connor excepted) but woman am I indebted for many a kind and benevolent favor during the voyage . . . In England, I am sorry to say, the talents of woman are not held in a proper degree of consideration. But when I came to this free and happy land, I found them duly appreciated.

In the sixth week, another disease broke out among the passengers—the diarrhea—(a disease as malignant, and almost as fatal as ship fever) caused by the impure state of our water, which was in such a state of decomposition, that no human being could drink it, until forced by being placed in similar circumstances with ourselves. Having no doctor on board, the disorders raged unchecked among them. The captain did not know what to prescribe for them; the medicine that seemed to do one person good, made another worse; you may easily conceive the panic this created among us. Such sweeping calamities exercised a baneful influence on the minds of many; every generous emotion, every tender feeling of the heart was dried up, while every selfish feeling in human nature, seemed called into full play.

Despair was depicted in every countenance, and desolation spread throughout the ship. To have a friend well this hour, sick the next, and in a few hours more, dead, and thrown overboard before his remains are cold, is indeed awful! Never, while I live, can I forget these fearful scenes; they taught me a lesson of the frailty and vanity of life, which will never be erased from my memory. How true are the words of Holy Writ: 'Thou turnest man to destruction; they are like grass which groweth up; in the morning it flourished!, in the evening it is cut down and withereth.' (Ps. xc. 3, 5, 6.) May the merciful God, who spared my life, spare me from such dreadful scenes.

I stated at the commencement of this narrative that the ship sprung a leak as she was leaving the dock. The carpenters could not repair this leak until the water-casks or hogsheads were removed; he therefore had to scuttle a number of them, letting the water run into the hold, which was pumped up by the sailors. When the leak was repaired, the hogsheads were replaced, and the hose being attached to the hydrant on the dock, we supposed they were all refilled; but when we had been a month at sea, the steward discovered that four hogs-heads, by oversight or neglect, had not been refilled. On the following morning, by Captain Thompson's order, our water was reduced from two quarts to one quart per day for an adult and one pint for a child. The week following, the captain died. Mr. Connor upon succeeding him, showed us the necessity of his reducing our allowance of water from a quart to a pint per day. My health, which had hitherto been good, notwithstanding all the hardships I had suffered, began to fail me. My provisions were consumed, and I had nothing but ship allowance to subsist upon, which was scarcely sufficient to keep us from perishing, being only a pound of sea-biscuit (full of maggots) and a pint of such water as I have before described.

I began to get so weak that if I walked upon deck for a short time, I was compelled to sit down from fatigue. From the time the fever broke out in the ship to this time, (the sixth week) I had kept upon deck as much as possible. I had frequently been all day and all night upon deck; the night I spent by remaining a few hours with the man at the helm, a few hours with the watch upon the fore-castle. At break of day I would then go to my berth, sleep a few hours, and then remain upon deck again. But I now lost all spirit, I felt as though I had no life in me. A listlessness came upon me, produced, no doubt, by suffering from extreme want. I had been in this state two days, when I was seized with the ship-fever; at first I was so dizzy that I could not walk without danger of falling. I was suffering much from a violent pain in my head, my brains felt as if they were on fire, my tongue clove to the roof of my mouth and my lips were parched with excessive thirst. Cheerfully would I have given the world, had I possessed it, for one draught of water. In this state I went to the captain and implored him to give me a draught of water. He said that water would make me worse, and that my only chance for life was in taking some medicine, which he instantly prepared for me. I still earnestly entreated him to give me a little water, but he replied that should he give to all the applicants, he would, in a few days be entirely out, and that he could not give to one unless he gave to all. I drank the medicine eagerly, as any fluid, however nauseous, was a boon not to be despised under existing circumstances. I remained in bed a few hours, but became so sick that I could neither sit nor stand, and was therefore compelled to keep to my berth, which was a double one. One of my bed-fellows had died a week before, another was sick with the diarrhea, and the third one was afraid to come near us, he therefore stayed on deck most of the time. I do not blame him for this, for, beside the fever, the stench in the steerage was horrid: the causes of which, it is neither necessary nor proper to state. Every day I felt weaker, and became exhausted upon the least exertion, and, as if to increase my misery, another storm arose and continued three nights and three days. I had to use all the little strength I had to prevent being thrown out of bed by the heaving of the ship. My strength failed me. I got two persons to put my bed in such a position that I could remain in it without having to grasp the boards of my berth; the hatchways were again closed up on us; a solitary lamp suspended from the roof, sent a glimmering light along the steerage. To hear the groans of the sick, the despairing cries of their kindred, the misery of all, and the dismal prospect of everything around me, conspired to fill my heart with gloomy forebodings.

My mind was busy imagining scenes at home. With my mind's eye, I beheld those which I hold most dear, gathered around the cheerful fire; I was the subject of their conversation; they hoped I had long since landed, and were in daily expectation of a letter from me. At one time they all seemed elevated with the hope that I had landed safe; the next moment they were cast down with the idea that I had, perhaps, perished at sea, or that some other calamity had befallen me.

Such was the scenes of home I pictured to my mind. My wife too, was I never more to see her; never more to see my lovely infant—lovely at least in our eyes? Alas no, death was already busy in our midst, already had he cut down the finest specimens of humanity among us. What hope, then, could I have? none! I was, I believed, already marked as one of the many victims. No language can express the agony of mind I suffered. Truly I may say with the poet,

'I thought upon my distant home,
The visions of my childhood came
Like fairy visons to my mind,
Of loved ones I had left behind;
A parent who saw me with tears,
Sisters who whispered of their fears,
And my heart's jewel, her last kiss,
I felt it now, in scenes like this.'

On the second day, the storm had sufficiently abated to admit of both hatchways being opened. With inexpressible joy did I behold the welcome light of Heaven. Nothing unless it had been the sight of land could have been more welcome. Our captain came again among us, ministering to our wants as far as lay in his power, giving medicine to one, and nourishment to another, (brought from the cabin). His generosity and unaffected humanity endeared him to the hearts of all on board. Captain Thompson, by being among the sick, had caught the fever, and died, and yet, notwithstanding this appalling fact, combined with the sight of the coffin over his roof, did this noble minded man fearlessly do the same, doomed, alas, to the same fate. But stay, let me not be too precipitate. 'Sufficient for the day is the evil thereof.'

At the end of this (the seventh) week, some of the passengers saw a great quantity of sea-weed floating on the ocean. The captain told us that it was a sure sign that we were near land, and assured us that we were in the gulf stream, and in about four days we should cast anchor. What transport of joy this imparted to all on board can be better imagined than described. Scarcely had the burst of joy, caused by this announcement subsided, before a rumor that Captain Connor had the ship-fever, ran among the passengers, causing a great panic. It was also said that if the captain died, or became delirious, there would be no one capable of taking command of the ship, as the second mate had not been to New York. I was very loth to believe these reports, but several passengers who had just seen and spoke to him, assured me it was too true. I could not get out of bed to go and see the captain, but the general alarm depicted in the countenance of the passengers, left me no room to doubt them. We had been kept in a continual state of excitement day after day, and week after week, and now, a prospect of a termination to this unfortunate voyage, and amelioration to my sufferings, came the long dreaded sickness of our second captain, an event which we had expected, but had hitherto been spared by a merciful God. I now gave myself up as lost; I was so weak that I could not raise myself up in bed. My eyes were dismal and sunken, and my bones seemed ready to burst through the skin. I could not take any of the nourishment that our humane captain sent to the sick.

In this state, I felt persuaded that the period for my dissolution had nearly arrived. The thoughts of my home, of my wife, of my child, of my father, of my sisters, was a source of great grief to me, but not so much as the dreadful anxiety I felt on account of my sins, which began to crowd upon my mind. Prepare to meet thy God is an injunction I had never obeyed.

'I never had my God address'd
In grateful praise, or humble prayer;
And if his word was not my jest,
(Dread thought) it never was my care.'—[Crabbe].[3]

The prospect of being thrown into the deep, the little flesh I had left to be devoured by sharks, my bones to be rising and sinking, suspended in mid-ocean, for ages, and on the judgment day, my soul to be cast into a deeper gulf, 'Where there is weeping, wailing, and gnashing of teeth,' 'Where the worm dieth not, and the fire is not quenched.' I essayed many times in a day to pray that God in mercy would spare my soul through the merits of a crucified Saviour. But alas, I felt that my prayers were rejected. My repentance of the sins I had committed through life was sincere; but that repentance I could not believe would avail me aught, because it was a death-bed repentance, and I felt as though my petition was rejected with scorn. To have felt a hope for mercy, to have felt my heart renewed, to have my Saviour's assurance that 'Thy sins, which are many, are all forgiven thee,' how gladly would I have given millions of worlds, had it been in my power. But I had no such cheering consolations to rob death of its terrors. The Scriptures assure me that 'The wicked shall be turned into hell.' (Ps. ix. 17.) 'Indignation and wrath, tribulation and anguish, upon every soul that doeth evil.' (Rom. ii. 8, 9.) The fate of my soul was thus revealed to me by the preceding quotations.

I was, as I believed, dying, and sent for Felix McQuade to come to me, (he often came to see and converse with me during my sickness). 'Felix,' said I, 'There is a favor I want you to do me. I feel my time is short. I do not think I shall live to see land, as for my wife and child, I am sure I shall not see them again. You are the only one on board from Manchester, (my native city). The favor that I want you to do is this: Take my pocket-book, in it you will find the residence of my wife, also the residence of my father and sisters; write to my wife, tell her I sent my dying love to her and my last request was that she would prepare to meet her

God, and bring up our child in the way she should go, that when she is old she will not depart from it. In my pocket-book you will find a few shillings, which is all I have except a few clothes in my box; you are welcome to them, only promise me solemnly that when you get in New York you will write to them. As a husband, as a man, I adjure you to do this favor for me.'

He promised me in the most solemn manner to perform this request if he lived to arrive in New York. He was recovering from a long sickness; he had been confined to his bed three weeks, and for several days he was considered delirious, and not expected to recover, but being one of the few who had a good stock of provisions, he, by giving some to a poor family, had every care and attention paid to him by them. It was fortunate for him that he had a little food to spare, otherwise I do not believe he would now be in the land of the living. But to return. From the time he promised to comply with my request, my mind was greatly relieved. He remained with me several hours every day. The fever had abated, but I was still unable to leave my bed: the hope of living till I should see land, and be buried on shore, again revived my spirits, for beyond that blessing I had no greater one to expect. The idea of being buried in the ocean I could not bear.

We were now in the eighth week of our voyage, and the prospect of seeing land in a few days caused great joy among all. Every day during this week, some of the passengers remained upon the fore-castle from daylight in the morning till dark in the evening, in hopes of seeing the long looked for land. About the middle of this week three men were seen by a sailor greedily eating the slush out of the slush-barrel. This occurred about midnight; the sailors sent them away, and next morning he told the ship-cook of it. The slush, it appears, is usually given to the cook as one of the perquisites of his office; it consists of all kinds of fat and greasy substances thrown into a barrel. This horrid stuff the sailor declared they eat with the greatest avidity. The captain, upon being informed of this, put a man to guard the barrel in the day time, and one to guard it during the night. Many of the half-starved wretched beings among us, envied them their good luck, as they called it, and would have been glad to have had this disgusting stuff given them to alleviate the pangs of hunger.

The day after this occurrence, Captain Connor came down among us for the last time, leaning upon the shoulders of two seamen. He visited every sick person—a task that eventually took him two hours to perform, having so many sick, as he had to stay a few moments with each person to ask questions and give medicine to them. He had not been able for a few days past to leave the cabin, and his visiting us the moment he was able, although still so weak that he could not walk without assistance, proved, if proof was needed, his determination to save as many of the lives of the passengers as lay in his power, if there was anything on board that he thought would be instrumental in doing so. As I have just said, I had not seen him for the last few days. What a change in that short time had taken place; pale, thin and exhausted, he had to rest many times before he could visit all the sick. Like myself, he was suffering from a violent dysentery as well as the ship-fever. When he reached my berth, he seemed somewhat surprised, and exclaimed.

WILLIAM SMITH, *AN EMIGRANT'S NARRATIVE*

'What, Smith! you alive yet!'

'Yes, sir,' said I, 'Thank God, I am, but I don't think I can live many days longer.'

'Don't be down-hearted about that,' said he, 'For I expect a pilot on board to-morrow, and you will soon be in Staten Island Hospital, where you will have good doctors to attend to you. I see the fever has left you, and if you live to land you will get cured of the dysentery, and perhaps outlive me.'

These were the last words he spoke to me, and alas, they proved too prophetic. I never saw him more, but I hope to meet him in the region of eternal bliss, where, I doubt not, he already is.

About nine o'clock next morning, the pilot came on board amid the huzzas of those who were able to shout for joy. Early in the afternoon, the exciting cry of 'Land!' 'Land!' 'Land!' ran through the ship like wild fire. A number of passengers came down from the deck to tell their sick relatives and friends that they had seen it, and yet such were my feelings, vacillating between hope and fear, that I could scarcely believe it. The effect it had upon the passengers, baffles all description. Some fell upon their knees and thanked God for his mercy to them, some wept for joy, others capered about, exhibiting extravagant demonstrations of joy. In a short time the anchor was let down, and we were visited by the Health Officer from Quarantine, who ordered all the sick to be brought into the hospital as quick as possible.

Thus was this disastrous voyage at an end, after an absence of exactly eight weeks from the shores of my native land, (the day we arrived at Staten Island being Friday, the 21st of January, 1848. My whole lifetime did not seem so long as the last two months appeared to me. When I was carried out of bed by two sailors, and brought upon deck and beheld the glorious sight of land, my feelings were indescribable. In the ecstacy of the moment I felt as if willing to die (if it was God's will) that instant. My prayer to be delivered from the monsters of the deep was granted, what more durst I ask? I felt my whole soul filled with a sense of gratitude to Almighty God for having preserved my life amid pestilence, famine, and the dangers of the sea. Such moments as these repay months of suffering. I anxiously looked on deck for Captain Connor, as I wished to bid him farewell, and thank him for the many acts of kindness I had experienced at his hands. Mr. Grey, the second mate, informed me that he was taken to the Mariner's Retreat, (a hospital on Staten Island expressly for seamen). Felix came and returned the articles I had given him on conditions before stated. He promised me that he would come to the hospital in a few days to see if I was living or not. But as I have not seen or heard of him since, I suppose he changed his mind, thinking it best to keep away from a hospital filled with persons afflicted with all kinds of contagious diseases, or, if he did come, he had not been admitted into it.

As the sailors were lifting me over the gangway, I cast a look upon the coffin, containing the remains of Captain Thompson, it was a mournful sight; he had told the cabin passengers that this should be his last voyage, and that when he arrived home [his residence was in St. John, New Brunswick] he would renounce a sea-faring life forever, and live upon land, in the bosom of his family. Alas, alas, he was fated never more to see them: his voyage of life was over, nought now remained but cold inanimate clay. Many were the tears of gratitude shed to his memory. Death had indeed been busy and relentless among us; already had we buried twenty-six at sea, and one hundred were taken into the hospital, many of them in a dying state. We were taken to the pier and then lifted into carts containing some straw, we lay extended upon it, and in that manner were conveyed into the hospital. Oh with what buoyant feelings of joy did I enter it. The thoughts that I should have plenty to eat and drink, and medicine to ease my bodily sufferings, a little nourishment to revive my exhausted frame, sent a thrill of joy to my heart, that none but those similarly situated can have an idea of. These are invaluable blessings under any circumstances, but to me, who had been deprived of them, lying prostrate upon a bed of sickness, surrounded by pestilence and famine, such blessings were indeed invaluable. Such were my thoughts and feelings upon being carried into that institution. Little did I think that new trials and sufferings awaited me, the continuance of which—for a lengthened period—would have made death preferable.

It was in the depth of winter when we landed at Staten Island, and upon reaching the sick room, I was immediately undressed, put into a hot bath, and then carried into what they called a bed. I had not been many minutes in it before I began to feel cold. The room was a very long one, containing a great number of beds; at one end of the room was a stove, the pipe attached to it extended to the other end for the purpose of heating it. The bed I was in being a long distance from the stove, and too far from the pipe to feel any heat from either, the feelings of coldness increased, till, in the course of half an hour, I was trembling violently, and notwithstanding every effort, I could not keep my teeth from striking each other.

The nurse asked me in a rough unfeeling manner, 'What the d—l are you making that moaning noise for?' I said I could not help it, that I was as cold as if I were freezing, and asked him to put me in a bed near to the stove. This he refused, saying he durst not without the doctor's leave. I earnestly entreated him to go and ask the doctor's permission: he did so, and returned with him. He gave me some medicine and ordered the nurse to carry me to one of the beds near the fire, where, in a short time, I felt much warmer, and enjoyed a refreshing sleep, from which I received much benefit and felt my spirits revived. Next morning I was so sore that I could not lie many minutes in one posture. I will explain the reason. The bed-posts were made of iron, with iron bars for the bottom, (similar to wooden laths). Upon these bars was put a coarse fabric, containing a little straw: this they called a bed. While lying upon it, I felt the bars almost as distinctly as though there was no bed under me. I was so thin that I was a mere living skeleton. In this state, being compelled to lie, as it were, upon iron bars, my sufferings were great from that cause alone. The nurse would not put more straw in the bed, although I begged of him many times to do so. I then mentioned it to the doctor when he came to visit me, but he hurried away without noticing my request. My clothes I could not get to put under me, as they were in the wardrobe, being unable to get out of bed and having to lie in it night and day, my sufferings may be easily imagined. In a few days I was removed into the recovery room, a room where convalescent persons are sent. Here my bed was the same as the one I had just left; the same doctor attended me, but being under the care of another nurse, (from such nurses and doctors deliver me,) I hoped to find him more humane than the other, but soon found myself in the hands of the most hard-hearted and cruel set of men it ever was, and I hope ever will be my lot to mingle with. When I was taken into the room my clothes were given me, and I kept out of bed as long as possible every day, in order to gather strength, and to avoid as much as possible the suffering attendant upon lying in such a bed; but when I felt exhausted, and unable to remain any longer out of bed, I undressed and put my clothes under me. The nurse happening to see me doing this, came and dragged me out, took my clothes from under me, threw them on the floor under the bed, and then, in the most savage manner, pushed me in the bed again. Other patients were treated in like manner for the same offense. The reader may exclaim,

'What offense! surely there is no law, human or divine, to prevent a man who was mere skin and bones from putting his clothes under him to keep him from lying on iron bars!'

To this I reply, true; but any trifle is an offense in the eyes of these avaricious villains, if you have no money to secure kind treatment, although they are in the receipt of regular salaries. If I were to give every instance of cruelty practiced upon the poor immigrants during my stay in that hospital, I might fill a volume; but it is impossible for me to remember a tenth part of what I saw there. Let one or two more instances suffice to show what kind of treatment we experienced: There were two rows of wooden benches, one on each side of the room; these benches are placed along the foot of the beds. Each patient is ordered to sit upon the bench which is close to the foot of his bed. My bed in this room was like the one in the sick room, a long distance from the fire. Every morning, before I could half dress myself, my hands and fingers became so cold that I could not finish dressing, and had to get any patient I could to do me the favor. As soon as we were dressed we were shivering with intense cold, while those whose bed was near to the stove were suffering equal hardships from the heat.

The moment the nurse and the overseer (as he was called) went out of the room, we would hurry to the stove to warm ourselves. Those who were too warm also gladly seized the opportunity to leave their seats. The instant that either the nurse or overseer was seen coming, we hurried to our seats again, and if either of them got to a patient before he reached his seat, he was sure to receive unmerciful treatment of some kind. By keeping a strict lookout I had hitherto managed to get to my seat in time to escape the ill usage of these villains; but it was my fate to receive a little of this treatment as well as others. We were as usual, around the stove, when one day the overseer came suddenly upon us by entering at one of the side-doors that led into the yard. This door being right opposite the stove, he got among us before half of us could get to our seats. I was the one nearest to him when he reached us; he seized me by the coat collar, dragged me to my seat, shaking me with all the vengeance of a demon; when he got me to my seat, he threw me upon it with such force that I fell with my back upon the iron rail at the foot of the bed, receiving a severe injury in the spine, from the effects of which, it was a long time before I was free, causing severe pains in my back upon the least exertion, and at one time I had every symptom of a rupture, which, however, to my great joy, gradually wore away in about two months.

A few days after this, a German was treated in the same brutal manner, for having dared to leave his seat to go and warm himself by the stove. He could not speak a word of the English language—he was about fifty years old, and his hair was beginning to whiten. He was decently attired, and his whole appearance convinced me that he had moved in respectable society in his own native land.

'Is it their object to kill or cure the patients?' was a question I asked myself more than once during my stay there. From the moment I entered the hospital to the time of leaving it, I saw no kind feelings, no generous actions shown to us, but on the contrary, every opportunity was taken by these miscreants to display their little brief authority. Our food, too, was of the most meager description, in the sick room the patients are allowed nothing but dry bread and what they called tea, which is little else than hot water and a little sugar in it. When I was removed into the recovery room, my food was the same, with the addition of a little flesh meat. Such was the nourishment given to men who, with famine and disease, were reduced to the verge of the grave.

The doctor's mode of visiting a patient appeared to me to be ridiculous. He came hurrying to a patient with a book in his hand; the instant he got to the patient he would ask him to put out his tongue, then ask him how he felt, and hurry off without waiting for an answer, or hearing anything the patient wished to say. Thus, from the doctor down to the lowest menial, the poor immigrant is treated with contempt and cruelty, which seemed to be the order of the day. This treatment is the more uncalled for, when the fact is borne in mind that this hospital is supported by immigrants, each one having to pay one dollar, which is charged to them in their fare. For instance, a ship arrives with four hundred immigrants and not one sent into the hospital, all being in good health. Here then, is four hundred dollars from that ship alone, without the immigrants putting the hospital to one cent of expense.

Another ship, like us, may be very unfortunate, and send a great many into the hospital, putting it to more expense than it receives from these immigrants, but the sum received from the other, more than counterbalances the loss by these; so that, if it is viewed in the light of dollars and cents, there is no justifiable reason for such treatment. When we left Liverpool we had three hundred immigrants on board, one half I am convinced, are now in their cold graves, beyond the cares of this world, and the inhumanity of their fellow men. Emaciated from long confinement within the narrow limits of a ship, disease, and all the horrors attendant upon the want of water and provisions, ought to have entitled us to their commiseration. But oh, how bitterly was I disappointed; little did I think that in this glorious land of freedom I should meet with such a reception under such circumstances. From my childhood upward, I had felt an increasing love for America—in political opinion I was always a thorough republican. How many happy hours had I spent in reading a history of the United States, and contemplating the circumstances which had given a Washington to the world; the noble devotion of Americans to the cause of liberty, their struggle with their tyrants in 1776, and the declaration of Independence, all were treasured up in my memory.

These were events unequaled in the world's history, and to which I was proud to refer, hoping they would prove a beacon to guide a downtrodden world to freedom and happiness. Such were my feelings and sentiments toward this country. Judge then, how galling to my feelings was the cruel treatment I received when I landed upon its hospitable shores, which, if I had not experienced, I could not have believed. In a country blessed with a free government, with a people possessing the highest order of intelligence, and in the highest state of civilization, the existence of such a system of heartless cruelty, perpetrated upon poor unoffending immigrants, and that too in the hour of sickness, and on the confines of eternity, may well indeed be doubted. But experience has taught me that neither the character nor the manners of a nation are to be judged by what may be found to exist in some of its institutions, particularly in a hospital. But at that time I had no other means of judging what kind of people the Americans were, than what I saw there. They were the first Americans I had ever seen, and I fell into the common error of blaming the many for the crimes of the few. But to return to my narrative.

Finding myself much better in health, and being able to walk without assistance, I determined to leave this place, and venture into New York, although unable to work and only a few shillings in my pocket, which would not last more than a week. What was to be my fate after that time, I knew not, but was willing to risk anything rather than remain here in worse than Egyptian bondage. I informed the doctor of my resolution to leave, and asked him for my discharge, my other clothes, and the little trifle in money that was put in his care at the time I entered the hospital. To this request he replied that he could not allow me to leave, as I was not in a fit state to do so, and that it would be several weeks before I should be able to leave. Saying this, he hurried off as usual. However, next day, I again requested my discharge, which, after some hesitation, he promised to do on the following day, as that was the day fixed for sending those who had recovered sufficiently, to New York. Next day, according to promise, I was discharged in company with about forty others, mostly Germans.

We were sent on board the *Cinderella* tow boat, which conveyed us to New York. Upon landing at the slip we were besieged by a number of carmen desirous to convey our boxes and baggage.

Not knowing where to go, and to avoid expense, I abandoned my box on the slip, taking out the chief contents, which I put into a bag, and then attempted to walk a short distance at a time, but was soon compelled to give up the idea of walking into the heart of the city, as I soon became so exhausted, a faintness came on me in spite of every effort to shake it off, and worse than all, had very little use or feeling in my limbs. Finding myself unable to walk, I sat down to reflect upon what course to pursue. While doing so, a girl passed by with a pitcher of water, from which I drank freely. Feeling somewhat revived by it, I again attempted to walk. I had not got more than twenty yards before I found it utterly impossible to proceed further. I sat down upon a stoop, where, in a short time my appearance attracted the attention of some children that were playing near me. They stood looking very earnestly, which caused several persons to stop and look at me, some of them asking me many questions. One of them took me to a boarding house, where, he told me, I could get lodgings. He also cautioned me not to say that I had had the ship-fever, for if I did, no one would give me a shelter in his house; I might say that I was ill with the dysentery, (which was true,) but by no means to admit that I had ever had the ship-fever. He assisted me until I reached the door, when I went in and inquired if he could accommodate me with lodgings, to which he replied in the affirmative. I remained with Mr. H—m about four days, when Mr. S—n—r, one of his transient boarders, took me to his home in Bloomfield, N. J., with the intention of keeping me for a month or six weeks to recover my health, and then if I was able, to work in his woolen factory. When we arrived at his residence he told his parents his intentions toward me, but they became so alarmed at my appearance that they said I must go back next day, declaring I should give all the family the ship-fever. I never saw persons so scared in my life, (except those on board the ship). They put the bag containing my clothes into the yard among the snow. I tried to reason with them, assuring them there could be no danger, as it was many weeks since I was seized with it. But it was no use to say anything to them, for they said my looks were enough to frighten anyone, and if their neighbors saw me, they would say I had just broke loose from the grave. The following day I was sent to the railway cars for the purpose of returning to New York. No sooner was I seated than several persons rose from their seats and retired to the other end of the car, keeping their eyes fixed on me till the cars stopped. When I left the cars I could not help giving vent to my feelings in a flood of tears, at the thoughts of my protracted sufferings, and being compelled to return to New York, with only a few cents in my possession. Little did I think that being sent on that day would prove the most fortunate event of my life, so little do we know of the ways of Providence. When I got on the ferry-boat at Jersey City, a gentleman came up to me and asked me if I had just left the cars. I told him I had, that I had been to Bloomfield, and was returning to New York. He told me that he saw me on the cars, but had lost sight of me in getting out, and that he had been seeking me, but could not find out which way I had gone, and was glad to meet me again, as he thought from my appearance I had suffered much from severe sickness, and stood in need of assistance. I then informed him of the chief events that had occurred during our voyage, our sufferings in the hospital, and my present pecuniary circumstances. He told me to give my whole heart entirely to that God by whose boundless mercy I had survived so many dreadful scenes and sufferings.

He then gave me pecuniary relief, and told me to call upon him at his residence in a day or two. He then left me, giving me a slip of paper, upon which was written, 'John Wilson, Attorney-street, New York.'

In a few days, Mr. H—m finding my money was nearly gone, told me my bed was occupied by another person, and he had no room for me. I left him, and went to find my late friend's residence, distant about a mile and a half, which took me nearly three hours to walk that distance. When I reached his house, I was almost benumbed with cold, but a cheerful fire soon had a genial influence upon me. A supper was soon prepared, and for the first time since I left England, I sat down to a comfortable meal. Everything bespoke neatness and order. After supper, everything was prepared for the following day, which was the first Sabbath I had been in New York. The command to keep the Sabbath holy, and to do no manner of work, was most religiously kept by this family, which consisted of my benefactor, his wife, her father, Mr. Maltbey, her brother and sister. After a prayer had been offered up to the throne of mercy on my behalf, I retired to rest upon a good bed – a luxury I had long been a stranger to.

In a short time I wrote to my wife, informing her of my arrival in New York, also informing her that I had been eight weeks at sea, and in consequence of sickness, had been in the Staten Island Hospital two weeks, also stating that I was still sick and unable to work, but that I had found a good home in the bosom of this family. I requested an immediate answer, as my benefactors were going upon a farm they had purchased, and I wished to receive the answer before I became again a wanderer upon the face of the earth. In that letter I carefully avoided saying much respecting the ship-fever, and still less concerning my sufferings, as I was well aware that to inform her of a hundreth part of what had befallen me, would be sufficient to cause the deepest anguish, not only to my wife, but to every member of the family. How often were my drooping spirits revived when I recollected that not one of them knew anything of what had occurred, except the little I had told them, which was as a drop in the ocean. Even to this good family I was equally cautious and reserved. The caution of the stranger while taking me to H—m, the fright of the S—n—r family, and the expectation that this family would pursue the same course toward me if they knew I had been afflicted by the ship-fever, kept my mind in a state of great anxiety.

But in this I was mistaken. They were the followers of [John Wesley] one who, while on earth, went about doing good, and, thank God, not one of them suffered a moment's sickness through taking me under their roof, although there was but little danger of that, yet few would be willing to risk it. But to return.

While I was congratulating myself at the supposed ignorance of my wife and relatives respecting the events of the voyage they were thrown into the deepest distress caused by a circumstance which I had not the remotest idea of. The reader will remember that Felix returned the pocket-book which contained the residence of my wife and relatives, and could not write to them. I had never seen him before I met him on the ship, immigrating to this country. He had resided a few years in Manchester, and knew a few of my acquaintances. When I became so sick that

I had no hope of recovery, it was natural that I should select him as the proper person to write and inform them of my fate, for I could not endure the idea that my wife should think I was living and had deserted her, and my child, when it grew up, to scorn its father's memory, while in fact I had sacrificed my life in attempting to better their condition. My father and sisters too would think of me as a villain unworthy of a moment's thought. These were my reasons for imploring him to write to them, and let them know the truth. When he arrived in the city of New York, he wrote back to his wife, informing her of the death of my bedfellow, and also that I was lying in the hospital so sick that long before that letter reached England I should be dead, and as she did not know my wife, she must send that information to the factory where I had worked for several years and was well known, and the news spreading among the workmen, my wife would hear of it. Mrs. McQuade did so, and the report had spread among so many that when my wife heard of it, and partially recovered from the shock which this news was calculated to produce, she could not trace the report to its author.

However, in a few days she saw Mrs. McQuade, (wives will surmount any difficulties to hear of absent husbands) who read to her that part of the letter just related. The distress this news caused among them may be easily conceived, particularly to my wife, who had buried her sister a few weeks before I left home, and in a fortnight after I left Liverpool had followed to the grave her last relative—her mother—whose dying prayer was offered up to God, beseeching him to bring me safe through the perils of the deep. The propriety of going in mourning as a mark of respect to my memory was spoken of, but my wife clung to the hope that I was not dead. Felix had not said I really was, but what he said concerning the voyage left little hope that I was living, and she felt assured that if such was the case, I would get some one to write and let her know it. But when days passed into weeks and no letter came from me, it was thought high time to pay the last tribute of respect to me. As they were about to do so, my wife received the letter I wrote, the chief contents of which I have already informed the reader. When the postman delivered it, although sealed with red, she had not power or courage to read it, but took it to my father, who instantly broke the seal, eager to know the best or worst. Oh, could I have seen my aged father with my letter in his hands, reading it to all the family; could I have seen them surrounding him and my wife, mingling their tears of joy together, and when he came to that part of it that stated I had for the present found a good home and was fast recovering my health, to have seen him unable to read farther for some time, the emotions of joy being too strong for him; what would I not have given to have been among them at that moment.

Such scenes may be seen and felt, but not described. While I was awaiting an answer to this letter, I was recruiting very fast. My limbs, of which I had nearly lost the use, were coming to a natural state of feeling, and in the course of a month, I felt as though I was able to do some light work, and, as I did not wish to be a burthen to these good people, proposed to go to Philadelphia to seek employment in the cotton factories.

This my benefactor strongly opposed, as my state of health and circumstances would not warrant my undertaking such a step. My friend Wilson advised me to remain with him until I got employment in the city, and said he would endeavor to procure me a situation by speaking to some of his friends in my behalf. I yielded to his request, and shortly after, he introduced me to Mr. W. H. P—w, who, upon learning a few particulars concerning my misfortunes, took me into his employ, and learned me the straw hat pressing trade, by which, in a few months, I was enabled to send for my wife and child, and had the inexpressible pleasure of seeing them arrive safe. Thus in five short months at this employment, I was again in possession of a domestic home. Such was the contrast in my condition and prospects in that short time, the result of falling into good hands. How true is it that the darkest hour is just before day. My friends have long since gone into the country upon their little farm, where my warm wishes for their happiness and prosperity follow them. I shall ever remember with gratitude, the disinterested anxiety he manifested in my future welfare, nor shall I forget the many cheerful hours I enjoyed beneath his hospitable roof, and trust I am not altogether wanting in gratitude to God for so many undeserved blessings. A few more words and I have done.

I had long felt an anxiety to know the fate of Captain Connor. I remembered hearing him say he had once lived on Staten Island. I went there a few weeks ago, (2d Oct. 1849) and inquired among the watermen if they knew him. A few of them instantly replied they did, but that he was dead, having died about two years ago, in the hospital called the Retreat. I told them that it was not so long ago as that, and that perhaps it was not the same man, and I asked them to describe him to me. They did so, and I was convinced that it was the same man. I was not ashamed to drop a tear to his memory. He had, like his noble commander before him, died a victim to his generous disposition, by venturing among the sick passengers.

I told them I was one of the unfortunate passengers, and having received many acts of kindness from him, had come to learn his fate. They told me a few anecdotes concerning him which it gratified me to hear. Two years have now elapsed, but the scenes I have witnessed, and the sufferings I have endured, are still as vivid in my memory as they were at the time of their occurrence. Never, while memory holds her empire, can I forget them.

Gentle reader, my humble narrative is told. 'Tis no more than hundreds of thousands who have left their native land, could tell; who, after exchanging the most painful adieus with their families and friends, the objects of their affections and solicitude, have relinquished all those social and domestic comforts which ever exist in the endearments of home, and all those feelings so dear to the human heart, have thrown themselves upon the trackless ocean, to meet a watery grave, or death in a foreign land, unknown, uncared for.

Reader, if you are an American, let your sympathy be extended to the honest immigrants, whom tyranny, overpopulation, and taxation has forced upon your shores, and may the star-spangled banner protect your noble institutions, and triumph over liberty's foes till time shall be no more. Adieu.

Notes

1 Robert Southey (1774–1843), an English Romantic poet and poet laureate (1813–1843).
2 John Ledyard (1751–1789), American explorer and adventurer.
3 George Crabbe, (1754–1832), an English poet, surgeon, and clergyman.

8

HENRY JOHNSON TO JANE JOHNSON, 18 SEPTEMBER 1848, IN L.WYATT (ED.), 'THE JOHNSON LETTERS', *ONTARIO HISTORY* (1948), PP. 7–52, ON PP. 34–38

Henry Johnson's (1820–1849) letter of 18 September 1848 to his wife Jane Johnson in Dungonnell, County Antrim offers a detailed account of the Irish Famine migration and of confessional tensions that emerged over the course of the voyage. The letter is extracted from a bound type script of emigrant letters from 26 May 1848 to 7 February 1888 of the McConnell family that was published by Louise Wyatt, ed. 'The Johnson Letters', *Ontario History* v. XI (1948), 7–52. According to Stephen Davison, 'Johnson left Ireland for Canada after being imprisoned for debt and his letters from to his wife describe his voyage to New York and his experience looking for work in Canada West. His account of the social and working conditions in southern Ontario is particularly vivid and detailed. Following her husband's urgent plea to join him in Canada, Jane left Ireland with their two children in 1849, but Henry died of cholera in Montreal, Quebec, before they could be reunited . . . The originals [of the letters] are held at the University of Western Ontario'.[1] Henry Johnson's death certificate, after he died from cholera in Montreal, was found in 1946, although an entry in a Family Bible noted the date of his death as 5 July. His death certificate is noted in the registry of Christ Church (Anglican) Montreal, as follows:

Henry Johnson died on the 4th day of July, one thousand eight hundred and forty nine, aged 29 years and was buried the same day by me.

Signed J. Ellegood, assistant minister.[2]

Hamilton Canada West, Sept. 18, 1848.

My dearest Jane,

Since I wrote a letter to you from Liverpool enclosing a gold Heart for Alex which I hope you received, I have had rather a rough time of it. I was a week in Liverpool before the ship sailed, which was on the 7th of July. We started with a fine fair breeze and got along well until the third day when it came on to blow very hard. I was lying in my berth sleeping when I was wakened with a cry and shouts of ship's lost the ship's sinking – I started up and such a sight: Men, women & children rushing to the upper deck. Some praying & crossing themselves others with faces as white as a corpse. On deck they were gathered like sheep in a pen crying on the Captain to save them. I asked some of them what was wrong but they were so frightened they couldn't speak. However I seen the sailors rushing down to the lower deck & I followed determined to know for myself and there sure enough the water was coming in through one of the portholes at the bow as thick as a large barrel. For a long time all the efforts of the sailors & two mates were unavailing to stop it and they gave it up in despair and came and told the Captain to lower the boats. He cursed them & told them to try it again but the first mate refused & told him to go to himself which he did telling the man at the helm at the same time to put the ship before the wind, a very dangerous experiment at the time as we were near rocks on the Irish coast. However, he went down & got it partially stopped which partly quieted the fears of the passengers although some of them didn't get over it until the end of the voyage. There re fur-five hundred on board all Roman Catholics with the exception of about forty protestants and a more Cowardly Set of hounds than the same papists I never seen. In the time of danger they would do nothing but sprinkle holy water, cry, pray, cross themselves and all sorts of Tomfoolery instead of giving a hand to pump the ship and then when the danger was over they would Carry on all sorts of wickedness and they are just the same any place you meet them at home or abroad. I took the matter cooly enough. I knew if we were to go down I might as well take it Kindly as not as crying wouldn't help me. Under this impression I enjoyed the Scene about me well. One old fellow Kept me laughing nearly the whole time at the way he was getting on. The very Senses were frightened out of him Cursing & praying in one breath. I got such a disgust at the party of papists at this Scene that I felt almost as if I could have submitted to go down if I had got them all with me. 'God forgive me.' We got all right again and went on our right Course. Up to this time I had not opened my provision box as it was lowered into the hold but when I did get at it I found the ham alive with maggots & was obliged to throw it overboard. The remainder of the stuff I eat as sparingly of as possible but Could not spin them out longer than four weeks at the end of which time I was obliged to subsist on the ship's allowance which was two pounds of meal or flour and five pounds of biscuit in the week. The pigs wouldn't eat the biscuit So that for the remainder of the passage I got a right good starving. There was not a Soul on board I knew or I might have got a little assistance 'but it was every man for himself'. Altogether it was nearly eight weeks from [the time when] we started from Liverpool untill we got to New York, the longest passage Captains Said ever he had. Six days before we got in a regular storm came on with nothing to this. We had some very hard gales before but this surpassed anything I ever thought of. Although there was some danger yet the wind being with us and going at the rate of 13 miles an hour through mountains of sea I enjoyed it well. In the Six days the Storm lasted we made more than we had done for Six weeks before. This was the pleasantest time I had although not for some others. One poor family in the next berth to me

HENRY JOHNSON TO JANE JOHNSON

whose father had been ill all the time of a bowell Complaint I thought great pity of. He died the first night of the storm and was laid outside of his berth. The ship began to roll and pitch dreadfully. After a while the boxes barrels etc began to roll from one side to the other, the men at the helm were thrown from the wheel, and the ship became almost unmanageable. All this time I was pitched right into the Corpse, the poor mother and two daughters were thrown on top of us, and there Corpse, boxes barrel women & children in all one mess were Knocked from side to side for about fifteen minutes. 'Pleasant that, wasn't it Jane Dear.'

Shortly after the ship got righted and the Captain came down we sowed the body up, took it on deck, and amid the raging of the storm he read the funeral Service for the dead and pitched him overboard. When I got into New York I eat too freely and the second day I took dysentery, a very Common Complaint here which lasted 14 days. I went to a doctor and he gave me a Small bottle told me to use with it a glass of burnt brandy three times a day. This I done but it still continued untill I was scarcely able to stand on my feet. I made application to get into the hospital but on account of a wrong name being on the ship's books they would not let me and were going to fine me into the bargain only I started off as fast as my legs would carry me. I stopped in New York about ten days and in that time made every exertion to get a situation of some kind. John McKillop, John Johnson, and another were on the look out every day but unless by accident I might remain there until doomsday & not get one. I told John McKillop I had a letter to a young man in this country and he advised me to start off direct as business was better and there wasn't the slightest chance in New York. Business is so very bad in it at present. I was very ready to take his advice as I felt me money slipping away from me very fast and I thought I would try the end of it rather than hang any longer on a mere chance. I got packed up & started for the place I had Bristow's letter for. I passed through a great variety of Scenery coming here & through a great deal of annoyance also. The space I have here will not allow me to describe it to you but I may have another opportunity Soon. When I came here I was very much disappointed to hear that the young man to whom I have the letter died in July last of a bowel complaint in two days sickness leaving his father & mother & sister entirely helpless. They had only come over a short time before entirely depending on him. If you have any opportunity of letting Bristow Know this send word to him. The young man's master is at present in New York and will not return for a week. When he does return I intend showing him Bristow's letter and making application to him myself either for a situation with himself or in some of the mills about here and I think very likely will get one. At any rate I intend to Settle down here in one Shape or another as I am tired of being tossed about such as I have been this long time and besides it is a great waste of money travelling. If you had a thousand eyes you couldn't watch the rascals that are on the way from New York to Canada unless you have been this way before. It is scarcely fair for the short time I have been in the Country to give an opinion upon it one way or the other; however as far as I have Observed the Country the people their Manners and Customs I will give it to you. In ten days travelling through the state of New York I came in contact with a good many characters of the Yankees and from New York to the Canada Shore I did not meet one that I Could like. They have no regard for religion, children have very little respect for their parents, and they Carry what they call the spirit of independence So far as even in their speech to defy God himself. The Canal boats carry on their trade on Sunday Same as another day. If you were dying they would Scarcely give you a cup of water without paying and for everything you do get they charge very high although the first cost price is very low. There are better and worse but any I came in Contact with are of this Stamp. Labour is very well paid but I don't know that some tradesmen wouldn't save much at home if they would take Care. The people of Canada are quite different. They are all Scotch and North of Ireland people, homely and civil in this part. When I came into it first I felt almost as if I was getting home again. It is most decidedly a better place to rear a family in than the States if you wish them to have any regard to religion or any respect for their parents. You must forgive me not writing to you immediately on landing as I promised to do as I wanted to be settled in Some place where you would Know where to write to me and also I did not wish to Send any word until I could Send Something encouraging to you as I am Sure My Dearest Jane, you would require Something by this time to keep your Spirits up. If I had got into a situation I intended sending some money with the letter but I hope you are not yet in want of any. I will write again immediately I get settled in any place so that you may Know where to direct your letter to as I am Sure by this time you must have a great deal of news to tell me. I hope you heard good news from Wm. McKeen & family & Isabella. Give my love to all your family & Kiss the two little children for me. You and them has never once been out of my mind and heart since I left you. I have been very anxious on your account and I do think if I had Known all I have suffered since on account of being Separated I would either have had you with Me in spite of everything or else remained and suffered the worst they Could do on Me but don't be discouraged Dear Jane. I am at present in right good health and determined to do all that lies in my power for you and if possible to redeem Some of the past errors of my life. I don't wish this letter to be shown. It is only for yourself as there are few others Care anything for Me. So I wish to be forgotten by them. God bless you!

I am as ever My Dear & beloved Jane

Your faithful & devoted Husband

For ever

Henry Johnson

P.S. I will be able in my next letter to give Some description of the Country. This I merely intend for yourself.

Notes

1 S. Davison (ed.), *Northern Ireland and Canada: A Guide to Northern Ireland Sources For The Study of Canadian History C.1705–1992* (Belfast: Queen's University Belfast and the Public Record Office of Northern Ireland, 1994), pp, 57–58.

2 Henry Johnson to Jane Johnson, 18 September 1848, in L.Wyatt (ed.), 'The Johnson Letters', *Ontario History* (1948), pp. 7–52, on p. 51.

9

JANE WHITE TO ELEANOR, 29 JUNE, 1849. PUBLIC RECORD OFFICE OF NORTHERN IRELAND. D.1195/3/5, 8B, 9–15

Jane White's letter from the quarantine station at Grosse Isle, Quebec to Eleanor Wallace on 29 June, 1849 is part of a collection of 17 letters between them from 1849–1860 held by the Public Record Office, Northern Ireland (D.1195/3/5, 8B, 9–15). According to Stephen Davison, Jane White's letters 'comment on a wide range of matters including: the voyage from Belfast, the quarantine station at Grosse Isle; the first impression of the country'.[1] Her correspondence is also reproduced in Cecil J. Houston and William J. Smyth's *Irish Emigration and Canadian Settlement: Patterns, Links, and Letters* (1990).[2] They observe that:

> Jane White was a proper young lady, an only child, suitably schooled in County Down in the late 1830s in the niceties and haughtiness of bourgeois respectability. She was eighteen when she waited with her parents for the medical examination at Grosse Isle emigration quarantine station. The family had left Ireland at the beginning of May 1849, toward the end of the Famine, 'the time of the potato rot' Jane called it, and they travelled in relative comfort as cabin passengers on the *Eliza Morrison* from Belfast. In their luggage was Jane's piano, and they were accompanied by a servant. The journey had taken eight weeks through gales and rough seas, but passengers and crews arrived safely and in generally good health. Their boat passed inspection, and Jane, instead of being isolated in quarantine – the lot of thousands of less fortunate people – was allowed to go ashore on Grosse Isle for a picnic and a ramble in the woods. She also found there the time and peace to write her first letter home to a friend, Eleanor, in Newtownards, County Down.[3]

I am glad to inform you that we are so far on, in our long tedious journey. We are anchored at Grose Isle about 36 miles below Quebec. It is an island in the St. Lawrence; the quarantine station is here and I assure you the passengers all feel very discontented at being kept here. We have been detained since our arrival on Saturday evening and it is now Wednesday. We have had fever and smallpox on board so that is the reason. The sick persons were taken on shore in a boat to the hospital. There are a great many sheds erected in the island that have been very useful for sick persons. There was a doctor here on Sunday from shore who examined the ship and was convinced there was not any sickness among the cabin or poop cabin passengers, which is a very great blessing for us. My Mama's health is pretty good. She was very very ill since we left home greatly owing to the extremely severe heaving of the ship. No one could have any idea of the inconvenience but those who have felt it. One is so tossed about and sometimes cannot keep on their feet. There are two families from Co. Antrim in the poop, besides ourselves. One room is boarded in so we are comfortable in that respect. There are two nice girls here who have kept me in company since I came here.

We have had many fearful days on our long voyage. It is eight weeks on Saturday last since we embarked in Belfast Lough. I could not describe to you all our perils, such fearful gales as we had, a constant succession of them I may say without erring much. One morning we had a narrow escape from being shipwrecked. There was a heavy gale set in from the northwest that carried away our bulwarks, cabin skylight etc . . . washing two of the sailors down the main hatchway and laying our ship for a short time under water nor was she ever expecting to rise. She did rise thank God and very shortly after we picked up the . . . crew of a schooner that the same gale had broken to pieces. She had her broadside actually driven in by the sea. Such gales are dreadful.

Our captain had been above 20 years at sea and confessed we had seen as much desperate weather as had seen in his time, but I should not tire you with too long a description.

A great number of ships have been lost in the ice here early in the spring. One was wrecked in the gulf of St. Lawrence here during the gales. It contained four hundred passengers who all perished except one child who picked up by a vessel passing the spot.

I can only say *Eliza Morrison* has been slow but sure. The weather is very warm. The scenery on the banks of the river is delightful especially at this season of the year, hill and valley and beautiful towns and villages slooping to the river's edge together with fertile islands, form the most beautiful landscape I ever saw. The houses are of wood and very white. The inhabitants are mostly of French descent and speak the French language. The Roman Catholic religion is established here.

I saw a very pretty steam boat on Sunday afternoon last which was St. John's Day. It came passed here on a pleasure excursion from Quebec, full of people gaily dressed. They stopped here and came past our ship. They were accompanied by a . . . band and played The Trubadour, Garry Owen and other tunes. It was a very handsome sight. The day was warm and the sun . . . bright but it showed a very bad respect for the Lord's Day. They are only to be excused on account of being Papists.

You would be surprised to see the number of brigs crowded here all full of emigrants from Britain trying their fortunes in America. We are all in good health thank God. I was scarcely sea sick at all but my mama was an Abigail was very sick the first week but is quite well now and has had the offer of two or three places already . . . Hope your dear mama is recovered. Tell her I will ever remember her kindness. Please give my kind love to her and to Miss Orr and if you see Miss Harriet Dobson please to tell her I am safe arrived here and please say I will write to her very shortly and give her my very kind love.

I hope I will soon be able to send you my direction and if there are any questions you wish to ask me about the voyage, do so. I am writing but in a confused manner but I hope you will excuse me as I merely snatched the opportunity to let you know I am safely landed at last.

The land is near. I was over in the island today and had a nice walk through the trees with my mama and dad and two young ladies. Their servant man came along with a basket so we had a sort of picnic.

Remember me to Miss Jane Gelston. Tell her I cannot give her much information about Canada yet but the time may come . . . My dear friend yours ever sincerely and affectionately.

Jane White.

Notes

1 Davison, *Northern Ireland and Canada*, p. 16.
2 C. J. Houston and W. J. Smyth, *Irish Emigration and Canadian Settlement: Patterns, Links, and Letters* (Toronto: University of Toronto Press, 1990), pp. 287–301.
3 Houston and Smyth, *Irish Emigration and Canadian Settlement*, p. 287.

10

SIR ROBERT GORE-BOOTH LETTERS (1846–1849), *APPENDIX X, MINUTES OF EVIDENCE BEFORE SELECT COMMITTEE ON COLONISATION FROM IRELAND, SUBMITTED BY SIR ROBERT GORE-BOOTH, BRITISH PARLIAMENTARY PAPERS, EMIGRATION, V 5,* PP. 122–132

Sir Robert Gore-Booth was landlord of Lissadell House, County Sligo, who assisted his tenants to emigrate in 1847 and then submitted some of their letters from Saint John, New Brunswick, to be published, along with the testimony of Stephen De Vere, by the House of Lords Select Committee on Colonisation from Ireland. Like his neighbouring Sligo landlord. Lord Palmerston, Gore-Booth has been accused of clearing his estate, but most of the historical evidence is exculpatory. Tyler Anbinder and Gerard Moran argue persuasively that he was a progressive landlord whose tenants fared much better than most during the Great Hunger.[1] Nevertheless, they faced considerable hardship and often perished during the Famine voyage and in Saint John, New Brunswick, as their letters attest, though they did not blame their landlord for their misfortune. Their letters are also written in the vernacular of the steerage class in contrast with most accounts of the Famine migration.

Letter from Patt and Cathorine McGowan, Saint John, N.B., to 'Brother Roger,' 25 December, 1847.
Brother Roger,
I take the Apertunity of sending yow Those few lines hoping to find yow all In as good health as this leaves us at preasit thanks be to god for his mercy towards us As for the time past I cannot tell yow the One half of my sickness and disease when I left Ierlad I never was stranger or in better Health until we were 15 days on ship Board Moly Mew died which lay in the bearth under mine and I took the fevour of her and bidy Conolly and also Cathorine Relly And Cathorine tom own,

neither of us was able To bring the other A drop of drink for nine days And Each of us was relapsed onely as tug dan would bring it to us and honour Mc Gowns Childrin I took the bowel complaint And Continued with me for 3 three weeks On the ship until we landed at the End Of five weeks and one day we passed the Inspector doctor for three days by the Enterference of The Captain and Mrs. Yates we had to go to qarrenteen Isilan to Ospital and I was given up by the doctor I passed blood trough me for Three days and the skin and flesh busted off My teeth and gave Blood on my mouth I was Attend by one docter murfy from County galway cured me in six days and also Betty By the assistance of god and was Annointed And Every day from that Back I was getting better After being five weeks on the Island I Came out to saint Johns and was warmly received By Andrew Kerigan who dyed of a fevour and buryed o the twenty second of this month and all the Neaburs and took Ahouse but could get nothing to do with my trade I went to Mr. John Robeson Merchant who is Joined in Merchandise with henery gore of greenack trough means Of my carractor from ser boothe gore gave me work But continued seven days until I took A second favour and could Not do one hands turn for Eight weeks I did not work but Eight days until the 1st day of december I Agreed with one James Murfy from waterford town for six months until June at fifteen pounds sterling and A Kitchen and Room and plenty fire wood direct your letter to Patt MGown cooper of the strait shore In care of Mr. Peter Rogan Portland street saint Johns new brumswick Roger if in case that you entend to Come out here Come early in spring And let me know aboutit firm contitucional men has from four to five shillings Each day 10s. and 6d. for your weeks boarding or 2s. for your bed and washing cooking I felt A great deal of pleasure in hearing About the reverent James Conolly How is all freends and neibours particularly those who reminded me Patt Conolly Gortnahowla Michael Ewny own Carlis M'morrow and frank danown It is sorowful to hear all of your neibours that died here which was already dear to us The Rate of flour 18s. and indea meal 10s. A hundred plinty of Earning until now Nomore at preasent but We Remain in good health.
PATT AND CATHORINE MCGOWAN.

Letter from Bryan Clancy and his sister, Saint John, N.B., to their mother and brother, 17 November 1847.
Dear mother and brother,
I take the favourable opportunity of writting these few lines to you hoping to find you are all in as good health as this laves me and my sister at present thanks be God for all his mercies to us Dear mother we were very uneasy for ever coming to this country for we were in a bad State of health During The Voiage their was a very bad fever aboard Pebby was taken to the Cabbin by the Captains wife and was there from we were a week on Sea till we came to quarentine and took the fever on the Ship then all the passengers that did not pass the Doctor was sent to the Isleand and She was kept by the Captains wife then on laving the ship.

Pebby was relapsed again and sent to Hospital and remained their nine or ten days but thanks be to God we got over all the Disorders belonging the Ship I was at work at A Dollar per day But the place got very bad and no regard for new passengers even a nights Lodgeing could be easy found I met with Andy Kerrigan and he took me with him to his house and remained their for amounth Boarding Mary took a very Bad fever and was Despaired of Both by priest and Doctor And as soon as She got well Andy took the Same disease I am Sorry to relate that poor Biddy Claney And Catharine McGowan Died in Hospital and A great many of our friends there is A prospect of the winter Been very bad and I offten wished to be a home again Bad and all as we were we offten wished we never Seen St. John

Dear Mother I hope you will Let me now as soon as possible how are you all my Sisters and poor Brother and all in good health it is all we are Sorry for that we cannot Send any relief to you But this place is Different to our opinions at home any new pasengers except the have friends before them are in Distress its very to get work here except them that are in Steady employment The goverment are about to Send all the passengers that were Sent out here by Lord Pamistown and Sir Robert Home again Because the the are sure that all of them that did not perish that the surely will this Winter Dear mother let us now how ye are getting on or are you all in good health I am very glad that Catharine did not come to this place for a great deal of our neighbours Died here I am Sorry to inform ye that James Connolly of Glaniff and wife Died and three children Thady Freely Died in hospital and Daniel Gallangher and wife of Coolagrapy and Roger McGowan of Drinaghan Patt Giblin and his Brother Domnick and I was very when I herd that Thady Giblin Died Let us now how is Mr. and Misses Likely and not Forgetting Baby Pebby Sends her love and Best respects them Let us now how is our neighbours Dan McGowan and Patt Connolly and family and also Patt Quin Let us now how is Honor Flanigan I am sorry to teel that a great deal of our Comrad passengers did in Hospital Mick Waters of Grange Died and James Gilmartin of Newtown We have a right To Return God thanks for his Mercy to us Let us now how does the markets Rate or is the publick works in force or any relief given Since we left that Country or is Fill or Mary in Service Thanks be to God I was not one hour Since I came to this Country but Pebby was a long time comeing round which gave me great trouble and uneasiness Bridget Conoly was given up and was in the quarentien Isleand Six weeks and her child Died in the Isleand A great many of the passengers went out to the country and could get no employ Bad as the City is it is better than the Country We expect to Spend the Winter here Patt McGowan and his wife and us is together and his wife works for the Shops at 2l. 5s. Amth The day I rote this Letter Peby got good Service at two Dollars A mounth if God Spares we we Soon be able to send some help to you and if either Boy or Girl had Had Any Sort of good Service it would Be Better than Here No more at present But remains your Loving and affectionate

BRYAN CLANCY AND SISTER.

When you write Direct your Letter To Thomas Camel Publican Portland Dear Mother and Brother Answer this as Soon as possible.

SIR ROBERT GORE-BOOTH LETTERS (1846–1849)

Letter from Ference McGowan, Saint John, N.B., to 'Father and Mother', 13 October, 1847.

Dear Father & Mother,

I take the Liberty of writing those few Lines to you hoping to find you in good Health as this Leaves me in at present thanks be to God I had good Health since I arived here and plenty of work You will have to Excuse me for not writing before now indeed it was neglect on my Part for not doing so I am very glad that you did not come out here it is better stop by the Land they are comeing here and dieing in Dozens their is not a vessal comes here but the feaver is on Board, write when you receive this and Let me know how the Family is and also all my Old neighbors, Catherine McGovan of Gurthnahowle died of feaver also Paddy McGowan of Drynahon Paddy Clanceys Daughter Biddy Frank McSharey's wife, Paddy McGowan of Gurthnahowle is Lyin ill of the Feaver, Lit Molly McGowan know that Denis O'Donnell & Wife are well, I stop with them and Margaret went to Boston the day Before Landed here their is no account from her as yet Let me know how the times are at home and how the markets rate and if the crops are good. Let none of you attempt to come here this season as there are so many here and the Feaver is in every House almost It is a good place for young people but there are Enough at present until next summer, tell Andey McSharry he would do Better here than at home Let come next Summer the People are Lying out here on the shores under sheads and going to the grave numbers of them every day. Let Paddey Connoley know that his Son & Daughter are in good health I intend to go to the states in Springs if I dont Change my mind.

Markets rate as follows Potatoes 1s.3d. p stone Butter 1s. 3d. p Pound flower for 196 Pounds 35 shillings Eggs 8d. Write Imedeately and direct to the care of John Koen Portland Bridge st.John NB., for me.

P.S. Biddy McSharrey is in good Health. Frank McSharrey and Family are getting well of Feaver. Larry Runian and wife are on the Iland and sister ill of feaver. Mrs. Dolan Connor and familey are well the Husband is in the states.

No more at Present But remains

Your Son truly

FERENCE MCGOWAN.

Letter from Catherine Hennagan, Saint John, N.B., to her mother and father, 15 February, 1848.

Dear Father & Mother.

I take the present opportunity of letting you know that I am in good health hoping this will find you and all friends in the same. I wrote you shortly after I came here but recevid no answer which makes me very uneasy untill I hear from you and how you are and all friends. Dear Father we had a pretty favourable passage we Cast Anchor at Partridge Island after 5 weeks passage there were 4 Deaths on the passage but the Second day after we arrived here and after the Doctor came on Board the Sickness commenced we were then put on the Island for 3 Weeks at the end of which time my dear Litle Biddy died thank God I got safe off and continues to enjoy good health since Dear Father Pen could not write the distress of the Irish Passengers which arrived here thro Sickness death and distress of every Kind the Irish I know have suffered much and is still suffering but the Situation of them here even the Survivors at that awful time was lamentable in the extreme there are thousands of them buried on the Island and those who could not go to the States are in the Poorhouse or begging thro the Streets of St John, let me know how James Burns and Sister are and let me know how John Burns is, and Biddy Kelly and family I am living 10 miles from St John Churchland when you write direct the Care of the Revd Edmund Quin C.C. forwarded to Neal Quin Church Land St. John N.B. If you would wish to come here I would like you was here as I think times will mend here after some time and dear Father I will soon send you some help let me know if Catherine Bradley Mary McGowan and Mary Kinloghlan wrote home as I do not know where they went to or where they are. Milk and Butter is very dear here 4d. per quart and 15d. per lb. I went to the country with my uncle but he went off to the States since let uncle Paddy know that Thos. went to Boston with his uncle Thos. got a place for the Boys in Boston Biddy's two Sons do not neglect but write as soon as you can as I will be uneasy untill I hear from you.

No more at Present But remains your affectionate Daughter till Death,
CATHERINE HENNAGAN.

Letter from Owen and Honr. Henigan, Hallowell State of Maine, to their son, 17 March, 1848.

Dear Son,

We Take this Favourable opertunity of writing these few lines hoping to Find ye in as good a State of health as the writing of this letter leaves us in at present thanks be to God for his mercies to us. Dear Son we wish to Let you know how we are geting on in this Country since we left miserable St Johns it is allmost as bad as Ireland we are getting on very well since we Came to the State of Maine Peter and Thomas is Geting on well Peter sent us as much money to us as suported in Saints Johns and paid our passage on the Coach five Hundreds and had a good house for us and the rent of it paid untill Sumer he had two barrells of flour one barrell of beef and fire wood and has three pounds Sterling to you and that is only a Token of our love to you we will send of the first of the month and it is only now itself we are begining to do to our likeing and after the frost and snow is over we will be Able to Send you Some thing that will be worth naming it would be our wish that you would Come out here but you may do as you please and do not for get John and we will not for get you after a little my Father and Mother Sends their Love and best Respects to you and to Nelly for her Kindness to their children and their best Respects to your Mother and Brothrs in Law my mother sends her best respects to her only Brother and family Molly Healy and family is well in saints Johns Molly Scanlon is well Let john Cristol know that at the time we were in Boston his Doughter hired with a farmer we can give no further Acount of her Let John Hennigans Doughter is hired out in the Country from Saint John Let

Paday Hennigan know that his Son Tomy is here and Left John Hark in Boston with Michl Mc Loughnin that lived Between Carney and Oxfield in Ireland and has Patt out here in a farmers house and the Legacy was let run to Long we could Not recover it after it was let run 21 years we are as happy as the day is Long we have as much of our own Country pole here Let Edward Hennigan of Patch know that if he was here it would be better for him there is Some trouble betwixt Irish folks here you need not send Now Answer for this Leter But be on the Look out for the next Letter we will send it on the first of the next month and there will be some money in it.

No more at pressent, but here remains your Affectionate Parents

OWEN AND HONR. HENIGAN

Till Death.

Note

1 T. Anbinder, 'Lord Palmerston and the Irish Famine Emigration', *Historical Journal*, 44.2 (2001), pp. 441–469, on pp. 450–51; G. Moran, *Sir Robert Gore-Booth and His Landed Estate in County Sligo, 1814–1876* (Dublin: Four Courts, 2006).

11

HENRY DAVID THOREAU, *THE SHIPWRECK, PUTNAM'S MONTHLY* 5.30 (1855), PP. 632–637

Henry David Thoreau (1817–1862) is one of the best known American romantic or transcendentalist authors, who is most famous for *Walden; or, Life in the Woods* (1854). In his essay *'The Shipwreck'*, published the following year, Thoreau reacts to the wreck of the brig *St. John*, which had sailed from Galway on 7 September, 1849 bound for Boston, but foundered on the rocks in Cohasset Bay, Massachusetts, on 7 October, with over a hundred fatalities.

We left Concord, Massachusetts, on Tuesday, October 9th, 1849. On reaching Boston, we found that the Provincetown steamer, which should have got in the day before, had not yet arrived, on account of a violent storm; and, as we noticed in the streets a handbill headed, 'Death! one hundred and forty-five lives lost at Cohasset,' we decided to go by way of Cohasset. We found many Irish in the cars, going to identify bodies and to sympathize with the survivors, and also to attend the funeral which was to take place in the afternoon;— and when we arrived at Cohasset, it appeared that nearly all the passengers were bound for the beach, which was about a mile distant, and many other persons were flocking in from the neighbouring country. There were several hundreds of them streaming off over Cohasset common in that direction, some on foot and some in wagons,—and among them were some sportsmen in their hunting-jackets, with their guns, and game-bags, and dogs. As we passed the graveyard we saw a large hole, like a cellar, freshly dug there, and, just before reaching the shore, by a pleasantly winding and rocky road, we met several hay-riggings and farm-wagons coming away toward the meeting-house, each loaded with three large, rough deal boxes. We did not need to ask what was in them. The owners of the wagons were made the undertakers. Many horses in carriages were fastened to the fences near the shore, and, for a mile or more, up and down, the beach was covered with people looking out for bodies, and examining the fragments of the wreck. There was a small island called Brook Island, with a hut on it, lying just off the shore. This is said to be the rockiest shore in Massachusetts, from Nantasket to Scituate,—hard sienitic rocks, which the waves have laid bare, but have not been able to crumble. It has been the scene of many a shipwreck.

The brig *St. John*, from Galway, Ireland, laden with emigrants, was wrecked on Sunday morning; it was now Tuesday morning, and the sea was still breaking violently on the rocks. There were eighteen or twenty of the same large boxes that I have mentioned, lying on a green hillside, a few rods from the water, and surrounded by a crowd. The bodies which had been recovered, twenty-seven or eight in all, had been collected there. Some were rapidly nailing down the lids, others were carting the boxes away, and others were lifting the lids, which were yet loose, and peeping under the cloths, for each body, with such rags as still adhered to it, was covered loosely with a white sheet. I witnessed no signs of grief, but there was a sober dispatch of business which was affecting. One man was seeking to identify a particular body, and one undertaker or carpenter was calling to another to know in what box a certain child was put. I saw many marble feet and matted heads as the cloths were raised, and one livid, swollen, and mangled body of a drowned girl,—who probably had intended to go out to service in some American family,—to which some rags still adhered, with a string, half concealed by the flesh, about its swollen neck; the coiled-up wreck of a human hulk, gashed by the rocks or fishes, so that the bone and muscle were exposed, but quite bloodless,—merely red and white,—with wide-open and staring eyes, yet lustreless, dead-lights; or like the cabin windows of a stranded vessel, filled with sand. Sometimes there were two or more children, or a parent and child, in the same box, and on the lid would perhaps be written with red chalk, 'Bridget such-a-one, and sister's child.' The surrounding sward was covered with bits of sails and clothing. I have since heard, from one who lives by this beach, that a woman who had come over before, but had left her infant behind for her sister to bring, came and looked into these boxes and saw in one,—probably the same whose superscription I have quoted,—her child in her sister's arms, as if the sister had meant to be found thus; and within three days after, the mother died from the effect of that sight.

We turned from this and walked along the rocky shore. In the first cove were strewn what seemed the fragments of a vessel, in small pieces mixed with sand and sea-weed, and great quantities of feathers; but it looked so old and rusty, that I at first took it to be some old wreck which had lain there many years. I even thought of Captain Kidd,[1] and that the feathers were those which sea-fowl had cast there; and perhaps there might be some tradition about it in the neighbourhood. I asked a sailor if that was the *St. John*. He said it was. I asked him where she struck. He pointed to a rock in front of us, a mile from the shore, called the Grampus Rock, and added:

'You can see a part of her now sticking up; it looks like a small boat.'

I saw it. It was thought to be held by the chain-cables and the anchors.

I asked if the bodies which I saw were all that were drowned.

'Not a quarter of them,' said he.

'Where are the rest?'

'Most of them right underneath that piece you see.'

It appeared to us that there was enough rubbish to make the wreck of a large vessel in this cove alone, and that it would take many days to cart it off. It was several feet deep, and here and there was a bonnet or a jacket on it. In the very midst of the crowd about this wreck, there were men with carts busily collecting the sea-weed which the storm had cast up, and conveying it beyond the reach of the tide, though they were often obliged to separate fragments of clothing from it, and they might at any moment have found a human body under it. Drown who might, they did not forget that this weed was a valuable manure. This shipwreck had not produced a visible vibration in the fabric of society.

About a mile south we could see, rising above the rocks, the masts of the British brig which the *St. John* had endeavoured to follow, which had slipped her cables and, by good luck, run into the mouth of Cohasset Harbor. A little further along the shore we saw a man's clothes on a rock; further, a woman's scarf, a gown, a straw bonnet, the brig's caboose, and one of her masts high and dry, broken into several pieces. In another rocky cove, several rods from the water, and behind rocks twenty feet high, lay a part of one side of the vessel, still hanging together. It was, perhaps, forty feet long, by fourteen wide. I was even more surprised at the power of the waves, exhibited on this shattered fragment, than I had been at the sight of the smaller fragments before. The largest timbers and iron braces were broken superfluously, and I saw that no material could withstand the power of the waves; that iron must go to pieces in such a case, and an iron vessel would be cracked up like an egg-shell on the rocks. Some of these timbers, however, were so rotten that I could almost thrust my umbrella through them. They told us that some were saved on this piece, and also showed where the sea had heaved it into this cove, which was now dry. When I saw where it had come in, and in what condition, I wondered that any had been saved on it. A little further on a crowd of men was collected around the mate of the *St. John*, who was telling his story. He was a slim-looking youth, who spoke of the captain as the master, and seemed a little excited. He was saying that when they jumped into the boat, she filled, and, the vessel lurching, the weight of the water in the boat caused the painter to break, and so they were separated. Whereat one man came away, saying:—

'Well, I don't see but he tells a straight story enough. You see, the weight of the water in the boat broke the painter. A boat full of water is very heavy,' – and so on, in a loud and impertinently earnest tone, as if he had a bet depending on it, but had no humane interest in the matter.

Another, a large man, stood nearby upon a rock, gazing into the sea, and chewing large quids of tobacco, as if that habit were forever confirmed with him.

'Come,' says another to his companion, 'Let's be off. We've seen the whole of it. It's no use to stay to the funeral.'

Further, we saw one standing upon a rock, who, we were told, was one that was saved. He was a sober-looking man, dressed in a jacket and gray pantaloons, with his hands in the pockets. I asked him a few questions, which he answered; but he seemed unwilling to talk about it, and soon walked away. By his side stood one of the life-boatmen, in an oil-cloth jacket, who told us how they went to the relief of the British brig, thinking that the boat of the *St. John*, which they passed on the way, held all her crew,—for the waves prevented their seeing those who were on the vessel, though they might have saved some had they known there were any there. A little further was the flag of the *St. John* spread on a rock to dry, and held down by stones at the corners. This frail, but essential and significant portion of the vessel, which had so long been the sport of the winds, was sure to reach the shore. There were one or two houses visible from these rocks, in which were some of the survivors recovering from the shock which their bodies and minds had sustained. One was not expected to live.

We kept on down the shore as far as a promontory called Whitehead, that we might see more of the Cohasset Rocks. In a little cove, within half a mile, there were an old man and his son collecting, with their team, the sea-weed which that fatal storm had cast up, as serenely employed as if there had never been a wreck in the world, though they were within sight of the Grampus Rock, on which the *St. John* had struck. The old man had heard that there was a wreck, and knew most of the particulars, but he said that he had not been up there since it happened. It was the wrecked weed that concerned him most, rock-weed, kelp, and sea-weed, as he named them, which he carted to his barn-yard; and those bodies were to him but other weeds which the tide cast up, but which were of no use to him. We afterwards came to the life-boat in its harbor, waiting for another emergency,—and in the afternoon we saw the funeral procession at a distance, at the head of which walked the captain with the other survivors.

On the whole, it was not so impressive a scene as I might have expected. If I had found one body cast upon the beach in some lonely place, it would have affected me more. I sympathized rather with the winds and waves, as if to toss and mangle these poor human bodies was the order of the day. If this was the law of Nature, why waste any time in awe or pity? If the last day were come, we should not think so much about the separation of friends or the blighted prospects of individuals. I saw that corpses might be multiplied, as on the field of battle, till they no longer affected us in any degree, as exceptions to the common lot of humanity. Take all the graveyards together, they are always the majority. It is the individual and private that demands our sympathy. A man can attend but one funeral in the course of his life, can behold but one corpse. Yet I saw that the inhabitants of the shore would be not a little affected by this event. They would watch there many days and nights for the sea to give up its dead, and their imaginations and sympathies would supply the place of mourners far away, who as yet knew not of the wreck. Many days after this, something white was seen floating on the water by one who was sauntering on the beach. It was approached in a boat, and found to be the body of a woman, which had risen in an upright position, whose white cap was blown back with the wind. I saw that the beauty of the shore itself was wrecked for many a lonely walker there, until he could perceive, at last, how its beauty was enhanced by wrecks like this, and it acquired thus a rarer and sublimer beauty still.

Why care for these dead bodies? They really have no friends but the worms or fishes. Their owners were coming to the New World, as Columbus and the

Pilgrims did,—they were within a mile of its shores; but, before they could reach it, they emigrated to a newer world than ever Columbus dreamed of, yet one of whose existence we believe that there is far more universal and convincing evidence—though it has not yet been discovered by science—than Columbus had of this; not merely mariners' tales and some paltry drift-wood and sea-weed, but a continual drift and instinct to all our shores. I saw their empty hulks that came to land; but they themselves, meanwhile, were cast upon some shore yet further west, toward which we are all tending, and which we shall reach at last, it may be through storm and darkness, as they did. No doubt, we have reason to thank God that they have not been 'Shipwrecked into life again.' The mariner who makes the safest port in Heaven, perchance, seems to his friends on earth to be shipwrecked, for they deem Boston Harbor the better place; though perhaps invisible to them, a skilful pilot comes to meet him, and the fairest and balmiest gales blow off that coast, his good ship makes the land in halcyon days, and he kisses the shore in rapture there, while his old hulk tosses in the surf here. It is hard to part with one's body, but, no doubt, it is easy enough to do without it when once it is gone. All their plans and hopes burst like a bubble! Infants by the score dashed on the rocks by the enraged Atlantic Ocean! No, no! If the *St. John* did not make her port here, she has been telegraphed there. The strongest wind cannot stagger a Spirit; it is a Spirit's breath. A just man's purpose cannot be split on any Grampus or material rock, but itself will split rocks till it succeeds.

Note

1 William Kidd (1645–1701), a Scottish sailor executed for piracy in 1701.

Part II

EYEWITNESS TESTIMONIES
Famine Irish Caregivers

The second part of *Irish Famine Migration Narratives* comprises eyewitness testimonies of those who cared for Famine emigrants and Irish orphans, especially French-Canadian female religious such as the Grey Nuns and Sisters of Providence in the fever sheds of Montreal. The most compelling, continuous, and detailed accounts can be found in the annals of the Sisters of Charity, or Grey Nuns, which are little known because they were unpublished and written in French. They were not digitized, transcribed and translated until 2012,[1] and appear in print in this book for the first time. The Grey Nuns kept three sets of annals, based on earlier records, about their experiences of caring for Famine emigrants in the summer of 1847 and 1848. They are held in Archival Services and Collections, Maison de Mère d'Youville, Sisters of Charity of Montreal, 'Grey Nuns', and are internally classified as follows: *Ancien Journal*, vol. I, 1847, 491–515; *Ancien Journal*, vol. II; *Le Typhus de 1847*, 319–510; and (not yet translated into English, or included here) *La terrible épidémie de 1847*', 1–150. The Grey Nuns also wrote an account of the *Foundation of St Patrick's Orphan Asylum* for Famine emigrants that is also published here for the first time. Their annals are supplemented with Protestant female charitable writing to support Famine Irish emigrants in the form of the anonymously published *The Emigrant Ship. Written for the Protestant Orphan Bazaar* (1850).

Note

1 See Jason King (ed.), Irish Famine Archive, http://faminearchive.nuigalway.ie.

12

GREY NUNS, OR SISTERS OF CHARITY, FAMINE ANNAL, *ANCIEN JOURNAL*, VOL. I. TRANSLATED BY JEAN-FRANÇOIS BERNARD

TYPHUS EPISODE (1847)

There has been an extraordinary emigration this year, the likes of which had never been seen. During the voyage, an outbreak of the plague declared itself in all the vessels carrying the poor Irish to Canada, so that upon arriving at GROSSE ILE where they were to be quarantined, a great number of plague victims died upon exiting the vessels, in addition to those that had been dumped at sea during the voyage. Those that had not yet been struck down by the sickness were sent to Montreal where hundreds of them would arrive every day. The pestilential disease, of which they carried the seed, usually manifested itself on the way, so that when they did arrive here, they were as sick as those that had remained on GROSSE ILE.

On June Seventh (7), our mother Superior[1] heard that there were a great number of sick people lying outdoors along the pier and that they found themselves in the saddest of shape. Before undertaking anything for their relief, she went to the SEMINARY to consult Mister Superior. Mister Superior being on the Mountain, our mother came back without having seen him. Later on the day, the Venerable M. JOHN RICHARDS, P.S.S.,[2] came to the Order accompanied by M. Connolly,[3] to ask for the sister's assistance with these unfortunates. At that moment, our mother superior, who was only waiting on the permission and approbation of the good Fathers of the Seminary to go help these unfortunates, left with sister St Croix for the Emigrants' Office to obtain the AGENT OF GOVERNMENT'S consent so as to be able to act more freely. The Office's gentlemen welcomed them very politely: they were granted full liberties to act as best they could. They authorized them to hire men and women to help them in the burdensome TASK they were to undertake. Our Mother was not surprised by the gracious welcome she had received when she learned that the venerable M. John Richards (Jean Richard) had preceded her. This good father, seeing that the Office's gentlemen were somewhat embarrassed by the great number of sick individuals that came in endlessly, and did not know how to provide them with the care that their state imperiously required, had suggested that they ask the SISTERS OF CHARITY to care for the sick. MISTER THE INTENDANT, a Protestant, welcomed the suggestion of M. John Richards (Jean Richard), for whom all these gentlemen had a singular veneration, most graciously; but they apparently did not know where to go to find the sisters that M. Richard had mentioned; great was his joy when he saw us come in to offer our services.

Our Mother was immediately led by an employee of the office to the main hospital (if we can give it that name). GOOD GOD! What a spectacle. Hundreds of people, most of them lying naked on planks haphazardly, men, women and children, sick, moribund and cadavers; all of this confusion hit the eyes at once. Our Mother there met MISTER THE SUPERIOR of the Seminary as well as the good M. MORGAN[4] who, at the moment, was occupied trying to lift from the ground a sick person who was choked up by his own vomiting in order to place him on a near-by cot.

Our Mother and my sister St Croix,[5] their hearts broken by the spectacle they had just beheld, headed back to the Order incapable of rendering all the horror that the sight of these infected emigrants, recalling a vast tomb, has inspired in them.

On the eve of that same day, after dinner, our Mother, after having depicted the deplorable state of these unfortunates, called upon the Order to help them since she did not wish to force anyone to do so. She did not need to do so more than once, since our dear sisters came in large numbers and put themselves at the service of our Mother to be sent there, when she would deem it fit.

JUNE 9 1847.- Consequently, on JUNE 9, EIGHT (8) of our sisters, accompanied by FIVE (5) hired women to assist them, made their way to the SHEDS and began on this day their strenuous function. However, the number of sisters was far from sufficient, as new ones would go every day, so much so that on Sunday, the 13th of the month, we found ourselves TWENTY-THREE (23) caring for the plague victims.

The number of hired, men and women, did not suffice since every day, due to the great number of incoming sick people, new sheds had to be erected, and we came eventually to have EIGHTEEN (18) of them. We think it suitable and of the highest order, to come to an agreement with the gentlemen of the OFFICE regarding the price we would offer them before increasing the number of hires so as to avoid the intrusion of any suspicious character, our MOTHER SUPERIOR alone is authorized to HIRE or FIRE employees. These gentlemen willingly granted what our Mother requested. A wage was established. Our Mother, overloaded with tasks, immediately designated a Sister whose primary occupation would be to monitor employees' conduct, to keep the books for each of them; when it was time to get paid, they would come to the Office with a note from the Sister and were immediately paid. The Sisters enjoyed a considerable influence upon the AGENTS of the Government. They obtained all they requested for the sick from the Office.

Each Sister held her post and supervised exclusively the department that our Mother had given her. She had the necessary men and women to assist her.

The government simultaneously had SOUP prepared and distributed it to emigrants and convalescents, per its order. Only Priests, Sisters and Doctors could provide emigrants with tickets required to receive this help.

After having cared for the plague victims all day, the Sisters headed back to the Order in the evening, leaving behind them trustworthy individuals that were paid to watch through the night.

In the evening, upon their arrival at the Order, the Sisters changed their habits in one of the hangars. In the morning, we would reprise the habits we had cast off the previous day.

The situation was different for our good fathers of the Seminary who, after having breathed the sheds' pestiferous air all day, usually remained by the sick at night. The good M. PIERRE RICHARD[6] spent many nights acting as a nurse, especially in the first few days, where the service had yet to be organized. When we came in in the morning to begin the day, we would encounter him in a shed, M. CAROFF[7] in another, pale and exhausted from the previous night's work; yet calm and sweet merriment always upon their faces. The angelic behaviour of those two saintly priests while we were with them at the sheds will never be erased from our memory, and the examples of all the virtue they gave greatly contributed to our courage in lieu of the most lamentable of disasters to be seen.

Additionally, in order to go from one shed to the other, we had to cross the area that separated them, often with mud up to our knees, sometime under heavy rainfall; several days in a row . . . One day, one of our sisters who was making her way to a more remote shed, decided, so as to not get stuck in the mud, to climb up on the hill that bordered the shore. As she was painstakingly making her way, a great gust of wind toppled her over and made her tumble to the bottom of the hill. It is unnecessary to relate in detail the state in which she found herself. Scenes of this nature occurred often, but our good Lord gave us the strength and the courage to bear all of this gaily. In fact, as we had mentioned before, the example of our dear Fathers supported us and the works of encouragement that they mercifully addressed us whenever the occasion presented itself, singularly excited our devotion. One day, one of our sisters, drenched by the rain, and covered with mud, encountered, while crossing the courtyard, M. PIERRE RICHARD who himself was not in his best state. Since the rain was falling heavily at that moment, this SISTER said to him: 'Father, what awful weather, will this rain last forever?' . . . 'Eh! Sister,' he answered kindly with his usual tranquillity, 'these are but pearls that are falling. Let us not let them get lost' . . .

What transpired at the SHEDS where the plague victims lodged was soon known throughout the town; while they had no desire, to frequent these infected sites, several people sent sweets for the sick. The Sisters of the congregation were not the last to display their generosity for the relief of the unfortunate. The commiseration for the poor victims of this tragedy was so wide, that even soldiers deprived themselves of part of their rations and came to deliver them AT THE GATES every day, without fear of contracting the contagion.

EYEWITNESS TESTIMONIES

Words are lacking to express the hideous state in which the sick found themselves, up to three of them in the same bed, or cots to be more exact, that had been hastily fashioned and gave the impression that they were caskets. When touring the SHEDS, we would find cadavers exhaling an insufferable infection, lying in the same bed as those that still breathed; the number of sick was so considerable, that we at some point counted ELEVEN HUNDERD (1100) of them, some of whom had been dead for a few hours before we had noticed. One day, a Sister, passing one of those sheds, saw a poor afflicted that appeared restless; she came near his cot and saw that he was attempting to push off two dead bodies between which he was lying down. In spite of the delirium that deprived him of some of his faculties, the sight of those cadavers, one black as coal, the other, in contrast, yellow like saffron, caused him such fright that it momentarily brought him back to his senses; once delivered from his two companions, he fell back in his previous state of insensibility, and the next day, it was his turn to join the ranks of the dead . . . we could cite a thousand traits of this kind; but it is impossible to report all of them. Before we could build a hangar to store the dead bodies as the sick expired, we would take them outside of the sheds and the bodies would be left in the open air on planks prepared to that effect in a courtyard, and since the CEMETERY was some distance from here, we waited until there was a sufficient number to fill up the cart that conveyed them to the tomb. What a spectacle when entering the courtyard, to see on one side all these inanimate CORPSES, and on the other all the caskets ready to receive them. . .

One day came a man from GROSSE ILE, where he had remained upon his arrival, being too sick to be transported to Montreal, where his wife, who was in good health, was sent with everyone else who had yet to be infected with the contagion. This poor man was looking everywhere for his wife without being able to find her; finally, he enters the SHEDS and looks on every cot to no avail. Finally, he goes out to pursue his search; while crossing the courtyard, he sees a great number of dead bodies. He comes nearer to examine them more closely. What does he see? . . . The inanimate body of his wife whom he was looking for all this time. He takes her in his arms, seeming to doubt that she is in fact dead; he wants to bring her back to life, talks to her, calls her by her name, kisses her tenderly; but for all these demonstrations, the only answer he receives is death's silence. Once he is convinced that she no longer exists, he abandons himself to his pain, the air is filled with his cries and sobs, the spectacle was most heart wrenching. Scenes of this nature occur several times a day. What is even more heart wrenching is to see little children, only a few months old, abandoned due to the death of their mothers. When arriving at the SHEDS in the morning, we looked in every corner to make sure of the number of deaths that had occurred during the night; the Sisters were expected to deliver to the Doctors a daily report of their respective departments. During these visits, we found more than one young child lying with mothers who no longer existed, suckling their breasts, to find some nourishment.

The venerable M. Jean Richard, filled with compassion upon seeing the fate of these little innocents, the number of which was considerably increasing, and

GREY NUNS, OR SISTERS OF CHARITY

fearing that the Protestants would seize them, did not rest until the Commissary agreed to build a SHED exclusively for CHILDREN. He put them all together and, like a good father, tended to their more urgent needs. Realizing that these children were almost naked and that we did not have anything to change them, he allows the SISTERS to clothe them using rags that belong to orphans from the seminary. We could see this venerable priest, almost every day among these little afflicted, searching for ways to improve their fate. While we went to the sheds, we would cease to attend the OFFICES OF THE PARISH and on June 17, the Sacred-Heart Day, the Sisters, too tired, and absent in great numbers, were unable to sing the Offices. We used EULOGISTS for the Great Mass and the Vespers, and orphans sang the Salvation; which they continued doing so all the while that the sickness persisted.

We continued so until the TWENTY-FOUR (24) of JUNE. At that time, exhausted Sisters began crumbling under the weight of their tasks; already two of them were victims of the contagion. Our Mother Superior, seeing the pestiferous disease enter the house, warned us that we could not go on for long supporting the care of the SHEDS. She alerted Mister Superior of the state of our Sisters stricken by the epidemic evil as well to her fears she bore concerning the others. This revered Father thinks it best to confer with his Eminence Monsignor of Montreal[8] who, after having talked with our Mother Superior, decided that the Sisters of Providence would come to our assistance; that the GENERAL INSPECTION would remain in our care, that we would have to deal with all of the affairs with INTENDANTS, DOCTORS, and employees of the Government: finally, that the Sisters of Providence would only act as helpers. During a small assembly held in order to organize our work at the SHEDS, over which Monsignor presided, his Eminence expressed the desire to establish regulations for the occasion. However, our MOTHER humbly objected that there was no possibility to restrain ourselves to Regulations in the current state of things. His Eminence did not insist further.

On the TWENTY-SIX (26) of JUNE, TEN (10) Sisters of Providence came to our assistance. The apartment serving as a pre-novitiate was offered to them as a dormitory. They attended exercises of piety with us, and those of them that were novices followed the exercises of the novitiate.

When our Sisters returned from the sheds in the evening, they washed themselves and changed clothes; despite these hygienic precautions, they were infected by the odour they brought back from the SHEDS.

In order to continue caring for the sick, it was decided that a portion of the Sisters would spend half of their day at the House of Pointe-Saint Charles and, after having rested there, would take the place of the others so that they could then rest as well.

JUNE 29, THRITEEN (13) of our Sisters were stopped by the disease. ELEVEN (11) of them HAD THE TYPHUS that they contracted at the SHEDS.

The day after, THIRTIETH (30) of the month, the Governor General, LORD ELGIN CAME WITH HIS LADY[9] AND A BRILLANT PROCESSION, to offer condolences to the Order. He appeared quite moved upon learning that a great number of our Sisters were grievously sick, being victims of their devotion to serving the plague victims. His Excellency was accompanied by Monsignor PHELAN, bishop of Kingston, who was currently in Montreal.

At this time, the Monsignors of Saint-Sulpice that had tended to the plague victims, were also becoming ill from TYPHUS. We then saw his EMINENCE Monsignor of Montreal himself, who had returned from his trip to Rome but a few days before, visit, administer and tend to all sorts of cares for the poor victims of the epidemic. On JULY 3, he spent the night at the sheds with Monsignor Phelan, to help the sick and at day break, being exhausted, the two saintly bishops went to our house in Pointe Saint Charles to rest a little. Since the number of our Sisters present at the sheds was decreasing from day to day, due to the number of sick people at the Order, which increased every day, Monsignor of Montreal called upon the NUNS of the HOTEL-DIEU, allowing them to exit the cloister in order to help the Sisters of Providence who were about to be left alone . . . We saw these good NUNS, SIX (6) of them, come as well, endangering their own lives to relieve their brothers.

On JULY FIFTH (5), TWENTY-THREE (23) of our Sisters were bed ridden; of them, SEVENTEEN (17) were victims of the horrors of the plague. Those who were still standing collapsed from exhaustion in caring for their Sisters, before having to rely on seculars in order to care for them; but everyone avoided our house that now seemed like a tomb, and we were able with difficulty to gather but a few devoted individuals to come and expose themselves by performing this service. However we must not forget the devotion and sincere affection that a few respectable LADIES displayed for our Order during these days of gloomy memories.

Despite this terrible ordeal that struck our house, a good deal of young people came to ask admittance in our novitiate. FOUR OF THEM were admitted and ENTERED DURING THE PINNACLE OF THE EPIDEMIC. The courage of these good POSTULANTS was heroic to us. One of them came to replace her sister, who at the moment, gave no hope of recovery.

On JULY SIXTH (6), ONE of our Sisters received the last rites. We deemed it prudent to isolate the sick, putting together those that showed a more severe affliction. We carried a portion of them in the CHAMBER OF STATUES, leaving those less sick in the infirmary. The novitiate was converted into an infirmary for novices who were cared from by their Mistress, aided by those that were not victims of the disease. At the same time, with Monsignor's approval, we called in a second doctor to assist Doctor CHARLEBOIS in caring for our sick sisters.

Our Mother Superior, stricken with the exhaustion that came with overseeing the sheds, which she visited regularly every day, and burdened with a thousand cares from issues that arose at the time, succumbed under the weight of this dual burden. A disease of the entrails, coupled with total exhaustion, caused us to worry for her for several days.

On JULY SEVENTH (7), OUR SISTERS STOPPED GOING TO THE SHEDS, and FIFTEEN (15) of our sick received the holy Viaticum; several of them were in great danger of dying.

On the EIGHTH (8), our Mother's birthday, death entered the Seminary and the Reverend Mister MORGAN, after having caught a fever while caring for the plague ridden, was the first victim. This good gentleman was struck by the contagion after just a few days with the sick. He endured horrible sufferings before dying and was delirious nearly the whole time. He was THRITY-SEVEN years old.

On the 10th, at 9.30 in the evening, our good little sister ADELINE LIMOGES,[10] after a few days of suffering, passed away amidst the most horrible pains. This dear Sister, having donned the saintly habit a mere two months earlier, had distinguished herself through great obedience. Of a merry and constant humour, she endeared herself to all of her companions through her sweet gaiety and her considerate manner for all. When her Mistress announced to her that she had been designated to go care for the plague victims, her happiness was so great that she immediately went to Church to thank the good Lord. She was TWENTY years, ONE month and TWENTY-FOUR days old. She was buried the following day at one (1) in the afternoon. Her LIBERA was sung by eulogists.

On JULY ELEVENTH (11), our Mother gathered the Sisters in the Sisterhood after dinner, to propose that we all do a novena at NOTRE DAME de BON SECOURS . . . Two Sisters would go to attend Mass on behalf of the Sisterhood every day. Moreover, our Mother suggested we give this Church a STATUE of the Virgin Mary, made by our sisters. This novena was made in the hope of STOPPING this scourge. The proposal was accepted with joy by all the Sisters. It was not possible to have mass at Bonsecours; Monsignor, upon approving the novena, told our Mother that mass would be held in our Church and that candles would be lit at Notre-Dame de Bonsecours; and that once the disease had been stopped, we would all go on a pilgrimage to this Church where he would say Holy Mass himself . . . With the same intention, we kept candles lit in front of the Virgin Mary's altar, in our chapel.

The same day (11), bore witness to the TRAGIC DEATH of the priest M. J.-B.S. GOTTOFREY, p.s.s.[11] He departed at HALF PAST SIX in the evening, after having confessed himself to a postulant that did not speak French. He appeared merrier than usual; a few of our sisters came to see him, he told them with his natural vivacity: 'Courage, my dear Sisters, our sufferings are short-lived, but our reward is eternal.' Saying good night to our Mother, he told her: 'Take care not to kill yourself!', meaning not to exhaust herself caring for the sick. This dear gentleman was unaware of the accident that was to befall him AN HOUR AND A HALF LATER. He left to go visit a few sick people that called for him and, having gone to the Church of NOTRE-DAME de BONSECOURS to get the Holy Viaticum, he went up on the side of the Sacristy, which was on the third floor, wanting to go out on a balcony where we would often go, but that had been demolished in order to construct other buildings. He firmly opened this poor door that, foolishly, had not been nailed shut, and fell to the pavement on pieces of stone that were to be used for the buildings. His body was taken to the HOUSE OF THE VERGER and later to the HOTEL-DIEU. He was buried on the 12th.

On the TWELFTH (12), we began the novena at SAINT ROCH. The statue of this saint had been placed on the altar of the chapel of the Virgin Mary. At ONE in the afternoon, we went to the Church, in the same order as for the MISERERE, low habits. The poor and the children attended with us.

On the THIRTEENTH (13) after a few days of horrible suffering due to the epidemic disease that he had caught caring for the plague victims, died M. REMI CAROF, a priest at the Seminary. His limitless devotion and charity with which he helped the sick were truly moving. On more than one occasion we had seen him lie down between two dying individuals, to hear their confession; since, as we have previously said, they were lying TWO or THREE per bed, and these cots were so close to one another that one could not pass between them. It is important to note that an insufferable odour emanated from the sick, that they were covered in vermin, and surrounded by the most repugnant that dirtiness could offer. In this shameful position, we saw him take in the confession of a dying woman, hold in his arms the small child that was preventing her from confessing. Other times, he would himself go get stacks of hay so that the sick who were lying naked on the floor could climb unto them. Finally, this priest would stop at nothing to contribute to the salvation of their souls and the relief of their body.

During this time, we noticed, with a singular edification, the sweet joy that accompanied all of his gestures. Every time we would meet him, he would always have a few encouraging remarks to address us. This dear Gentleman, whose memory is dear to us, was but THIRTY (30) YEARS and three months old.

On the FOURTEENTH (14), our good Sister ANGELIQUE CHEVREFILS, known as Sister PRIMEAU,[12] having donned the habit only EIGHTEEN DAYS prior, died at FIVE in the evening. She experienced the joy of pronouncing her vows before dying, being sane of mind. Sister MATHILDE DENIS (SAINT JOSEPH) who was, at the same time, in mortal danger, also pronounced her vows conditionally. Our good Sister PRIMEAU was a promising candidate, she displayed great punctuality in all little observances, was thoughtful of her companions, she was always willing to do what disgusted others. The good Lord contented himself with the willingness she had shown while caring for the sick, since she caught the contagious disease as soon as she began to do so, and endured it with admirable patience and resignation. She was buried the next morning. One of her sisters who was a teacher, was also victim of the scourge at the time; we kept the news of her sister's death hidden and she learned of it only after her recovery.

It is difficult to have an idea of the pitiable state of the house during the epidemic. The regular spots were deserted, or rather non-existent, since we had put up beds in the communal room. However, our elder, Sister HARDY, who was a stickler for rules, was always punctual in ringing the exercises, and those that could afford to leave the care of the sick at that time would not miss them; sometimes there would be only THREE or FOUR attending, sometimes only TWO. The service of the poor in the rooms was interrupted for almost the entire duration of the epidemic. However, the Hospitaller Sisters constantly kept their offices, or if they came to miss them, were replaced by others. As we have said before, everyone fled the house; with the exception of Monsignor of Montreal, M. the Superior of the Seminary, and our good Father Larré who would sometimes come up to three times in a day. We will never forget the paternal care that Monsignor deigned grant us in those difficult circumstances. Every time his eminence would enter the house, it's as if he would bring us life. One of our Sisters that had been on the brink of the tomb, had begun her recovery but had yet to recover her senses; this poor Sister pursued Monsignor and implored him to cure her. 'If you would wish it so, Monsignor, she would tell him with an air that clearly showed she was still under the delirium's influence, if you wish it so, you could cure me.' This good Father could help but laugh.

Every one so abhorred our house that we had trouble finding someone to come and wash the clothes of the sick; even our hired help abandoned us and, a poor young gentleman that we had taken in was the only person willing to nail the coffins of our Sisters. We had taken the care of filling the coffins with lime and, as soon as the body of a Sister had been removed, we would cleanse the apartment where she had died immediately.

On JULY FIFTEENTH (15), died the good M. Pierre Richards. P.S.S. whose conduct at the SHEDS seemed to us more angelic than human. The Lord only knows all the acts of charity that this saintly Priest did for the plague victims during his laborious ministry at the SHEDS.

He always seemed preoccupied with the elements of eternity, and on every occasion, his words would support this interest. One day, we pointed out to him that his cassock was filled with vermin, he gently replied: 'That is nothing, leave them, soon they will be jewels.'

The last day we saw him at the sheds, we noticed he was more pensive and slightly more exhausted, the disease beginning to take a hold of him; one of our sisters came near the window where he standing, contemplating a heap of COFFINS which were piled up in the yard. She asked him if he was sick. After answering that he was not well, he said to her: 'Do you think our coffins are already made?' She answered him with an air of certainty: 'They are yet to be made, but it is certain that their planks have already been sawed.' She then told him that a great number of Sisters were victims of the contagion. 'That is good,' he continued, 'They will go to heaven, and I hope I will not delay in joining them'. A few days later, this dear Gentleman, along with Sister Ste Croix with whom he also spent time, were among the dead. . .

M. PIERRE RICHARD and SR STE CROIX, the memories tell us, greeted each other with these words: 'Is today the day where we'll meet the Eternal father?'

SISTER REID'S REFLEXIONS.[13]'Seeing the Sisters go by each morning on their way to the sheds, the people were enthusiastic. Miss E. KOLYMER, a young Protestant, was determined to embrace Catholicism and to enter our noviciate. The Typhus era was the starting point of the development of our religious family and of our undertakings; in sacrifice as well as in fecundity'. The Sisterhood was composed of THIRTY-EIGHT (38) Sisters, when my Sister REID entered, on November 8th, 1845.

The next day, July 16th, our good sister JANE COLLINS,[14] a novice for THREE months and EIGHTEEN (18) days, succumbed to the pestiferous disease following the cruellest of sufferance, accompanied by a near-continuous delirium. This dear Sister had laboured tremendously while caring for the sick. Her main task was to exhort them and prepare for their imminent deaths. When she would see them with Protestant ministers that had entered our hospitals, she would not let them out of her sight even for an instant, for fear that they would attempt to pervert these poor unfortunates; and on more than one occasion, she had to fight off these ministers of error; but through the wisdom of her reasoning, would always manage to confound them. She was TWENTY (20) years, NINE (9) months and EIGHTEEN days old. She was buried the next day, at half past SEVEN (7) in the morning.

On the TWENTY-FIRST (21) our dear Sister MARIE-ROSALIE BARBEAU,[15] known as SR MARIE, died at midnight and was buried the next day at FIVE (5) in the evening.

According to the doctor, to stop the disease's progress (contagion), it was decided that those in recovery needed fresh air and a change of locale. The idea was to find a house in a convenient location, after several days of fruitless search, our fathers at the Seminary offered their house at the GREGORY farm, situated in a very beautiful location, and in proximity to the town, with all the desirable advantages: ISOLATION, FRESH AIR, EASY AND SPACIOUS LODGING; nothing was lacking of all that could make the stay suitable for the sick. Our good Sisters of the Congregation were thinking of offering us their house in Ile Saint-Paul. Their hired help, upon hearing that our sick would be transported to the island, all wanted to leave, fearing they would contract the sickness. Our good Sisters of the Congregation were disposed to lose the entire harvest for the year; they brought it up to Monsignor who refused to have them expose themselves to such a considerable loss.

After a few difficulties, Monsignor allowed the Sisterhood to transport our recovering SISTERS to the GREGORY farm (or ST GABRIEL). The sisters of the Congregation took upon themselves to clean the house and even the furniture. They set up EIGHTEEN or TWENTY good beds, and got the house ready to welcome our Sisters. Monsignor allowed us to have a chapel in the house and to hold the Holy Sacrament. These dear Sisters, whose devotion we will never forget, paid for everything, and all was set up perfectly.

On the TWENTY-THIRD (23), at SIX IN THE EVENING, our good sister ALODIE BRUYIERE,[16] a postulant for EIGHT months and EIGHT days, passed away at the age of TWENTY (20) years, ELEVEN months and FIVE days, after THREE weeks of sickness, Typhus contracted at the sheds, which presented all of the most serious symptoms. Before dying, her entire body was but a wound which produced an insufferable infection. She was a good person who would have made a saintly nun. She only appeared at the sheds, where she has been sent to care for the sick and subsequently contracted the disease.

The same day, a victim of his devotion for the sick, died the venerable M. Jean Richard (M. JACKSON-JOHN RICHARDS, P. S. S.).

A few days before his death, TWO of our Sisters went to see him at the Hotel-Dieu where he was sick. This good father insistently recommends to them the care of poor little children, for which he had taken great pains: 'Do not lose sight of them,' he said to them, 'For Protestants will seize them.'

To properly praise this venerable priest is beyond all expression. The wisdom of his advice and the caution he exercised in his proceedings rendered him singularly respected by employees of the government who went to him with all their difficulties. So, the slightest of his desire was for them an order. As soon as the venerable Mr Richards had pronounced himself, regardless of any divergence of opinion, all yielded to his word. One day this good father sent to the Administrator[17] a request to receive an order of hay for a shelter which lacked some. Mr. the Administrator responded to the request: 'An order of hay for the reverend Father Richards. Ah! Had I an order of gold to send him.' A few days later, both had gone where gold and hay are of equal worth since Mr. the Administrator was struck by the contagious disease and soon followed Mr. Richards into the grave.

Notes

1 Sister Elizabeth Forbes-McMullen, Mother Superior of the Sisters of Charity (1843–1848).

2 Father John Jackson Richards (1787–1847), also known as Jean Richard, was a Sulpitician priest in Montreal who died caring for Irish emigrants on 23 July, 1847. Originally from Alexandria, Virginia, he had come to Montreal as a Methodist minister in 1807 to proselytise, but instead converted to Catholicism, was ordained in 1838, and presided over the city's first English language services for Irish Catholics in 1817.

3 John Joseph Connolly (1816–1863), first pastor of Montreal's St. Patrick's Church (now basilica) when it was consecrated in 1847.

4 Father Patrick Morgan (1810–1847), died caring for Irish emigrants on 8 July, 1847.

5 Marie-Charlotte Pommainville, called Sister Ste Croix (1811–1847), died caring for Irish emigrants on 31 July, 1847.

6 Father Pierre Richard (1817–1847), died caring for Irish emigrants on 15 July, 1847.

7 Father Rémi Carof (1815–1847), died caring for Irish emigrants on 14 July, 1847.

8 Ignace Bourget (1799–1885), Bishop of Montreal (1840–1876).

9 James Bruce, Lord Elgin (1811–1863), Governor General of the Province of Canada (1847–1854), married to Lady Mary-Louisa Lambton (1819–1898).

10 Sister Marie-Adeline Limoges (1827–1847), died caring for Irish emigrants on 10 July, 1847.

11 Father Jean-Baptiste-Etienne Gottofrey (1815–1847), died caring for Irish emigrants on 11 July, 1847.

12 Marie-Angelique Chevrefils, called Sister Primault (1846–1847), died caring for Irish emigrants on 12 July, 1847.

13 Sister Mary Martine Reid (1809-?) survived the fever sheds in 1847 and decades later in 1899 she testified about her experiences in a notarised deposition that is catalogued as 'Typhus 1847 46' in the Grey Nuns' archive (Archival Services and Collections, Maison de Mère d'Youville, Sisters of Charity of Montreal, 'Grey Nuns'). In her deposition, Sister Reid gave sworn testimony that:

> I am now shown by Mr Kavanagh, Q.C. an extract made by Mr J.A.U Beaudry of a plan deposited in the minutes of the late Theodore Doucet Esq., Notary, on the nineteenth of August one thousand eight hundred and fifty-three (1853)

the immigrant sheds that I speak of appear in this place, and to the west of these sheds, or in the direction of the present St Etienne Street, is situate the present lot where the monument stands to the memory of the immigrants who died and were buried there, I remember the place very well. The terrible scenes that I have witnessed in these sheds made such an impression upon my mind that I can never forget them, nor the place where they occurred. I remember the cemetry very well, I have frequently passed there since, and I have never passed there and seen the stone without thinking of the scenes that I witnessed there in 1847 – and I am absolutely certain that the enclosure where the monument now stands is the cemetry where the bodies of those who died in the immigrant sheds at that time were buried.

Hundreds and hundreds of the ship fever patients were buried in that enclosure where the monument now stands, I believe there were over six thousand, I saw numbers of bodies taken there to be buried. I am absolutely certain to the facts now stated by me.

Each body was placed in a separate coffin and then (though I have no personal knowledge of the fact) I believe that quicklime was put into each coffin, I never saw the quicklime put into the coffins but still I have no doubt that it was. I believe that the immigrants were almost altogether Irish.

This land, of which the cemetry forms part, was sold by our community on the thirty-first of December one thousand eight hundred and fifty-three (1853). It is to my knowledge that our sisters have since then expressed their regret that there was no reservation on the land where the cemetry is situate – it was an oversight on the part of our community I am certain.

(signed) Mary Martine Reid.

Witness J.H. Kenehan

Dated at Montreal this 13th day of November 1899.

14 Sister Jane Collins (1826–1847), died caring for Irish emigrants on 16 July, 1847.
15 Sister Marie-Rosalie Barbeau (1801–1847), died caring for Irish emigrants on 21 July, 1847.
16 Sister Marie-Alodie Bruyère (1826–1847), died caring for Irish emigrants on 23 July, 1847.
17 A reference to the mayor of Montreal, John Easton Mills (1796–1847), who died caring for Irish emigrants on 12 November, 1847.

13

GREY NUNS, OR SISTERS OF CHARITY, FAMINE ANNAL, *ANCIEN JOURNAL*, VOL. II. *THE TYPHUS OF 1847*. TRANSLATED BY PHILIP O'GORMAN

The Grey nuns of the General Hospital feel beating in their chests a heart already open to the generous aspiration to follow their venerable founder to the fields of suffering and death. They wait upon a single word, one order. The revered mother Forbes-McMullen, worthy superior of their community at this time, joining in strong and active faith, was tender, generous and compassionate towards the unfortunate. She learned some details on the situation of the emigrants who arrived on our shores, she was deeply moved, and, understanding with only one glance the duty owed to this community, conceived a bright desire to rush to the relief of this misery with her girls. . .

They were welcomed with great courtesy and deference by the government steward, who gave all authorization necessary to the Grey Nuns to visit and take care of the pestilent, authorizing them to engage faithful men and women. The venerated Mother superior, almost surprised by this cordial welcome, is not surprised when she learned that she was preceded by the good M.J. Richard. Seeing the embarrassment of the steward in finding sufficient personnel to tend to the needs of the sick and dying, he suggested asking the Sisters of Charity if they would provide aid. This steward was Protestant; he knew little about catholic institutions, and did not know who to address himself to; we understand his satisfaction in seeing the Grey Nuns offer themselves. He hastened to conduct them to a home almost in ruin by the river, under the name of the hospital.

What a spectacle unravelled in the eyes of this good mother and her company! Hundreds of people were laying there, most of them on bare planks, pell-mell, men, women and children. The moribund and cadavers are crowded in the same shelter, while there are those that lie on the quays or on pieces of wood thrown here and there along the river. It was a spectacle that should have discouraged Mother McMULLEN and her generous companion. On the contrary, they felt their souls lifted to the heights of the mission that the heavens were preparing for them. The meeting they are in at this moment with the Seminary superior and the intrepid M. Morgan fills them with enlightenment. The latter has occupied himself with a poor sick individual that he covers in earth, suffocated by his own vomit;

EYEWITNESS TESTIMONIES

he puts them with such charity on a poor pallet, that they feel animated by a new ardour to come themselves, to save these unfortunate poor.

Once returned to the community, they have no expressions powerful enough to retell what they have seen. After supper, the venerated mother calls on the courage and the generosity of her girls, convinces them to combat in a new field of sacrifice; they are free nevertheless to appeal to their own strengths. The whole Community has but one heart and one soul to offer to the provision of its superior. . .

'June 9th, say the old manuscripts, EIGHT sisters and FIVE women left for the SHEDS, and the following Sunday, the 13th, there were 23. . . The community numbered at this time, thirty-seven sisters and eighteen novices.' . . . The names of the first Sisters who went to the SHEDS are barely mentioned in the convent annals; what a regrettable gap. However, do we ignore them? Is it not the entire community, as we have just mentioned, that we see on its feet?

Let us continue . . . The first shelters that the fellowship built to receive the emigrants stretched along the canal, this territory belonging to the General Hospital. Point-Saint-Charles, where it was situated, was once a rural valley, and very swampy, as this year saw torrential rains. Despite the mud and other inconveniences, the sisters made their journey within twenty minutes, already hearing the groans of the ill and the wails of the dying . . . We disperse ourselves in this unfamiliar maze . . . Could we imagine for a moment the spectacle this multitude of men and women piled pell-mell offered, up to three or four in the same bed, indifferent to everything, groaning, however, heartbreakingly? We were running here, running there . . . supporting a poor, dying woman, ripping away from her the poor infant she clung to so close to her heart . . . We point out the heavens to another while wiping away his agonizing sweat. We have the cadavers taken away from those still breathing, and we took a look around us . . . We step outside the shelter only to find more of the miserable poor, recumbent without salvation, we eagerly go to their aid, multiplying our steps without counting. What misery! Who could describe them? This is not just a family, or one hundred that are ill, but almost an entire nation feeling the anxieties of this agony.

Unfortunate Ireland persecuted for its faith and exhausted with hunger on its soils, comes to a strange land to drink the dregs of its chalice. O Heaven, open yourself to us, and show us the palms of these new martyrs! In the first hours of our sisters in the SHEDS, do not make them feel the wrath of all the evils that are housed there. All day long, they seek to find prompt and salutary ways to face such suffering. These sheds are usually 100 to 200 feet long and 25 by 30 in size, separated by walls and contiguous from one another. Some, however, are separated by a distance of 30 to 30 feet; this proximity renders service easier. They are furnished but with poor beds made from simple planks, attached to the walls and more or less inclined in the same way seen in barracks or in police stations. We will substitute them soon with bunks; these are poles with crude planks around the circumference of which a layer of straw makes a soft bed.

GREY NUNS, OR SISTERS OF CHARITY

Some of the emigrants brought cots and blankets with them, but we no longer have these little furnishings or other objects today to help serve the ill. We simply draw water from the river and add broth in a huge pot or cauldron with a capacity of twelve gallons which is boiled over a fire lit in the middle of the court. Doctors and sisters take a pot or a bowl for the needs of their ill.

The government supplies fresh bread, tea and meat, and many charitable people from the city send provisions. The reverend Sisters of the Congregation, regretting not being able to follow their Sisters of Charity to the hospitals, provided sugar, cookies, tea and other sweets for the ill.

We see soldiers directing themselves towards the barrier at the entrance to the SHEDS to bring a portion of their rations. It is in these infirmaries infested with fever, where hundreds have caught the contagion and have died, that our good sisters go and in doing so, threaten their health and their lives.

Every day will be laborious and rich in all sorts of merits, and the night, in trusting their ill to people staying overnight, the sisters embark on their journey back to the community; but what precautions were needed to ensure that they did not take the contagion of this malignant fever with them . . . They venture to only the least inhabited areas, and there they hurry to rid themselves of their habits and of the vermin attached to them, and communicating only minimally with the other sisters, take their rest. . .

They are not the least bit surprised to find at the dawn of this new day the priests who were watching over the shelters when they left: it was the good Father Richards and the excellent M. Caroff, the two of them still standing after a night passed in the exercising of their holy ministry; they were pale and unkempt. Veritable sentinels, they did not whatsoever wish to abandon these poor souls at the final moment that would decide their eternities. The good sisters, more numerous today than yesterday, hurry to complete the general visit of this immense dormitory, in order to assess the conditions of their sick. Alas! Many are no longer any more than cadavers. We see poor little children still searching for the substance of life from the breast of their poor mother whom death had frozen. We meet here and there poor little creatures stiffened by death.

This expression cannot faithfully convey the terrible state in which these sick were strewn, as we have said, up to THREE in the same bed, next to those who died during the night.

A poor, dying individual was very agitated, a sister passing by, believed he was in his life's last moments of suffering; but to her horror she discovered this unfortunate was lying between two cadavers! One was all black, and the other livid, yellow, a hideous sight. She had the cadavers removed, and as soon as the moribund calmed down, agony came to strike him, and he was soon nothing more than a cadaver that we hastened to remove. Since we had not yet constructed a mortuary for the dead, the corpses were exposed in the outdoors, and once there was a great enough number of them, we made a cemetery for the bodies in the neighbouring fields.

The odour that these cadavers produced and the horror they naturally caused add to the distressing picture of this situation. We nevertheless see the sisters calmly patrolling around the diverse enclosures; they take charge of the department Mother McMullen trusted them with. Sister BRAULT expends energy, as well as showing remarkable strength to gently care for her beloved sick. She is in charge of a SHED, and since it must be enlarged from time to time, she helps to transport the poor patients to the vehicle that will transfer them to another department, and then with satisfaction she returns to the bedside of the others to have them take the remedies which she prepared with care and to relieve them in any possible way. Sister Desjardins appears to us as an unchanged, flowering figure. Oh! If she had in this moment her brushes and a canvas, she would faithfully reproduce the gloomy scenes of our sad shelters. But it is to these poor sick individuals that she presently gives all her time. Over there, at the end of the dark corridor, I see the silhouette of Sister Marie (Barbeau). She strives to find the most miserable.

In effect, in this isolated place can be found a shed faintly lit by some glass. The hardened ground makes its floor.

A number of convalescents which varies from day to day have taken charge of shredding cable, earning a small ration as a result. The good sister is among them; taking care of their needs with solicitude and she remains dedicated to this task without worrying herself with the humidity or the other inconveniences.

This valiant sister, who is not physically imposing, exerts an astonishing energy. We love seeing her by the bedsides of the ill, what care! What attention! What thoughtfulness! The most repugnant are those that she offers to care for with most haste. One day, she was working in a department that contained five hundred pestilent. Her gaze suddenly stopped on a poor dying woman; she ran to her side to prepare for her to receive the Extreme Unction; the moribund emitted a repugnant odour. Right after our dear sister removed the woman from the fetid pallet she hastened to put her on another. A young doctor arrived at this moment, offering to help the good sister in this service, but with hardly having moved this rotting body he felt such strong nausea that he went outdoors without delay to relieve himself through copious vomiting. He had no expression with which to sufficiently praise this little nun who had mastered nature's repugnances. Shortly after, the young doctor, caught the illness himself, wanted to have sisters by his bedside, and since he is Protestant, abjured his errors and did not cease to repeat that he owed his conversion to the beautiful example set by the Sisters of Charity. One morning when Sister Marie was sweeping the SHED under direction, an officer came with a squad of soldiers. Surprised to see this little nun in charge of this task, he commanded his soldiers who immediately seized the broom and cleaned the apartment in an instant.

Let us turn to Sister Croix-Pominville, who is so ardent in her offering of services to the hospitals; yes! Let us see her in action in this hospital on the river – an old house that was the first refuge of the emigrants. She was among a great number of sick whom she consoled with the expression of her pious sentiments. . .

Sister Saint-Joseph-Denis has not the least part to play in these miserable shelters. But let us go up to the attic, and see her in the middle of a great number of small children. The good sister cares for them with a faithful spirit, because otherwise, the nauseating odour, and all the repulsive care that the poor little ones require would turn her off, but she does not believe this to be too much of a price to pay for the cross of the religious order she will soon receive . . . few weeks sufficed in order for the priests and nuns to establish order and regularity. The shelters were divided into several apartments, one for men, one for women, one for children.

There was a SHED especially for welcoming arrivals.

It is in this shed that we recognize sister COLLINS, a young novice full of ardour and the spirit of sacrifice. We see her in the middle of a crowd of emigrants, keeping her calm, listening with deference and gentleness, to the lamentations of the poor strangers.

She greets them with compassion, encourages them, makes them hope for better days.

All those who were denied access to other shelters, she keeps near here, multiplying her efforts to improve their sad situation. How many times did she hold herself back from bathing these poor dying souls with her tears?

The hangar which she was able to use was very low and very narrow, lacking beds, without doubt, since one had needed to lie down next to the poor to have them drink; but her great courage did not weaken; if she could not relieve their bodies, she knew at least that she could relieve their souls by making them foresee the eternal life. Oh! How her discourses were sympathetic to the dying! She had a gift to touch their hearts . . . What souls she pulled out of heresy! . . . In seeing Protestant ministers circulating in the shelters, she made a good guard against those who wished to indoctrinate; she confounded with her responses full of sense and doctrine those who asked her reckless questions.

Another affliction distressed her heart when she saw the arrival of emigrants: it was the heart wrenching goodbyes they said to each other when men, women and children were separated to be placed in their respective shelters. Similar scenes were repeated often within and outside the shelters, and the hearts of our dear sisters were often crushed with pain.

One day, a poor Irishman who had disembarked that day arrived at the SHEDS and asked about his wife who had preceded him on his journey to Montreal. No one was able to give him news: he ran about the shelters worried and disconsolate without finding her; he finally arrived at the place where the cadavers of those who had died during the night were put; he examined them one by one: he stopped and threw himself on the ground while screaming in lament, dragging himself to one of the cadavers which he covered in kisses and tears. He had found the one who had been his companion and his consolation in life. His despair knew no bounds and he left at a slow pace, convinced that he was the only one left of his family.

EYEWITNESS TESTIMONIES

These scenes repeat themselves every day, when we proceed to the sepulchre of the dead; fathers, mothers, husbands, wives, and children, surrounding those who are so dear to them, so opposed to their departure, letting out cries that provoke tears.

The priests, the nuns linger in these scenes of desolation to temper the bitterness with words of peace and resignation. Sister MONTGOLFIER traversing the enclosure met a little girl of 11 or 12 years old who was looking for her mother; she had been transported to Montreal before her. The good Sister took her affectionately by the hand and went with her from bedside to bedside. All anxious, the little one looked left and right, her little heart beating with fear and hope. All of a sudden she heard a most tender exclamation 'O Mother!' but in embracing her mother, her little arms held a moribund on her last breaths. Another morning, Sister MONTGOLFIER was completing her usual visits when she noticed that young children had entered the enclosure where their dead father lay; these poor little ones were calling him caressing him and playing amongst themselves.

Worried about the fatigue that this illness could cause, the vigilant sister hastened to make the young children back away, but, what pain! Their father was but a cadaver! Such force did she need to take these children away while hearing their heart breaking cries; she guided them to the SHEDS designated for children and a few days later, she placed them happily with a family.

The following autumn, sister Montgolfier was once again in the SHEDS when an Irishwoman recovering from typhus arrived searching for her husband and children. After many questions, the sister recognized the unfortunate mother of the little orphans she was caring for. With haste she gave her all the details to satisfy her. This poor woman put her hands together and raised her gaze towards the heavens: Ah! My sister, said she, with the deepest of pain; I am consoled to learn that my children are still alive and that they have been returned to me! Blessed be the Lord! This family's name was McKay. As we have seen, there was a shed specifically designated for children. It was M. J. Richard who solicited it from the government, in the fear that the Protestants would seize these poor little ones. He had little bunks transported and wished to. . . . help fill the benches. It is without doubt on this occasion that he requested hay from the emigration intendant: 'With pleasure, replied the latter, if only I had a load of gold to send this holy man instead' . . .

Let us add a few details on the goodness and the patience of this holy priest. One day, after giving confession to a poor woman lying on a pallet serving equally as the home of her children, he left covered in filth; he was then obliged to go clean his cassock at great cost to him. In another meeting, again giving confession to a poor dying mother, who was holding a little girl with great concern, the good priest took the child in his arms and held it, all the while lending an ear to the dying. These good Sulpician priests and many other priests who shared their ministry, were well practiced in the role of nurses, and performed all kinds of services for the patients.

14

GREY NUNS, OR SISTERS OF CHARITY, FAMINE ANNALS, *FOUNDATION OF ST. PATRICK'S ORPHAN ASYLUM* (1849). TRANSLATED BY PHILIP O'GORMAN

It was the month of October 1847. . . . One hundred and nineteen children from the fever sheds who had not been claimed by their parents were gathered with the orphans in this house . . . Meanwhile the small colony could not enjoy its new resting place for long. As the incumbent priests of St. Patrick's church had no presbytery, it became necessary to give it up to them. From the 21st of May 1848, twelve children from the Rocheblave refuge were transferred to the Mother House. The others were evacuated on the 13th of July, and were placed in good families or trusted to the care of Mr. Dowd,[1] a young sulpician who arrived in Montreal on the 21st of June previous, and after three weeks was named chaplain of the poor Irish. . .

Very recently, an excellent widow named Suzanne Brown arrived in the country. Born in Ireland to an affluent family, who were stripped of their assets by misfortune, she was widowed with her three (3) children: Georges (Jacques), Brigitte and Rose, and the courageous woman left her homeland to seek fortune abroad. She was travelling to Quebec with a group of Irish immigrants when she was struck down at sea by the contagion. From Quebec, she could nevertheless be transported to Montreal, but on her arrival she became so sick that as it was unlikely she would recover and she seemed unconscious, we entrusted her son Jacques to Mr. Louis-Misael Archambault, curate of Saint Hugues, her eldest daughter Brigitte to the Grey Nuns, and Rose, her youngest, was adopted by a courageous Irishwoman whose name we unfortunately did not retain.

Having returned to health against all odds, Mrs. Brown was delighted to see her son in the parish priest of Saint Hugue's home and her eldest daughter with the Grey Nuns. But where to find her little Rose? Days and weeks passed with no clues to enlighten her. It was under these circumstances full of anguish that Father Du Merle met this brave woman. Touched by the courage which she showed amidst so many trials and hardships, and moreover, seeing she was educated, pious and was ready and willing to devote herself, he proposed that she take care of the children in the refuge on Colburn street, to spend the night with them and catechise them.

Mrs. Brown, delighted to add her resources to this beautiful work, eagerly accepted the Reverend Father's request. A lower level of the house was transformed into a school, and was used as such, until 1849. When she found herself surrounded by the orphans who absorbed her teachings like thirsty earth absorbs the dew, she thought of her little Rose. 'If I had her here with me, she said, I would teach her with all the others.' With this weighing on her mind, one March evening, she attended a Lenten prayer service or a benediction of the Holy Sacrament in St Patrick's church. In the silence of the ceremony, she was disturbed from her contemplation by the sound of a marble rolling on the floor which came to rest in the folds of her clothes. She had barely raised her eyes when she saw a little girl aged three (3) or four (4) running to collect it. 'Is this not my little Rose,' she said trembling with emotion. Indeed, it was this child who she mourned and thought she had lost forever, now returned to her at this moment by our Lord, and by instinct, she reached out. However, her adoptive mother who had missed nothing of what happened, intervened and protested. Before the ceremony had even finished both women went to the sacristy to submit the case to Father Dowd. He did not delay in resolving the issue, and that very evening, Madame Brown triumphed, coming back to the refuge with little Rose.

Note

1 Father Patrick Dowd (1813–1891), Sulpician priest in Montreal (1848–1891).

15

ANON. *THE EMIGRANT SHIP. WRITTEN FOR THE PROTESTANT ORPHAN BAZAAR*, IN THE *LITERARY GARLAND, AND THE BRITISH NORTH AMERICAN MUSEUM* (MONTREAL: LOWELL AND GIBSON, 1850)

THERE was a crowd looking on, one bright morning in early Spring, while an Emigrant ship weighed anchor, and spreading her white sails, moved slowly out to sea. A loud cheer broke from the spectators, and it was answered by a farewell shout—a wailing cry rather, it was so sad and plaintive—which burst from the full heart of those poor emigrants, who crowded the deck to take a last look of their native land.

A last look! and who ever looked for the last time on any spot endeared by memories of joy or sorrow, without a pang, keener than words can express?

'That ship is too heavily laden,' said a hard faced man, whose thoughts dwelt on the risks of Insurance, in which he was deeply concerned.

'Too much – too much crowded,' replied a bustling, active man, 'there will be sickness on board, and it will be detained in Quarantine, till the demand for Spring goods is passed.'

He spoke feelingly, for he had consigned a large amount of goods to the chances of that crowded bark.

'God be with the poor creatures,' fervently ejaculated another; one who wore a priestly garb, beneath which, beat the heart of a true Samaritan. And his prayers followed those whom poverty and despair had driven away, to find new homes in a far off, stranger land.

'God bless your reverence,' said an old woman, wiping a tear from her eye, 'there go our friends and neighbors, who would have lived and toiled honestly on their own bits of land, if the bread had not been taken from their mouths, and they were left to starve entire—God help them.'

'Let them go, mother,' said a young man huskily, 'Why should they stay here till the black rot comes, and the bailiffs turn them out of doors? When I have saved enough, mother dear, *we* will go too.'

The crowd dispersed; the ship ploughed heavily along, farther, farther off—it became a mere speck, and was then lost to sight. And, save in a few forsaken homes, or a few desolate hearts, who thought of, or cared for the fate of that heavy burdened Emigrant Ship?

The ship went on its way bravely, ploughing the smooth sea with deep furrows, and steady progress, though the wind was capricious and often drove it from its course. Twenty days it had already been at sea; it was alone in the midst of the broad Atlantic, and a hundred and thirty living souls were pent up within its narrow limits. And there was not a heart there, however seared with wretchedness, or hardened by degradation, or chilled by disappointment and poverty, but throbbed with a feeling of hope that some better destiny awaited them in the land they were approaching, than had fallen to their hard lot in that which they left behind.

Another week passed away, but storms had arisen, and adverse winds bent the ship about, while drenching rains swept the deck, which only experienced seamen could tread in safety. The nights were dismally dark, and the angry waves lashing the sides of the vessel, which pitched fearfully on the stormy sea, struck terror into the hearts of the ignorant and superstitious. Provisions also began to grow scarce, for with habitual improvidence, many had neglected to prepare for the exigencies of a long voyage, and others had been sent from their homes almost destitute. The captain, a selfish and grasping man, doled out a scanty supply from his private stores, for which he exacted a most unjust compensation, and those who had no money to give, became a burden on the charity of the compassionate. During the week in which the storm continued, a fearful change had taken place among the unfortunate Emigrants. Shut out from the fresh air, crowded together in a small space, and destitute of wholesome food, a fearful disease was generated, and when the sun again broke out cheerfully, and all were called on deck, not one half their number were able to obey the summons. Pale, dispirited, worn by fasting and confinement, they crawled forward; even those who had been cleanly and robust, were but the shadows of their former selves, and on the face of childhood, was imprinted those most painful lines—the traces of premature suffering and hardship.

Amidst a silence which seemed sad and ominous, two of the ship's crew followed, staggering under the weight of a dead human body; and when another and another was brought forward, and cast, with little outward form, into the fathomless deep, a cry of anguish burst from the survivors, and the chillness of despair settled on every heart. The work of death went on among that devoted company; in quick succession, fifty passed away, and their bodies were consigned to a watery grave.

It was a joyful sound when a man at the mast head cried out, 'Land!' and the faint outlines of Newfoundland might be seen through a glass, in the far distance. The cry was repeated by every lip, and the saddest face lighted up with a glow of pleasure. The sun had just sunk below the waves, and the broad sea, mingling with the horizon, lay like a smooth mirror beneath the glowing sky. Eagerly, but vainly the poor Emigrants strained their sight to catch a glimpse of the wished for land;—it still lay far beyond the ken of any but the most experienced eye. They were dispersed with rude jests by the sailors, and returned disappointed to their allotted places. Seated on the bulkhead there remained one group, apparently too much absorbed by their own sorrows, to observe anything passing around them. A young man of perhaps thirty years, was holding on one knee a sickly looking little girl, and on the other, an infant of some eighteen months sat quietly nibbling a crust, and vainly trying to win a smile by holding it coaxingly to her father's lips. A sturdy little boy nodded at his feet, while the mother, sitting beside her husband, leaned her head on his shoulder, and wept bitterly. That day, her mother and an only brother had been consigned to the deep.

'Do not fret so, Bessy dear,' said the husband tenderly, 'It cannot call back the dead, and fretting only wears the life out of you. Just think of the bairns now,—you will make them grit too.'

'The poor bairns, God keep them,' sobbed the wife, 'and you too Allan, but you do look so pale! Sore enough times we had at home, but then we kept all together, — and now they are gone—gone!' and she burst into a fresh flood of tears.

Allan soothed his wife with all the arguments which his kind heart could suggest, and her tears gradually dried and she tried to answer him with a smile, but her heart was sadly oppressed, poor thing, for her gentle but not very strong spirit had sunk under the distresses of that sad voyage.

An early marriage and the demands of a growing family, had kept Allan and his young wife poor; and how can the Irish peasantry hope to grow rich amidst the accumulated social evils which grind them to the earth! They rented a small cabin; and a patch of potato ground and a cow were their chief dependence; yet Allan and his wife belonged to the decent poor who prized independence and looked forward to better days. But the potato rot came, and took away from them the staff of life; labor was scarce and poorly remunerated, and the cow was sold to pay their rent and taxes. So they scraped together the little that was left, and it barely sufficed to pay for a passage to America after setting aside a few pounds for the outfit of a new home, or any exigencies that might arise. From this small sum some coins had already been abstracted to relieve the necessities of their suffering fellow passengers, for Allan and Bessy had kind hearts and could not resist an appeal to their sympathies. And, however deficient the unsophisticated Irish may be in prudential virtues, and in worldly wisdom, for generosity and self-sacrificing kindheartedness, no people in the world can equal them.

The Emigrant Ship, still infected with the baleful fever, reached Grosse Isle in due season and was detained the usual time in quarantine. Many carried the seeds of the dreaded fever to the shelters provided for them on the island, and before the ship was purified and suffered to proceed to Quebec, more than half the remaining Emigrants rested under the sod. On the very day that they were preparing to depart, poor Allan was taken ill and carried to the hospital. Bessy's agony amounted to despair, for in her weak, fond heart was the strong love of a devoted wife, and the superstition of her uncultured race. It is well remembered what terror the progress of *ship fever* spread on every side, and how reluctant any but the devoted Nuns, or the most mercenary nurses, were found, to attend upon the sick. But Bessy's love was stronger than her fear, and nothing could keep her from her husband's side. The medical men, touched with her distress allowed her to attend upon him, and though almost unconscious of her presence, his sufferings were mitigated by her vain, but tender care. Poor Bessy's painful watchings, aggravated by distress of mind, brought on her the same terrible disease, and for some weeks after Allan's death, her life seemed to hang by a single thread.

It was a bright summer morning, when Bessy and her little children mingled in with a crowd of Emigrants, landed from a steamer on the wharf at Montreal. She looked round on the cheerful, active scene, and a sense of loneliness smote upon her heart. This then was the city which she had looked forward to, with such earnest longing, when they parted from their native shore. This was the end of the long travel which she had commenced with such unambitious but sanguine hopes! And he who had set out with her, and on whose stronger arm she leaned for support, had fallen by her side, and henceforth she must tread the world alone! Poor Bessy! *she had not time to grieve;* the poor have never time to grieve. In the midst of bereavement they must rise up and struggle for existence, and with stricken hearts bear the burden of the day, and crush down the sorrow which would unnerve their hands for that labor on which their life depends! Often we may look at them, and wonder at their apathy, when, could we see their hearts, we might read there a tale of patient endurance and of unforgetting sorrow, which would far outweigh all external badges, and all conventional forms.

In an obscure court, leading from a narrow street, in the heart of the city, might be seen a few wooden houses close packed together, and the words 'Room to Let' written in large characters on one dilapidated window-shutter, attracted the attention of the passing idler. The houses were swarming with children, and every room, save that one which had just lost a tenant, was occupied by a family. The court was small, closed in by those over-crowded tenements, and the air stifling and polluted. In the middle of the yard was a pool of water kept full by the emptying of dirty suds and other questionable slops, and some half dozen ragged children were gathered round it with boisterous mirth, floating chips upon the stagnant water. From almost every window some untidy female looked out, or a meager baby was held up to find amusement in gazing at the noisy children without. All manner of rubbish littered up the sides, and the feet slipped over decaying vegetables thrown out before the doors. It seemed strange that life could be supported in such a fetid atmosphere and pent up in such close apartments. Yet in these places the poor of cities are obliged to live, for rents are too dear where there is fresh air and comfortable lodgings!

In that 'Room to Let,' poor Bessy found shelter for herself and children. Her money was nearly exhausted; scarcely two sovereigns remained of all her little store. There she deposited her chest, her bed, and the few articles of comfort she had brought from her childhood's home. The poor children fretted sadly, for they had been used to fresh air, and the little cabin where they first saw the light, was clean, and stood alone on a breezy hill side. Bessy soothed their complaints and though her own heart was *crushed,* love for them gave her courage and endurance. Patiently she sought employment, and though often ill requited, day after day found her toiling in cheerful hope and earning enough to keep want from the door, and to pay the rent of her little room. If anxious thoughts would sometimes intrude, hope came to her aid, and she looked forward to the time when her children would be old enough to help her, and they could then earn more, and live in a better place. Poor Bessy, this was the extent of her ambition.

Autumn came on with its chilling blasts and dismal rains. The children needed warmer clothes, and the wind blew so sharply through the broad cracks and shattered windows, that another stick must be added to the fire, and even then their teeth chattered, and the small dipped candle at night, flickered painfully to the eyes. Bessy had no peat-bog to go to now, where fuel might be had for digging, and the long, long winter came on fast and found her ill prepared to meet its severity. Work was not as plenty as it had been in warmer weather. A family for whom she had done washing, left town suddenly and forgot to pay her a dollar which was due. Alas! a few shillings which the rich think so lightly of, or spend in selfish extravagance, if given to the poor, or applied to the just payment of honest industry, how many hearts would be gladdened, how many abodes of poverty made comfortable!

That dollar Bessy had appropriated to purchase fuel; for a week they had had no warmth except from the blaze of a few chips which the children picked up about some unfinished buildings, and the mother's heart ached as she looked on their poor little frozen fingers and their bare feet, pinched with cold. And when they came crying round the few dying embers, her thoughts turned reproachfully to the rich man in his abundance, who had so cruelly forgotten the claims of justice and humanity.

It was the midst of winter. Bessy sat with aching eyes by the dim candle, finishing some slop work that she had procured from a dealer in *cheap labor.* Sixpence for a garment neatly made! It was a bargain which brought *him* ample remuneration, but left *her* only a few farthings for her strained sight and wasted strength. A threadbare cloak, which was the pride of her happier days, slightly screened her from the wind that whistled through every crevice; but still her feet ached, and her fingers were so numb she could scarce hold the needle. A few chips still lay on the hearth; they were all that were left to warm the little ones the next day, when she must leave them alone to go and work at Mrs S's. No, she could not rob the children of the warmth they so much needed; so she drew the cloak more closely round her, and at a late hour her task was finished, and poor Bessy lay down to rest with a more quiet mind and a far more confiding spirit, than many are blessed with, whose easy lot leaves them no anxious thoughts for the morrow.

The next day Bessy returned home thoroughly chilled from her day's work. She had gone far out of her way to ask for a few shillings due for some sewing which she took home in the morning; for she was very hard pressed, and Mrs. S. could not make the change when she left her house, but told her to call again the next day. Mrs. S.—with all her kindly feelings, knew little of the wants of the poor, and Bessy never complained to anyone. She bore her lot with patient submission, and felt an honest pride in concealing her wants from every eye. So she could not make up her mind to tell Mrs. S. that she and her children were suffering from cold and want, but gratefully took the fragments of broken meat offered her, and in weariness, threaded the cold streets, half blinded by driving sleet, to obtain the paltry sum due for her midnight labor. It was then too late to purchase any thing that night, so Bessy went home and groped her way up the crazy stairs, to her cold silent room: for a charitable neighbor in the next apartment had looked after the children and put them to bed. Bessy ached in every limb, and her head throbbed painfully. It was of no use to kindle up the embers at that late hour, so she laid down beside the children, cold and damp, and vainly tried to sleep. It seemed very long, that weary night, as she tossed from side to side, and could find no relief in change. Hardship, anxiety and exposure had done their work, and a burning fever raged in every vein. In the morning she was unable to rise.

It was well for poor Bessy that she had a kind friend in her neighbor of the next apartment, who, with the warm sympathy that almost invariably springs up, fresh and genial among the weeds of poverty,—rendered her every needful assistance, and watched beside her with the tenderest care. Mrs. S. also, when two or three days passed away, and Bessy did not return for her money, neither came on the usual day to work for her, sent to enquire the cause. Greatly shocked to learn that her own thoughtlessness had, in part, occasioned Bessy's illness, she endeavored to repair the error by every possible attention which her situation demanded; and the suggestions of self-reproach led her, ever after, to regard more seriously the claims of those whose labor contributes so materially to domestic comfort.

Bessy had struggled hard with poverty and her constitution was unable to bear so severe a shock. The violence of the disease yielded to medical skill, but a rapid decline followed which left no hope of recovery. The world could offer her few allurements, and the grave had no terrors to her imagination. But one strong tie still held her to life, and the mother forgot all suffering in her earnest prayer to live a little longer for the children's sake. 'My children, what will become of them?' was the constant burthen of her heart; and the doubt, 'Who will care for the poor creatures when I am gone?' rose before her with painful pertinacity.

Happily Mrs. S. was enabled to soothe her fears, and give peace to her dying moments. She explained to her that there was a place provided, where such little ones were received and kindly cared for, and promised that her children should all find a home there, when she could no longer care for them. Poor Bessy's gratitude was unbounded; she had no higher boon to ask in life, and death came to her without a sting. The little orphans were welcomed to the Protestant Orphan Asylum, where their brief troubles were soon forgotten; and here, subjected to kind discipline, and instructed in all good and useful knowledge suited to their condition, it is hoped they will grow up to usefulness, and reflect credit on the Institution which has embraced them in its noble charity.

Friends of this Orphan Asylum! It is no tale of fictitious sorrow which we have laid before you. In your own experience, similar cases most have often called forth your generous sympathies. At every turn, you meet the poor, the sorrowful and the forsaken. In all the by-ways and obscure corners of this city are hungry, weeping orphans, left to the cold charity of a world that deigns not to look upon them, but whom Providence calls on you to rescue and redeem for the service of mankind.

And to others, the gay, the prosperous and the happy, who come here this day to pass an idle hour, or to please the fancy and gratify the taste,—let a deeper thought and a more earnest desire take possession of their minds, and lead them more faithfully, to perform the mission which our Heavenly Father has appointed to every child of humanity.

These orphan children appeal to every Christian heart, not for themselves alone, but for all little ones who are destitute of food and shelter,—care for their bodies, and training for their immortal minds. And to every one whom Providence has blessed with means and opportunity, is addressed the touching language of the Savior. 'In as much as ye have done it unto one of the least of these, ye have done it unto me.'

Note

1 See J. King, 'L'historiographie irlando-québécoise: Conflits et conciliations entre Canadiens français et Irlandais', translated by Simon Jolivet, *Bulletin d'histoire politique du Québec* 18:3 (2010), pp. 13–36, on pp. 19–21; J. King, 'The Genealogy of *Famine Diary* in Ireland and Quebec: Ireland's Famine Migration in Historical Fiction, Historiography, and Memory', *Éire-Ireland*, 47 (2012), pp. 45–69, on pp. 53–66.

16

FR. BERNARD O'REILLY TO *QUEBEC MERCURY* (LETTER WRITTEN ON GROSSE ISLE QUARANTINE STATION, 11 JULY, 1847; PUBLISHED IN THE *QUEBEC MERCURY* ON 27 JULY, 1847)

Fr. Bernard O'Reilly (1818–1907).

Bernard O'Reilly was born in Tuam, County Galway, and studied for the seminary in Nicolet and Quebec City before he was ordained in 1842. He served on Grosse Isle from July 6–14, 1847 and then testified about his experiences in Montreal on 23 July. He was so moved by the suffering of Famine emigrants that he founded a political association to prevent his French-Canadian parishioners from suffering a similar fate.[1] O'Reilly often revisited his experiences in his later writings such as 'The Irish Emigration of 1847' (1852) and *The Mirror of True Womanhood; A Book of Instruction for Women in the World* (1877) which are reproduced here. In later life he settled in the United States and became a supporter of Home Rule, as expressed in *The Cause of Ireland Pleaded Before the Civilized World* (1885).

My Dear Sir,

I cannot allow the Reverend Mr. Halle to leave the island without writing you a few words. You may consider this letter as private or not, and make such use of it as circumstances may prescribe or your own judgement consider expedient.

With the scenes that I have every hour of the day and night under my eyes, it may be allowed me to make a few observations on the state of things here.

Dr. Douglas is blamed, it is said, for all the unalleviated misery that prevails on the island, and on him the press and the giddy tongue of rumor make to fall all the censure which should be brought home to another quarter.

Now the facts are these: Dr. Douglas is making superhuman exertions to provide for the comforts of the wretched hundreds that are thrown into this charnel house. He is at the present moment unable to walk, yet he finds the means to see everything. But what can he do? Emigrants arrive in the tents, and the new hospitals continually, but they are *for days and nights* without a bed under them or a covering over them, wasting and *melting*, under the united influence of fever and dysentery, without a nurse or any other person to give them a drink during their long hours of raging thirst and horrible suffering. Whose fault is it if medical attendance is not provided for the unfortunates who are thus thrown helpless and friendless on this rock? Whose fault is it if the medical gentlemen who devote themselves to the cure of the plague-stricken thousands can neither get servants, nor medicine, nor drink for their respective patients? Who is, who ought to be, blamed if we are here since last Tuesday morning without ever seeing a sight of the steamboat chartered by the Government for the regular service of this station while it is absolutely necessary that the steamboat should in the present dreadful emergency perform a daily trip to Grosse Isle? I leave it to you, and the public, what must be the consequence of all this neglect?

The consequence is that for the want of bed and bedding, for want of attendance, hundreds of poor creatures, after a long sea-voyage, consumed by confinement and hunger, thirst and disease, are brought here and compelled to spend the long, long night, and the sultry melting day, lying on hard boards, without a pillow under their burning heads, without a hand to parch their wet lips, and fevered brow, without a hand to their tottering steps to any place where they can satisfy nature's most urgent wants, under the wasting influence of dysentery.

The consequence is that every day my reverend fellow-laborers and devoted medical gentlemen who imperil their lives in the same cause are compelled to behold hundreds that a little providential precaution and ordinary care might have restored to their large and helpless, houseless families and distracted relations, hurried away in a few hours to their premature and unhonoured grave, while those who should at once provide for their salvation, at every cost and sacrifice, are higgling about the means.

Is it encouraging to a young professional man to expose himself to almost certain death, for the paltry remuneration . . . held out to those who tender their services? Can it be hoped or expected that servants can be found for the trifle of payment . . . offered as wages to those who are willing to come and spend their nights and their days in a fever hospital?

I say it is my solemn conviction that money should be spared to enlist the services of every person whom money may entice to this theatre of disease and death. It is my unalterable conviction, shared, I am sure, by all who now witness or have formerly seen the state of things here, that no sacrifice should be deemed great by the Government, or the Legislature, which might save to humanity so many lives, to Ireland so many grateful children, to the Empire so many subjects.

I am not to be told that the Imperial Government would hesitate for a single moment to refund the Province for every shilling expended in a cause so sacred in an emergency unparalleled in the history of nations. Why then all this frothing and talking and examining when the Government should be effectually doing everything for the wretch ship-loads cast upon our shores? Where is the use of committees or commissions or inquiries or abuse of the Ministry, when that Ministry and Opposition should be unanimous in the suggestion and adoption of every measure which may afford a remedy proportionate to the appalling calamity?

This is strong language, but the language of a priest and an Irishman who is now in the midst of disease and death; who speaks out his heart and his mind with a hope of doing a little good where so much is imperiously required; who writes on the coffins of the hecatombs slaughtered by legislative neglect, much more than by the hand of sickness; who writes without the intention of wounding any or blaming, but with that of warning all concerned, with timely and salutary exertion: who writes, too, as if the line he pens were to be his last, and that on the truth it contains were to rest his reputation in life, his hopes for eternity.

With many thanks for your constant and warm advocacy for poor, suffering, heart-broken Ireland and Irish-men.

I remain, ever sincerely yours,

B. O'Reilly

17

FR. BERNARD O'REILLY, TESTIMONY FOR *REPORT OF THE SPECIAL COMMITTEE APPOINTED TO INQUIRE INTO THE MANAGEMENT OF THE QUARANTINE STATION AT GROSSE ISLE, . . . ON BEHALF OF THE BOARD OF HEALTH OF THE CITY OF MONTREAL* (23 JULY 1847). CANADA. LEGISLATURE. LEGISLATIVE ASSEMBLY. SPECIAL COMMITTEE APPOINTED TO INQUIRE INTO THE MANAGEMENT OF THE QUARANTINE STATION AT GROSSE ISLE

I only visited two ships, the *Avon* and the *Triton* [while serving at the quarantine station on Grosse Isle from 8 to July 14, 1847]. The *Avon* lost one hundred and thirty-six passengers on her voyage and the *Triton* eighty-seven, according to the Masters' statements. We administered the last rites of religion to about two hundred on board these two ships, and many others were in a state of great debility. . . .

No delay occurred in the burials [of the dead]. The Rev. Mr. Harper, who usually buried the dead, informed me that the graves were only dug four feet deep, and that three tier of coffins lain in; consequently there could not be sufficient quantity of earth to cover them. . . . As to the management of the Quarantine Station, it struck me during my stay at the Island, (and this feeling was shared by my Reverend fellow laborers,) that there *was* mismanagements somewhere. – The Medical staff at Grosse Isle were inadequate to the multifold and unceasing duties they had to face. The means provided for the comfort of the sick and the restoration of their health was sadly deficient. In a word, without determining to whom blame is to attach, it cannot be denied that if the Station had been established to prevent the inroads of disease and pestilence, to preserve the lives of the famine and fever-stricken thousands, the tide of Emigration was to leave on our shores; it cannot be denied that the result has been quite contrary to the general hope and the general expectation. Fever has at the present hour found its way into town and country in the Upper and Lower Provinces; and Legislators and citizens must come to the conclusion that either the system established to prevent the ravages of sickness was in itself imperfect, or that some egregious deficiency must have taken place in carrying out the same. I was under the impression while at Quarantine, that the Provincial Government had provided very insufficient means for the reception and care of the sick Emigrants, for the attendance of the requisite number of Physicians, and, above all, for the obtaining of the necessary number of nurses. I left Grosse Isle with the belief that Dr. Douglas had only very limited powers; that if there were not physicians enough, nurses enough; if both Physicians and nurses were not in possession of even a <u>scanty</u> supply of what was <u>absolutely necessary</u> for the proper discharge of their respective duties, it was because Dr. Douglas could not get the same; because his hands were tied. I saw the medical gentlemen indefatigable in their exertions, but I always heard them complain that, in the first place, they could not attend to the number of sick allotted to them; in the second, that they had not at their disposal medicines or diet to insure the cure of their patients, or attendants to see to their comforts. I here repeat what I have previously, though not so distinctly asserted: there was not a sufficient number of sheds erected. Moreover, those that are standing, have been got up without a proper regard to site and ventilation, to the recovery of the sick, the promoting of convalescence, and to the health of the persons whose duties compel them to visit these sheds. I have visited the sheds near the Lachine Canal [in Montreal] this morning, and I feel quite sure they are better furnished with every comfort and attendance required by their unfortunate inmates, than the sheds and tents occupied by the sick at Grosse Isle. At the time of my departure from the latter place, there was not a bundle of straw to be had on the Island. There was no spring water, no lime juice; at least we saw none. At a time when there should be a steamboat chartered to make a daily trip to the Station, we were a whole week without seeing the *St. George*; and even then, although the boat was at a distance of two acres from the shore, the Captain left the Rev. Mr. Harper and myself behind, while his very crew only answered our request for a boat by laughing at us. Were it not that we prevailed by dint of entreaties on the crew of the *Jessie* to bring us on board the steamer *Quebec*, we should have been compelled to remain another week at the Station. This is only one instance of the inconvenience to which the Clergymen in charge of the Station are exposed for want of a boat. Vessels came daily crowded with sick, and unless some person, through kindness, bring us on board, the wretched Emigrants are allowed to die in sight of their clergy, without the supreme consolation of an Irish Catholic, the last rites of his Church. . .

Again, I would respectfully solicit the attention of the proper authorities, in order that every precaution may be taken to preserve the property and money of those who are landed on Grosse Isle, together with an exact record of deaths and discharges. I was eight days at Grosse Isle, and during that period I could convince myself that, if things continue as they now exist, very few of those who land on its rocky shores, shall ever leave them. Thousands have already found there a premature and unhonoured grave – thousands must yet swell the present list of victims, if the Legislature and the Government do not immediately take the necessary steps, not indeed to repair the irreparable errors of the past, but to prevent, at least, their recurrence in the future. No sacrifice, no pains should be spared to remunerate the services of those physicians who imperil their lives in the hot-beds of pestilence, and no money should be refused to induce all these whom money might entice to attend the sick-bed of the homeless and friendless Emigrant. . .

Thus the spectre-like wretches who daily come up from Quarantine, without health, home, friends or money, would, by proper care and diet, recruit their strength, and either settle in the vicinity or continue their journey upwards without danger to others, and with comfort to themselves. The authorities must sooner or later adopt some similar plan at Grosse Isle or near Quebec, if they do not choose to consent to the wholesale murder of thousands who are just now on the ocean, or preparing to leave home for Canada. These remarks are made with the sole intention of pointing out where the evil lies, and of enabling the competent authority to apply at once the proper remedy. I wish to blame none, for I know not who is to be blamed in this sad matter. I cannot, however, forbear from expressing my grief that some many thousands of my fellow-creatures, my fellow countrymen, and subjects of this Empire, should have been sacrificed to *neglect* and *improvidence*. Nor is it to be imagined that the prospects before us can be much brighter, or that mortality can, to any extent decrease among the Emigrants. So long as they are sent away from the ports of Great Britain and Ireland crammed up by hundreds in the hold of a ship, without air, food, or the necessary means of procuring cleanliness and ventilation, as on board the *Avon* and the *Triton*, they must die by hundreds; disease must seize on the strongest frames and soon consume them. The fever-tainted remnant, on landing at Grosse Isle, will find a very slight change for the better in their condition. The greater number must sink under the united influence of fever and dysentery; those who are healthy, if sent up as hitherto to Montreal, must bring with them seeds of sickness, and become the inmates of the sheds in that City; while out of the numbers who can leave Montreal for a further destination, the large majority are pre-doomed to expire on the wharves of Kingston and Toronto, and to carry with them whithersoever they direct their steps, the dreadful malady that now hangs over the country like a funeral pall. I repeat it; let energetic steps be at once taken for the proper accommodation of the sick and the healthy on their landing and arrival; let more hospitals be erected at Grosse Isle, and in a more healthy situation; let the sick be carefully separated from the healthy, and proper lodgings prepared for the latter at Grosse Isle or some other place, while undergoing a quarantine, which experience must *now*, if ever, have taught us to be of indispensable necessity for all before they are sent up to Quebec or Montreal. I feel confident that the outlay required for this purpose, even were it not refunded by the Home Government, would be in a way repaid by the preservation of the public health, and the preservation too of many, many lives, precious to their own families and valuable to the Colony. . . .

I do wish it to be understood that if proper means were taken to make the healthy as well as the sick undergo a delay at Quarantine, the lives of hundreds of them, perhaps of thousands, would be thereby preserved: And this will be the more apparent, when it is considered that ships casting anchor at Quarantine in the condition in which I saw the *Avon*, and the *Triton*, have scarcely a single truly healthy person on board; those who were very sick could not and were not landed when I left. Sickness, under these circumstances, must increase on board the ships; the healthier portion of these passengers cannot but get enfeebled by their being detained on board: their predisposition to typhus caused by the length of their sea voyage, the poor quality of their food, and the pestilential atmosphere they were constantly inhaling, as a matter of course, was increased, and they were placed in the most imminent danger of contracting the disease. When they left the station, they were *literally crammed* on board the steamers, exposed to the cold night air, or the burning summer's sun, and in this state the most robust constitution must soon give way to an unbroken series of hardships.

Montreal and the whole Province have learned the consequences of thus allowing Emigrants to leave Grosse Isle without a sufficient sanitary probation, as well as the effects of permitting 800, 900, or 1000 persons in a state of uncleanliness and debility to be huddled for 48 hours together on the deck of a steamboat. I therefore contend that if any provision could be made to land all Emigrants *immediately* after their arrival, to afford them comfortable and healthy accommodation and diet, to make them attend the rules of cleanliness; when it was found it was safe to permit them to depart, a great change might be observable in their condition, on arriving in our cities and country places.

18

FR. BERNARD O'REILLY, 'SETTLEMENT OF THE EASTERN TOWNSHIPS', *QUEBEC MERCURY* (30 MARCH. 1848)

If political motives are to be imputed because the welfare of *one* class or *one* race is especially advocated, it ought to be borne in mind, that it is among *that class alone*, that lies the deep and inveterate evil I would fain remedy. If, in fine, by claiming for my flock, and for the French Canadian inhabitants of Lower Canada, some reparation for the neglect or the injustice of the Colonial administration during half a century, I am to be impeached with betraying the interests of my own countrymen at large,—I must not submit in silence to the accusation. Were it a crime in the eyes of Irishmen for an Irish priest, to promote the welfare of his flock, I should blush to bear an Irish name. And, if it be a sin to foster kindly feeling, and brotherly affection among Irishmen and Canadians, and – as I shall ever do among Irishmen and men of every other origin, with whom they live – then do I plead guilty. But certain I am, there is not a truly Irish heart, a truly noble soul here present, that does not acquit me of the charge.

Should I, think you, be worthy of the sacred character I bear, did I attempt to sow animosity between those who come from my own native land, and those who boast their English blood, no matter how deep the causes of hatred one country may have against the other? And should I not be still more guilty if I attempted to stir up strife between the Irish exile on the banks of the St. Lawrence and his Canadian brother, when I cannot pass a threshold in town or country where I may not see some fatherless, motherless orphan from Ireland, seated at the fireside, and enjoying the sunshine and warmth of French Canadian sympathy and cordial affection? Should I do so, seven hundred of these little children of misfortune, whom pestilence and famine have deprived of a mother's love – of a father's protection, would raise their voices to declare, that among the generous-hearted population of the cities and parishes, they have found a mother's bosom, upon which to rest their fevered brows – a father's hand to wipe away the tears of sorrow and suffering from their pale and bony cheek, and in a Canadian home! The noble Canadian Clergymen who descended to an early grave, the victims of their devotedness to my poor stricken countrymen, would they not raise their voices from the tomb to accuse me of unnatural, unparalleled, ingratitude? How could I visit Montreal where I saw those heroic nuns attending by night and by day the death bed of the emigrant; and, day after day, laying down their lives in the performance of the work of Charity? It is only a week ago, that I heard the death-knell of another of these angels of earth, who caught the contagion whilst attending upon our poor little orphans. And how many more of these noble victims will fall next summer? How many more of that devoted French Canadian clergy will be torn from their flocks and their heartbroken parishioners by the hand of pestilence? And all this for the sake of the Irish emigrant! Could there be a pulse in my heart that would not throb for such a people? No! If I loved them not, praised them not, blessed them not, you would spurn me from you to some other shore where I could no longer see the emigrant's unhonoured grave, and beside it the grave of the Canadian priest and Canadian nun, who cheered the lonely exile's last hour – who caught the pestilence from his poisoned breath, as they wiped the cold sweat from his brow, and poured the balmy word of peace into his departing soul.

But the scenes of Grosse Isle and Montreal would follow me thither: the spectacle I beheld at Three Rivers and in the neighbouring parishes, would come back to my mind's eye; – those Canadian women as I landed on the wharf, with my orphan charge, craving them from me, unappalled by their squalor and the dread sickness that spoke through every wan feature – taking them in their arms, pressing them to their bosoms with more than maternal fondness and heroism, and bedewing them with tears of sympathy! Oh! How many parishes have witnessed scenes like these? Even a fortnight ago in Montreal, when the saint-like bishop of that city appealed in favour of our little emigrant orphans in that beautiful letter in which the melancholy plaintiveness of a Jeremiah is blended with the eloquence and charity of a Paul, did I not behold in one week two hundred and twenty nine of our orphans taken to the homes and bosoms of French Canadians? Why add more?

There may be a field for similar acts of heroic charity before the year '49 dawns on us. Well I know that those who proved mothers to the orphans, and protectors to the widow, and comforters to the agonized patient, shall be again true to their former character of devotedness and piety. When, therefore, charity proves itself by those acts which divine wisdom makes the best test of its excellence – the harbouring of the widow and the orphans and the periling of one's life for the stranger and the exile, – shall we not deeply feel, and gratefully acknowledge it? Ever has it been my constant duty to inculcate both in this city, and wherever the hand of Providence hath placed me, brotherly affection towards all creeds and all origins: from that rule, I cannot with any semblance of reason be said to now depart, to promote ill-feelings towards those who worship with me at the same altar, and in whose affectionate kindness the friendless, helpless children of my wretched country to sure refuge on this side of the broad Atlantic.

19

FR. BERNARD O'REILLY, 'THE IRISH EMIGRATION OF 1847', *TRUE WITNESS AND CATHOLIC CHRONICLE* (17 DECEMBER 1852)[1]

About five years ago, while surrounded on the shores of the St. Laurence, with the victims of hunger and ship fever, I was given a copy of a lecture delivered in New York on 'The Antecedent Causes of the Irish Famine.' I had then before me a truthful commentary to these elegant pages; my only regret in perusing them was, that their illustrious author had not been an eye witness of the scenes in which I was nightly and daily privileged to take an active part. What an inspired energy his eloquence would have caught from their contemplation! What a lesson his revered voice could have read to Europe and America on the working of that government, which but a very short time ago we heard praised up in our midst as the very perfection of political liberality, wisdom, and enlightenment! How the dungeons of Naples and the cruelties of Sicily would have sunk into the shade before the horrid realities of Grosse-Isle!

Still is it not on these horrors that I wish to dwell. I only mean to touch them lightly. But I do intend even that little to remain on record as an irrefutable instance of the practical philanthropy of that model government, whose great men have overflowing sympathies for the down-trodden of every clime save their own, and who love the negro so ostentatiously and noisily in order to dispense themselves from loving their own brethren.

My purpose in appearing before you is a higher one. I wish to disburden my soul of the conviction which I felt even in the lazar-houses and fetid ship-holds of Canada—that Providence would bring some mighty good out of all that suffering. Yes, I read that assurance in the sublime virtues which it was then given me to witness. That alone enabled me not to curse the oppressor—and this was much; it gave me also hope for Ireland—and this was more; but, above all, it made me rejoice for America.

Nor must you deem this be the illusion of a youthful enthusiasm, on the effect of an overweening love of country. I had not then touched the soil of the United States. But since that happiness has been vouchsafed me, my previous convictions have acquired the evidence of a mathematical demonstration.

They have assumed the form of this consoling truth. That the heart of a nation tried by suffering so unparalleled in duration and intensity, and giving all the whole unfailing evidence of superhuman fortitude, is destined for some great end;

and that, moreover, where Providence forces . . . a nation, under such pressure, to diffuse abroad a portion, and a large portion, of her vital energies, it must be in a design of kindness to the regions towards which these energies are made to flow . . .

Early in the spring of 1847 the tide of emigration set in through the valley of the St. Laurence. The local authorities in every part of Ireland had been anxiously watching for the time when the Canadian navigation usually opens, in order to rid their wharves, poorhouses, crowded hospitals, and the hulks at anchor in every seaport of the living mass of misery for which they could not or would not find shelter and relief. The landlords, too, throughout the country had begun their work of wholesale demolition and extermination; some gave to their famishing tenants a mere trifle, on condition that they should take the road to the nearest place of embarkation; others put into their hands pretended cheques on Canadian mercantile houses, to induce them to give up their little farms, while all employed every means of persuasion and coercion to urge their dependents to the sea side.

And sooth to say the tenants, whether they found themselves absolutely penniless, or still possessed of some little money, were not loath to hurry away to the great Republic of the West, where loving friends awaited them, and whence, during that dreadful winter, they had been sent such generous, although insufficient assistance. They crowded, therefore, improvidently and recklessly into every vessel that was advertised to sail for America. Nor did the ship owners, nor the emigrant agents, make any scruple of receiving more passengers than the law permitted; the law was notoriously and most shamefully violated.

In the colonies, meanwhile Government and people were quite unprepared for the frightful amount of sickness and destitution which the eastern winds were hurrying to their doors. More than ordinary precautions had indeed been taken, and I am confident no necessary expense and pains would have been spared by the Canadian executive had timely notice been sent, and it was so easy and so urgent to do so. But as it was there was not accommodation for one-fifth of the sick and dying that the months of April and May deposited on the barren rocks of Quarantine.

The military authorities at the first fearful tidings, with characteristic promptness and generosity, sent every tent which their stores contained. But the workmen hired to erect sheds had soon caught the contagion. Higher, and the very highest wages were offered to others, who, in their turn, sickened and died after a few days, so that, at the very height of the disease, no bribe could induce mechanics to approach the island.

The fierce Canadian summer had now come, attended with unusual sultriness. Thousands upon thousands of the sick, melting under the united influences of long confinement, hunger, fever, and dysentery, kept pouring in at Grosse Isle.

Not one drop of fresh water was to be had on the island—there was no lime juice, no clean straw even to protect the patients from the wet ground in the tents, or the rough boards in the hospitals; while in the beginning of July, with the thermometer at 98° in the shade, I have seen hundreds landed from the ships, and thrown rudely by the unfeeling crews on the burning rocks, and there I have known them to remain two whole nights and days without shelter or care of any kind.

Without shelter or care of any kind—for the few trustworthy persons whom the zeal of the Clergy, or the prospect of a large salary, induced to go down at the beginning, were soon exhausted; want of sleep, of proper nourishment, and the pestilential atmosphere in which they had to move continually, had soon laid them prostrate. How, then, were skilful, careful sick-nurses to be found? I blush, I weep to say it, the common gaol was opened, and its loathsome inmates were sent to watch the death-bed of our pure, helpless emigrant youth.

This it was—together with the hope of earning fully the crown which they all expected – that made the Clergymen who attended the station in turns multiply themselves by day in ministering to the wants of both soul and body, and spend their nights in relieving, as they might, the unspeakable wretchedness of that multitude whose groans arose like a hoarse and mighty murmur in the stillness, making sleep a thing not to be thought of. One devoted Priest—the Rev. Hubert Robson[2]—an only son, too, of an infirm and doting mother—after the fatigues of confessing, anointing, consoling the sufferers, was wont to spend his few recreation hours in carrying in his arms and on his back the sick from the beach to the hospitals. One very sultry day, overcome by this labour of love, he lay himself down on the shore, beside a rock, to snatch a moment's sleep. Alas! he awoke with a raging fever, and, the first of the long list of those Canadian Priests who laid down their lives for the emigrant, he went to his early reward in Heaven. The grief of the poor people on learning his death was as moving as it was universal.

Meanwhile the multitudes who had strength enough to baffle the scrutiny of the visiting physicians proceeded to Quebec, Montreal, and the cities of the upper province, spreading the infection on their way. The hardships of their long exposure on a steamboat deck had soon developed the latent germs of the malady. Alarm and death were everywhere.

The cholera, in its most malignant form, did not visit with death and desolation half the families which ship fever caused to mourn. It was sufficient to give the new-comers, how healthy so ever in appearance, hospitality for a single night, to meet them even on the road, or to inhale the miasmas which clung to their persons and luggage, in order to contract the pestilence. Whole families were swept away in return for a single act of kindness done the passing emigrants.

Despite the vigilance of the municipal officers, every Canadian city soon presented the same spectacle of disease and suffering as Quarantine.

From the outset, the Canadian Clergy felt that an opportunity had come for them to display the sublime virtues which Catholic charity inspires. Their presentiments and hopes were not disappointed. Every one of the Clergymen who had been summoned, or who had volunteered, to meet the danger, during the two first months and a half, was either dead or dying, or slowly recovering. The Bishop of Montreal and his coadjutor gave the example of spending the entire night in confessing and anointing the sick who came up by the evening boats. The Nuns of the General Hospital and the Sisters of the Asylum of Providence were the first to offer themselves to share in the good work. Although very numerous, their whole community could not suffice, and their cloistered Sisters of the *Hotel Dieu* soon came to relieve them at the pillow of the emigrant. For months did the whole city behold these devoted women, moving like angels of light and peace through the crowded sheds, and wading literally knee deep in the mire from tent to tent on the low and marshy ground, until at length the nunneries themselves were converted into hospitals for the perishing Sisterhood, where the few who retained their strength could scarcely tend their own sick and dying.

I cannot trust myself longer on this part of my narrative. Yet, before I turn away from it I owe it to truth and holiest gratitude to declare:—That with the facts of every plague and epidemic of ancient and modern times vividly present to my memory, I do believe such suffering never before existed, and that such an instance of devotedness and magnanimity has never been exhibited to the world as by the Bishops, Priests, Nuns, and people of Canada, in 1847.

I say the *French Canadian people*; for, not satisfied with collecting for the relief of Ireland some £8,000 sterling – so strongly were their sympathies aroused towards the emigrant—that although most parishes already wept for their dead, or feared for their sick Pastor, and that it appeared certain death to take an emigrant under one's roof; still, as each Parish Priest returned from Quarantine, or from Montreal, the parishioners came to meet them at the landing places with long trains of carriages, to escort the Priests and his numerous orphans home. And touching was the meeting of these French mothers with the little children misfortune gave them; and warm and happy the homes they were brought to. But these recollections unnerve me.

There is, however, one other instance of generosity that I must place on record. I do so the more willingly, as the whole course of this narrative must tell the more severely against other official personages. The Governor General of Canada, the Right Honourable, the Lord of Elgin, at the very moment when the thought of approaching Grosse Isle appalled the stoutest hearts, went down himself to examine into the state of things; and he went through every ward and tent fearlessly and cheerfully.

During the winter he zealously adopted every suggestion made for the relief of the sick and poor, and provided with a fatherly solicitude against the contingencies of the approaching spring. The Sisters of Charity of the *Asylums of Providence* who had borne a conspicuous part in the labours and sacrifices of the two Sisterhoods already mentioned, now offered to go down to Quarantine, and superintend the hospital department; they were destined to an equally meritorious duty in the hospitals of Montreal.

The spring did, indeed, bring fever; and with it came the dreaded cholera. The noble-hearted governor would trust to no one but himself the duty of securing the comfort of the emigrant sick. When cholera and ship fever were raging together at 'The Sheds', he would be seen passing through the wards, going with the Nuns from bed to bed, to inquire into the condition of the patients. But this is only what we should expect from the descendant and representative of the Royal Bruce.

FR. BERNARD O'REILLY, *TRUE WITNESS*

Thus passed the spring and summer in one continuous influx of pestilence, terror, and misery indescribable; fleet after fleet of passenger vessels, bearing their cargoes of dead and dying up the Canadian waters. Some ships had lost 100, some 200 persons, since they had sailed; some had lost all, or nearly all their crew; so that they lay below in the stream, carried up and down with the tide, until discovered by chance from the shore, or until pity induced the Canadians from the neighbouring villages to work them up to port.

In many cases, as where these ships had been laden from the hulks and poorhouses, the passengers had never left the hold, very many had never stirred from their berths, from the hour they had lost sight of Ireland to their casting anchor at Grosse Isle. The dead were dragged up by means of a grapnel or boat-hook, and cast into the deep. You may fill up the picture that met the eyes of the Missionaries when they descended into this living mass of putrefaction to strive and strengthen the living.

And now the autumn had arrived. Many a parish was left without its Pastor. Montreal had wept its Vicar General; its two Bishops were long despaired of; well-nigh twenty of its Priests, with a far greater number of Nuns, had died in the work of mercy. Quebec, too, saw many of its most pious and promising Clergymen sink under their labours; Bytown, Kingston, and Toronto, paid also their tribute to death and charity. The indefatigable Bishop Power closed the heroic list. He went to join his fellow-martyrs, after months of obstinate and superhuman fatigue, leaving his young diocese long widowed and inconsolable.

About the beginning of September two emigrant ships were obliged to put in to the nearest ports of Nova Scotia and New Brunswick. They had taken out the tenants of a minister of the imperial crown;[3] but so dreadful was the state of all on board, that the municipal authorities, after furnishing the captains with the most pressing necessaries, compelled them to put once more to sea.

In the beginning of November, when the St. Laurence was already covered with floating ice, a vessel was observed beating about the mouth of the Saguenay; she was evidently in distress. The Canadian pilots, whose Catholic sympathies had been already so nobly tested, boarded her. The crew were disabled to a man: the hold was a sepulchre. Every assistance that could be procured was speedily sent, and the ship was brought up the river. As it was found impossible to provide hospital-room for these new-comers at Quebec, the Rev. Bernard McGauran,[4] who had been the first at Quarantine in the spring, and the last to leave it in the fall, embarked with these last sufferers and had them towed up to Montreal. At their arrival, so indescribably loathsome was their condition that as soon as the living had been extracted from the heap of death in which they had been buried for months, the vessel was burned to the water's edge, and sunk.

Now, who, think you, was the noble landlord who treated his tenants with such exemplary tenderness? Heard you of a British statesman, who, scarcely a twelve months ago, endorsed a pamphlet written by one of his former associates in the ministry, on the cruelties, real, imaginary, or exaggerated, committed against a few political prisoners at Naples—who denounced those cruelties from his place in parliament at a time when any means of getting up excitement against the people, or creating prejudice against Catholic cruelties, was deemed of paramount importance in England? Who sent copies of that same pamphlet, accompanied with an insolent official note, to all the cabinets of Europe? Who could suspect that this nobleman, this minister so jealous of the rights of liberty and humanity in other countries, so tender-hearted towards Sicilian political prisoners, would allow, if he did not order, the subject of the crown he served, his fellow-countrymen, his own tenantry, to be shipped off more carelessly and treated more inhumanly than the slave-seller would ship off or the slave-buyer treat, his cargo? What do you say if this man is Lord Palmerston?

But what was the behaviour of the emigrants under privations and sufferings so unequalled? Let me state to you, that you will only get one answer from every point of the provinces. The Prelates, the Priests, and those incomparable women whom I have mentioned, are unanimous in asserting :—'That such a spectacle of meekness, of uncomplaining, unwavering patience, purity, piety, and faith, they have never heard of, and had never hoped to see on earth.'

This opinion had also spread among the country people; their Priests had told them that these fever-stricken emigrants were religious heroes, and hence the eagerness with which they took to their bosoms the Irish orphans, and the affectionate reverence with which they still regard them, as the children of martyrs in Heaven, the offspring of a martyred Church.

Turn we now to the Church of Ireland herself; what was her attitude all this while? That which we might expect from the mother of such a race; an attitude of moral sublimity to which nothing in any age can be found superior. Her fields were blighted; her populous villages had become a howling wilderness in which dogs fought for their masters' unburied bones; her highways were covered with multitudes whose cabins had been levelled before their eyes, and themselves and their little ones left to perish with hunger and fever on the road-side; or to find their way, as best they might, to the far distant coast of the Western World. There she sat, amidst solitude and sickness, surrounded with the corpses of one portion of her children, and the ghastly forms of the remainder writhing in the last throes of starvation; her heart pierced with ten thousand sorrows, but her calm blue eye fixed with unfaltering gaze on Heaven. . .

Now, sons of Ireland, what say you to your mother?

Then, her spirit has not been broken—her soul has not grown old midst the trials of centuries? Her teeming church yards, her depopulated districts, where silence sits heavier on her heart than the earth on the bosom of the dead; the uncounted thousands of Grosse Isle, with the uncoffined copses over which the spirits of the deep keep respectful watch; all, all this has not, then, weighed down the heart of dear old Ireland. – You are proud of her, it is a lawful and a holy pride.

For there is more than life in that heart so full of Faith, and in that unconquered soil there is divinest charity. . .

What was Ireland's answer? In every pulpit, in every country church to which the famishing congregation could scarce crawl, his voice was drowned with the sobs and cries that ascended to Heaven for the Church of St. Austin and St. Anselm.

This was Ireland's revenge.

And we have this generous heart in America. We possess it in the hundreds of thousands of working men whom the Atlantic wave deposits yearly upon our shores, with their livery of abject wretchedness it is true, and their awkward gait and unseemly accent—with their haggard look, their emaciated cheek, their fevered eye, it is also true; but with minds enlightened with the clear belief and the understanding of the heart—with the soul capable—America wilt not gainsay me—capable of every ennobling virtue, of every duty of citizenship. We possess that pure, incorruptible heart, that patient, invincible heart, in these poor Irish maidens, the glory of Ireland, the apostles' of England in our day; who turn away from its godless coal mines, and manufactures, from its pampered middle classes, and its self-adoring aristocracy, the wrath of Heaven; and draw on the land the eye, the love, and intercession of the countless host of England's and Ireland's Saints. We, too, have them scattered through every household these hard-working daughters of holy poverty and honourable exile, who, by their faithfulness, their generosity, their love of Ireland, their gratitude to America, by their self-denying spirit, their devotedness to the friends whom they have left behind them, and, above all, by their lion-hearted chastity, teach woman where is her true sphere and place, and on the basis of what virtues she can build up her empire over the respect and affections of the world.

No, Catholics do not expect the model woman the type of her sex. She has been found, since the Son of God was born of a woman; since lowly-mindedness, love of poverty, obscurity, and toil, and the spirit of sacrifice, have raised a daughter of mankind to be mother of the Most High. And, to find her faithful followers, we have only to recollect our mothers and sisters.

Yes, they are to be found everywhere, from the opulent Mansions of New York to the newest sheds of San Francisco and Australia, these daughters of St. Patrick, always and everywhere modest, mild, and true to the service of their Heavenly Mistress, and the interests of their earthly masters.

Surely the mighty heart of America will not beat less free, or bold, or pure, because such blood will mingle with it.

Am I wrong then in supposing that the energies of this mass of men and women, unceasingly poured in upon our land, form a most important element in the future destinies of our Republic!

This is a fact already felt, acknowledged even, we have only to glance at its most obvious results.

There is, therefore, in the influx of strangers brought us by the famine and Emigration of 1847 an element of strength for the Constitution, as well as of prosperity for the land.

We are not dreamy, discontented, ever-seeking theorists in politics, no more so than in religion. We have well defined, unvarying duties towards the Law and the Magistrate entrusted with its execution. It is hard in any case to make us rise against authority; but when we have found rational liberty with institutions that protect industry, and interfere not with conscience, then our hearts and lives are at the command of authority.

We find such here: liberty to worship the God of our fathers; liberty to advance in all the paths of honour and wealth; liberty for the exercise of every lawful faculty of mind, heart, and conscience. . .

But while enjoying this noble share of freedom, or awaiting quietly, though watchfully, the balance of our Christian liberties, we never will join in any dissatisfaction from within, or sanction any unholy agitation from without.

Already have the sons of Ireland approved themselves not unworthy brothers of the ancient Catholics of the land; steadfast friends of union, as well as determined foes to all revolutionary extravagance. . .

It is time that we should proclaim it; she, too, is the mother of civilisation and liberty. The remedy for the social evils of a portion of our country is not in agitation, in unjust and angry invective. The political quacks who have poisoned Jamaica, who allow Ireland's sores to remain without binding up, would not cure, but kill. . .

I believe God has implanted the Church in this land, and sent the Irish emigrant to multiply her temples everywhere, in order that when other doctrines will have borne and ripened their fruits of death and disorganisation, she may be there with her fruit of life and communion. . .

But will she have no other return to expect from us? Most certainly shall there be another. It is in this country, in every Irish—No! in every American heart, that Providence elaborates and prepares, for its own good time, the freedom of Ireland. This is the debt America owes the Emerald Isle, and she will know when and how to pay it.

It is well, then, that God has allowed human events to hold on their course. The sufferings of 1847 will have their own purpose, their own memorable result on both sides of the Atlantic.

Let us, children of Ireland, hold up our heads, and strengthen our hearts with the high hopes which I have set before you. When the Hebrew giant of old was compelled to the ignominy of the servile toil, deprived of his sight and shorn of the strength which he held from on high, he confessed himself punished for having betrayed the secret of that strength.

Ireland never has betrayed the secret. She will not have, like the Israelite Samson, to sacrifice herself in order to pull down destruction on her oppressors. But, like him in his innocence, while welled in by the foe from every outward succour, and seemingly beset with inextricable difficulties, she may be seen bearing far away beyond the reach of the pursuers the very gates of her prison.

When the dawn of that blessed day will have come to gladden our hearts, when the young giant of Ireland's liberty, will wake with his tread the echoes of the American hills, on that day we shall not forget the 'Famine and Emigration of 1847.'

Notes

1 Bernard O'Reilly's article is based on a lecture that he delivered in New York City.
2 Father Hubert Robson (1808–1847), died caring for Irish emigrants on Grosse Isle on 1 July, 1847.
3 Henry John Temple, Lord Palmerston (1784–1865), Foreign Secretary in 1847 and Prime Minister (1855–58, 1859–65). The burned vessel that O'Reilly refers to is the *Lord Ashburton* which transported 481 assisted emigrants from Palmerston's estate in Sligo via Liverpool to Quebec, 65 of whom perished at sea.
4 Father Bernard McGauran (1821–1882), chaplain of Grosse Isle in 1847.

20

FR. BERNARD O'REILLY, *THE MIRROR OF TRUE WOMANHOOD; A BOOK OF INSTRUCTION FOR WOMEN IN THE WORLD* (NEW YORK: P. J. KENNEDY, EXCELSIOR PUBLISHING HOUSE, 1877), PP. 96–99

In the City of Quebec itself but comparatively few ravages were committed by this dreaded 'Ship-fever,' the steamers which conveyed the healthier immigrants to Montreal and the upper St. Lawrence not being permitted to land. In Montreal, however, and in Kingston and Toronto their arrival and passage were marked by a fearful mortality. In the first-named Bishop Bourget, his coadjutor, Bishop Prince, his vicar-general, and some thirty priests were stricken down by the plague. The seminary of St. Sulpice alone lost eight of its members. The Bishop Power of Toronto fell a victim to it, and its ravages were such, during the early summer, that they far outstripped those of the cholera.

Of course thousands upon thousands of orphans were left behind, and that, too, at a time when to give them a refuge in any home in town and country, appeared to be bringing certain death into the family. Yet, – and this is what must redound to the eternal honor of the French Canadian population of the present province of Quebec, – not only was there no hesitation manifested in adopting these little cast-aways, but at the voice of their bishops and priests the people of the country parishes vied with each other in their zeal to share their homes with them.

The author remembers returning from the quarantine, in the second week of July, with the Rev. John Harper, rector of St. Grégoire, opposite Three Rivers. They had spent a fortnight among the fever-sheds, and had, at the urgent request of their parishioners, brought home with them a large number of orphans. The parishioners of St. Grégoire (the descendants of the noble Acadians eulogized by the author of 'Evangeline'[1]) had chartered a little steamer to convey us and our orphans across the river. We had been delayed perforce on our way upward, and on our arrival about midnight at Three Rivers, we found a crowd of eager and excited women, mothers of families all of them, waiting and watching for us. Mr. Harper was among his parishioners, and on the spot these noble mothers were allowed to satisfy the yearning of their Christian hearts, and to take each her little orphans to her embrace. It was a spectacle worthy of the admiration of angels, which was beheld on that wharf at that sultry midnight in July, these farmers' wives, weeping every one of them with their holy emotion which sweetest charity creates, pressing around their pastor and choosing, when they could, in the uncertain light, the child that pleased them best, or accepting joyously and folding in a motherly embrace the little orphan allotted to them. The ladies of Three Rivers were also there, jealous of the happiness of their sisters and neighbours, and employing in the darkness some pious stratagems to decoy to their homes some of the weary, wasted, or fevered little creatures.

The author was a hundred miles distant from his own parish of Sherbrooke, and had only dared to select a few orphans to take with him all the way. So, after an hour of confusion and excitement we were all content to rest till the approaching daylight. When the dawn came, and we left our resting places for the ferry, all Three Rivers and its neighbourhood were abroad to see the priests, their orphans, and the happy mothers to whom God had given the prize of an orphan, wending their way in a procession to the steamer and to the ferry-boat. The heat of the preceding days, and the sultry night with its excitement, had told on more than one of the bewildered little strangers: there were several cases of declared fever. But no one seemed to mind. The charity of Jesus Christ was abroad, like a river overflowing its banks. Two children who had fallen to the author's charge were especially ill; one, a little boy, clung to his cassock as we set out from the hotel; the other, a little girl of four, he had to carry in his arms, as she was too sick to walk.

The scene has remained indelibly impressed upon heart and memory. We were wending our way through the crowd of weeping or pitying spectators when the wife of a distinguished lawyer of Three Rivers, childless herself as we were told, approached the author to caress the little motherless one who clung to him in apparent insensibility. As she kissed the child again and again, addressing it in the sweetest tones of womanly tenderness, the little sufferer looked into those appealing, tearful eyes, and stretched out her arms to that hungry heart which would not be refused. They were only separated by death thereafter.

But when we reached the other shore we found the Rev. J.C. Marquis, with the entire population of St. Grégoire, and every available mode of conveyance waiting for us; and so we proceeded some two or three miles to the beautiful parish church, where priests and people knelt in devout thanksgiving, – the priests grateful for their preservation from the plague, the people thanking God for the precious boon charity had bestowed on them. They did not rest contented with this, however: hundreds of other orphans were sought after subsequently and added to the happiness, and – let us hope – the prosperity of this excellent people. Not one of these stranger-children but became in every sense the child of the home into which it was received.

All through the remaining months of summer, the autumn, and the early winter, this generous flame of charity spread and burned among the French Canadian parishes along both shores of the St. Lawrence; and, strange to say, the good souls

243

who thus vied with each other in opening their homes and hearts to the orphans of Ireland's exiles, were wont to say that while the plague spared the families into which the strangers were admitted, it swept away pitilessly such as gave them a passing or a mercenary refuge. Ah, generous people of New France, may the Saints of Ireland obtain for you length of days, with the richest blessings of true freedom, a constant increase in the noblest gifts of soul, and all the rewards of true piety!

Note

1 American poet Henry Wadsworth Longfellow's (1807–1882) epic poem *Evangeline, A Tale of Acadie* was published in 1847.

21

JOHN FRANCIS MAGUIRE, *THE IRISH IN AMERICA* (NEW YORK: D & J SADLIER AND CO, 1868), PP. 134–153

John Francis Maguire (1815–1872) was the founder and editor of the *Cork Examiner* (1841–1872) and an MP for Dungarvan (1852) and Cork City (1865–1872). He published *The Irish in America* in Montreal and London with D & J Sadlier and Co. on both sides of the Atlantic in 1868. The book is based on his travels and interviews with Famine survivors in Canada and the United States in 1866–67. He was a moderate, constitutional nationalist who argued in *The Irish in America* that Irish Catholics fare better abroad than in their native land when not subject to British misgovernment in Ireland.

The Irish Exodus – The Quarantine at Grosse Isle – The Fever Sheds – Horrors of the Plague – The 'Unknown' – The Irish Orphans – The good Canadians – Resistless Eloquence – One of the Orphans – The Forgotten Name – The Plague in Montreal – How the Irish died – The Monument at Point St. Charles – The Grave-mound in Kingston – An illustrious Victim in Toronto – How the Survivors pushed on.

I HAVE more than once referred to the unfavourable circumstances under which the vast majority of the Irish arrived in America, and the difficulties with which, in a special degree, they had to contend; but the picture would be most imperfect were not some reference made to the disastrous emigration of the years 1847 and 1848 – to that blind and desperate rush across the Atlantic known and described, and to be recognised for time to come, as the Irish Exodus. We shall confine our present reference to the emigration to Canada, and track its course up the waters of the St. Lawrence. A glance even at a single quarantine – that of Grosse Isle, in the St. Lawrence, about thirty miles below Quebec – while affording a faint idea of the horrors crowded into a few months, may enable the reader to understand with what alarm the advent of the Irish was regarded by the well-to-do colonists of British America; and how the natural terror they inspired, through the terrible disease brought with them across the ocean, deepened the prejudice against them, notwithstanding that their sufferings and misery appealed to the best sympathies of the human heart.

EYEWITNESS TESTIMONIES

On the 8th of May, 1847, the 'Urania,' from Cork, with several hundred immigrants on board, a large proportion of them sick and dying of the ship-fever, was put into quarantine at Grosse Isle. This was the first of the plague-smitten ships from Ireland which that year sailed up the St. Lawrence. But before the first week of June as many as eighty-four ships of various tonnage were driven in by an easterly wind; and of that enormous number of vessels there was not one free from the taint of malignant typhus, the offspring of famine and of the foul ship-hold. This fleet of vessels literally reeked with pestilence. All sailing vessels, – the merciful speed of the well-appointed steamer being unknown to the emigrant of those days, – a tolerably quick passage occupied from six to eight weeks; while passages of ten or twelve weeks, and even a longer time, were not considered at all extraordinary at a period when craft of every kind, the most unsuited as well as the least seaworthy, were pressed into the service of human deportation.

Who can imagine the horrors of even the shortest passage in an emigrant ship crowded beyond its utmost capability of stowage with unhappy beings of all ages, with fever raging in their midst? Under the most favourable circumstances it is impossible to maintain perfect purity of atmosphere between decks, even when ports are open, and every device is adopted to secure the greatest amount of ventilation. But a crowded emigrant sailing ship of twenty years since, with fever on board! – the crew sullen or brutal from very desperation, or paralysed with terror of the plague – the miserable passengers unable to help themselves, or afford the least relief to each other; one-fourth, or one-third, or one-half of the entire number in different stages of the disease; many dying, some dead; the fatal poison intensified by the indescribable foulness of the air breathed and rebreathed by the gasping sufferers – the wails of children, the ravings of the delirious, the cries and groans of those in mortal agony! Of the eighty-four emigrant ships that anchored at Grosse Isle in the summer of 1847, there was not a single one to which this description might not rightly apply.

The authorities were taken by surprise, owing to the sudden arrival of this plague-smitten fleet, and, save the sheds that remained since 1832, there was no accommodation of any kind on the island. These sheds were rapidly filled with the miserable people, the sick and the dying, and round their walls lay groups of half-naked men, women, and children, in the same condition – sick or dying. Hundreds were literally flung on the beach, left amid the mud and stones, to crawl on the dry land how they could. 'I have seen,' says the priest who was then chaplain of the quarantine, and who had been but one year on the mission, 'I have one day seen thirty-seven people lying on the beach, crawling on the mud, and dying like fish out of water.'[1] Many of these, and many more besides, gasped out their last breath on that fatal shore, not able to drag themselves from the slime in which they lay. Death was doing its work everywhere – in the sheds, around the sheds, where the victims lay in hundreds under the canopy of heaven, and in the poisonous holds of the plague-ships, all of which were declared to be, and treated as, hospitals.

From ship to ship the young Irish priest carried the consolations of religion to the dying. Amidst shrieks, and groans, and wild ravings, and heart-rending lamentations, – over prostrate sufferers in every stage of the sickness – from loathsome berth to loathsome berth, he pursued his holy task. So noxious was the pent-up atmosphere of these floating pest-houses, that he had frequently to rush on deck, to breathe the pure air, or to relieve his overtaxed stomach: then he would again plunge into the foul den, and resume his interrupted labours.

There being, at first, no organisation, no staff, no available resources, it may be imagined why the mortality rose to a prodigious rate, and how at one time as many as 150 bodies, most of them in a half-naked state, would be piled up in the dead-house, awaiting such sepulture as a huge pit could afford. Poor creatures would crawl out of the sheds, and being too exhausted to return, would be found lying in the open air, not a few of them rigid in death. When the authorities were enabled to erect sheds sufficient for the reception of the sick, and provide a staff of physicians and nurses, and the Archbishop of Quebec[2] had appointed a number of priests, who took the hospital duty in turn, there was of course more order and regularity; but the mortality was for a time scarcely diminished. The deaths were as many as 100, and 150, and even 200 a day, and this for a considerable period during the summer. The masters of the quarantine-bound ships were naturally desirous of getting rid as speedily as possible of their dangerous and unprofitable freight; and the manner in which the helpless people were landed, or thrown, on the island, aggravated their sufferings, and in a vast number of instances precipitated their fate. Then the hunger and thirst from which they suffered in the badly-found ships, between whose crowded and stifling decks they had been so long pent up, had so far destroyed their vital energy that they had but little chance of life when once struck down.

About the middle of June the young chaplain was attacked by the pestilence. For ten days he had not taken off his clothes, and his boots, which he constantly wore for all that time, had to be cut from his feet. A couple of months elapsed before he resumed his duties; but when he returned to his post of danger the mortality was still of fearful magnitude. Several priests, a few Irish, the majority French Canadians, caught the infection; and of the twenty-five who were attacked, seven paid with their lives the penalty of their devotion. Not a few of these men were professors in colleges; but at the appeal of the Archbishop they left their classes and their studies for the horrors and perils of the fever sheds.

It was not until the 1st of November that the quarantine of Grosse Isle was closed. Upon that barren isle as many as 10,000 of the Irish race were consigned to the grave-pit. By some the estimate is made much higher, and 12,000 is considered nearer the actual number. A register was kept, and is still in existence, but it does not commence earlier than June 16, when the mortality was nearly at its height. According to this death-roll, there were buried, between the 16th and 30th of June, 487 Irish immigrants 'Whose names could not be ascertained.' In July, 941 were thrown into nameless graves; and in August, 918 were entered in the register under the comprehensive description – 'Unknown.' There were interred, from the 16th of June to the closing of the quarantine for *that* year, 2,905 of a Christian people, whose names could not be discovered amidst the confusion and carnage of that fatal summer. In the following year, 2,000 additional victims were entered in the same register, without name or trace of any kind, to tell who they were, or whence they had come. Thus 5,000 out of the total number of victims were simply described as 'Unknown.'

This deplorable havoc of human life left hundreds of orphans dependent on the compassion of the public; and nobly was the unconscious appeal of this multitude of destitute little ones responded to by the French Canadians. Half naked, squalid, covered with vermin generated by hunger, fever, and the foulness of the ship's hold, perhaps with the germs of the plague lurking in their vitiated blood, these helpless innocents of every age – from the infant taken from the bosom of its dead mother to the child that could barely tell the name of its parents – were gathered under the fostering protection of the Church. They were washed, and clad, and fed; and every effort was made by the clergy and the nuns who took them into their charge to discover who they were, what their names, and which of them were related the one to the other, so that, if possible, children of the same family might not be separated for ever. A difficult thing it was to learn from mere infants whether, among more than 600 orphans, they had brothers or sisters. But by patiently observing the little creatures when they found strength and courage to play, their watchful protectors were enabled to find out relationships which, without such care, would have been otherwise unknown. If one infant ran to meet another, or caught its hand, or smiled at it, or kissed it, or showed pleasure in its society, here was a clue to be followed; and in many instances children of the same parents were thus preserved to each other. Many more, of course, were separated for ever, as these children were too young to tell their own names, or do anything save cry in piteous accents for 'Mammy, mammy!' until soothed to slumber in the arms of a compassionate Sister.

The greater portion of the orphans of the Grosse Isle tragedy were adopted by the French Canadians, who were appealed to by their curés at the earnest request of Father Cazeau,[3] then Secretary to the Archbishop, and now one of the Vicars General of the Archdiocese of Quebec. M. Cazeau is one of the ablest of the ecclesiastics of the Canadian Church, and is no less remarkable for worth and ability than for the generous interest he has ever exhibited for the Irish people. Father Cazeau had employed his powerful influence with the country clergy to provide for the greater number of the children; but some 200 still remained in a building specially set apart for them, and this is how these 200 Irish orphans were likewise provided for:

Monsignor Baillargeon,[4] Bishop of Quebec, was then curé of the city. He had received three or four of the orphans into his own house, and among them a beautiful boy of two years, or perhaps somewhat younger. The others had been taken from him and adopted by the kindly *habitans*, and become part of their families; but the little fellow, who was the curé's special pet, remained with him for nearly two years. From creeping up and down stairs, and toddling about in every direction, he soon began to grow strong, and bold, and noisy, as a fine healthy child would be; but though his fond protector rejoiced in the health and beauty of the boy, he found him rather unsuited to the quiet gravity of a priest's house, and a decided obstacle to study and meditation. In the midst of his perplexity, of which

248

JOHN FRANCIS MAGUIRE, *THE IRISH IN AMERICA*

the child was the unconscious cause to the Curé of Quebec, a clergyman from the country arrived in town. This priest visited M. Baillargeon, who told him that he had 200 poor orphan children – the children of 'The faithful Catholic Irish' – still unprovided with a home, and he was most anxious that his visitor should call on his parishioners to take them. 'Come,' said he, 'I will show you a sample of them, and you can tell your people what they are like.' Saying this, M. Baillargeon led his visitor up-stairs, and into the room where, in a little cot, the orphan child was lying in rosy sleep. As the light fell upon the features of the beautiful boy, who was reposing in all the unrivalled grace of infancy, the country curé was greatly touched: he had never, he said, seen a 'Lovelier little angel' in his life. 'Well,' said M. Baillargeon, 'I have 200 more as handsome. Take him with you, show him to your people, and tell them to come for the others.' That very night the boat in which he was to reach his parish was to start; and the curé wrapped the infant carefully in the blanket in which he lay, and, without disturbing his slumber, bore him off to the boat, a valued prize.

The next Sunday a strange sight was witnessed in the parish church of which the curé was the pastor. The priest was seen issuing from the sacristy, holding in his arms a boy of singular beauty, whose little hands were tightly clasped, half in terror, half in excitement, round the neck of his bearer. Every eye was turned towards this strange spectacle, and the most intense curiosity was felt by the congregation, in a greater degree by the women, especially those who were mothers, to learn what it meant. It was soon explained by their pastor, who said: – 'Look at this little boy! Poor infant!' (Here the curé embraced him.) 'Look at his noble forehead, his bright eyes, his curling hair, his mouth like a cherub's! Oh, what a beautiful boy!' (Another embrace, the half-terrified child clinging closer to the priest's breast, his tears dropping fast upon the surplice.) 'Look, my dear friends, at this beautiful child, who has been sent by God to our care. There are 200 as beautiful children as this poor forlorn infant. They were starved out of their own country by bad laws, and their fathers and their poor mothers now lie in the great grave at Grosse Isle. Poor mothers! they could not remain with their little ones. You will be mothers to them. The father died, and the mother died; but before she died, the pious mother – the Irish Catholic mother – left them to the good God, and the good God now gives them to you. Mothers, you will not refuse the gift of the good God!' (The kindly people responded to this appeal with tears and gestures of passionate assent.) 'Go quickly to Quebec; there you will find these orphan children – these gifts offered to you by the good God – go quickly – go to-morrow – lose not a moment – take them and carry them to your homes, and they will bring a blessing on you and your families. I say, go to-morrow without fail, or others may be before you. Yes, dear friends, they will be a blessing to you as they grow up, a strong healthy race – fine women, and fine men, like this beautiful boy. Poor child, you will be sure to find a second mother in this congregation.' (Another embrace, the little fellow's tears flowing more abundantly; every eye in the church glistening with responsive sympathy.)

This was the curé's sermon, and it may be doubted if Bossuet or Fenelon ever produced a like effect. Next day there was to be seen a long procession of waggons moving towards Quebec; and on the evening of that day there was not one of the 200 Irish orphans that had not been brought to a Canadian home, there to be nurtured with tenderness and love, as the gift of the *Bon Dieu*. Possibly, in some instances that tenderness and love were not requited in after life, but in most instances the Irish orphan brought a blessing to the hearth of its adopted parents. The boy whose beauty and whose tears so powerfully assisted the simple oratory of the good curé is now one of the ablest lawyers in Quebec – but a French Canadian in every respect save in birth and blood.

As soon as good food and tender care had restored vigour to their youthful limbs, the majority of the orphans played in happy unconsciousness of their bereavement; but there were others, a few years older, on whom the horrors of Grosse Isle had made a lasting impression.

A decent couple had sailed in one of the ships, bringing with them two girls and a boy, the elder of the former being about thirteen, the boy not more than seven or eight. The father died first, the mother next. As the affrighted children knelt by their dying mother, the poor woman, strong in her faith, with her last accents confided her helpless offspring to 'The protection of God and His Blessed Mother,' and told them to have confidence in the Father of the widow and the orphan. Lovingly did the cold hand linger on the head of her boy, as, with expiring energy, she invoked a blessing upon him and his weeping sisters. Thus the pious mother died in the fever-shed of Grosse Isle. The children were taken care of, and sent to the same district, so as not to be separated from each other. The boy[5] was received into the home of a French Canadian; his sisters were adopted by another family in the neighbourhood. For two weeks the boy never uttered a word, never smiled, never appeared conscious of the presence of those around him, or of the attention lavished on him by his generous protectors, who had almost come to believe that they had adopted a little mute, or that he had momentarily lost the power of speech through fright or starvation. But at the end of the fortnight he relieved them of their fears by uttering some words of, to them, an unknown language; and from that moment the spell, wrought, as it were, by the cold hand of his dying mother, passed from the spirit of the boy, and he thenceforth clung with the fondness of youth to his second parents. The Irish orphan soon spoke the language of his new home, though he never lost the memory of the fever-sheds and the awful death-bed, or of his weeping sisters, and the last words spoken by the faithful Christian woman who commended him to the protection of God and His Blessed Mother. He grew up a youth of extraordinary promise, and was received into the college of Nicolet, then in the diocese of Quebec, where he graduated with the greatest honours. His vocation being for the Church, he became a priest; and it was in 1865 that, as a deacon, he entered the College of St. Michael, near Toronto, to learn the language of his parents, of which he had lost all remembrance. He is now one of the most distinguished professors of the college in which he was educated; and, in order to pay back the debt incurred by his support and education, he does not accept more than a small stipend for his services. Of his Irish name, which he was able to retain, he is very proud; and though his tongue is more that of a French Canadian, his feelings and sympathies are with the people and the country of his birth. The prayers of the dying mother were indeed heard; for the elder of the girls was married by the gentleman who received them both into his house, and the younger is in a convent.

Absorbed thus into the families of the French-speaking population, even the older Irish orphans soon lost almost every memory of their former home and of their parents, and grew up French Canadians in every respect save the more vigorous constitution for which they were indebted to nature. It is not, therefore, a rare thing to behold a tall, strapping, fair-skinned young fellow, with an unmistakable Irish name, and an unmistakable Irish face, who speaks and thinks as a French Canadian. Thus genuine Irish names – as Cassidy, or Lonergan, or Sullivan, or Quinn, or Murphy – are to be heard of at this day in many of the homes of the kindly *habitans* of Lower Canada.

Though it was the humane policy of those who took care of the orphans of Grosse Isle to keep the same family in the same neighbourhood, so as not to separate brother from sister, it has happened that a brother has been reared by a French family, and a sister by an Irish, or English-speaking, family; and when the orphans have been brought together by their adopted parents, they could only express their emotions by embraces and tears – the language of the heart.

In some, but rare instances, visions of the past have haunted the memory of Irish orphans in their new homes. One of these, a young girl who bore the name of her protectors, was possessed with a passionate longing to learn her real name, and to know something of her parents. A once familiar sound, which she somehow associated with her former name, floated through her brain, vague and indistinct, but ever present. The longing to ascertain who she was, and whether either of her parents was still living, grew into an absorbing passion, which preyed upon her health. She would frequently write what expressed her recollection of the name she had once borne, and which she thought she had been called in her infancy by those who loved her. The desire to clear up the doubt becoming at length uncontrollable, she implored the curé of her parish to institute inquiries in her behalf. Written in French characters, nearly all resemblance to the supposed name was lost; but through the aid of inquiries set on foot by Father Dowd, the Parish Priest of St. Patrick's, in Montreal, and guided by the faint indication afforded by what resembled a sound more than a surname, it was discovered that her mother had taken her out to America in 1847, and that her father had never quitted Ireland. A communication was at once established between father and child; and from that moment the girl began to recover her health, which had been nearly sacrificed to her passionate yearning.

The horrors of Grosse Isle had their counterpart in Montreal.

As in Quebec, the mortality was greater in 1847 than in the year following; but it was not till the close of 1848 that the plague might be said to be extinguished, not without fearful sacrifice of life. During the months of June, July,

August, and September, the season when nature wears her most glorious garb of loveliness, as many as eleven hundred of 'The faithful Irish,' as the Canadian priest truly described them, were lying at one time in the fever-sheds at Point St. Charles, in which rough wooden beds were placed in rows, and so close as scarcely to admit of room to pass. In these miserable cribs the patients lay, sometimes two together, looking, as a Sister of Charity since wrote, 'as if they were in their coffins,' from the box-like appearance of their wretched beds. Throughout those glorious months, while the sun shone brightly, and the majestic river rolled along in golden waves, hundreds of the poor Irish were dying daily. The world outside was gay and glad, but death was rioting in the fever-sheds. It was a moment to try the devotion which religion inspires, to test the courage with which it animates the gentlest breast. First came the Grey Nuns, strong in love and faith; but so malignant was the disease that thirty of their number were stricken down, and thirteen died the death of martyrs. There was no faltering, no holding back; no sooner were the ranks thinned by death than the gaps were quickly filled; and when the Grey Nuns were driven to the last extremity, the Sisters of Providence came to their assistance, and took their place by the side of the dying strangers. But when even their aid did not suffice to meet the emergency, the Sisters of St. Joseph, though cloistered nuns, received the permission of the Bishop to share with their sister religious the hardships and dangers of labour by day and night.

'I am the only one left,' were the thrilling words in which the surviving priest announced from the pulpit the ravages that the 'Ocean plague' had made in the ranks of the clergy. With a single exception, the local priests were either sick or dead. Eight of the number fell at their post, true to their duty. The good Bishop, Monsigneur Bourget, then went himself, to take his turn in the lazar-house; but the enemy was too mighty for his zeal, and having remained in the discharge of his self-imposed task for a day and a night, he contracted the fever, and was carried home to a sick-bed, where he lay for weeks, hovering between life and death, amid the tears and prayers of his people, to whom Providence restored him after a period of intense anxiety to them, and long and weary suffering to him.

When the city priests were found inadequate to the discharge of their pressing duties, the country priests cheerfully responded to the call of their Bishop, and came to the assistance of their brethren; and of the country priests not a few found the grave and the crown of the martyr.

Among the priests who fell a sacrifice to their duty in the fever-sheds of Montreal was Father Richards, a venerable man, long past the time of active service. A convert from Methodism in early life, he had specially devoted his services to the Irish, then but a very small proportion of the population; and now, when the cry of distress from the same race was heard, the good old man could not be restrained from ministering to their wants. Not only did he mainly provide for the safety of the hundreds of orphan children, whom the death of their parents had left to the mercy of the charitable, but, in spite of his great age, he laboured in the sheds with a zeal which could not be excelled.

'Certainly, he shall have it: I wish it was gold, for his sake,' replied the mayor.

A few days after both Protestant mayor and Catholic priest 'had gone where straw and gold are of equal value,' wrote the Sister already mentioned. Both had died martyrs of charity.

Only a few days before Father Richards was seized with his fatal illness he preached on Sunday in St. Patrick's, and none who heard him on that occasion could forget the venerable appearance and impressive words of that noble servant of God. Addressing a hushed and sorrow-stricken audience, as the tears rolled down his aged cheeks, he thus spoke of the sufferings and the faith of the Irish: –

'Oh, my beloved brethren, grieve not, I beseech you, for the sufferings and death of so many of your race, perchance your kindred, who have fallen, and are still to fall, victims to this fearful pestilence. Their patience, their faith, have edified all whose privilege it was to witness it. Their faith, their resignation to the will of God under such unprecedented misery, is something so extraordinary that, to realise it, it requires to be seen. Oh, my brethren, grieve not for them; they did but pass from earth to the glory of heaven. True, they were cast in heaps into the earth, their place of sepulture marked by no name or epitaph; but I tell you, my clearly beloved brethren, that from their ashes the faith will spring up along the St. Lawrence, for they died martyrs, as they lived confessors, to the faith.'

The whole city, Protestant and Catholic, mourned the death of this fine old man, one of the most illustrious, victims of the scourge in Montreal.

The orphan children were gathered to the homes and hearts of the generous Canadians and the loving Irish; and most of them had grown up to manhood and womanhood before either monument or epitaph marked the spot in which the bones of their dead parents were mingling with the dust. But there is a monument and a record, the pious work of English workmen, inspired by the humane suggestion of English gentlemen. In the centre of a railed-in spot of land at Point St. Charles, within a hundred yards or so of the Victoria Bridge, that wondrous structure which spans the broad St. Lawrence, there is a huge boulder, taken from the bed of the river, and placed on a platform of roughly hewn stone; and on that boulder there is this inscription: –

TO
Preserve from desecration
THE REMAINS OF SIX THOUSAND IMMIGRANTS,
Who died of Ship-fever,
A.D. 1847–8, This stone is erected by the
WORKMEN OF MESSRS. PETO, BRASSEY, AND BETTS,
Employed in the
Construction of the Victoria Bridge,
A.D. 1859.

In the church of the Bon Secour one may see a memorial picture,[6] representing with all the painter's art the horrors and the glories of the fever-shed – the dying Irish, strong in their faith – the ministering Sisters, shedding peace on the pillow of suffering – the holy Bishop, affording the last consolations of religion to those to whom the world was then as nothing: but, in its terrible significance, the rude monument by that mighty river's side is far more impressive.

Let us follow the Irish emigrant – 'the faithful Irish' – farther up the St. Lawrence. In the grounds of the General Hospital of Kingston there is an artificial mound, of gentle swell and moderate elevation, the grass on which is ever green, as if owing to some peculiar richness of the soil. When verdure has been elsewhere burned up or parched, on this soft-swelling mound greenness is perpetual. Beneath that verdant shroud lie mouldering the bones of 1,900 Irish immigrants, victims of the same awful scourge of their race – the ship-fever. With the intention of pushing on to the West, the goal of their hopes, multitudes of the Irish reached Kingston, 350 miles up the St. Lawrence from Quebec; but the plague broke out amongst this mass of human misery, and they rotted away like sheep. So fast did they die, that there were not means to provide coffins in which to inter them. There was timber more than sufficient for the purpose, but the hands to fashion the plank into the coffin were too few, and Death was too rapid in his stroke; and so a huge pit of circular form was dug, and in it were laid, in tiers, piled one upon the other, the bodies of 1,000 men, women, and children: and even to the hour when I beheld the light of the setting sun imparting additional beauty to its vivid greenness, there was neither rail, nor fence, nor stone, nor cross, nor inscription, to tell that 1,900 of a Christian people slept beneath the turf of that gigantic grave.

Twenty years ago Kingston was a small place, with little more than half its present population; and the Irish, who now form an important portion of its community, were then comparatively few in number. But in no part of British America did the Irish display a more heroic devotion to humanity and country than in that city, from which the greater number of the inhabitants had fled in terror, at the presence of the migratory hordes who brought pestilence with them in their march. The Irish of the town stood their ground bravely; and not only were their houses thrown open to their afflicted country people, and their means placed unreservedly at their disposal, but they tended the sick and dying, and ministered to them in the holiest spirit of charity. Among the best and bravest of those who succoured the plague-smitten of that dreadful time were three Irish Protestants – Mr. Kirkpatrick, then Mayor of Kingston[7]; Alderman Robert Anglin[8]; and Mr. William Ford,[9] afterwards Mayor – who were in the sheds both day and night, and by their ceaseless efforts to relieve the sufferers inspired others with increased courage and still greater self-devotion.

Father Dollard,[10] an Irish clergyman, had to bear the chief share of the priestly duty; and from the first moment that the fever broke out, until the earth was beaten down on the top of the grave-mound, he was in the midst of the danger. So shocking was the condition in which the unhappy people reached Kingston, the last resting-place of many of them, that the clergymen, three at the most, had to change their own clothes repeatedly in the day. One of the three priests, who had been only just ordained, died of the contagion.

When the plague abated, and the danger no longer existed, the inhabitants returned; and now there began an unseemly scramble for the orphan children of the Catholic parents who slept beneath the mound in the grounds of the Hospital. The Irish Catholics of the surrounding locality strained every resource in order to afford a home to the orphans of their native country and religion, and through their charity the greater number of them were well provided for; but others of a different faith secured a certain proportion of the children, who are now perhaps bitter opponents of the creed of their fathers.

The same scenes of suffering and death were to be witnessed in the city of Toronto, as in the other cities of Canada during those memorable years 1847 and 1848. Sheds were constructed, and hearses and dead-carts were in hourly requisition. The panic was universal; but the humane and high-spirited, of all denominations, did their duty manfully. Two and three coffins were constantly to be seen on the hearse or waggon used for bearing the dead to the grave-pit outside the town. One day the horse drawing this hearse got restive, and, breaking from his conductor, upset the three coffins, which, falling into pieces, literally gave up their dead. This occurred near the Market Square, about the most public thoroughfare in Toronto, and at once a crowd assembled, horror-stricken but fascinated by the awful spectacle. Every effort was made to repair as speedily as possible the momentary disaster; but it was some time before the three wasted bodies of the poor Irish could be hidden from sight.

The priests, as in all similar cases, were ceaselessly at work, with the usual result – the sacrifice of several of their number.

Among the losses which the Catholic Church had to deplore during this crisis was that of a venerable Irishman, Dr. Power, Bishop of Toronto. He was implored by his people not to expose a life so valuable to his flock; but he replied, that where the souls of Christians, and these the natives of his own country, were in peril, it was his duty to be there. 'My good priests are down in sickness, and the duty devolves on me. The poor souls are going to heaven, and I will do all I can to assist them,' said the Bishop. And, in spite of the most earnest and affectionate remonstrance, he persevered in performing the same labours as the youngest of his priests. The Bishop prepared for his post of danger by making his will, and appointing an administrator. The letters of administration were lengthy, and of much importance, embracing necessarily the financial and other concerns of the diocese. This document, most precious from its association with the voluntary martyrdom of the venerable Prelate, is preserved among the episcopal archives of Toronto. It was commenced with a bold firm hand; but as it proceeded amid frequent interruptions – his visits to console the dying being their chief cause – the writing became more and more feeble, until one might mark, in the faint and trembling characters of the concluding lines, the near approach of death, which soon consigned him to the tomb, another martyr to duty. Rarely, if ever, has a larger funeral procession been seen in Toronto, and never has there been a more universal manifestation of public sorrow than was witnessed on that mournful occasion. Every place of business in the streets through which the procession passed was closed, and Protestant vied with Catholic in doing honour to the memory of a holy and brave-hearted prelate.

Partridge Island, opposite the city of St. John, New Brunswick, was the scene of more horrors, more destruction of human life. In fact, wherever an emigrant ship touched the shores of the British Provinces, or sailed into their rivers, there is the same awful carnage to be recorded.

A portion of the survivors pushed on to the West, their march still tracked by fever, and marked by new-made graves. The majority stopped at various places on the way, or spread over Central and Western Canada, many settling on Crown lands placed at their disposal by the Government, but others hiring themselves as farm labourers, not having, as yet, the energy to face the forest, and engage in a struggle for which disease and sorrow had rendered them for a time unequal. But in half a dozen years after might be seen, along the shores of the lakes, and on the banks of the great rivers and their tributaries, prosperous settlements of those fever-hunted exiles, who, flying in terror from their own country, carried plague and desolation with them to the country of their adoption. It was remarked of them that, though they bravely rallied, and set about their work as settlers with an energy almost desperate, many seemed to be prematurely old, and broke down after some years of ceaseless toil; but not before they had achieved the great object of their ambition – made a home and realised a property for those who, with them, survived the horrors of the passage, and the havoc of the quarantine and the fever-shed.

Even to this day the terror inspired in the minds of the inhabitants through whose districts the Irish emigrants passed in the terrible years of 1847 and 1848 has not died out. I was told of one instance where, little more than a year since, whole villages were scared at the announcement, happily untrue, that 'The poor Irish were coming, and were bringing the fever with them.'

Notes

1 The quote is attributed to Father Bernard McGauran (1821–1882).
2 Joseph Signay (1778–1850), Archbishop of Quebec (1833–1850).
3 Father Charles-Félix Cazeau (1807–1881), secretary to the Archbishop of Quebec.
4 Charles-François Baillargeon (1798–1870), Archbishop of Quebec (1867–1870).
5 The orphan is Robert Walsh, whose writing is also published in this volume.
6 Théophile Hamel's *Le Typhus* (1847); see J. King, 'Mortuary Spectacles: The Genealogy of the Images of the Famine Irish Coffin Ships and Montreal's Fever Sheds' in M. Corporaal, O. Frawley, E. Mark-FitzGerald (eds.), *The Great Irish Famine: Visual and Material Cultures*, (Liverpool: Liverpool University Press, 2018), pp. 88–109.
7 Thomas Kirkpatrick (1805–1870), mayor of Kingston, Ontario in 1847.
8 Robert Anglin (1806–1874), Common Councilman in Kingston from 1843.
9 William Ford (1811–1893), mayor of Kingston in 1848.
10 Fr. Patrick Dollard (1808–1868), parish priest in Kingston.

22

ROBERT WALSH TO UNNAMED IRISH BISHOP (1857). (ARCHIVES DU SÉMINAIRE DE NICOLET, F091/B1/5/2 & F091/B1/5/3). TRANSLATED BY JASON KING

Robert Walsh is the Irish Famine orphan 'Who momentarily lost the power of speech through fright or starvation' after the death of his parents on Grosse Isle, alluded to but not named by John Francis Maguire in *The Irish in America* above. The first traces of him can be found in the 'Emigration Agent Returns of Emigrant Orphans, 1847' as well as the register of orphans, 1847–1848, compiled by of La Société charitable des Dames catholiques de Québec.[1] His family had most likely sailed on the *Avon* from Cork, and Reverends Bernard O'Reilly and John Harper escorted Robert Walsh and his surviving sisters Mary and Anne from Grosse Isle on 14 July, 1847[2] to Ste. Grégoire, Quebec, where they were adopted. Robert Walsh was given a good education and entered into the seminary of nearby Nicolet. After he was ordained, Walsh learned English at St. Michael's College in Toronto.

As an Irish famine orphan who became a member of the clergy, Robert Walsh left extensive records at Archives du Séminaire de Nicolet. One of the most poignant of these is the letter below that he wrote both in English and in French to a bishop in Ireland in 1857, asking him for help in tracing his relatives and a little sister who did not make the voyage to Canada with them ten years earlier, but was left behind in Ireland. There is no evidence that Robert Walsh ever received a reply to his letter. He did, however, embark on his own voyage to Ireland in 1872 to find his younger sister, but was sorely disappointed because nobody remembered his family or where they had lived. He returned to Quebec and died soon thereafter on 31 January, 1873, at the age of 33. Although he was unsuccessful in finding his younger sister, it is entirely possible that she survived the Famine and efforts are being made to trace her.

Reverend Sir,

In the horrendous emigration of 1847, my father, David Walsh, and my mother, Honora O'Donnell resolved to go with their family to the new world where they had relatives. They had five children; but they left in Ireland with relatives or acquaintances a little girl,[3] aged roughly five to six months, if I remember well. She could have been more or less, for I then was but seven years old and had experienced a long voyage so my misfortunes made me lose the exact memory of these things. My oldest sister was ten and called Mary, the youngest was eight and is called Anny; I had a younger brother called Patrick; I think he was only four years old.

We all arrived in Quebec on the St. Lawrence at the end of June or beginning of July 1847. There, my father, my mother, and my brother Patrick died. They were sick of the typhus which caused so much devastation in this year in Canada. We were three, my two sisters and me, without any support in a foreign country. Providence alone remained for us. Also, He did not forsake us. We were helped by a Catholic priest who was very good to us and ensured that we were adopted into a French-Canadian family and provided with an excellent education. My two sisters are teaching in a good school and receive sufficient wages for their needs. As for me, I am now studying in a Canadian college and I will finish my studies within two years. Also, I am not more than ten or fifteen miles distant from my sisters so that we can write easily and even see each other sometimes, especially during the two months of holidays we are given in the fine season of summer that we spend together.

The purpose of the present letter is then to inform your greatness the particular account of these things in order that you can be moved to take an interest in the fate of these three orphans, to search and discover if they still have any relations left in Ireland. For a decade we have learned nothing of them, and we are like those who have no relatives or acquaintances. I hope that you will do all that is in your power to find some people, if any, who will be dear to us. We were of Kilkenny, if I am right, and there must still be some of our relations there.

My father was the intendant of the lord Montgomery who lived very near Kilkenny then I believe. It was he who conveyed labourers in the lord's service. I was then an infant and I remember that I would go sometimes with my mother and sisters and the lord to a magnificent orchard near his estate. How I love to recall these memories which are for me like a fair dream! Yes, I had a father, a mother, and now they are no more. If only I learned one day that we have relations who think of us, who know the details of our misfortune, and who would write to me, then I would be a little comforted; for they also have learned nothing of us for ten years. They would be glad to know something of us. My sister, my dear sister, if she exists, when she would learn that she has a brother and sisters in Canada who are thinking of her she would write to them, although she does not know them! Oh! how much these words would mean in our hearts! We will see then we are not alone in the world, and it is this thought that will give us courage to endure our separation here.

I hope that your Lordship will take into consideration my questions and that you will do all that charity permits on this occasion. I will be in your debt if you may discover some of my relations and let me know of them soon.

I still have something else to ask of you if you will permit me, on what I have said lately. It is that, as I said, my father was a steward of Lord Montgomery, and also that his Lordship had given him a letter of recommendation. I think that if he was still living, he would be glad to know the fate that has befallen his old friend. So then, if you had the noble goodness to tell him of that, if you can, I will remember always with gratitude your charity towards me.

There is the task I am endeavouring to impose on you; you will find me certainly impudent, but I think that you will praise at least my purpose. You will excuse my English composition because I have forgotten my native tongue in Canada.

It is with the greatest respect that I am your fellow countryman and your son in Jesus Christ.

Robert Walsh.

Notes

1 See M. O'Gallagher, *Grosse Ile: Gateway to Canada, 1832–1937* (Sainte-Foy, Quebec: Carraig Books, 1984), p. 143.
2 See J. King, 'Finding a Voice: Irish Famine orphan Robert Walsh's search for his younger sister', in C. Kinealy, J. King, and G. Moran (eds.), *Children and the Great Hunger* (Cork and Hamden, Connecticut: Cork University Press and Quinnipiac University Press, 2018), 123–138.
3 Although Robert Walsh never discovered her name or whereabouts, she was in fact given her mother's name Honora Walsh and baptized on 12 August 1846.

23

THOMAS QUINN, 'UNE VOIX D'IRLANDE', IN *PREMIER CONGRÈS DE LA LANGUE FRANÇAIS AU CANADA. QUÉBEC 24–30 JUIN 1912* (QUÉBEC, 1913), PP. 227–232. TRANSLATED BY JASON KING

Patrick (12) and Thomas (6) Quinn were forced to emigrate in May 1847 with their family from Lissonuffy on the Strokestown estate of Major Denis Mahon in County Roscommon, which is now the site of the Irish National Famine Museum. They sailed on board the *Naomi*, which was one of the worst of the 'coffin ships'. It arrived in Quebec on 10 August, 1847, after carrying 421 steerage passengers from Liverpool on a journey to Grosse Isle that lasted forty five days, of whom 196 or slightly under fifty percent perished, including 78 at sea, 31 at quarantine, and a further 87 in the quarantine hospital on the island. The boys were left orphans on Grosse Isle, adopted by a French-Canadian family, and both became priests who served mixed French-Canadian and Irish Catholic congregations. On 25 June 1912, Thomas Quinn thanked the French-Canadian people for their generosity in an address at the First Congress of the French Language in Canada, held in Quebec City. His speech was titled 'Une Voix d'Irlande' ('A Voice from Ireland') and published in *Premier Congrès de La Langue Français au Canada. Québec 24–30 Juin 1912* (Québec: Imprimerie de l'Action Sociale Limitée, 1913).[1] It is published in English in this book for the first time.[2]

I do not belong by birth to the French family. The language of my childhood is a foreign language, and if I am afforded the great honor to speak before this patriotic gathering, then it is as an adopted child and son of Ireland.

But, ladies and gentlemen, the adoption was a complete success and I claim my place at the paternal table. The French language, it is mine as it is yours. Those dedicated priests spoke the language through which my father could die in peace in the land of exile, forgiving his persecutors in Ireland! My adoptive parents spoke that language when they took me in at five years of age; they spoke it when they instructed me in my youth! It is still the tongue of old, and it is in this language that I am here today to recognize the people of French-Canada who adopted and took in an Irish son...

French Canadians, you can proudly claim the right to speak your language. It is a right for which you have made sacrifices!

This right so long disputed, and sanctioned by royal authority itself, seemed now safe from hostile forces.

But after coming out victorious from this long struggle, the French-Canadian race had to contend with something still more painful, the ingratitude and treachery of ostensible friends. And I come, ladies and gentlemen, to this troubling question of the relationship between my original and my adopted race.

Cruel irony! Deplorable contradiction! Both races seem to live next to one another, in this land of America, their ancestors were in Europe, inseparable allies. Cremona, Fontenoy, Laugfeld,[3] you have witnessed the warriors of the Emerald Isle who amazed you with their bravery and heroism, and ensured that France had brilliant victories....

Why, in changing countries, do these paragons of justice and law break their alliance with the old sons of France? Why, above all, does that noble patient, chivalrous people, which has suffered from oppression, want to be oppressive to turn? And that in circumstances marked by the blackest and most revolting ingratitude?

I spoke of evil and oppression. What people underwent the weight of evil and oppression as much as did those in Ireland? It is not my intention, on this occasion, to recall its history of bloodshed which is so ingrained in the Irish story.

Allow me, however, ladies and gentlemen, to describe an incident in which I was involved, an incident in which I was myself an actor and victim.

It was in 1847. A famine, even worse than the one which had preceded it, threatened the Irish people with total extinction. The most astonishing part of the awful spectacle was, not to see the people die, but to see them live through such great distress.

During the course of three years, more than four million unfortunates, miraculously escaping death, took the road of exile from their native country. Like walking skeletons they went, in tears, seeking hospitality from more favored lands.

In the designs of Providence, we were cast upon the shores of Grosse-Ile after a stormy passage of two months at sea. A malady, known nowhere else to science, – the famine fever – came to add its untold terrors to so much other suffering and misery.

Canada, however, had foreseen the advent of these people and had acknowledged them as brothers in Christ. Stirred with compassion, French-Canadian priests, braving the epidemic, contended for the glory of rushing to their relief. French-Canadian clergymen, be eternally blessed for your heroism! You, above all, who fell victims to your devotedness! Glorious martyrs of charity, enjoy forever in glory the reward you so justly merit!

Thanks to your untiring charity, my unfortunate parents were able to sleep their last sleep in peace with God, pardoning their enemies, and carrying with them to the grave the ineffable consolation of leaving their children in the care of French-Canadian priests. I still remember one of these admirable clergymen who led us to the bedside of my dying father. As he saw us, my father with his failing voice repeated the old Irish adage, 'Remember your soul and your liberty'.

Sixty-six years have passed since then, but my soul belongs to the French-Canadian people, and my spirit jealously guards their rights and freedoms.

If the episode I just recounted was not enough to instil a love of French-Canadians, there was another incident from my youth that would forever determine my preference for my country of adoption.

My adoptive parents to allow me to retain my mother tongue enrolled me in an English school, run by two old women, who were imbued with a sense of narrow bigotry.

One day when the Blessed Sacrament passed in the street, led by a priest, I wanted to kneel, following the Catholic custom. My mistress reacted violently with an expression I will not repeat. I was forced to obey her, but never returned to the school. My education in English was over. It was not the language of my soul or my freedom!

The people of French-Canada, too, were once abandoned by their mother country, and so they became orphaned. They had imposed on them a foreign language, unknown, and said: 'It is not the language of our soul or our freedom!' After long and perseverant efforts, they finally obtained the privilege to speak French on an equal basis with English. But even where it was strongest, they never attempted to impose on others who lived near them their ideas and language. They wanted their freedom, but never sought to restrict the freedom of others. This is my ideal! And that is why these people have my affections and my preferences!

Dear descendants, God thank you, for your fathers cared for those starving and shivering with fever, and you are now seeking the right to speak your language, in the name and under the guise of religion, not to have imposed on you a foreign idiom!

I regret them deeply, but these attacks will succeed only in strengthening your national feeling and love of your mother tongue.

And if a man who is highly placed and venerable dares to speak out against the French in the preaching of the Gospel, there will always be some eloquent patriot to embody in himself the claims of his race, with a noble and respectful firmness.

Your language has been entrusted with a glorious mission and not a bankrupt one. . .

This right all must recognize, and my countrymen first. The Irishman is by nature a generous soul.

Just as O'Connell, defending his unhappy country, crushed by oppression unnamed, still found the time and means to claim religious freedom for his co-religionists in England and Scotland, who had been banished from these lands for three centuries, I recognize in his words the voice of Ireland, because he spreads the word of justice and freedom.

THOMAS QUINN, 'UNE VOIX D'IRLANDE'

Ireland, real as God made it, by the ministries of Patrick, the Columbans and their successors, deserves and will always have my admiration and love. From it and not a bastard Ireland that is disfigured by unhealthy contact I proclaim myself a proud and devoted son.

Ladies and gentlemen, in this celebration of speaking French, I will, I believe, be the faithful interpreter of the feelings of us all, in expressing the wish and hope to see an end soon to the unfortunate and disastrous divisions between us. In this hospitable land of Canada, there must be a place in the sun for all races, for all languages, without any group seeking to stifle or limit the rights of another.

The Irish and French-Canadian races, both of them Catholic, are walking hand in hand towards the same ideal: the extension of Christ's kingdom, what a wonderful sight it would give the world! And is religious progress the principle of their union?

Is this a dream or a mirage that lies before me? The future will tell.

In any event, I, as the child of a courageous mother, who struggled against her oppressors, bit by bit, to preserve his heritage and freedom, tell my French-Canadian friends and my benefactors: struggle without fear, like O'Connell[4] and Redmond,[5] because your cause is right and just and cannot perish.

Notes

1 T. Quinn, 'Une Voix d'Irlande', *Premier Congrès de La Langue Français au Canada. Québec 24–30 Juin 1912* (Québec: Imprimerie de l'Action Sociale Limitée, 1913), pp. 227–232.

2 See J. King, 'Une Voix d'Irlande: Integration, Migration, and Travelling Nationalism Between Famine Ireland and Quebec in the Long Nineteenth Century', in C. Reilly (ed.), *The Famine Irish: Emigration and the Great Hunger* (Dublin: History Press, 2016), pp. 193–208.

3 The Irish Brigade helped the French defeat the Austrians in the Battle of Cremona during the War of Spanish Succession on 1 February, 1702. It also helped the French defeat Dutch, British, and Hanoverian troops in the Battle of Fontenoy fought on 11 May, 1745 during the War of Austrian Succession.

4 Daniel O'Connell (1775–1847), often referred to as 'the liberator', O'Connell led the campaigns for Catholic Emancipation (1829) and repeal of the Union between Great Britain and Ireland.

5 John Redmond (1856–1918), leader of the Irish Parliamentary Party (1900–1918) that campaigned for Irish Home Rule.

BIBLIOGRAPHY

Anbinder, T., 'Lord Palmerston and the Irish Famine Emigration', *Historical Journal*, 44.2 (2001), pp. 441–469.

Anon., 'Notes of a trip to Canada East', *Toronto Globe* (September 1, 1847).

Anon., 'The emigrant ship. Written for the protestant orphan bazaar', in *The Literary Garland, and the British North American Magazine* (Montreal: Lowell and Gibson, 1850).

Burke, J., MS John Burke, *Reminiscences* (New York: New York Historical Society Library).

Charbonneau, A., and A. Sévigny (eds), *1847, Grosse Île: A Record of Daily Events* (Ottawa: Parks Canada, 1997).

Corporaal, M., *Relocated Memories: The Great Famine in Irish and Diaspora Fiction, 1846–1870* (Syracuse, NY: Syracuse University Press, 2017).

Corporaal, M., and C. Cusack, 'Rites of passage: The coffin ship as a site of immigrants' identity formation in Irish and Irish American fiction, 1855–85', *Atlantic Studies*, 8.3 (2011), pp. 343–359.

Corporaal, M., and J. King, 'Irish Global Migration and Memory: Transnational Perspectives on Ireland's Great Hunger and Exodus', *Atlantic Studies: Global Currents*, 11.3 (2014), pp. 301–320.

Craigy, S. H., 'Journal of a Passage from Belfast to New York'. Public Record Office, Northern Ireland, reference number: T 3258/66.

Davison, S (ed.), *Northern Ireland and Canada: A Guide to Northern Ireland Sources For The Study of Canadian History C.1705–1992* (Belfast: Queen's University Belfast and the Public Record Office of Northern Ireland, 1994).

de Launay, M. E. L. C., *History of The Religious Hospitallers of Saint Joseph*, vol. II, 3rd edition, translated and revised by Sister F. C. Kerr, LIB2000.607. Reference library, St. Joseph Region Archives of the Religious Hospitallers of St. Joseph, Kingston, Ontario.

De Vere, A., *Recollections of Aubrey De Vere* (London: Edward Arnold, 1897).

De Vere, S., 'Minutes of evidence before select committee on colonisation from Ireland, letter to the Select committee (November 30, 1847)', in *British Parliamentary Papers, Emigration*, vol. 5 (Shannon: Irish University Press, 1968), pp. 45–48.

De Vere, S., '1847–1848 America Journals', Vols. I–II. Trinity College Library Dublin. Manuscripts Department, MSS 5061–5062.

———, '1847–1848 Letter-book', Trinity College Library Dublin. Manuscripts Department, MS 5075a.

Donnelly, J. S. Jr., 'The Construction of the Memory of the Famine in Ireland and the Irish Diaspora, 1850–1900', *Éire-Ireland*, 31.1–2 (1996), pp. 26–61.

BIBLIOGRAPHY

Gallman, M. J., *Receiving Erin's Children. Philadelphia, Liverpool, and the Irish Famine Migration, 1845–1855* (Chapel Hill, NC: University of North Carolina Press, 2000).

Gilman, W., *Melville's Early Life and Redburn* (London: Oxford University Press, 1951).

Gore-Booth, R., 'Gore-Booth letters, appendix x, minutes of evidence before select committee on colonisation from Ireland', in *British Parliamentary Papers, Emigration*, vol. 5 (Shannon: Irish University Press, 1968), pp. 122–132.

Gray, P., 'Shovelling out Your Paupers': The British State and Irish Famine Migration, 1846–50', *Patterns of Prejudice*, 33.4 (1999), pp. 47–65.

Gwynn Jones, J., *The Abiding Enchantment of Curragh Chase: The Big House Remembered* (Cork: Clo Duanaire, 1983).

Hirota, H., *Expelling the Poor: American Seaboard States & the 19th Century Origins of American Immigration Policy* (Oxford: Oxford University Press, 2017).

Horner, D., 'If The Evil Now Growing Around Us Be Not Staid': Montreal and Liverpool Confront the Irish Famine Migration as a Transnational Crisis in Urban Governance', *Histoire Sociale/Social History*, 46.92 (2013), pp. 349–366.

Houston, C. J., and W. J. Smyth. *Irish Emigration and Canadian Settlement: Patterns, Links, and Letters* (Toronto: University of Toronto Press), 1990.

Johnson, H., letter from Henry Johnson, Hamilton, Canada West, to Jane Johnson, Dungonnell, Antrim, September 18, 1848, in L. Wyatt (ed.), 'The Johnson Letters', *Ontario History*, 5.11 (1948), pp. 7–52.

Kinealy, C., *This Great Calamity: The Irish Famine, 1845–52*. Boulder: Roberts Rinehart, 1995.

King, J., 'L'historiographie irlando-québécoise: Conflits et conciliations entre Canadiens français et Irlandais', Translated by S. Jolivet, *Bulletin d'histoire politique du Québec*, 18.3 (2010), pp. 13–36.

——, 'The Genealogy of *Famine Diary* in Ireland and Quebec: Ireland's Famine Migration in Historical Fiction, Historiography, and Memory', *Éire-Ireland*, 47 (2012), pp. 45–69.

——, 'Remembering famine orphans: The transmission of famine memory between Ireland and Québec', in C. Noack, L. Janssen, and V. Comerford (eds), *Holodomor and Gorta Mór: Histories, Memories, and Representations of Famine in Ukraine and Ireland* (New York: Anthem Press, 2012), pp. 115–144.

——, 'Remembering and Forgetting the Famine Irish in Quebec: Genuine and False Memoirs, Communal Memory and Migration', *Irish Review*, 44 (2012), pp. 20–41.

——, 'The remembrance of Irish famine migrants in the fever sheds of Montreal', in M. Corporaal, C. Cusack, L. Janssen, and R. van den Beuken (eds), *Global Legacies of the Great Irish Famine: Transnational and Interdisciplinary Perspectives* (Brussels: Peter Lang, 2014), pp. 245–266.

——, 'The famine Irish, the Grey Nuns, and the fever sheds of Montreal: Prostitution and female religious institution building', in C. Kinealy, J. King, and C. Reilly (eds), *Women and the Great Hunger* (Hamden, CT: Quinnipiac University Press, 2016), pp. 95–108.

——, 'Une Voix d'Irlande: Integration, migration, and travelling nationalism between famine Ireland and Quebec in the long nineteenth century', in C. Reilly (ed.), *The Famine Irish: Emigration and the Great Hunger* (Dublin: History Press, 2016), pp. 193–208.

——, 'The famine Irish migration to Canada in 1847–1848: Assisted emigration, colonisation, and the unpublished famine diaries of Stephen De Vere', in P. Fitzgerald, and A. Russell (eds), *John Mitchel, Ulster, and the Great Irish Famine* (Dublin: Irish Academic Press, 2017), pp. 30–45.

BIBLIOGRAPHY

———, 'Mortuary spectacles: The genealogy of the images of the Famine Irish coffin ships and Montreal's fever sheds', in M. Corporaal, O. Frawley, and E. Mark-FitzGerald (eds), *The Great Irish Famine: Visual and Material Cultures* (Liverpool: Liverpool University Press, 2018), pp. 88–109.

——— (ed.), Irish Famine Archive. http://faminearchive.nuigalway.ie.

——— (ed.), Grey Nuns Famine Annal. *Ancien Journal*, Vol. I. Translated by J. F. Bernard. http://faminearchive.nuigalway.ie/docs/greynuns/GreyNunsFamineAnnalAncienJournalVolu meI.1847.pdf

——— (ed.), Grey Nuns Famine Annal. *Ancien Journal*, Vol. II; *The Typhus of 1847*. Translated by P. O'Gorman. http://faminearchive.nuigalway.ie/docs/grey-nuns/TheTyphusof1847.pdf.

——— (ed.), Grey Nuns Famine Annal. *Foundation of St. Patrick's Asylum*. Translated by P. O'Gorman. http://faminearchive.nuigalway.ie/docs/grey- nuns/GreyNunsFamineAnnalFoundationofStPatricksOrphanAsylum.pdf

Leda, J., *The Melville Log: A Documentary Life of Herman Melville 1819–1891*. (New York: Gordian Press, 1969).

MacDonagh, O., *A Pattern of Government Growth: Passenger Acts and their Enforcement, 1800–1860* (London: MacGibbon & Gee, 1961).

Maguire, J. F., *The Irish in America* (New York: D & J Sadlier, 1868).

Mark-Fitzgerald, E., *Commemorating the Irish Famine: Memory and the Monument* (Liverpool: Liverpool University Press, 2013).

McGowan, M., *Creating Canadian Historical Memory: The Case of the Famine Migration of 1847* (Ottawa: Canadian Historical Association, 2006).

———, 'Famine, Facts, and Fabrication: An Examination of Diaries from the Irish Famine Migration to Canada', *The Canadian Journal of Irish Studies*, 33.2 (2007), pp. 48–55.

———, *Death or Canada: The Irish Famine Migration to Toronto, 1847* (Toronto: Novalis Publishing, 2009).

McMahon, C., 'Recrimination and Reconciliation: Great Famine Memory in Liverpool and Montreal at the Turn of the Twentieth Century', *Atlantic Studies*, 11.3 (2014), pp. 344–364.

Melville, H., *Redburn: His First Voyage* (New York: Harper & Brothers, 1849).

Miller, K. A., 'Emigration to North America in the era of the great famine, 1845–55', in J. Crowley, W. J. Smyth, and M. Murphy (eds), *Atlas of the Great Irish Famine* (Cork: Cork University Press, 2012), pp. 214–227.

———, *Emigrants and Exiles: Ireland and the Irish Exodus to North America* (Oxford: Oxford University Press, 1985).

Mitchel, J., *Jail Journal; or, Five Years in British Prisons* (New York: Published at the Office of The Citizen, 1854).

Moran, G., *Sending Out Ireland's Poor: Assisted Emigration to North America in the Nineteenth Century* (Dublin: Four Courts, 2004).

———, *Sir Robert Gore-Booth and His Landed Estate in County Sligo, 1814–1876* (Dublin: Four Courts, 2006).

O'Gallagher, M., *Grosse Ile: Gateway to Canada, 1832–1937* (Sainte-Foy, Quebec: Carraig Books, 1984).

O'Gallagher, M., and R. M., Dompierre (eds), *Eyewitness : Grosse Isle, 1847* (Sainte-Foy, Quebec: Carraig Books, 1995).

O'Neill, P., *Famine Irish and the American Racial State* (London: Routledge, 2017).

O'Reilly, B., *The Mirror of True Womanhood; A Book of Instruction for Women in the World* (New York: P. J. Kennedy, Excelsior Publishing House, 1877).

BIBLIOGRAPHY

Pugliese, J., 'Crisis Heterotopias and Border Zones of the Dead', *Continuum*, 23.5 (2009), pp. 663–679.

Quinn, T., 'Une Voix d'Irlande', in *Premier Congrès de La Langue Français au Canada. Québec 24–30 Juin 1912* (Québec: Imprimerie de l'Action Sociale Limitée, 1913), pp. 227–232.

Sadlier, A. T., *Life of Mother Gamelin: Foundress and First Superior of the Sisters of Charity of Providence* (Montreal: Mother House of Providence, 1912).

Sadlier, M. A., *Willy Burke; or, The Irish Orphan in America* (Boston: Thomas B. Noonan and Co, 1850).

———, *New Lights; or, Life in Galway* (New York: D & J Sadlier, 1853).

———, *The Blakes and Flanagans* (New York: D & J Sadlier, 1855).

———, *Con O'Regan; or, Emigrant Life in the New World* (New York: D & J Sadlier, 1856).

———, *Elinor Preston; or, Scenes at Home and Abroad* (New York: D & J Sadlier, 1857).

———, *Bessy Conway; or, The Irish Girl in America* (New York: D & J Sadlier, 1861).

———, 'The Plague of 1847', in *Messenger of the Sacred Heart* (Montreal: League of the Sacred Heart, 1891), pp. 204–208.

Smith, W., *An Emigrant's Narrative, Or, A Voice from the Steerage: Being a Brief Account of the Sufferings of the Emigrants in the Ship "India," on Her Voyage from Liverpool to New-York, in the Winter of 1847–8, Together with a Statement of the Cruelties Practiced Upon the Emigrants in the Staten Island Hospital* (New York: Published by the Author, 1850).

Southam, P., *Irish settlement and National identity in the Lower St. Francis Valley* (Richmond, Quebec: Richmond St. Patrick's Society, 2012).

Thoreau, H. D., 'The shipwreck', *Putnam's Monthly*, 5.30 (1855).

van Hear, N., *New Diasporas: The Mass Exodus, Dispersal and Regrouping of Migrant Communities.*(Seattle: University of Washington Press, 1998).

White, J., letter from 'Grosse Island to Eleanor Wallace, Newtownards', 29 June, 1849. Public Record Office, Northern Ireland, document 1195/3/5.

Whyte, R., *The Ocean Plague: A Voyage to Quebec in an Irish Emigrant Vessel* (Boston, MA: Coolidge and Wiley, 1848).

Wilson, D., *Thomas D'Arcy McGee: Passion, Reason, and Politics – 1825–1857*. vol. 1 (Montreal & Kingston: McGill-Queens University Press, 2008).

Woodham-Smith, C., *The Great Hunger: Ireland, 1845–1849* (Harmondsworth: Penguin, 1962).

Young, J., *MSS 'Diary of John Young'. Nancy Mallett Archive and Museum of St. James Cathedral* (Toronto: c. 1847).

KEYWORDS

An Emigrant's Narrative, or, a Voice from the Steerage

Atlantic crossing
Black Rock
Boston
brig *St John*
British North America
Burke, John
Canada
cholera
coffin ships
Deer Island, Boston
De Vere, Stephen
dysentery
emigrant letters
emigrants
Famine annals
Famine diaries
Famine exodus
Famine migration
Famine orphans
fever sheds
French-Canadians
Gore-Booth, Robert
Great Hunger migration
Grey Nuns
Grosse Isle
Hospitaller Sisters of St Joseph
Ireland
Irish exodus
Irish National Famine Museum
Irish orphans
Johnson, Henry

Kingston, Ontario
Maguire, John Francis
Melville, Herman
Montreal
New York
O'Reilly, Bernard
Passenger Acts
Philadelphia
quarantine station
Quebec
Quinn, Thomas
Redburn
ship fever
Sisters of Charity
Sisters of Providence
Smith, William
Staten Island Fever Hospital
Strokestown Park House
Sulpician fathers
The Irish in America
The Ocean Plague
The Shipwreck
Thorough, Henry David
Toronto
typhus
typhus orphans
Walsh, Robert
White, Jane
Whyte, Robert
Windmill Point
Young, John